Cliff White

**Bibliography of North American Invertebrate Paleontology**

Cliff White

**Bibliography of North American Invertebrate Paleontology**

ISBN/EAN: 9783744666503

Printed in Europe, USA, Canada, Australia, Japan

Cover: Foto ©ninafisch / pixelio.de

More available books at **www.hansebooks.com**

DEPARTMENT OF THE INTERIOR.
UNITED STATES GEOLOGICAL SURVEY OF THE TERRITORIES.
F. V. HAYDEN, U. S. GEOLOGIST.

MISCELLANEOUS PUBLICATIONS, No. 9

DESCRIPTIVE CATALOGUE

OF

# PHOTOGRAPHS

OF

NORTH AMERICAN INDIANS.

BY

W. H. JACKSON,

PHOTOGRAPHER OF THE SURVEY.

WASHINGTON:
GOVERNMENT PRINTING OFFICE.
1877.

# PREFATORY NOTE.

OFFICE OF UNITED STATES GEOLOGICAL AND
GEOGRAPHICAL SURVEY OF THE TERRITORIES,
*Washington, D. C., November* 1, 1877.

The collection of photographic portraits of North American Indians described in the following "Catalogue" is undoubtedly the largest and most valuable one extant. It has been made at great labor and expense, during a period of about twenty-five years, and now embraces over one thousand negatives, representing no less than twenty-five tribes. Many of the individuals portrayed have meanwhile died; others, from various causes, are not now accessible; the opportunity of securing many of the subjects, such as scenes and incidents, has of course passed away. The collection being thus unique, and not to be reproduced at any expenditure of money, time, or labor, its value for ethnological purposes cannot easily be overestimated.

Now that the tribal relations of these Indians are fast being successively sundered by the process of removal to reservations, which so greatly modifies the habits and particularly the style of dress of the aborigines, the value of such a graphic record of the past increases year by year; and there will remain no more trustworthy evidence of what the Indians have been than that afforded by these faithful sun-pictures, many of which represent the villages, dwellings, and modes of life of these most interesting people, and historical incidents of the respective tribes, as well as the faces, dresses, and accoutrements of many prominent individuals.

Those who have never attempted to secure photographs and measurememts or other details of the physique of Indians, in short, any reliable statistics of individuals or bands, can hardly realize the obstacles to be overcome. The American Indian is extremely superstitious, and every attempt to take his picture is rendered difficult if not entirely frustrated by his deeply-rooted belief that the process places some portion of himself in the power of the white man, and his suspicion that such control may be used to his injury. No prescribed regulations for the taking of photographs, therefore, are likely to be fully carried out. As a rule, front and profile views have been secured whenever practicable. Usually it is only when an Indian is subjected to confinement that those measurements of his person which are suitable for anthropological purposes can be secured. In most cases the Indian will not allow his person to be handled at all, nor submit to any inconvenience whatever. Much tact and perseverance are required to overcome his superstitious notions, and in many cases, even of the most noted chiefs of several tribes, no portrait can be obtained by any inducement whatever. If, therefore, the collection fails to meet the full requirements of the anthropologist, it must be remembered that the obstacles in the way of realizing his ideal of a perfect collection are insurmountable.

About two hundred of the portraits, or one-fifth of the whole collection, have been derived from various sources, and most of these are pictures of Indians composing the several delegations that have visited Washington from time to time during the past ten years. Such individuals are usually among the most prominent and influential members of the respective tribes, of which they consequently furnish the best samples. The greater portion of the whole collection is derived from the munificent liberality of William Blackmore, esq., of London, England, the eminent anthropologist who has for many years studied closely the history, habits, and manners of the North American Indians. The Blackmore portion of the collection consists of a number of smaller lots from various sources; and it is Mr. Blackmore's intention to enlarge it to include, if possible, all the tribes of the North American continent.

The entire collection, at the present time consisting of upward of a thousand negatives, represents ten leading "families" of Indians, besides seven independent tribes, the families being divisible into fifty-four "tribes," subdivision of which gives forty-three "bands." The collection continues to increase as opportunity offers.

The present "Catalogue," prepared by Mr. W. H. Jackson, the well-known and skilful photographer of the Survey, is far more than a mere enumeration of the negatives. It gives in full, yet in concise and convenient form, the information which the Survey has acquired respecting the subjects of the pictures, and is believed to represent an acceptable contribution to anthropological literature.

F. V. HAYDEN,
*United States Geologist.*

# PREFACE.

The following Descriptive Catalogue is intended to systematize the collection of Photographic Portraits of Indians now in the possession of the United States Geological Survey of the Territories, and to place on record all the information we have been able to obtain of the various individuals and scenes represented. It is of course far from complete; but it is a beginning, and every new fact that comes to light will be added to what has already been secured., This information has been gathered from many sources, principally from Indian delegates visiting Washington, and by correspondence with agents and others living in the Indian country.

Particular attention has been paid to proving the authenticity of the portraits of the various individuals represented, and it is believed that few, if any, mistakes occur in that respect.

The historical notices are mainly compilations from standard works on the subject.

All of the following portraits and views are photographed direct from nature, and are in nearly every case from the original plates, the exceptions being good copies from original daguerreotypes or photographs that are not now accessible.

The portraits made under the supervision of the Survey are generally accompanied by measurements that are as nearly accurate as it has been possible to make them.

The pictures vary in size from the ordinary small card to groups on plates 16 by 20 inches square. The majority, however, are on plates $6\frac{1}{2}$ by $8\frac{1}{2}$ inches square; these are usually trimmed to 4 by $5\frac{1}{2}$ inches, and mounted on cabinet cards.

All the photographs are numbered upon their faces, and as these numbers do not occur in regular order in the text a Numerical Index is appended, by means of which the name of any picture, and the page on which the subject is treated, may be readily found.

W. H. J.

# ADVERTISEMENT.

Miscellaneous Publications No. 5, entitled "Descriptive Catalogue of the Photographs of the United States Geological Survey of the Territories for the years 1869 to 1873, inclusive," published in 1874, contains, on pages 67–83, a "Catalogue of Photographs of Indians, [etc.]" This, however, is a mere enumeration of the negatives then in the possession of the survey, and is now superseded by the present independent publication.

# CATALOGUE OF PHOTOGRAPHS OF NORTH AMERICAN INDIANS.

## LIST OF FAMILIES, TRIBES, AND BANDS.

### I. ALGONKINS.

CHEYENNES.
CHIPPEWAS.
   *Pembina.*
   *Red Lake.*
   *Rabbit Lake.*
   *Mille Lac.*
   *Wisconsin.*
DELAWARES.
MENOMONEES.
MIAMIS.
OTTAWAS.
POTTAWATOMIES.
SACS AND FOXES.
SHAWNEES.
PEQUODS.
   *Stockbridge.*
   *Brotherton.*

### II. ATHABASCAS.

APACHES.
   *Coyotero.*
   *Essaqueta.*
   *Jicarilla.*
   *Mohave.*
   *Pinal.*
   *Yuma.*
   *Chiricahua.*
NAVAJOS.

CATALOGUE OF INDIAN PHOTOGRAPHS.

### III. DAKOTAS.

CROWS.
DAKOTAS.
    *Blackfeet.*
    *Brulé.*
    *Cut Head.*
    *Mdewakanton.*
    *Ogalalla.*
    *Oncpapa.*
    *Sans Arc.*
    *Santee.*
    *Sisseton.*
    *Two Kettle.*
    *Wahpeton.*
    *Yankton.*
    *Upper Yanktonais.*
    *Lower Yanktonais.*
IOWAS.
KAWS or KANSAS.
MANDANS.
MISSOURIAS.
OMAHAS.
OSAGES.
OTOES.
PONCAS.
WINNEBAGOES.

### IV. PAWNEES.

ARICKAREES or REES.
KEECHIES.
PAWNEES.
    *Chowee.*
    *Kit-ka-hoct.*
    *Peta-howerat.*
    *Skee-dee.*
WACOS.
WICHITAS.

### V. SHOSHONES.

BANNACKS.
COMANCHES.
KIOWAS.

SHOSHONES.
UTAHS.
    *Capote.*
    *Muache.*
    *Tabeguache.*
    *Yampa.*
    *Uinta.*

### VI. SAHAPTINS.

NEZ-PERCÉS.
WARM SPRINGS.
WASCOS.

### VII. KLAMATHS.

KLAMATHS.
MODOCS.
ROGUE RIVER.

### VIII. PIMAS.

PAPAGOS.
PIMAS.

### IX. IROQUOIS.

SENECAS.
WYANDOTS or HURONS.

### X. MUSKOGEES.

CREEKS.
SEMINOLES.
CHICKASAWS.
CHOCTAWS.

### XI. INDEPENDENT TRIBES.

ARAPAHOES.
CADDOS.
CHEROKEES.
MOQUIS.
PUEBLOS.
TAWACANIES.
TONKAWAYS.

# HISTORY OF FAMILIES, TRIBES, AND INDIVIDUALS.

## I. ALGONKINS.

Early in the seventeenth century, the Algonkins were the largest family of North American Indians within the present limits of the United States, extending from Newfoundland to the Mississippi, and from the waters of the Ohio to Hudson's Bay and Lake Winnipeg. Northeast and northwest of them were the Eskimos and the Athabascas; the Dakotas bounded them on the west, and the Mobilian tribes, Catawbas, Natchez, &c., on the south. Within this region also dwelt the Iroquois and many detached tribes from other families. All the tribes of the Algonkins were nomadic, shifting from place to place as the fishing and hunting upon which they depended required. There has been some difficulty in properly locating the tribe from which the family has taken its name, but it is generally believed they lived on the Ottawa River, in Canada, where they were nearly exterminated by their enemies, the Iroquois. The only remnant of the tribe at this time is at the Lake of the Two Mountains.

Of the large number of tribes forming this family, many are now extinct, others so reduced and merged into neighboring tribes as to be lost, while nearly all of the rest have been removed far from their original hunting-grounds. The Lenni Lenape, from the Delaware, are now leading a civilized life far out on the great plains west of the Missouri, and with them are the Shawnees from the south and the once powerful Pottawatamies, Ottawas, and Miamis from the Ohio Valley. Of the many nations forming this great family, we have a very full representation in the following catalogue, about equally divided between the wild hunters and the civilized agriculturists.

### 1. CHEYENNES.

"This nation has received a variety of names from travellers and the neighboring tribes, as Shyennes, Shiennes, Cheyennes,

Chayennes, Sharas, Shawhays, Sharshas, and by the different bands of Dakotas, Shai-en-a or Shai-é-la. With the Blackfeet, they are the most western branch of the great Algonkin family. When first known, they were living on the Chayenne or Cayenne River, a branch of the Red River of the North, but were driven west of the Mississippi by the Sioux, and about the close of the last century still farther west across the Missouri, where they were found by those enterprising travelers Lewis and Clark in 1803. On their map attached to their report they locate them near the eastern face of the Black Hills, in the valley of the great Sheyenne River, and state their number at 1,500 souls." Their first treaty with the United States was made in 1825, at the mouth of the Teton River. They were then at peace with the Dakotas, but warring against the Pawnees and others. Were then estimated, by Drake, to number 3,250.

During the time of Long's expedition to the Rocky Mountains, in 1819 and 1820, a small portion of the Cheyennes seem to have separated themselves from the rest of their nation on the Missouri, and to have associated themselves with the Arapahoes who wandered about the tributaries of the Platte and Arkansas, while those who remained affiliated with the Ogalallas, these two divisions remaining separated until the present time. Steps are now being taken, however, to bring them together on a new reservation in the Indian Territory.

Up to 1862, they were generally friendly to the white settlers, when outbreaks occurred, and then for three or four years a costly and bloody war was carried on against them, a notable feature of which was the Sand Creek or Chivington massacre, November 29, 1864. "Since that time there has been constant trouble. * * * In '67, General Hancock burned the village of the Dog Soldiers, on Pawnee Fork, and another war began, in which General Custer defeated them at Washita, killing Black Kettle and 37 others." The northern bands have been generally at peace with the whites, resisting many overtures to join their southern brethren.

*List of illustrations.*

118, 120. HAH-KET-HOME-MAH. *Little Robe.* (Front.)
SOUTHERN CHEYENNE.
119, 121. HAH-KET-HOME-MAH. *Little Robe.* (Profile.)
SOUTHERN CHEYENNE.
109. HAH-KET-HOME-MAH. *Little Robe.* SOUTHERN CHEYENNE.

110. MIN-NIN-NE-WAH. *Whirlwind.* SOUTHERN CHEYENNE.
111. WHOAK-POO-NO-BATS. *White Shield.*
                                                         SOUTHERN CHEYENNE.
112. WO-PO-HAM. *White Horse.* SOUTHERN CHEYENNE.
113. BAH-TA-CHE. *Medicine Man.* SOUTHERN CHEYENNE.
114. PAWNEE. SOUTHERN CHEYENNE.
115. ED. GUERRIER. *Interpreter.* SOUTHERN CHEYENNE.
26. LAME WHITE MAN. NORTHERN CHEYENNE.
    WILD HOG. NORTHERN CHEYENNE.
27. BALD BEAR. NORTHERN CHEYENNE.
    CUT FOOT. NORTHERN CHEYENNE.
28. DULL KNIFE. NORTHERN CHEYENNE.
    LITTLE WOLF. NORTHERN CHEYENNE.
29. CRAZY HEAD. NORTHERN CHEYENNE.
    SPOTTED WOLF. NORTHERN CHEYENNE.
30, 31. STONE CALF and WIFE. SOUTHERN CHEYENNE.
116. WHIRLWIND and PAWNEE. SOUTHERN CHEYENNE.
117. LITTLE ROBE and WHITE HORSE.
                                                         SOUTHERN CHEYENNE.
122. HIGH TOE.
123–4. GROUPS AT AGENCY.

## 2. CHIPPEWAS.

Migrating from the East late in the sixteenth or early in the seventeenth century, the Chippewas, or Ojibwas, settled first about the Falls of Saint Mary, from which point they pushed still farther westward, and eventually compelled the Dakotas to relinquish their ancient hunting-grounds about the headwaters of the Mississippi and of the Red River of the North. Were first known to the French, about 1640, who called them *Sauteux,* from the place of their residence about Sault Ste. Marie, a name still applied to them by the Canadian French. They were then living in scattered bands on the banks of Lake Superior and Lake Huron, and at war with the Foxes, Iroquois, and Dakotas, becoming thereby much reduced in numbers. Were firm allies of the French in all of their operations against the English, and took a prominent part in Pontiac's uprising. During the revolutionary war they were hostile to the colonists, but made a treaty of peace with them at its close. They again sided with the English in the war of 1812, but joined in a general pacification with a number of other tribes in 1816. Like other tribes, they gradually ceded their lands to the Government, receiving in return annuities and goods, until in 1851 all but a few bands, retaining but moderate reservations, had removed west of the Mississippi.

"The Chippewas, now numbering 19,606, formerly ranged over Michigan, Wisconsin, and Minnesota, and with common interests, and acknowledging more or less the leadership of one controlling mind, formed a homogeneous and powerful nation; a formidable foe to the Sioux, with whom they waged incessant warfare, which was checked only by the removal of the Minnesota Sioux to Dakota after the outbreak of 1863."

The collecting of the Chippewas upon thirteen reservations, scattered over the above-named States, under five different agencies, has so modified the *esprit du corps* of the tribe that, though speaking the same language and holding the same traditions and customs, the bands located in different sections of the country have few interests and no property in common, and little influence or intercourse with each other. The agency has taken the place of the nation, and is in turn developing the individual man, who, owning house, stock, and farm, has learned to look solely to his own exertions for support. No tribe by unswerving loyalty deserves more of the Government, or is making, under favorable conditions, more gratifying progress; 9,850 of the tribe live in houses, 9,345 are engaged in agriculture and other civilized occupations; and 13,202 wear citizen's dress. Fifty-seven per cent. of their subsistence is obtained by their own labor, mainly in farming; for the rest, they depend on game and fish, especially the latter, of which they readily obtain large quantities.

The Chippewas are extensively intermarried with the Ottawas, and are thrifty and worthy citizens of the United States, as are also those of Saginaw, and of Keewenaw Bay in Michigan. The Bad River, Red Cliff, Red Lake, and Mississippi bands are likewise making rapid progress in civilization. Of those which have made but little or no progress are the Leech Lake, White Earth, Mille Lac, and other scattered bands in remote and inaccessible regions of Minnesota and Wisconsin, the older chiefs resolutely opposing any attempt on the part of the younger men to begin a civilized life.

*List of Illustrations.*

1001. ES-EN-CE. *Little Shell.* PEMBINA.

Head chief of the Pembinas, residing at Turtle Mountain, in Dakota. His father and grandfather were chiefs of the same band before him. Took an active part against the Sioux in the Minnesota massacres in 1863. Visited Washington in 1874, at the head of a delegation in behalf of their bands, to protest against being removed from their old homes about Turtle Mountain.

1002. MIS-TO-YA-BE. *Little Bull.* PEMBINA.

Head brave of the Pembinas, and resides at Pembina. Is a man of considerable influence, his word being law with his band. Has good common sense and fine executive ability. Was removed by the Government to White Earth reservation, but refuses to live there, and has gone back to his old home. Has fought the Sioux frequently, and has been quite successful in stealing horses from them. Has two wives. Does no farming.

1003. KA-EES-PA. *Something Blown Up by the Wind.* PEMBINA.

A half-breed, but lives and dresses like an Indian. His father was made a chief of the Pembinas by the English and Americans, and upon his death succeeded him. Is a very successful hunter, and is looked upon as a representative man of the tribe.

1004. KE-WOE-SAIS-WE-RO. *The Man Who Knows How to Hunt.* PEMBINA.

A half-breed and third brave of the band. Always joined the Chippewas in fighting the Sioux—the Pembinas fighting on horseback—and counts four scalps. Is a trader. Is thought very much of by his tribe, and has a reputation for moral worth and straightforward dealing.

851. LARGE GROUP of the preceeding four numbers.

1068. SHAY-WI-ZICK. *Sour Spittle.* RED LAKE.

A brave of the Red Lake band of Chippewas and younger brother of the head chief. His wife and children were killed by the Sioux, and he fought them frequently in return, killing two. Was a good speaker and farmed a good deal. Died last winter, aged about 70.

80, 1069. QUI-WI-ZHEN-SHISH.  *Bad Boy.*  RED LAKE.

Foremost brave of the Red Lake band. His father was chief, which office is now held by his older brother. Was ranked as one of the bravest of the Chippewas in their battles with the Sioux, and took many scalps. Was a fine speaker and a man of much influence. Farmed very successfully and raised considerable corn, and was also a good hunter. Had two wives. Died in 1872.

1070. QUI-WI-ZENS.  *The Boy.*  RED LAKE.

A brave and a leading warrior in the battles of his tribe with the Sioux. A good speaker, hunter, and farmer, although the farming is done almost entirely by his wife and children, as is the case with all these Indians. Is now dead.

1071. AUGUSTE.  PEMBINA.

A brave of the Pembinas, formerly residing near the British line, but now removed, with his band, to the White Earth reservation. Has the reputation of being a miserable, worthless Indian, unwilling to work, and adhering with great tenacity to the heathenish customs of his tribe. Was baptized in his infancy by the Roman Catholics, but has renounced his Christianity. Has had his skull broken three times in quarrels with his own people, and has been twice wounded in fights with the Sioux.

1072. MOOZOMO.  *Moose's Dung.*  RED LAKE.

A petty chief of the Red Lake band. Died some years ago at a very old age. Was a great hunter, and farmed considerably also. Was much respected by the Red Lake bands, and especially so by the whites.

1073. ME-JAW-KEY-OSH.  *Something in the Air Gradually Falling to the Earth.*  RED LAKE.

A brave but recently made a chief of the Red Lake Chippewas, and is ranked as the very bravest of all his tribe. Had always been accustomed to fight the Sioux, but after the massacre of 1862-'63 re-organized and led a small party of from six to ten of his bravest men against them every summer for some time, killing with his own hand fifteen of their enemies and bringing home their scalps. Was a crafty warrior and knew well how to slay his foe without losing his own life. He still lives, farming and hunting for a living, and is a man of great influence in his band.

1074. ESSINIWUB OGWISSUN. *The Son of Essiniwub.*
RED LAKE.

A quiet, peaceable young man, never on the war-path, peace having been declared with the Sioux before he came of age.

1075. MAIADJIAUSH. *Something Beginning to Sail Off.*
RED LAKE.

A brave residing at Red Lake. His father was a chief and his younger brother the present head chief of the Red Lake band. Ten years ago had the reputation of being a bad man, and has the same suspicion still hanging about him; is ill-natured, cross-grained, and always striking and quarrelling with his fellow-Indians.

1076. NABONIQUEAUSH. *A Yellow-haired One Sailing Along.*
RED LAKE.

1077. TIBISHKO-BINESS. *Like a Bird.* RED LAKE.

A petty chief and brother of Bad Boy. Has often fought the Sioux as a leading brave. Hunts for a living, while his family cultivate corn and potatoes. Is a good speaker and much respected by the Red Lakes.

78, 79. PO-GO-NAY-GE-SHICK. *Hole in the Day.*
81. AH-AH-SHAW-WE-KE-SHICK. *Crossing Sky.* RABBIT LAKE.
82. NAH-GUN-A-GOW-BOW. *Standing Forward.* RABBIT LAKE.
83. KISH-KA-NA-CUT. *Stump.* MILLE LAC.
84. MIS-KO-PE-NEN-SHA. *Red Bird.* LAKE WINNIPEG.
85. NAW-YAW-NAB. *The Foremost Sitter.* WISCONSIN.
86. NOW-WE-GE-SHICK. *Noon Day.*

### 3. DELAWARES.

When first discovered by the whites, the Delawares were living on the banks of the Delaware, in detached bands under separate sachems, and called themselves Renappi—a collective term for men—or, as it is now written, Lenno Lenape. In 1616 the Dutch began trading with them, maintaining friendly relations most of the time, and buying so much of their land that they had to move inland for game and furs. Penn and his followers, succeeding, kept up the trade and bought large tracts of land, but the Indians claimed to have been defrauded and showed a reluctance to move. They then numbered about 6,000. With the assistance of the Indians of the Six Nations the authorities compelled the Delawares to retire. At the beginning of the Revolution there were none east of the Alleghanies. By treaty in 1789 lands were reserved to them between the Miami and Cuyahoga, and on the Muskingum. In 1818 the Delawares ceded all their lands to the Government and removed to White River, Missouri, to the number of 1,800, leaving a small number in Ohio. Another change followed eleven years after, when 1,000 settled by treaty on the Kansas and Missouri Rivers, the rest going south to Red River.

During the late civil war they furnished 170 soldiers out of an able-bodied male population of 201.

In 1866 sold their land to the railroad which ran across it, and buying land of the Cherokees, settled where the main body now resides, small bands being scattered about among the Wichitas and Kiowas.

In 1866, by a special treaty, they received and divided the funds held for their benefit, took lands in severalty, and ceased to be regarded as a tribe. They have given up their Indian ways and live in comfortable houses. Many of them are efficient farmers and good citizens. They are becoming so incorporated with other tribes that there has been no late enumeration made of them as a whole. During the late war they numbered 1,085.

*List of illustrations.*

181-2. BLACK BEAVER.

Is a full-blood Delaware. Has travelled very extensively through the mountains, serving at one time as a captain in the United States Army. Has a large farm under cultivation, and lives in a very comfortable manner, having good, substantial frontier buildings. He commenced life as a wild Indian trapper, until, becoming familiar with almost all of the unexplored region of the West, and being a remarkably truthful and reliable man, he was much sought after as a guide, and accompanied several expeditions in that capacity. His life has been one of bold adventure, fraught with many interesting incidents, which, if properly written out, would form an interesting and entertaining volume.— *Batty.*

186. GREAT BEAR.

### 4. MENOMONEES.

Were known to the French as early as 1640, and were then living on the Menomonee River, emptying into Green Bay, Wisconsin. Their name is that of the wild rice upon which they largely depend for their subsistence. This is one of the few tribes in the United States who have never been removed from their old home, and are still residing on the same spot where they were first known. Served with the French against the Foxes in 1712, and against the English up to 1763, participating in Braddock's defeat, battles of Fort William Henry and the Plains of Abraham. Were allies of the English during the Revolution, and also in the second war with Great Britain. In 1831 commenced ceding their lands to the Government for money payments, until they were finally located in 1854 in their present reservation in Shawano County, Wisconsin, consisting of 231,680 acres of very poor land. They are declining rapidly in numbers. In 1822 were estimated at 3,900; the present count makes them 1,522. Are now living in a civilized way, with a large proportion of their children attending school regularly. Their main dependence is upon the lumber trade, cutting during the last winter over 5,000,000 feet of logs, netting them $4 per 1,000.

*List of illustrations.*

852. MOSES LADD.

An intelligent and influential man in the tribe, a grandson of Corrow and nephew of Shu-na-ma-shu-na-ne, noted chiefs of the Menomonees. In 1876 Mr. Ladd was sent as a delegate from his tribe to Washington to settle various complications before the Departments and Congress. Was born at Green Bay, Wis., in 1828. Is of mixed blood.

## 5. MIAMIES.

In 1658 were found on Green Bay, Wisconsin, and in 1670 near the head of Fox River, and were then said to number 8,000 warriors, living in mat houses within a palisade. Their early history is full of their many engagements with Iroquois, Sioux, and the French, in all of which they lost heavily. Sided with the English in the revolutionary war, continuing hostile to the United States until 1815. They then numbered 3,000, but their wars had left them in a badly demoralized condition, leading to broils among themselves, in which nearly 500 perished in eighteen years. In 1835 a portion, numbering 384, were removed from Indiana to the south side of the Kansas River. By 1838 the Miamies remaining in Indiana, then numbering 1,100, sold the rest of their lands; and in 1846 500 of them removed to Kansas, where in twenty-two years they were reduced to 92. In 1873 their lands were sold, when most of the tribe confederated with the Peorias, a few remaining in Kansas as citizens. Are now very much scattered, with no agency of their own, and number, as near as can be ascertained, less than 100. The subjects of the following photographs are of mixed blood:

*List of illustrations.*

419. LUM-KI-KOM.
420. THOS. MILLER.
421. JOE DICK.
422-4. ROUBIDEAUX.
425. THOS. RICHARDWELL.
426. ROUBIDEAUX and RICHARDWELL.

## 6. OTTAWAS.

When first discovered by the early French explorers were residing on the northwest shore of the peninsula of Michigan. After the defeat of the Hurons in 1649, they fled before the Iroquois to beyond the Mississippi, but were soon compelled to retrace their steps by the Dakotas, and finally settled at Mackinaw, where they joined the French in many of their operations and in their contest for Canada. At its close, Pontiac, head chief of the Detroit Ottawas, organized a great conspiracy for the destruction of the English, which was only partially successful. During the Revolution were with the English. At its close a long series of treaties followed, until, in 1833, those in

Michigan ceded their lands and removed south of the Missouri River. In 1836 those in Ohio sold their lands and removed to the Indian Territory and prospered, becoming citizens of the United States in 1867. In 1870 made another move to a new reservation of 25,000 acres near the Shawnees, where they are now living, reduced to 140. A large number of Ottawas are now living on the shore of Lake Superior, so intermarried and confederated with the Chippewas that there is no attempt at any distinction between them, the two combined numbering over 6,000. In Canada there are about 1,000 more, all self-supporting.

*List of illustrations.*

504. SUCKER.

505. CHE-PO-QUA. *Lightning.*

English name, Henry Clay. Full-blood Ottawa. Uneducated, but of considerable executive ability. Is a councilman and an energetic, unselfish worker for the advancement of the tribe. Was born in 1830, and this photograph taken in 1868.

506. PARTEE. *John Wilson.*

Chief of the tribe from 1867 to 1869, dying before the expiration of his term of office, aged about 60 years. Was but little versed in English, but was well educated in his own language. Was noted for amiability and hospitality, and made one of the very best of chiefs.

507. SHA-PON-DA. *Passing Through.* (James Wind.)

Succeeded John Wilson as chief for two years. Is a half-blood. Is well educated in native language, and an ordained minister in the Baptist church. Died in 1875.

1040. JOSEPH KING.

Successor of James Wind as chief of the Ottawas. Is well educated in both native and English languages. Age, 50 years.

1041. L. S. DAGNET.

Born as a Peoria, but was expelled from the tribe, and the Ottawas adopted him as one of their own.

1039. FRANK KING.

Also an adopted member of the tribe, being originally a Chippewa. Has been a counsellor, and also judge of the council.

## 7. POTTAWATOMIES.

Early in 1600 were occupying the lower peninsula of Michigan in scattered bands, whence they were finally driven westward by the Iroquois, and settled about Green Bay. The French acquired much influence over them, whom they joined in their wars with the Iroquois. Joined Pontiac in his uprising in 1763. Hostile to colonists during the Revolution, but made a peace in 1795, joining the English again, however, in 1812. New treaties followed by which their lands were almost entirely conveyed away, until in 1838 a reserve was allotted them on the Missouri, to which 800 were removed. The whole tribe then numbered about 4,000, some bands of which had made considerable progress in civilization, while a part, called the Pottawatomies of the Prairie, were roving and pagan. Those in Kansas made rapid progress in civilization. In 1867, 1,400 out of 2,180 elected to become citizens and take their lands in severalty; the others held to their tribal organization, but disintegration set in and many became wanderers, some even going to Mexico. It is difficult at the present time to estimate their whole number, owing to their scattered condition. There are only 450 in the Indian Territory, under the care of the Indian Bureau, and in Michigan 60. The others are citizens of roaming in Mexico. Of this once numerous and powerful nation we have but a single illustration, viz:

*List of illustrations.*

522. MZHIK-KI-AN. *Thunder Coming Down to the Ground.*

## 8. SACS AND FOXES.

The Sacs, Sauks, or Saukies, as it has been variously written—a word meaning white clay—and the Foxes, or Outagamies, or more properly the Musquakkink, (Red Clay), are now as one tribe. They were first discovered settled about Green Bay, Wis., but their possessions extended westward, so that the larger part was beyond the Mississippi. They partly subdued and admitted into their alliance the Iowas, a Dakota tribe. By 1804 they had ceded all their lands east of the Mississippi, and settled on the Des Moines River, moving subsequently to the Osage, and most of these finally to the Indian Territory. In 1822 the united bands numbered 8,000, but are now reduced to a little more than 1,000, of whom 341 are still

ALGONKINS—SACS AND FOXES. 17

in Iowa, 430 in the Indian Territory, 98 in Nebraska, and about 200 in Kansas. The Sacs and Foxes of the Mississippi in the Indian Territory have a reservation of 483,840 acres. Unsuccessful attempts have been made lately to induce those in Kansas to join them. Those in Iowa are living on a section of land purchased by themselves. The Sacs and Foxes of the Missouri have 4,863 acres of land in Nebraska, but it is proposed to remove them soon to the Indian Territory.

*List of illustrations.*

677. KEOKUK. *Watchful Fox.*

A chief of the Kiscoquah band of Sacs or Sauks, and head chief of the combined Sacs and Foxes.

"The entire absence of records by which the chronology of events might be ascertained, renders it impossible to trace, in the order of their date, the steps by which this remarkable man rose to the chief place of his nation, and acquired a commanding and permanent influence over his people.

"Keokuk is in all respects a magnificent savage. Bold, enterprising, and impulsive, he is also politic, and possesses an intimate knowledge of human nature, and a tact which enables him to bring the resources of his mind into prompt operation. His talents as a military chief and civil ruler are evident from the discipline which exists among his people."— *McKinney.*

678, 681-2, 705. KEOKUK, JR.

Son of the preceding, and succeeded him in the chieftainship.

679, 684. CHARLES KEOKUK.

Grandson of Keokuk, sr.

683. KEOKUK, JR., and CHARLES KEOKUK.

685-6. MO-LESS.

687-8. SAC-A-PE.

689. MO-LESS and SAC-A-PE.

692. QUA-QUA-OUF-PE-KA, or *Dead Indian.*

693. THE SEA.

694. BIG BEAR.

2

695–9. MO-KO-HO-KO.
700. MANO-TO-WA.
400. WAH-COM-MO.
401. NE-QUAW-HO-KO. *Grey Eyes.*
396, 691, 701. WAH-PAH-NAH-KA-NA KAH. *Bear Eating Acorns Up a Tree,* or *Geo. Gomez.*

A Mexican by birth, and interpreter for the Sacs and Foxes since 1858. Was sold to the Comanches when thirteen years of age, but ran away and joined the Kickapoos. Was captured again by the Comanches while he was out with the Kickapoos hunting, but was allowed to escape and rejoin his Indian friends. Drove Government teams for a while between Forts Leavenworth and Kearney. In 1852 joined the Sacs and Foxes, and participated in some of their battles on the plains.

He has been married into the following tribes: Caddoes, Kickapoos, Pawnees, Seminoles, Shawnees, Pottawatomies, Winnebagoes, Iowas, and Sacs and Foxes of Missouri; and speaks the languages of the Creeks, Caddo, Comanche, Pottawatomie, Kickapoo, Sac and Fox, Pawnee, Iowa, and Winnebago, besides English and Spanish.

708. SAC CHIEF.
709. GROUP OF SAC AND FOX CHIEFS.
805. GROUP OF FOX CHIEFS.
806. COMMISSIONER BOGY READING TREATY.
710. COMMISSIONER AND DELEGATION OF CHIEFS.
706–7. GROUPS OF DELEGATIONS.

## 9. SHAWNEE.

The Shawnees or Shawanoes are an erratic tribe of Algonkin stock, supposed to have been one primarily with the Kickapoos. Were first discovered in Wisconsin, but moved eastwardly, and, coming in contact with the Iroquois south of Lake Erie, were driven to the banks of the Cumberland. Some passed thence into South Carolina and Florida, and, by the early part of the eighteenth century, had spread into Pennsylvania and New York. At the close of the Spanish and English war those in Florida emigrated and joined the northern bands, and, again coming into contact with the Iroquois, were driven westward into Ohio. Joined in Pontiac's uprising in 1763, and rallied under the English flag during the Revolution. In 1795 the main body of the tribe were on the Scioto, but some had already crossed the Mississippi and others south. Those in Missouri ceded their lands to the Government in 1825, and those in Ohio in 1831, for new homes in the Indian Territory. In 1854 the main body in the Indian Territory disbanded their tribal organization and divided their lands in severalty.

The *Eastern Shawnees* are those who emigrated direct from Ohio to the Indian Territory, where they now are. They number 97, and are successful agriculturists.

The *Absentee Shawnees* are those who, thirty-five years since, seceded from the main portion of the tribe in Kansas and located in the northern part of the Indian Territory, where they have received no aid from Government, but are now in a highly prosperous condition. They number 563 at the present time.

*List of illustrations.*

711. WA-WA-SI-SI-MO.
712. F. A. ROGERS.
713. CHARLES TUCKER.
716. BERTRAM.

### 10. PEQUOD.

Of the five principal nations of New England in 1674, the Pequods or Mohegans, the two being considered as one, were tribes of considerable influence and strength of numbers, claiming authority over all the Indians of the Connecticut Valley. Jonathan Edwards states that the language of the Stockbridge or Muhhekanew (Mohegan) was spoken throughout New England. Nearly every tribe had a different dialect, but the language was radically the same. Elliot's translation of the Bible is in a particular dialect of this language. The Stockbridges, so named from the place of their residence, was originally a part of the Housatonic tribe of Massachusetts, to whom the legislature of that State granted a section of land in 1736. They were subsequently removed to New Stockbridge and Brotherton, in Western New York, many other tribes of New England and also of New York joining them. They had good lands and fine farms, and were rapidly becoming worthy of citizenship, when, in 1857, they were removed to a reservation near Green Bay, Wisconsin, on which, their agent reported, no white man could obtain a comfortable livelihood by farming. They have been divided for some time into two bands, known as the "citizen" and "Indian" factions, the former having lived off from the reservation for the past twelve years. In 1875, 134 of the "citizens" received their per capita share of the tribal property, and became private citizens of the United States. The tribe has 118 members remaining.

1050. NA-UN-NAUP-TAUK. *Jacob Jacobs.*     STOCKBRIDGE.

A delegate from the Stockbridge Indians to Washington in 1875, and again in 1876. Born in Wisconsin in 1834. Belongs to the "citizen" band, and participated in the late division of the tribal property and separation from the tribe.

1049. WAUN-NAUN-CON. *J. C. W. Adams.*     STOCKBRIDGE.

Born on the Seneca reservation in New York in 1843, and removed to Wisconsin in 1853. Received a collegiate education at the Lawrence University. In 1876 represented the Stockbridges and Munsees as a delegate in Washington.

1065. LYMAN P. FOWLER.     BROTHERTON.

A member of the Brotherton branch of the Pequod Nation. Born in Oneida County, New York, in 1823, but emigrated with some of the Stockbridges to Wisconsin in 1836. Chosen as a delegate to Washington on behalf of the Stockbridges and Munsees.

## II. ATHABASCAS.

A family of North American Indians, comprising two large divisions, one living in the British Possessions, between Hudson's Bay and the Pacific, and the other along the southern boundary of the United States, in Arizona, New Mexico, and Texas, with some smaller bands along the western coast, north of Oregon.

The name of the family is derived from Lake Athabasca, a Cree word, meaning "cords of hay." They are supposed by many to be of Tartar descent, and their language has been found to be somewhat analogous to that of Thibet. Their traditions point to an emigration from the West, over a series of islands, and amid much snow and ice. The southern branch includes the nomadic Apaches, the industrious Navajos, and a small remnant of Lipans in Texas, numbering, in all, over 20,000.

### 1. APACHES.

One of the most numerous branches of Athabascan stock are the *Apaches*, a fierce, nomadic nation, roaming over the Territories of New Mexico and Arizona, and Sonora and Chihuahua. Always a scourge and a terror to settlers, they have held in check for many years the civilization of the country covered by their depredations. In 1831 Gregg wrote of them: "They are the most extensive and powerful, and yet the most vagrant, of all the savage nations that inhabit the interior of Northern Mexico. They are supposed to number 15,000 souls, although they are subdivided into various petty bands and are scattered over an immense tract of country. They never construct houses, but live in the ordinary wigwam or tent of skins and blankets. They manufacture nothing, cultivate nothing. They seldom resort to the chase, as their country is destitute of game, but seem to depend entirely upon pillage for the support of their immense population, at least 2,000 of which are warriors."

Steadily resisting all attempts at conversion by the missionaries, they gathered about them many of the disaffected tribes and made frequent descents upon missions and towns, ravaging, destroying, and completely depopulating many of them. Since the annexation of their territory to the United States they have caused much trouble, and an almost constant warfare has been kept up against them until quite recently. Successful military campaigns broke up their predatory habits, and since then the efforts which have been made to gather them upon reservations, where they could be cared for until capable of self-sustenance, are proving entirely successful. At the present time more than half the whole nation are on the San Carlos reservation in Arizona, where they have nearly 4,000 square miles, or over 2,500,000 acres, situated upon both sides of the Rio Gila, between the one hundred and ninth and one hundred and eleventh meridians, 400 acres of which are now under cultivation by Indian labor entirely, producing 10,000 bushels of potatoes, 2,000 bushels of corn, and large quantities of other vegetables. They draw their entire subsistence from the Government, but only in return for labor performed, and under this law are doing much good in the way of making and repairing irrigating-ditches, clearing and fencing land, &c. Are now occupying 223 comfortable houses, built for them. "When it is considered that only 2,000 of these Indians have been on the reservation two years, most of whom were participants in the outbreaks of last year (1874); that the 1,400 Ponto, Yuma, and Mohave Apaches from Verde arrived in March last; and that the 1,800 Coyoteros from White Mountain agency arrived July last, after harvest, the above figures will be found a most striking exhibit of the results of the application of a firm control and common-sense treatment for one year."

Besides the San Carlos reservation in Arizona, there are two others in New Mexico, upon which are gathered most of the rest of the Apaches, with the exception of about 650 in the Indian Territory.

The Mescalero reservation, midway between the Rio Grande and the Pecos, contains some 570,000 acres, upon which are the Mescaleros and some other smaller bands, to the number of about 1,100. But little has been done in the way of civilizing them, and they depend almost entirely upon the Government for their subsistence.

The Jicarilla reservation, intended for the sub-tribe of that name, is of about the same dimensions as that of the Mescaleros, and lies between the San Juan River and the northern boundary-line of New Mexico. The Jicarillas, who number about 1,000, have not as yet been placed upon this reserve, but roam at will over the surrounding country, spending much of their time with the southern Utes, with whom they have intermarried to a considerable extent. They draw a portion of their subsistence from the Government and depend upon their own resources for the rest.

The Annual Report of the Commissioner of Indian Affairs for 1875 subdivides and enumerates the Apaches as follows:

| | |
|---|---|
| Apaches proper | 463 |
| Aribaipais | 389 |
| Coyoteros | 1,784 |
| Chiricahuas | 475 |
| Essa-queta | 180 |
| Gila | 800 |
| Jicarilla | 950 |
| Mescalero | 1,100 |
| Miembro | 800 |

## ATHABASCAS—APACHES. 23

| | |
|---|---|
| Mohave | 588 |
| Mogollon | 400 |
| Pinal | 435 |
| Tonto | 661 |
| Yuma | 376 |
| Miembre, Mogollon, and Coyoteros classed together | 490 |
| Total | 9,891 |

*List of illustrations.*

**853. ESKIMINZIN.** PINAL.

Height, 5 feet 8 inches; circumference of head, 22¼ inches; circumference of chest, 37 inches; age, 38 years. Head chief of San Carlos reservation and of the Pinal Apaches. His family was among those slain at the Camp Grant massacre in 1871. Is now taking the lead in living a civilized life, having taken up a farm on the San Carlos River.

**854. ESKIMINZIN AND WIFE.** PINAL.

**855. CASSADORA.** *A hunter.* PINAL.

Height, 5 feet 8½ inches; circumference of head, 23 inches; circumference of chest, 40 inches. Petty chief; was one of the most lawless and intractable of the tribe. Took part in the assault on a wagon-train in the Cañon Dolores in 1872.

**856. CASSADORA AND WIFE.** PINAL.

**857. ESKINILAY.** PINAL.

Height, 5 feet 2 inches; circumference of head, 22 inches; circumference of chest, 35 inches. A captain of the reservation police.

**858. ESKINILAY AND WIFE.** PINAL.

**860. CHIQUITO.** PINAL.

Height, 5 feet ¾ inches; circumference of head, 23 inches; circumference of chest, 36 inches. A petty chief.

**861. CHIQUITO AND WIFE.** PINAL.

**862. SAYGULLY.** PINAL.

Height, 5 feet 7¼ inches; circumference of head, 22¼ inches; circumference of chest, 36 inches.

863. Eskayelah. Coyotero.

Height, 5 feet 11 inches; circumference of head, 23 inches; circumference of chest, 36½ inches. An hereditary head chief of the Coyotero Apaches.

864. Skellegunney. Coyotero.

Height, 5 feet 8½ inches; circumference of head, 22½ inches; circumference of chest, 36½ inches. Is looked upon as being a hard case, and has the reputation of being a great horse-stealer.

865. Cullah. Chiricahua.

Height, 5 feet 6¼ inches; circumference of head, 22 inches; circumference of chest, 35½ inches.

866. Hautushnehay. Pinal.

Height, 5 feet 9 inches; circumference of head, 23 inches; circumference of chest, 36¼ inches. One of the reservation policemen appointed by the agent.

867. Napasgingush. Pinal.

Height, 5 feet 6½ inches; circumference of head, 21½ inches; circumference of chest, 34½ inches.

868. Cushshashado. Pinal.

Height, 5 feet 3¼ inches; circumference of head, 22 inches; circumference of chest, 33 inches. A clerk in the trader's store on the San Carlos reservation; speaks English fluently.

869. Pinal. Coyotero.

Height, 5 feet 3¼ inches; circumference of head, 21¾ inches; circumference of chest, 37 inches. A sub-chief.

870. Passalah. Pinal.

Height, 5 feet 11½ inches; circumference of head, 23 inches; circumference of chest, 37½ inches. A reservation policeman.

871. Marijildo Grijalva.

Interpreter. A native of Sonora, Mexico. Was captured when quite young by the Coyotero Apaches, and held by them in captivity until looked upon as one of the tribe.

ATHABASCAS—APACHES. 25

1. ESKEL-TA-SALA. (Front.)     COYOTERO.
2. ESKEL-TA-SALA. (Side.)     COYOTERO.
3. SANTO. (Front.)     COYOTERO.
4. SANTO. (Side.)     COYOTERO.
5. TA-HO. *Equestrian.* (Front.)     ESSA-QUETA.
6. TA-HO. *Equestrian.* (Side.)     ESSA-QUETA.

A sub-chief of his band. Age, about 50 years; height, 5 feet, 11 inches; circumference of head, 23 inches; chest, 45 inches.

7. GRAY EAGLE. (Front.)     ESSA-QUETA.
8. GRAY EAGLE. (Side.)     ESSA-QUETA.
9. CAPITAN. (Front.)     ESSA-QUETA.
10. CAPITAN. (Side.)     ESSA-QUETA.

Age, about 56 years; height, 5 feet 8 inches; circumference of head, 24 inches; chest, 37 inches.

11. PACER. (Front.)     ESSA-QUETA.
12. PACER. (Side.)     ESSA-QUETA.

Was the acknowledged leader of the Apaches in the Indian Territory, and at the same time friendly to the whites. He and his squaw are now both dead.

13. 'PACER'S SQUAW. (Front.)     ESSA-QUETA.
14. PACER'S SQUAW. (Side.)     ESSA-QUETA.
451. KLE-ZHEH.     JICARILLA.
449. GUACHINITO. *One who Dresses in Indian Clothes.*
    JICARILLA.
753, 442. GUERITO. *The Man with Yellow Hair.*     JICARILLA.

A young chief of the Jicarilla Apaches, and a son of old Guero, their principal chief. This tribe is intermarried with the Utes, and has always been on friendly terms with them. Young Guerito was sent to Washington in 1873, joining the Ute delegation, for the purpose of effecting some treaty whereby these Apaches might have set apart for them a piece of land of their own to cultivate, as now they roam on Ute land and have no home they can call their own. He is a relative of Ouray, the great chief of the Utes, and through the latter's influence some such arrangement was effected. Guerito is a quiet and peaceable young man, a representative of his tribe, who prefer farming, and shrink from all wars against either Indians or white men.

444. SON OF GUERITO. JICARILLA.
443, 5, 6, 8. YOUNG BRAVES. JICARILLA.
447. PAH-YEH, or *Hosea Martin.* JICARILLA.
18. SON OF VICENTI. JICARILLA.
125. PEDRO SCRADILICTO. (Front.) COYOTERO.
126. PEDRO SCRADILICTO. (Side.) COYOTERO.
127. ES-CHA-PA. *The One-eyed.* (Front.) COYOTERO.
652. ES-CHA-PA. *The One-eyed.* (Side.) COYOTERO.
414. JOSÉ POCATI. (Front.) YUMA.
415. JOSÉ POCATI. (Side.) YUMA.
749. CHARLIE ARRIWAWA. (Front.) MOHAVE.
750. CHARLIE ARRIWAWA. (Side.) MOHAVE.
872-3. GROUPS comprising all the above included within the Nos. 853-871.

2. NAVAJOS.

A very numerous band of the Apache Nation inhabiting the mountains and plateaus of Arizona and New Mexico, between the San Juan and Little Colorado Rivers, ever since our first knowledge of them. The Spaniards early recognized their relation to the Apaches, although they differ totally from them in their industrious habits, being by far the most civilized of any tribe of Athabascan descent. They have evidently been quick to take advantage of their contact with the semi-civilized Pueblos and Moquis, and from them have acquired many useful arts—chiefly in learning to spin and weave. Their blankets, woven in looms, are of great excellence, and frequently bring from $25 to $100. They cultivate the soil extensively, raising large quantities of corn, squashes, melons, &c. Colonel Baker, in 1859, estimated their farms at 20,000 acres, evidently too large an estimate, as their agent's report for 1875 places the cultivated lands at only 6,000 acres. Their principal wealth, however, is in horses, sheep, and goats, having acquired them at an early day and fostered their growth, so that they now count their horses by the thousand, and their sheep by hundreds of thousands. Notwithstanding the excellence of their manufactures, their houses are rude affairs, called by the Spaniards *jackals,* and by themselves *hogans*—small conical huts of poles, covered with branches, and in winter with earth. Like the Apaches, they have made incessant war on the Mexicans, who have made many unsuccessful attempts to subjugate them. The expeditions against them on the part of the United States by Doniphan in 1846, Wilkes in 1847, Newby in 1848, and Washington in 1849, were practically failures. Colonel Sumner established Fort Defiance in 1851, but was forced to retreat, and all other attempts to subdue them were defeated until the winter campaign in 1863, when Colonel Carson compelled them to remove to the Bosque Redondo, on the Pecos River, where 7,000 were held prisoners by the Government for several years. In 1868 a treaty was made with them under which they were removed to Fort Wingate, and the following year back to their old home around Fort Defiance and the cañon De Chelly, where a reservation of 5,200 square miles was assigned them. The latest count puts their number at 11,768—3,000 of whom are said to come directly under the civilizing influences of the agency. Schools are not well established yet, but few of their children attending, and then very irregularly. Although they produce largely, yet they are dependent upon the Government for two-thirds of their subsistence. They dress well, chiefly in materials of their own make, and covering the whole body.

*List of illustrations.*

1027. MANULITO.

The great war-chief of the Navajos. Has been engaged in many combats, and his breast shows the scars of a number of wounds received in battle; was in command of the Indians during their siege of Fort Defiance.

1028. JUANITA.

The favorite one of five wives of Manulito, the chief.

1029. MANULITO SEGUNDO.

Son of Manulito and Juanita.

1030. CAYATANITA.

A brother of Manulito's, and captain of a band of warriors.

1031. BARBAS HUERO. *Light Beard.*

Chief councillor of the tribe, and an earnest advocate of a settled peace policy.

1032. CABRA NEGRA.

A captain, and a sub-chief.

1033. NARBONA PRIMERO.

A sub-chief, noted as being a consistent total abstinence advocate, and who exerts himself to save his tribe from the curse of intemperance.

1034. CARNERO MUCHO. A captain of a band.

1035. { GRANADA MUCHO. A captain of a band.
TIENE-SU-SE. Third war-chief.
MARIANA. Second war-chief.

1038. JUANITA AND GOV. ARNY. Showing Navajo blanket and weaving implements.

1036 GROUP of the preceding, members of a delegation to Washington in 1874.

786. BARBAN CITO. *Little Beard.*

452-5. Miscellaneous men and boys.

## III. DAKOTAS.

A large family of North American Indians, embracing the Assinaboins or Stone Sioux, the Dakotas proper, or, as they are called by the Algonkins, Nadowesioux, from which is derived the word Sioux; Omahas, Otoes, Osages, Poncas, Iowas, Kansas, Missourias, Minatarees, and Crows. Until quite recently they occupied the larger portion of the country bounded on the east by the great lakes, on the north by the British Possessions, on the west by the Rocky Mountains, and on the south by the Platte River. According to their traditions they came eastward from the Pacific, and encountered the Algonkins about the headwaters of the Mississippi, where the mass of them were held in check. One of the tribes of this great family, called by the Chippewas Winnebagook (men from the fetid or salt water), pushed through their enemies and secured a foothold on the shores of Lake Michigan. The Quapaws, called by their Algonkin foes the Alkausas or Arkansas, settled on the Ohio, but were ultimately driven down the river by the Illinois to the region now bearing their name. A few of the tribes retain very nearly their original hunting-grounds; the principal migrations of those who have moved having been southwestwardly, from the headwaters of the Mississippi to the Missouri.

In 1875 the Indians of this family residing within the limits of the United States numbered nearly 68,000, with about 1,000 more within the British Possessions. If the estimates of early explorers are to be relied upon, they must have lost heavily in population within the last one hundred years—intestine wars, the aggressions of the whites, and the vices of civilization reducing many once powerful tribes to demoralized remnants that are fast fading out of our knowledge by absorption into the ranks of more powerful neighbors. The majority of the tribes of this family are settled on reservations under the direct care and support of the Government, and are fairly on the road to a civilized future. The exceptions are some of the wild bands of the Sioux, the Minatarees or Gros Ventres, and the Crows. At the present writing most of the first-named are at war with the United States forces, while the two latter are friendly.

### 1. CROWS.

The Crows, or, as they call themselves, *Absaroka*, meaning something or anything that flies, when first known occupied the Lower Yellowstone and the valleys of the Big Horn and Tongue Rivers, but roamed over much of the surrounding country, carrying their incursions even to the plains of Snake River and to the valley of the Green. Were originally one with the Minatarees or Gros Ventres, but separated from them, and were afterward driven from their territory by the Ogalallas and Cheyennes, settling finally about the head of the Yellowstone, dispossessing in their turn the Blackfeet and Flatheads. Are divided into three bands, with a dialect peculiar to each, viz: the Kikatsa or Crows proper, the Ahnahaways, and the Allakaweah, numbering in all, as estimated in 1820, 3,250 souls. Obtaining horses at an early day, they became great marauders. Irving writes of them in "Astoria:" "They are in fact notorious marauders and horse-stealers, crossing and recrossing the mountains (the Big Horn), robbing on one side and conveying their spoils to the other. Hence, we are told, is derived their name, given them on account of their unsettled and predatory habits, winging their flight, like the crows, from one side of the mountains to the other, and making free booty of everything that lies in their way. In 1851, joined in a treaty with the United States giving a right of way for roads to be built through their country. In 1868 a treaty was made, and an attempt made to place all the Crows on one reservation, but without success until 1875. They have been much exposed to incursions from some parties of Sioux at their new agency on the Rosebud as well as at their former one on the Yellowstone. "The Indians, full of war and revenge, have no thought to bestow upon farming or other peaceful employment, especially as the best farming lands of the reservation are most exposed to these hostile incursions. Six families, however, have been induced to tend small farms, and have succeeded well. A mile and a half of ditch, sufficient to irrigate several hundred acres, has been dug, and it is hoped that another season will see at least a beginning made toward the civilization of these 4,000 wild but always loyal Crows."

*List of illustrations.*

940. KAM-NE-BUT-SE. *Blackfoot and squaw.*
946. KAM-NE-BUT-SE. *Blackfoot.*

The principal chief of the Mountain Crows; a splendid specimen of manhood, standing 6 feet 2 inches in height and of very heavy frame; owes his position to his bravery and success in fighting the Sioux, their inveterate enemies. He also ranks high as an orator and councillor in the nation. The first picture, in which he is represented in an elaborate dress of buckskin, was made while on a visit, with a delegation of his tribe, to Washington, in 1873; the other represents him as he appears at his home on the Yellowstone, or in his natural every-day garb.

941. CHE-VE-TE-PU-MA-TA. *Iron Bull and squaw.*

One of the principal chiefs of the Mountain Crows.

942. SE-TA-PIT-SE. *Bear Wolf and squaw.*
943. PERITS-HAR-STS. *Old Crow and squaw.*
944. { KAM NE-BUT-SE. *Blackfoot.*
ECHE-HAS-KA. *Long Horse.*
TE-SHU-NZT. *White Calf.*
945. { MO-MUKH-PI-TCHE.
ELLA-CAUSS-SE. *Thin Belly.*
PISH-KI-HA-DI-RI-KY-ISH. *The One that Leads the Old Dog.*
859. GROUP OF CROW DELEGATION to Washington in 1872, including Agent Pease and the interpreters.
947. IN-TEE-US. *He Shows His Face.*
948. MIT-CHOO-ASH. *Old Onion.*
949. GROUP OF CHIEFS and headmen.

DAKOTA—DAKOTAS OR SIOUX. 31

950. GROUP OF SQUAWS.

The last four pictures were made at the old agency of the Crows, on the Yellowstone, near Shields River, in 1871. The following were also made at the same place and time, and represent the old mission buildings (lately destroyed by fire), in which the agent had his headquarters; their tents and manner of living, and their mode of burial.

953. THE MISSION, or agency buildings.
952. VILLAGE SCENE, showing new adobe houses built for the Indians.
951. INSIDE VIEW OF A SKIN LODGE.
954. MODE OF BURIAL.

2. DAKOTAS, OR SIOUX.

The word Dakota means united, confederated, or many in one, and designates the tribe from which the family takes its name. They seldom or never willingly acknowledge the title *Sioux*, first given them by the French, and now by all whites. There are many theories as to the origin of this latter name, the most acceptable of which is that it is a corruption of the word *Nadouessioux*—a general Chippewa designation for enemies—which was gradually applied by missionaries and traders, through an imperfect understanding of the language, to the tribes thus designated. Governor Ramsey, of Minnesota, thought that the word " originated upon the Upper Missouri, among the early French traders, hunters, and trappers, they deriving it, in all probability, from the name of a sub-band of the Ti-t'-wan (Teton), Dakotas, called *Sioune*, who hunted over the plains of that river, and with whom, consequently, they came most frequently in contact.

"In Lewis and Clark's travels in 1803, they are called the *Teton Saone*, and their villages are located on the Missouri, near Cannon-ball River.

"At least we find the term *Sioux* first used in the early maps to designate a large tribe, with various subdivisions, upon the Upper Missouri only."

Dakota traditions go back but a comparatively short time, and are vague and obscure in regard to their origin and early residence, which place it, however, in the Northwest, above the great lakes. In their progress eastward they early possessed themselves of the country about the headwaters of the Mississippi and the Red River of the North, where they remained as late as 1868, when they were in part dispossessed by the Chippewas, who were eventually the cause of their removal to the Missouri.

Up to 1860, the Dakotas were divided into two principal divisions, those east of the Missouri, who were known as the Minnesota or Mississippi Dakotas, composed of four bands, viz: The M'dewakantons, or those of the Village of the Spirt Lake; the Wa-pe-kutes, or Leaf-Shooters; the Wah-pe-tons, or Village in the Leaves; and the Sissetons, or those of the Village of the Marsh. Most of these have been long in contact with the whites, and, having disposed of the greater portion of their lands to the Government, have abandoned most of their old habits, and devote themselves to farming. Others of them, however, are restless and devoted to old prejudices, and cause much trouble to the settlers. The massacre of the whites in 1862 was inaugurated by the M'dewakantons, the Wahpetons and Sissetons afterwards joining them.

Along the Missouri, but living mostly on its eastern side, were the Shanktonwans (Yanktons), or the People of Village at the End, inhabiting originally the Sioux, Desmoines, and Jacques Rivers, and living now principally about the mouth of the Vermillion.

The Yanktonais, a diminutive of the preceding name, and meaning the lesser or the little people of the End Village. Lewis and Clark described them as the Yanktons of the Plains, or Big Devils, who were on the heads of the Sioux, Jacques, and Red Rivers. Their present range is on the Missouri, above the Yanktons. From one branch of this band the Assiniboines are said to have sprung.

Pabóksa, or Cutheads, a branch of the Yanktons, and ranging above them.

The I-san-teis, or Santees, another sub-band of the Yanktons, living originally in Minnesota and Iowa, but since lately on the Missouri, near the Yanktons.

West of the Missouri, occupying the greater portion of Dakota, Wyoming, and portions of Montana and Nebraska, the general name of Tetons, or Tetonwans ("Village of the Prairie") has been given to the seven principal bands of the Dakotas inhabiting that region. Lewis and Clark placed them on their map in only two principal divisions, viz: as the "Tetans of the

# DAKOTA—DAKOTAS OR SIOUX. 33

Burnt Woods" (Brulés), and the "Tetans Saone," from which some suppose the word Sioux has been derived for the whole Dakota nation. The seven subdivisions as now recognized are the—

1. *Siha sa-pas* or *Blackfeet*, on the Missouri in the neighborhood of the Cannonball River.
2. The *Si-chan-koo* or *Burnt Thighs*, (Brulés,) ranging on the Niobrara and White Rivers, from the Platte to the Cheyenne.
3. *Oncpapas*, or "those who camp by themselves," who roam over the country between the Cheyenne and Yellowstone Rivers.
4. *Minnekonjous*, "those who plant by the water," south of the Black Hills.
5. *Itá-zip cho*, or *Sans Arcs*, "without bows," affiliating with the Oncpapas and Blackfeet, and ranging over much the same country.
6. *Ogalallas*, occupy the country between Fort Laramie and the Platte, although they are now confined to a reservation in the northwestern corner of Nebraska. Have the reputation of being the most friendly disposed toward the whites of all the Titonwans. Red Cloud, so well known as an Indian diplomat, is chief of this band.
7. *O-he-nom pas*, or *Two Kettles*. Live principally about Fort Pierre; against whom it is said very few complaints have ever been made, they having always observed faithfully the stipulations of their treaties with the United States.

In the Report of the Commissioner of Indian Affairs for 1875, there are twenty-one sub-bands of Dakotas enumerated, numbering, in the aggregate, 53,044. Of these, there are fourteen represented by portraits of their leading men, viz:

| | |
|---|---|
| Blackfeet, numbering at the present time about | 1,750 |
| Brulés, numbering at the present time about | 8,420 |
| Cut Heads, numbering at the present time about | 200 |
| Mdewakauton, numbering at the present time about | |
| Ogalallas, numbering at the present time about | 9,136 |
| Oncpapas | 2,100 |
| Sans Arc | 1,778 |
| Santee | 800 |
| Sisseton | 903 |
| Santee and Sisseton at Fort Peck | 1,000 |
| Two Kettles | 2,261 |
| Wahpeton | 1,300 |
| Yanktons | 2,500 |
| Yanktonais, Upper and Lower | 8,129 |

3

"The Sioux are included under twelve agencies, nine in Dakota, two in Montana, and one in Nebraska, at all of which, except at Fort Belknap, a beginning in Indian farming has been made in spite of all discouragements by reason of unsuitable location and the demoralizing influence of 'the hostiles.'"

The Ogalallas at Red Cloud agency, who have almost entirely abandoned the chase on account of scarcity of game, depend almost entirely upon the Government for their support. Their small beginnings in cultivating the soil came to naught through the grasshoppers. The Brulés at Spotted Tail agency have a thriving school with 75 pupils, and cultivated some lands. At the Upper Missouri agencies but little has been done beyond feeding the Indians who report to them for that purpose, their attempts at farming resulting in failures on account of the grasshopper pest. The Yanktons, Santees, Sissetons, Wahpetons, and other Sioux on the Lower Missouri and in Eastern Dakota have made more substantial progress in civilization, many of them having permanently discarded their Indian habits and dress, and live in houses, and are nearly self-supporting. The Santees in Nebraska especially have entirely renounced their old form of life; have churches and sabbath-schools, which are regularly attended. They have a monthly paper, printed in their native language, with an edition of 1,200 copies.

*List of illustrations.*

252. PE-JI'. *Grass.* (Front.) BLACKFEET.
253. PE-JI'. *Grass.* (Profile.) BLACKFEET.
254. PE-JI'. *Grass.* (Full-length.) BLACKFEET.
255. KAN-GI'-I-YO'-TAN-KA. *Sitting Crow.* (Front.) BLACKFEET.
256. KAN-GI'-I-YO'-TAN-KA. *Sitting Crow.* (Profile.) BLACKFEET.
257. MA'-YA-WA-NA-PE-YA. *Iron Scare.* (Front.) BLACKFEET.
258. MA'-YA-WA-NA-PE-YA. *Iron Scare.* (Profile.) BLACKFEET.
259. WI'-YA-KA-SHA. *Red Plume.* (Copy.) BLACKFEET.
920. MA-GA'-SHA-PA. *Goose.* (Copy.) BLACKFEET.

With the exception of the last two numbers the above represent a portion of a delegation of prominent Sioux chiefs and warriors who visited Washington in 1872. The portraits were made in Washington, and represent them in their best attire.

336. CIN-TE-GI-LE-SKA. *Spotted Tail.* (Front.) BRULÉ.

337. CIN-TE-GI-LE-SKA. *Spotted Tail.* (Profile.) BRULÉ.

Spotted Tail has long been the chief of the Brulé Sioux, and since his conversion from an intense hostility to an unswerving friendship for the white people has by them been looked upon and considered as the great chief of all the Sioux. The honors of this position are equally divided between Red Cloud and Spotted Tail; each is chief of his band only, the Indians themselves not recognizing any one man as chief of the whole nation; but their great executive abilities, oratorical powers, and popularity with both whites and Indians, have been the means of putting them forward as the champions of their people.

In his younger days Spotted Tail was a daring and audacious chief, murdering and massacreing wherever he went. In 1854, he and his band attacked a coach, murdered all the passengers, and perpetrated horrible enormities on the dead. He was eventually captured, and imprisoned for about six months in the guardhouse at Fort Leavenworth, during which time his feelings underwent a great change. Instead of a determined foe of the pale-faces, he became their earnest friend and coadjutor in the work of pacification. It has been well said of him that "he is worth more to the Government than a dozen major-generals, with their armies to back them."

The following extract from a speech by Spotted Tail, before a board of Indian Commissioners at Fort Laramie in 1867, will be read with interest as showing his ability as an orator: "My father and friends, your Great Father has sent you here to learn what was going on. You have come. Your Great Father has sent you to listen. Will you listen well, or only listen to half that is good and to half that is bad, and not take the whole to our Great Father? He has sent you here to hear and talk. We know you have not come with presents, but you may have a little money in your pockets that you could give them. They are poor and need help. These men here, and the old men, women, and children, have not had much to eat since they have been here, and if you could give them something it would make my heart glad. Yesterday my friends hit me a good deal; but it does not matter. I have spoken."

Spotted Tail is of a large, commanding figure, and his face generally wears a pleasant, smiling expression. It is a difficult matter to arrive at the exact age of any Indian, and in this case it is uncertain, but is probably about 45 years. He has been to Washington four times, each time as a delegate representing the Sioux nation.

338. SPOTTED TAIL AND SQUAW. BRULÉ.
339. SQUAW OF SPOTTED TAIL. (Front.) BRULÉ.
340. SQUAW OF SPOTTED TAIL. (Profile.) BRULÉ.
341. I-API-OTAH. *Gassy.* (Front.) BRULÉ.
342. I-API-OTAH. *Gassy.* (Profile.) BRULÉ.
343. I-TE'-SAN-YAN. *Whitewash his Face.* (Front.) BRULÉ.
344. I-TE'-SAN-YAN. *Whitewash his Face.* (Profile.) BRULÉ.
345. CHE-TAN'-TA`-KPI'. *Charge on the Hawk.* (Front.) BRULÉ.
346. CHE-TAN'-TA`-KPI'. *Charge on the Hawk.* (Profile.) BRULÉ.
347. NOM-PA-AP'A. *Two Strikes.* (Front.) BRULÉ.
348. NOM-PA-AP'A. *Two Strikes.* (Profile.) BRULÉ.
349. SQUAW OF TWO STRIKES. (Front.) BRULÉ.
350. SQUAW OF TWO STRIKES. (Profile.) BRULÉ.
351. KAN-GI'-SHA'-PA. *Black Crow.* (Front.) BRULÉ.
352. KAN GI'-SHA'-PA. *Black Crow.* (Profile.) BRULÉ.
353. HE GMA-WA-KU-WA. *One who Runs the Tiger.* (Front.)
BRULÉ.
354. HE-GMA-WA-KU-WA. *One who Runs the Tiger.* (Profile.)
BRULÉ.
355. WANMBLE'-SHDA. *Bald Eagle.* (Front.) BRULÉ.
356. WANMBLE'-SHDA. *Bald Eagle.* (Profile.) BRULÉ.
357. CHE-CHA'-LU. *Thigh.* (Front.) BRULÉ.
358. CHE-CHA'-LU. *Thigh.* (Profile.) BRULÉ.
359. SQUAW OF THIGH. (Front.). BRULÉ.
360. SQUAW OF THIGH. (Profile.) BRULÉ.
361. TA-TAN'-KA-SHA'-PA. *Black Bull.* (Front.) BRULÉ.
362. TA-TAN'-KA-SHA'-PA. *Black Bull.* (Profile.) BRULÉ.
363. CHO-NI'-CHA-WA-NI'-CHA. *No Flesh.* (Front.) BRULÉ.

## DAKOTA—CUT-HEAD. 37

364. CHO-NI'-CHA-WA-NI'-CHA. *No Flesh.* (Profile.) BRULÉ.
365. MA'-ZA-PON-KIS'-KA. *Iron Shell.* (Front.) BRULÉ.
366. MA'-ZA-PON-KIS'-KA. *Iron Shell.* (Profile.) BRULÉ.
367. MA'-ZA-PON-KIS'-KA. *Iron Shell.* (Full length.) BRULÉ.
368. MA-TO'-SHI'-CHA. *Wicked Bear.* (Front.) BRULÉ.
369. MA-TO'-SHI'-CHA. *Wicked Bear.* (Profile.) BRULÉ.
370. PA'-HUI ZI-ZI. *Yellow Hairs.* (Front.) BRULÉ.
371. PA'-HUI-ZI-ZI. *Yellow Hairs.* (Profile.) BRULÉ.
372. I-SHTA'-SKA. *White Eyes.* (Front.) BRULÉ.
373. I-SHTA'-SKA. *White Eyes.* (Profile.) BRULÉ.
374. MA-TO'-DUSA. *Swift Bear.* (Front.) BRULÉ.
375. MA-TO'-DUSA. *Swift Bear.* (Profile.) BRULÉ.
376. WA-KIN'-YAN-SKA. *White Thunder.* (Front.) BRULÉ.
377. WA-KIN'-YAN-SKA. *White Thunder.* (Profile.) BRULÉ.
378. MA'-ZU-O-YA'-TE. *Iron Nation.* (Front.) BRULÉ.
379. MA'-ZU-O-YA'-TE. *Iron Nation.* (Profile.) BRULÉ.
380. MA'-ZU-O-YA'-TE. *Iron Nation.* (Full length.) BRULÉ.

All of the above, under the famous chief Spotted Tail, were members of a delegation who visited Washington in 1872, and were photographed while there.

282. MA-TO'-WA-KAN'. *Medicine Bear.* (Front.) CUT HEAD.
283. MA-TO'-WA-KAN'. *Medicine Bear.* (Profile.) CUT HEAD.
284. MA-TO'-KO-KI'-PA. *Afraid of the Bear.* (Front.) CUT HEAD.
285. MA-TO'-KO-KI'-PA. *Afraid of the Bear.* (Profile.) CUT HEAD.
286. MA-TO'-PO'-ZHE. *Bear's Nose.* (Front.) CUT HEAD.
287. MA-TO'-PO'-ZHE. *Bear's Nose.* (Profile.) CUT HEAD.
288. CHAN-TE'-HA. *Skin of the Heart.* (Front.) CUT HEAD.
289. CHAN-TE'-HA. *Skin of the Heart.* (Profile.) CUT HEAD.
290. PI'-PI-SHA. *Red Lodge.* (Front.) CUT HEAD.
291. PI'-PI-SHA. *Red Lodge.* (Profile.) CUT HEAD.
292. WI-CHA-WANMBLE'. *Man who packs the Eagle.* (Front.) CUT HEAD.
293. WI-CHA-WANMBLE'. *Man who packs the Eagle.* (Profile.) CUT HEAD.

294. SQUAW OF THE MAN WHO PACKS THE EAGLE. (Front.)
CUT HEAD.

295. SQUAW OF THE MAN WHO PACKS THE EAGLE. (Profile.)
CUT HEAD.

197-8. CHE-TAN'-WA-KU-TE-A-MA'-NI. *The Hawk that hunts Walking.* MDEWAKANTON.

Generally known as *Little Crow*. Leader of the hostile bands in the Sioux massacre of the whites in Minnesota in 1862. He had not only visited Washington, and was supposed to be friendly to the whites, but had promised to have his hair cut and become civilized; and at the time of the massacre the Government was engaged in building him a house. Upon the defeat of the Indians, Little Crow escaped into the British Territory, where he was killed the following year.

199. MEDICINE BOTTLE. Son of *Little Crow.* MDEWAKANTON.

200. SHA-KPE. *Six.* MDEWAKANTON.

The massacre spoken of in connection with No. 197 was inaugurated by *Sha-kpe* and his band; some of his young men killed some white men while intoxicated, and then, through fear of retaliation, resolved upon an uprising and the extermination of all the whites at the agency. Sha-kpe's band was re-enforced by the principal warriors from the Mdewakanton and Wahpeton bands, Little Crow taking the leadership. Before they were subdued, 644 men, women, and children were massacred, and 93 soldiers killed in battle.

296. MA-HPI'-YA-LU'-TA. *Red Cloud.* (Front.) OGALALLA.

297. MA-HPI'-YA-LU'-TA. *Red Cloud.* (Profile.) OGALALLA.

Red Cloud, who with Spotted Tail stands pre-eminently forward as the exponents of the peace-policy, is the great chief of the Ogalalla Sioux, and generally recognized by the military and civil authorities as the head chief of all the Sioux. Before he buried the tomahawk, Red Cloud was undoubtedly the most celebrated warrior of all the Indians now living on the American continent. He had over 10,000 people in his camps, and could put in the field 3,000 warriors. When he marched against the settlements he always went in force. He takes his name from the number of his warriors, and their red blankets and paints; it was said that his soldiers covered the hills like a red cloud.

He is now about 45 years of age, six feet in height, and straight as an arrow; his face, which is of a dark red, is indicative of indomitable courage and firmness, and his full, piercing eyes seem to take in at a glance the character of friend or foe.

Red Cloud has probably participated in more conventions, treaties, and large assemblies of his own and the white people, in which the greatest interests were involved, than any other living Indian. "A man of brains, a good ruler, an eloquent speaker, an able general, and a fair diplomat, the friendship of Red Cloud is of more importance than that of all the other chiefs combined." While Spotted Tail has a lively vein of humor in his character, and loves to indulge in a little joke, Red Cloud is all dignity and seriousness.

The following, clipped from the report of the proceedings of the Board of Indian Commissioners at Fort Laramie, in 1870, is indicative of his earnest and impressive manner:

"Red Cloud then arose, and walking toward the outside group, raised his hands toward the skies, and then touched the ground. Then all the Indians rose to their feet, as with uplifted hands Red Cloud uttered the following prayer:

"THE PRAYER OF RED CLOUD.

"O Great Spirit, I pray you to look at us. We are your children, and you placed us first in this land. We pray you to look down on us, so nothing but the truth will be spoken in this council. We don't ask for anything but what is right and just. When you made your red children, O Great Spirit, you made them to have mercy upon them. Now, we are before you to-day, praying you to look down on us, and take pity on your poor red children. We pray you to have nothing but the truth spoken here. We hope these things will be settled up right. You are the Protector of the people who use the bow and arrow, as well as of the people who wear hats and garments, and I hope we don't pray in vain. We are poor and ignorant. Our forefathers told us we would not be in misery if we asked you for assistance. O Great Spirit, look down on your children and take pity on them.'"

298. RED CLOUD and MR. BLACKMORE.    OGALALLA.
299. SHUN'-KA-LU'-TA. *Red Dog.* (Front.)    OGALALLA.
300. SHUN'-KA-LU'-TA. *Red Dog.* (Profile.)    OGALALLA.
301. SHUN-TO'-KE-CHA-ISH-NA-NA. *Lone Wolf.* (Front.)
   OGALALLA.
302. SHUN-TO'-KE-CHA-ISH NA-NA. *Lone Wolf.* (Profile.)
   OGALALLA.
303. WA-HU'-WA-PA. *Ear of Corn.* (Squaw of Lone Wolf. Front.)    OGALALLA.
304. WA-HU'-WA-PA. *Ear of Corn.* (Squaw of Lone Wolf. Profile.)    OGALALLA.
305. SI-HA'-TAN'-KA. *Big Foot.* (Front.)    OGALALLA.
306. SI-HA'-TAN'-KA. *Big Foot.* (Profile.)    OGALALLA.
307. CHE'-TAN-SKA. *White Hawk.* (Front.)    OGALALLA.
308. CHE'-TAN-SKA. *White Hawk.* (Profile.)    OGALALLA.
309. WANMB'LE-KO-KI'-PA. *Afraid of the Eagle.* (Front.)
   OGALALLA.
310. WANMB'LE-KO-KI'-PA. *Afraid of the Eagle.* (Profile.)
   OGALALLA.
311. SHUN'-KA-WA-KAN-TO. *Blue Horse.* (Front.)
   OGALALLA.
312. SHUN'-KA-WA-KAN-TO. *Blue Horse.* (Profile.)
   OGALALLA.
313. WA-CHA-PA. *Stabber.* (Front.)    OGALALLA.
314. WA-CHA-PA. *Stabber.* (Profile.)    OGALALLA.
315. I-TE'-SHA'-PA. *Dirty Face.* (Front.)    OGALALLA.
316. I-TE'-SHA'-PA. *Dirty Face.* (Profile.)    OGALALLA.
317. TA-TAN'-KA-WAS-TE'. *Good Buffalo.* (Front.)
   OGALALLA.
318. TA-TAN'-KA-WAS-TE'. *Good Buffalo.* (Profile.)
   OGALALLA.
319. HE-HA'-KA-TA'-MA-KA. *Poor Elk.* (Front.) OGALALLA.

DAKOTA—ONCPAPAS. 41

320. HE-HA'-KA-TA'-MA-KA. *Poor Elk.* (Profile.) OGALALLA.
321. HE-HA'-KA-NO'M-PA. *Two Elks.* (Front.) OGALALLA.
322. HE-HA'-KA-NO'M-PA. *Two Elks.* (Profile.) OGALALLA.
323. SHUN-TO'-KE-CHA-ISH-HAN-SKA. *High Wolf.* (Front.) OGALALLA.
324. SHUN-TO'-KE-CHA-ISH-HAN-SKA. *High Wolf.* (Profile.) OGALALLA.
325. SHUN'-KA-A-MA'-NA. *Coyote.* (Front.) OGALALLA.
326. SHUN'-KA-A-MA'-NA. *Coyote.* (Profile.) OGALALLA.
327. CHAU-TE'-SU-TA'. *Hard Heart.* (Front.) OGALALLA.
328. CHAU-TE'-SU-TA'. *Hard Heart.* (Profile.) OGALALLA.
329. TA-TAN'-KA-HUN'-KE SNI. *Slow Bull.* (Front.) OGALALLA.
330. TA-TAN'-KA-HUN'-KE-SNI. *Slow Bull.* (Profile.) OGALALLA.
331. HE-HA'-KA-HE-WAN'-ZHI. *One-Horned Elk.* (Copy.) OGALALLA.
332. CHU-TU'-HU-TAN'-KA. *Big Rib.* (Copy.) OGALALLA.
333. WANMBLE'-KI-CHI-ZU PI. *War Eagle.* (Copy.) OGALALLA.
334. TA-SHUN'-KA-KO-KI-PA. *Old Man Afraid of his Horses and his Chiefs.* OGALALLA.
874. CHA-SA-TONGA. *Little Big Man.* OGALALLA.
875. TA-SHUN'-KA-KO-KI'-PA. *Young Man Afraid of his Horses.* OGALALLA.
876. WASHI-TA-TONGA. *American Horse.* OGALALLA.
877. TA-OOP-CHE KA. *Little Wound.* OGALALLA.
878. SHUNKA-LA-LO-KA. *He Dog.* OGALALLA.
879. MATO'-ZI. *Yellow Bear.* OGALALLA.
880. MATO'-YU-MNI. *Three Bears.* OGALALLA.
881. MA-WA-KA-YU-NA. *Sword.* OGALALLA.
882. WM. GARNET, Interpreter.
883. GROUP of the preceding eight numbers.
260. MA-TO'-CHU-TU'-HU. *Bear's Rib.* (Front.) ONCPAPA.
261. MA-TO'-CHU-TU'-HU. *Bear's Rib.* (Profile.) ONCPAPA.
262. TA-TO'-KA-IN'-YAN-KA. *Running Antelope.* (Front.) ONCPAPA.

263. TA-TO' KA-IN'-YAN-KA. *Running Antelope.* (Profile.) ONCPAPA.
264. HE-MA'-ZA. *Iron Horn.* (Front.) ONCPAPA.
265. HE-MA'-ZA. *Iron Horn.* (Profile.) ONCPAPA.
266. WA-KU'-TA-A-MA'-NI. *Walking Shooter.* (Front.) ONCPAPA.
267. WA-KU'-TA-A-MA'-NI. *Walking Shooter.* (Profile.) ONCPAPA.
268. WA-KIN'-YAN-CHI'-TAN. *Thunder Hawk.* (Front.) ONCPAPA.
269. WA-KIN'-YAN-CHI'-TAN. *Thunder Hawk.* (Profile.) ONCPAPA.
797. WI-CHA'-I-WE. *Bloody Mouth.* (Front.) ONCPAPA.
798. WI-CHA'-I-WE. *Bloody Mouth.* (Profile.) ONCPAPA.
799. WA-KAN-TA-I-SHNI. *Lost Medicine.* (Front.) ONCPAPA.
800. WA-KAN-TA-I-SHNI. *Lost Medicine.* (Profile.) ONCPAPA.
801. HE-SHA'-PA. *Black Horn.* (Front.) ONCPAPA.
802. HE-SHA'-PA. *Black Horn.* (Profile.) ONCPAPA.
803. P'SA. *Bull Rushes.* (Front.) ONCPAPA.
804. P'SA. *Bull Rushes.* (Profile.) ONCPAPA.
194–6. CHE-TAN-ZHI. *Yellow Hawk.* SANS ARC.
201–2. WA-KU'-TA. *The Shooter.* SANTEE.
203, 209. WA'-PA-HA-SHA. *Red Ensign.* SANTEE.
204. WA KAN'-HDI-SHA'-PA. *Black Lightning.* SANTEE.
205. O'-WAN-CHA-DU'-TA. *Scarlet all Over.* SANTEE.
206. CHO'-TAN-KA-SHKA'-TA. *Flute-Player.* SANTEE.
207. A-KI'-CHI-TA-NA ZIN. *Standing Soldier.* SANTEE.
208. WAN-M'DI-TA-PA'-A-MA'-NI. *Walks following the Eagle.*
SANTEE.
210. TA'-SHUN-KA-WA-KAN'-WI-CHA. *His Man Horse.* SANTEE.
211. MA-HP'I-YA-I-HUA-N. *Coming among the Clouds.* SANTEE.
212. ZI-TKA'-DA-TO. *Bluebird.* SANTEE.
213. MA-HPI'-YA-NA'-ZIN. *Standing Cloud.* SANTEE.
214. HAN-YA'-TA-DU'-TU. *Scarlet Night.* SAÑTEE.
215. HU-SHA-SHA. *Red Legs.* SANTEE.
249. PE-HUI-UZA-TAN-KA. *Great Scalper.* SANTEE.
250. TA-TAN'KA-NA'-ZIN. *Standing Buffalo.* SANTEE.
381. WA-KAN'-DA. *Medicine.* SANTEE.

DAKOTA—YANKTONS. 43

248. YOUNG BRAVE. SANTEE.
251. OLD BETTS. (Squaw.) SANTEE.
216. SERAPHINE RENVILLE. (Interpreter.) SANTEE.
382–4. GROUPS with Rev. Mr. Hinman. SANTEE.
192. HE-PTE'-CHE'-CHI-KA-LA. *Little Short Horn.* SISSETON.
187–190. MA-WA'-TAN'-NA-HAN'-SKA. *Long Mandan.*
                                                      TWO KETTLE.
191. SUK-TAN'-KA-GE-LE-SKA. *Spotted Horse.* TWO KETTLE.
193. AU-PE'-TO'-KE-CHA. *Other Day.* WAHPETON.
217–239. PA-DA'-NI-A-PA'-A-PA'. *Struck by the Ree.* YANKTON.
218, 219. PSI-CHA-WA-KIN-YAN. *Jumping Thunder.* YANKTON.
220, 906–7. SI-HA'-HAN'-SKA. *Long Foot.* YANKTON.
222–4. PTE-WA-KAN'. *Medicine Cow.* YANKTON.
221. MA-GA'-SKA. *White Swan.* YANKTON.
225–8. WA-HU'-KE-ZI-NOM'-PA. *Two Lance.* YANKTON.
725. LIGHT FOOT. YANKTON.
229. WI'-YA-KA-NO-GE. *Feather in the Ear.* YANKTON.
230–1. ZIN-TKA'-CHI-STIN. *Little Bird.* YANKTON.
232–3. WAN-M'DI-SHA'-PA. *Black Eagle.* YANKTON.
234. MA-TO'-I-WAN-KA'. *Bear Lying Down.* YANKTON.
235. TA-TAN-KA-IN'-YAN-KA. *Running Bull.* YANKTON.
236. HE-HA'-KA-A-MA'-NA. *Walking Elk.* YANKTON.
237. HE-HA'-KA-A-NA'-ZIN. *Standing Elk.* YANKTON.
238. MA-TO'-SA-BI-CHA. *Smutty Bear.* YANKTON.
240–1. SMUTTY BEAR AND STRUCK BY THE REE. YANKTON.
890. ZIN-TKA-SHA'-PA-MA'ZA. *Iron Black Bird.* YANKTON.
891. CHON-NOM'-PA-KIN-YAN. *Flying Pipe.* YANKTON.
892. WA-KIN-YAN-CHIN-STIN. *Little Thunder.* YANKTON.
893. TA-TAN'-KA-WA-KAN'. *Sacred Bull.* YANKTON.
894. ZIN-TKA'-KIN-YAN. *Flying Bird.* YANKTON.
896. TO-KI'-YA-KTE. *He Kills First.* YANKTON.
897. NA-GI'-WA-KAN'. *Sacred Ghost.* YANKTON.
898–9. MA-TO'-HO-TAN'-KA. *Bear with Big Voice.* YANKTON.
900. IN'-YAN-WAS-TE', *Pretty Rock.* YANKTON.
901. TO'-KA-YA-YU'-ZA. *One who Catches the Enemy.* YANKTON.
902. KU-WA'S-CHIN-A-NIA-NI. *One who Walks Home.* YANKTON.

44        CATALOGUE OF INDIAN PHOTOGRAPHS.

903. MA-TO'-I-WAN-KA'-A-MA'-NI.  *Bear that Walks Lying Down.*
    YANKTON.
904–5. MA-TO'-WA-YU-MNI.  *The Bear that Turns Around.*
    YANKTON.
908. TA-TAN'-KA-WA'-KAN.  *Medicine Bull.*    YANKTON.
276. TA-TAN'-KA-WA-NA'-GI.  *Bull's Ghost.*  (Front.)
    LOWER YANKTONAIS.
277. TA-TAN'-KA-WA-NA'-GI.  *Bull's Ghost.*  (Profile.)
    LOWER YANKTONAIS.
278. MA-TO'-WI-TKO-TKO.  *Foolish Bear.* (Front.)
    LOWER YANKTONAIS.
279. MA-TO'-WI-TKO-TKO.  *Foolish Bear.* (Profile.)
    LOWER YANKTONAIS.
280. MA-TO'-NOM'-PA.  *Two Bears.* (Front.)
    LOWER YANKTONAIS.
281. MA-TO'-NOM'-PA.  *Two Bears.* (Profile.)
    LOWER YANKTONAIS.
270. NA-ZU-LA-TAN'-KA.  *Big Head.* (Front.)
    UPPER YANKTONAIS.
271. NA-ZU-LA-TAN'-KA.  *Big Head.* (Profile.)
    UPPER YANKTONAIS.
272. I'-STA-SHA'-PA.  *Black Eye.* (Front.)
    UPPER YANKTONAIS.
273. I'-STA-SHA'-PA.  *Black Eye.* (Profile.)
    UPPER YANKTONAIS.
274. I-CHA'-SAN-TAN'-KA.  *Big Razor.* (Front.)
    UPPER YANKTONAIS.
275. I-CHA'-SAN-TAN'-KA.  *Big Razor.* (Profile.)
    UPPER YANKTONAIS.
170. WA-KAN'-DU'-TA.  *Red Thunder.* (Front.)
171. WA-KAN'-DU'-TA.  *Red Thunder.* (Profile.)
172. HAV-KA-WASH-TI.  *Good Hawk.* (Front.)
173. HAV-KA-WASH-TI.  *Good Hawk.* (Profile.)
174. PE-HAN'-SA-A-MA'NI.  *Walking Crane.* (Front.)
175. PE-HAN'-SA-A-MA-N'I.  *Walking Crane.* (Profile.)
176. WANMDI-ZI.  *Yellow Eagle.* (Front.)
177. WANMDI-ZI.  *Yellow Eagle.* (Profile.)
732. HATONA.  *Many Horns.* (Front.)

DAKOTA—MISCELLANEOUS GROUPS. 45

733. HATONA. *Many Horns.* (Profile.)
734. I-STE-SA'-PA. *Black Eye.* (Front.)
735. I-STE-SA'-PA. *Black Eye.* (Profile.)
736. TA-TAN-KA-HAN-SKA. *Long Fox.* (Front.)
737. TA-TAN-KA-HAN-SKA. *Long Fox.* (Profile.)
908. TA-TAN'-KA-WA-KAN', *Medicine Bull.*
916. MA-ZA'-O-ZAN-ZAN.
917. HE-HA'-KA-MA-ZU'. *Iron Elk.*
919. WANMDI-YAN'-KA. *Great Eagle.*
923. HIN-KAN-DU'-TA. *Red Owl.*
925. CUT NOSE.
927. MA-ZU'-KU'-TA. *Iron Shooter.*
931. TALL FEATHER JOINING.
932. WA-KAN'-O-ZAN-ZAN. *Medicine Bottle.*
933. O-TA-DAN. *Plenty.*
895. CHIEF WITH THE BIG WAR BONNET.
244. WAR DANCE.
815. GENERAL SHERMAN AND COMMISSIONERS at Fort Laramie.
816. COMMISSIONERS IN COUNCIL, Fort Laramie.
817. OLD MAN AFRAID OF HIS HORSES, AND GROUP.
818-830. MISCELLANEOUS GROUPS ABOUT FORT LARAMIE.
831. SIOUX BURIAL.
832-5. GROUPS ABOUT FORT LARAMIE.
838. INDIAN DELEGATION AT THE WHITE HOUSE.
839-41. ST. MARY'S MISSION, KANSAS.
845. THE SERGEANT OF THE GUARD.

### 3. IOWAS.

A tribe of Indians of Dakota stock, inhabiting originally the interior of the State of the same name. Marquette in 1673 placed them on his map as the Pa-houtet. Some of the neighboring Algonkins called them Iowas—a name originally applied to a river, and said to mean "the beautiful land"—and others Mascoutin or Prairie Nadouessi. In their own tongue their name is Pahucha, meaning "Dusty Nose." They were famous as great pedestrians, being able to walk twenty-five or thirty leagues a day, and the names of many of their chiefs show that they prided themselves on their walking.

In 1700 they were on the Mankato, and constantly roaming with the Western Algonkins. Early in the present century they numbered about 1,500, and were involved in wars with the Osages, Omahas, and the Sioux, losing heavily. Later they became much decimated through the ravages of the small-pox and other diseases.

First treaty was made with them in 1815. In 1836 the tribe, numbering 992, were removed to the west bank of the Missouri, and from this time rapidly declined in numbers, many of them becoming vagrants in other tribes, and others killed themselves by intemperance. By 1846 had decreased to 700. In 1861 the tribe, now reduced to 305, ceded all their lands except 16,000 acres, which they subsequently, in 1869, shared with some of the Sacs and Foxes, their old friends.

Since the tribe has been placed under the charge of the Society of Friends they have improved somewhat, so that at the present time (1875), although reduced to 219 souls, they are all living in good houses on their fertile reservation in Southern Nebraska, and are raising much more than is needed for their own consumption. They have good schools, at which nearly one-fourth of the tribe attend, and nearly one-half of the whole number can read. They stand in the front rank of civilized Indian tribes.

*List of illustrations.*

385–6. NAG A-RASH. *British.*

Became first chief of the Iowas in 1862, upon the death of Nan-chee-ning-a. Has always taken a prominent place in favor of civilization and the advancement of his tribe by education and work. Has made four visits to Washington and two to New York, the first being in 1847, when he travelled from Saint Joseph, Mo., to Baltimore in a wagon. Took part once in a great battle between the Otoes, Pawnees, Kickapoos, Pottawatomies, and Sacs and Foxes on one side, and the Snakes, Crows, Cheyennes, Arapahoes, Comanches, and Kiowas on the other, lasting from early dawn until dark. British shot 160 balls; 150 of the enemy were left on the field. Age, 68; height, 5.8½; head, 22⅞; chest, 47½; weight, 193.

388–9. MAH-HEE. *Knife.*
Third chief of the Iowas. When young, lived in Missouri, but afterward removed to Kansas. Enjoyed the confidence of the whites to a marked degree, and was mail-carrier for some time between the frontier posts and the agency. Was among the first to take the lead in settling down to an agricultural life. Has always been a hard-working man, but at one time was dissipated, and once, when under the influence of liquor, killed his father. Is a strictly temperate man now, but his rapidly-failing health will soon unfit him for his usual labor, and his example in the tribe as an industrious man will soon be lost. Age, 56; height, 5.10; head, $22\frac{3}{4}$; chest, $39\frac{1}{2}$; weight, 172.

391, 395. TAH-RA-KEE. *Deer Ham.*
Was fourth chief of the tribe until October, 1876, when he was deposed for persistent interference with the business of the agency. He had been suspended before, but was reinstated by another agent. Age, 50 years; height, $5.8\frac{1}{2}$; head, 22; chest, $41\frac{1}{2}$; weight, 179.

390. KI-HE-GA-ING-A. *Little Chief.*
Fifth chief of the Iowas. Enlisted in the Northern Army and participated in the late war of the rebellion, serving two years. Was promised the position of a chief if he enlisted, and upon his return the promise was made good. Age, 43; height, 5.10; head, $22\frac{3}{4}$; chest, 43; weight, 192.

387. KRA-TEN-THA-WAH. *Black Hawk.*
Was sixth chief of the Iowas. Died January 1, 1871, aged about 30 years; height, 6 feet; weight, 170 pounds.

392–4. NAN-CHEE-NING-A. *No Heart.*
Was first chief of the Iowas. Died in 1862, aged 65; height, 5.10; weight, 170.

921. A CHIEF.

922. GROUP, comprising most of the above numbers.

### 4. KAW OR KANSAS.

The Kansas are an offshoot of the Osages, whom they resemble in many respects. In 1673 they were placed on Marquette's map as on the Missouri, above the Osages. After the cession of Louisiana, a treaty was made with them by the United States. They were then on the river Kansas at the mouth of the Saline, having been forced back from the Missouri by the Sioux, and numbered about 1,500 in 130 earthen lodges. Some of their chiefs visited Washington as early as 1820. In 1825 ceded their lands on the Missouri, retaining a reservation on the Kansas, where they were constantly subjected to attacks from the Pawnees, and on their hunts from other tribes, so that they lost rapidly in numbers. In 1846 they again ceded their lands, and a new reservation of 80,000 acres on the Neosho in Kansas assigned them; but this also soon becoming overrun by settlers, and as they would not cultivate it themselves, it was sold, and the proceeds invested for their benefit and for providing a new home among the Osages. The tribe in 1850 numbered 1,300; in 1860, 800; and in 1875 had dwindled to 516. Under the guidance of Orthodox Friends they are now cultivating 460 acres, and have broken more than as much again. They raised among other things 12,000 bushels of corn; 70 of them are regular church-attendants, and 54 of their children attend school.

*List of illustrations.*

397. LITTLE BEAR.
398. KA-KE-GA-SHA. (Standing.)
399. KA-KE-GA-SHA. (Sitting.)

5. MANDANS.

The Mandans, or Mi-ah'-ta-nees, "people on the bank," have resided on the Upper Missouri for a long time, occupying successively several different places along the river. In 1772 resided 1,500 miles above the mouth of the Missouri, in nine villages located on both sides of the river. Lewis and Clarke found them in 1804 100 miles farther up in only two villages, one on each side of the river; near them were three other villages belonging to the Minnitarees and Ahnahaways.

In the year 1833 these Indians were in their most prosperous state, industrious, well armed, good hunters and good warriors, in the midst of herds of buffalo mostly within sight of the village, with large corn-fields, and a trading-post from which they could at all times obtain supplies, and consequently at that time they might have been considered a happy people. In their personal appearance, prior to the ravages of the small-pox, they were not surpassed by any nation in the Northwest. The men were tall and well made, with regular features and a mild expression of countenance not usually seen among Indians. The complexion, also, was a shade lighter than that of other tribes, often approaching very near to some European nations, as the Spaniards. Another peculiarity was that some of them had fair hair, and some gray or blue eyes, which are very rarely met with among other tribes. A majority of the women, particularly the young, were quite handsome, with fair complexions, and modest in their deportment. They were also noted for their virtue. This was regarded as an honorable and most valuable quality among the young women, and each year a ceremony was performed, in the presence of the whole village, at which time all the females who had preserved their virginity came forward, struck a post, and challenged the world to say aught derogatory of their character.

In these palmy days of their prosperity much time and attention was given to dress, upon which they lavished much of their wealth. They were also very fond of dances, games, races, and other manly and athletic exercises. They are also a very devotional people, having many rites and ceremonies for propitiating the Great Spirit, practising upon themselves a self-torture but little less severe than that of Hindoo devotees.

In the spring of 1838 that dreaded scourge of the Indians, small-pox, made its appearance among the Mandans, brought among them by the employés of the fur company. All the tribes along the river suffered more or less, but none approached so near extinction as the Mandans. When the disease had abated, and when the remnant of this once powerful nation had recovered sufficiently to remove the decaying bodies from their cabins, the total number of grown men was twenty-three, of women forty, and of young persons sixty or seventy. These were all that were left of the eighteen hundred souls that composed the nation prior to the advent of that terrific disease.

The survivors took refuge with the Arickarees, who occupied one of their deserted villages, but retained their former tribal laws and customs, preserving their nationality intact, refusing any alliances with surrounding tribes. The two tribes have lived together since then upon terms of excellent friendship.

50   CATALOGUE OF INDIAN PHOTOGRAPHS.

They now number 420, living in dome-shaped earthen houses, like the Pawnees, which are, however, being gradually replaced by log houses.

The following representatives of the tribe were part of a joint delegation of Arickarees and Mandans to Washington in 1874:

*List of illustrations.*

1006. WA-SHÚ-NA-KOO-RÁ. *Rushing War Eagle.*

The present head chief of the Mandans, a man noted for kindliness and benevolence. Age, 43; height, 5.7¾; head, 24¼; chest, 38.

1005. ME-RA-PA-RA-PA. *Lance.*

Head soldier or brave. Age, 38; height, 5.8½; head, 22¾; chest, 38½.

1007. E-STA-POO-STA. *Running Face.*

Young warrior, son of Red Cow, a "big chief," who was too old to travel, and this son sent in his place. Age, 23; height, 5.6; head, 21½; chest, 37¾.

884. CHARLES PAPINEAU. *Interpreter.*

Born in Montreal in 1820. Has lived in the Mandan country since 1839. Speaks Arickaree, Crow, Sioux, Gros Ventres, Mandan, French, and English.

6. MISSOURIAS.

The Missourias are a tribe of Dakota descent, living on the Missouri River, their name being one given them by the Illinois, and means the people living by the muddy water. They style themselves *Nudarcha*. Were first heard of in 1673, as the first tribe up the river which bears their name. Became allies of the French at an early day, and assisted them in some of their operations against other tribes. Were hostile to the Spanish and also opposed to the ascendency of English influence. In 1805, when Lewis and Clarke passed through their country, they numbered only 300 in all, living in villages south of the Platte, and at war with most of the neighboring tribes. They were affiliated with the Otoes, having deserted their own villages near the mouth of the Grand some time previously in consequence of their almost entire destruction by small-pox. The two have ever since been classed as one tribe. In 1862 the combined tribes numbered 708, and in 1876 only 454. Since their consolidation with the Otoes their history has been the same as of that tribe.

*List of illustrations.*

481. THRACH-TCHE. *True Eagle.*

A full-blood Missouria, and nephew of Ah-ho-che-ka-thocka (Quapaw Indian Striker), a title gained by his bravery in battle against the Quapaws, and who was head chief. At his (Ah-he-cho-ka-thocka's) death, the hereditary successor, Good Talker, was assassinated by Shungech-boy and others, when the line of descent fell on True Eagle, who became chief in 1860, and held the position of Missouria chief in the confederated Otoes and Missourias until 1874, when he resigned in favor of his nephew. Is now about 80 years of age, 6 feet in height, with a stout, well-proportioned frame.

503. NOCH-PE-WORA. *The One they are Afraid of.*

Is a cousin of True Eagle, and chief of the Eagle band of Missourias. Is of a mild, genial disposition, with but little force of character. Age, 45; height, 5.8½; weight, 155; head, 22½; chest, 35.

484-5. WA-THOCK-A-RUCHY. *One who eats his Food Raw.*

His father was of the Bear band of Otoes, and his mother of the Eagle band of Missourias. He inherited a chieftaincy among the Missourias, and succeeded to that position upon the death of his uncle, White Water, in 1868, when he took the name of LOD-NOO-WAH-HOO-WA, or *Pipe-Stem.* Lacks force of character, but is of a mild disposition and well disposed. Is about 5 feet in height, and of a well-developed physical organization.

486. MUNCHA-HUNCHA. *Big Bear,* or *Joseph Powell.*

Is a full-blooded Missouria. Succeeded his grandfather, Cow-he-pa-ha, as chief of the Bear band, in 1870. When a young man he lived much of his time among the whites. Possessing more than ordinary intelligence, he is at present the leading spirit of the Otoes and Missourias in the industrial pursuits of civilized life. These qualities have engendered much jealousy in the breasts of the older chiefs, who throw many obstacles in his way. Besides his good mental qualities he possesses a splendid physique. Height, 5.11; weight, 225; head, 23½; chest, 42.

498. BLACK ELK.

### 7. OMAHAS.

The Omahas were one of the tribes noticed by Marquette in 1673, and by Carver in 1766, who found them located on the Saint Peter's River. They were divided into two bands, the Istasunda, or Grey Eyes, and the Hongashans, and cultivated corn, melons, beans, &c. In 1802, from a tribe numbering about 3,500, they were reduced to less than a tenth of that number by small-pox, when they burned their village and became wanderers, pursued by their relentless enemy, the Sioux. Lewis and Clarke found them on the L'Eau qui Court, numbering about 600. Since 1815 many treaties have been made with them, always accompanied by a cession of lands on their part in return for annuities and farming implements. In 1843 they returned to their village, between the Elkhorn and the Missouri, and made a peace with some of the Sioux, but their great chief, Logan Fontanelle, was killed by them not long after. Since then they have devoted themselves mainly to agriculture, and, under the fostering care of the Friends, are very much improved in their condition. In 1875 they numbered 1,005, depending entirely upon their crops for their subsistence, of which they have considerably more than enough for their own use. They have three good schools, which are largely and regularly attended. The older Indians are also abandoning their old habits 'and assisting in building for themselves upon forty-acre allotments of their lands.

*List of illustrations.*

885. SHU-DTHE-NUZHE. *Yellow Smoke.*

A leading and influential chief among the Omahas, and a man of more than ordinary intelligence and executive ability. Holds his position by hereditary descent. Is well off, possessing a large number of horses and a very well furnished house.

## DAKOTA—OMAHAS.

465. GRE-DTHE-NUZHE. *Standing Hawk and squaw.*

The oldest chief in the tribe, and consequently one whose words always command attention in their councils. This view represents him leading his pony, followed by his faithful squaw.

467. O-HUN-GA-NUZHE. *Standing at the End.*

A brave, nearly nude, decorated with "war-paint" and astride a characteristic Indian pony.

468. MO-HA-NUZHE. *Standing Bent.*

A policeman, or one appointed by the chiefs to preserve order in the village.

463. GI-HE-GA. *Chief.*

One of the nine chiefs who govern the tribe, holding their positions by hereditary descent.

469–470. BETSY.

A noted character among the Omahas, an exponent of women's rights. Has always accompanied the tribe on their annual buffalo-hunts, and participates in the chase with the men. Speaks three Indian languages, besides French and English.

457. AGENCY BUILDINGS.
462. THE VILLAGE OF THE OMAHAS. (1871.)
461. THE VILLAGE. Near view, showing lodges.
464. GI-HE-GA'S LODGE.
459–460. VIEW FROM BLACKBIRD HILL.

In Irving's Astoria is a short sketch of some of the romantic deeds of Wa-shinga-sah-ba, or Blackbird, a famous chief of the Omahas, who died in 1802, which concludes as follows: "His dominant spirit and his love for the white man were evinced in his latest breath with which he designated his place of sepulture. It was to be on a hill, or promontory, upward of 400 feet in height, overlooking a great extent of the Missouri, from which he had been accustomed to watch for the barks of the white men. The Missouri washes the base of the promontory, and after winding and doubling in many links and mazes in the plains below, returns to within 900 yards of its starting-place, so that for thirty miles, navigating with sail and oar, the voyager finds himself continually near to this singular promontory, as if spell-bound.

"It was the dying command of the Blackbird that his tomb should be upon the summit of this hill, in which he should be interred, seated on his favorite horse, that he might overlook his ancient domain, and behold the barks of the white men as they came up the river to trade with his people."

The river has now changed its course, running far to the eastward, leaving at the foot of the hill a lake in the old bed of the river. The mound which was raised over the chief and his horse is now nearly obliterated, " yet the hill of the Blackbird continues an object of veneration to the wandering savage, and a landmark to the voyager of the Missouri."

472–476. GROUPS OF SCHOOL-CHILDREN.
478. EBA-HOM-BA'S LODGE.
479. VILLAGE SCENE.
477. A BRAVE.
471. INDIAN CARPENTERS BUILDING HOUSES FOR THE TRIBE.

8. OSAGES.

The Osages were placed on the Missouri in 1673 by Marquette, who called them the Wasashe; were allies of the Illinois, and near the last of the past century had been driven down to the Arkansas. Coming in contact with the French, they became their firm allies, and joined them in many of their operations against Spanish and English and other Indians; in 1804, made peace with the Sacs and Foxes, with whom they had been at war, and settled on the Great Osage River. Their numbers were estimated then at 6,300. The usual succession of treaties ceding lands, and wars with neighboring Indians followed, reducing them very much in numbers, until the breaking out of the civil war, when 1,000 of them went South and joined the Confederacy. Treaties of 1865, 1866, and 1870 provided for the conveying of their lands in trust to the United States, and for their removal to the Indian Territory, where they have been placed under the care of the Society of Friends, and are now making rapid progress toward a self-supporting condition.

## DAKOTA—OSAGES.

They now number 3,001, of whom 323 are civilized, self-supporting mixed-bloods.

*List of illustrations.*

511. JOSEPH, PAW-NE-NO-PA-ZHE. *Not Afraid of the Pawnees.*

Governor or chief of the tribe. Was born on the Osage reservation when in Kansas, and when 12 years of age was placed in a Catholic mission, where he received a good English education. He still retains the old customs and habits of his tribe, however. Is a brave and warlike chief, but yet exerts all his influence to secure peace between his people and the whites. Is about 40 years of age, 6 feet in height, with a large and commanding physique; head, $22\frac{1}{4}$; chest, 41.

886. SHONGA-SA-PA. *Black Dog.*

The youngest of the six principal chiefs of the tribe. Is 28 years of age, and was born on the present reservation. Is the descendant of a long line of chiefs, one of whom was principal in establishing peace between the Government and the wild tribes. With the governor, Joseph, he visited Washington in 1876 to adjust various business matters in connection with his tribe. Age, 28; height, $5.11\frac{1}{2}$; head, $22\frac{3}{4}$; chest, 38.

887. GROUP representing the governor and some of the headmen or councillors of the nation, as follows:

JOSEPH PAW-NE-NO-PA-ZHE. See No. 511.

CHETOPAH.

Died in 1876, aged 38. Was among the first to commence farming and to live in the white man's way.

PA-TSA-LUN-KAH. *Strike Axe.*

Born on the Osage reservation in Kansas 45 years ago. Is one of the principal " peace chiefs," and also chief of one of the largest bands of the Osages, over whom he has unbounded influence.

CHE-ZHE-LUN-KAH. *Big Chief.*

Chief councillor of the nation, a man of good sense and much influence. Is the son of a chief; 45 years of age, and was born in Kansas.

HARD ROPE.
Head war chief of the nation, and a man of considerable ability as an orator. Served as a scout under General Custer during the Indian war in the Indian Territory. Is now 50 years old.

513. KAH-HE-KA-WAH-TI-AN-KA. *Saucy Chief.*
509. NOM-PA-WA-LE. *A Savage.*
510. KE-SI-SI-GRE. *A Distant Land.*
512. MAH-KEA-PU-AT-SEE. *One Who Reaches to the Sky.*
888. JOSEPH AND BLACK DOG.
889. JOSEPH, BLACK DOG, OGEAS CAPTAIN, AND J. N. FLORER.

### 9. OTOES.

The Otoes, callling themselves Watoohtahtah, were known to the French as early as 1673, under the name of Otontanta; were originally part of the Missourias, and, with the Iowas, claim to have migrated to the Missouri with the Winnebagoes. They have long resided on the south side of the Platte River, in mud lodges, confederated with the Missourias, who formed one village with them. The two tribes now number 457 souls. Under the care of the Friends, many are laying aside their Indian dress and habits, and learning to labor. In common with many other tribes, their annuities are payable only in return for labor performed, which exercises a most beneficial effect.

*List of illustrations.*

480. AR-KE-KE-TAH. *Stand by It.*
Is a full-blooded Otoe Indian. He was a leading warrior in his tribe, and during the early settlement of Nebraska, when an emigrant train had been attacked on Big Sandy Creek, and robbed of all they had by a party of Pawnees, Ar-ke-ke-tah, leading a band of Otoes, fell on them, and, killing the entire party, restored the goods back to the emigrants, for which he gained notoriety, and received papers commendatory of this and other valuable services rendered the whites. By being a man of deep scheming and cunning, he succeeded in gaining the position of head chief of the tribe, while on a visit to Washington, in 1854, when

the treaty was concluded, in which the Otoes ceded to the Government the southeastern part of Nebraska. He was deposed from his chiefship in 1872, re-instated in 1873, but has been inactive as a chief since, and has lost his influence in the tribe. He is still living, about 65 years of age, and 5 feet 8 inches high, with square, well-built frame.

482, 492-4, 502. SHUN-GECH-HOY. *Medicine Horse.*

His father was an Otoe, and his mother a Missouria Indian. By hereditary descent he became, in 1854, head chief of the Bear band of Otoes, and being ambitious, worked himself finally into the position of head chief of the Otoes and Missourias. In 1874 he led a portion of the tribe away from their reservation, in violation of law and agency regulations, for which he, with five others, was arrested and confined for a time at Fort Wallace. In consequence, he became alienated from the agency and main part of the tribe, and lost his position as chief. Has features remarkably coarse; has a very stern, fierce disposition; is a deep schemer; would be willing to sacrifice almost any interest of his tribe in order to maintain a supremacy over them, and has been engaged in many stratagems of the kind. He is tenacious of old Indian customs, opposed to improvement that makes innovations thereon, and is a heavy clog on the tribe in their endeavors to advance in civilized pursuits. In stature, he is about 5 feet 9 inches, with a heavy-set, well-developed muscular frame; about 60 years of age.

487, 489, 490. LOD-NOO-WA-INGA. *Little Pipe.*

Is a son of Hick-a-poo or Kick-a-poo, formerly a prominent chief of the tribe. The chiefship had been hereditary through many successors, and after the death of Hic-a-poo, the present Little Pipe, in 1858, took his place. He was one of the followers of Shun-gech-hoy in 1874; was arrested and imprisoned with him, and has not since been recognized as a chief. He is of a mild disposition, well disposed toward improvement, but quiet and without much individual force of character. Has been under unfavorable influences, and therefore makes but little progress. He is about

50 years of age, 5 feet 7½ inches in stature, head 23 inches, chest 36, and weighs 155.

488. PAH-HO-CHA-INGA. *Little Iowa.*

Generally known by his more proper name of Baptiste Devoin, is a son of John Devoin, who is half French and half Missouria Indian. His mother is half Omaha, one-quarter French, and one-quarter Iowa Indian. He was partially educated at the Pawnee Mission, at Belleview, Nebr.; can read, write, and speak the English language tolerably well; also speaks Pawnee, Omaha, and French. He married into the Otoe tribe, and has been employed at Otoe agency in the several positions of teamster, farmer, interpreter, and miller, under former agents. In 1869, he was employed as interpreter for the tribe, and has continued in that office until the present. In height he is 5 feet 9¾ inches, head measurement 23½ inches, chest 44 inches, and weighs 220 pounds. He is about 40 years of age, and quite corpulent.

495. TCHA-WAN-NA-GA-HE. *Buffalo Chief.*

Is an Otoe Indian, though his grandfather belonged to the Iowa tribe. He was, when a young man, a self-constituted chief, leading a portion of the Buffalo band of Otoes, at a time when Sack-a-pie was chief, and at whose death he became the recognized head chief of the band, which position he held until 1874. He is still living; is about 80 years of age, in stature 5 feet 6 inches, and weighs about 160 pounds. He is of rather a mild disposition, though decided in his ways; concilitory to the whites, and has gained many friends among them.

497. BAPTISTE DEVOIN AND TCHA-WAN-NA-GA-HE.

The same as given and described in Nos. 488 and 495.

500. { E'EN-BRICK-TO. *Blackbird.*
      { OP-PO-HOM-MON-NE. *Buck Elk Walking.*

The first is half Otoe and half Omaha; the second, who is represented sitting, is a full-blood Missouria.

## DAKOTA—WINNEBAGOES. 59

501. {
   INSTA-MUNTHA. *Iron Eagle.*
   KO-INGA. *Little Thunder.*
   UP-PO-HOM-MON-NE.
   E'EN-BRICK-TO.
}

491.—LITTLE PIPE, with Missouria chief and interpreter.
496.—MEDICINE HORSE, BABTISTE DEVOIN, and interpreter.

### 10. PONCAS.

The Poncas were originally part of the Omaha tribe, to whom they are related. Lived originally on the Red River of the North, but were driven southwestwardly across the Missouri by the Sioux, and fortified themselves on the Ponca River. United for a time with the Omahas for protection, but have generally lived apart. Were so exposed to the forays of the savage Sioux that they were almost exterminated at one time, but after the treaties of 1817 and 1825 rallied and began to increase. Were estimated then at 750, which has remained their average number ever since. In 1858 sold their lands and went on a reservation near the Yanktons, but being too near their old foes, and not being able to raise any crops, were in 1865 removed down to the mouth of the Niobrara, where they now have three villages. Are still exposed to raids from the Sioux, retarding very much their progress toward a self-supporting condition. Efforts are being made to have them join their relatives, the Omahas.

*List of illustrations.*

517-518. {
   ASH-NOM-E-KAH-GA-HE. *Lone Chief.*
   TA-TONKA-NUZHE. *Standing Buffalo.*
   WA-GA-SA-PI. *Iron Whip.*
   WASTE-CO-MANI. *Fast Walker.*
}

519. WA-GA-SA-PI. *Iron Whip.*

521. NATIVE DRAWING.

### 11. WINNEBAGOES.

The Winnebagoes are a branch of the great Dakota family, calling themselves O-tchun-gu-rah, and by the Sioux, Hotanke, or the Big-voiced People; by the Chippeways, Winnebagonk—

whence their common English name—a word meaning men from the fetid waters. The French knew them as La Puans (the Stinkers), supposed to have been given them in consequence of the great quantity of decaying and putrid fish in their camps when first visited by white men. With some others they formed the van of the eastward migration of the Dakotas, penetrating apparently some distance, but were forced back to Green Bay. This was some time previous to 1670, as the map of the French Jesuit missionaries, dated 1671, styles Green Bay the "Bayo des Puans," and the map accompanying Marquette's journal, dated 1681, notes a village of the " Puans" as near the north end of Winnebago Lake, on the west side.*

They were then numerous and powerful, holding in check the neighboring Algonkin tribes, but soon after an alliance of tribes attacked and very nearly exterminated them. Became firm friends of the French until the Revolution, when they joined the English; made peace with the colonists afterward, but sided with the English again in 1812.

In 1820 they numbered about 4,500, and were living in five villages on Winnebago Lake and fourteen on Rock River. By a treaty in 1832 they ceded all their lands south of the Wisconsin and Fox Rivers, for a reservation on the Mississippi, above the Upper Iowa, but here they became unsettled, wasteful, and scattered. In 1846 they surrendered this reservation for another above the Saint Peter's. This proved unfit, and they became badly demoralized, losing many of their number by disease, but were kept on it by force. In 1853 they were removed to Crow River, and in 1856 to Blue Earth, Minnesota, where they were just getting a start in civilized pursuits when the Sioux war broke out, and the people of Minnesota demanded their removal. Thus again they were put on the march, and this time landed at Crow Creek, on the Missouri, near Fort Randall, a place so utterly unfit, that the troops could not retain them on it. Out of 2,000 when taken there, only 1,200 reached the Omaha reserve, to which place they had fled for protection. They were then assigned a new reservation on the Omaha lands, and placed under the care of the Friends, and since then have prospered. At the time of their removal, in 1863, from Minnesota, many of the tribe who had taken up farms remained, receiving their share of the tribal funds. There were also last

---

*Alexander Ramsey.

year 860 in Wisconsin, of whom 204 have lately joined those in Nebraska, swelling their numbers to 1,667. Nearly all of these now dress in civilized attire, and many of them have taken farms, their lands being divided into 40-acre allotments for the purpose, upon which they are building neat and comfortable cottages. There is an industrial and three day schools on the reserve, which are attended by one-sixth of their whole number. Their chiefs are now elected anually by the tribe, who in turn appoints a force of twelve policemen from the Indians to preserve order.

1080. JNO. M. ST. CYR.

A delegate representing the Wisconsin Winnebagoes. Has been to Washington three times. His mother was a relative of Little Priest, one of the most prominent chiefs of the tribe, and his father a Frenchman.

808. { NAW-CHER-CHOO-NU-KAW.
{ BAD THUNDER.

812. WAH-KUNK-SCHA-KAW, and daughter.

Wife of "Martin Van Buren," a former prominent chief of the tribe.

814. KA-RA-CHO-WE-KAW. *A Blue Cloud Passing By.*

809, 813. WINNEBAGO CHILDREN.

## IV. PAWNEES.

### 1. ARICKAREES.

The Arickarees, Ricarees, or Rees, as variously written, call themselves Sa-nish, or Tanish, meaning "the people," a common form of expression among Indians to indicate their superiority. They were originally the same people as the Pawnees of the Platte River, their language being nearly the same. That they migrated upwards along the Missouri from their friends below is established by the remains of their dirt-villages, which are yet seen along that river, though at this time mostly overgrown with grass. At what time they separated from the parent stock is not correctly known, though some of their locations appear to have been of very ancient date, at least previous to the commencement of the fur-trade on the Upper Missouri. At the time when the old French and Spanish traders began their dealings with the Indians of the Upper Missouri, the Arickaree village was situated a little above the mouth of Grand River, since which time they have made several removals, and are now located at Fort Clark, in a former village of the Mandans.

The cabins or huts of the Arickarees and other stationary tribes are built by planting four posts in the ground in the form of a square, the posts being forked at the top to receive transverse beams. Against the beams other timbers are inclined the lower extremities of which describe a circle, or nearly so, the interstices being filled with small twigs, the whole thickly overlaid with willows, rushes, and grass, and plastered over with mud laid on very thick. A hole is left in the top for smoke to pass out, and another at the side for a door. The door opens a few steps distant from the main building on the surface of the ground, from which, by a gradual descent through a covered passage, the interior of the hut is reached. The door is of wood, and the aperture large enough to admit a favorite horse to the family circle, which is often done. These buildings are located within fifteen or twenty feet of each other without any regard to regularity.

They cultivate considerable land, each family separating its little farm from their neighbors' by rush fences. Corn is their principal dependence, of which they raise considerable quantities. The work is done entirely by the women, the primitive hoe being their only implement. They generally have quite a surplus, which they trade to the Dakotas and to the fur companies.

The Arickarees are quite expert in manufacturing a very serviceable kind of pottery, neatly shaped, and well adapted for cooking purposes. They are of clay, hand wrought, but not glazed.

At the present time they number 900, and are associated with 600 Gros Ventres and 420 Mandans at the Fort Berthold agency on the Upper Missouri, where 13,000 square miles has been set apart for them as their reservation. They have 500 acres under cultivation, and are receiving considerable assistance from the Government in the way of improved implements. Many houses are being built, and the more progressive Indians are abandoning the old mud-lodges for them.

*List of illustrations.*

1042. KU-NUGH-NA-GIYE-NUK. *Rushing Bear.*

Head chief; age, 56; height, 5.8½; head, 22¾; chest, 39½.

1044. E-GUS-PAH. *Bull Head.*

Age, 57; height, 5.4½; head, 23¼; chest, 42½.

1043. CHE-WA-KOO-KA-TI. *Black Fox.*

Son of Black Bear, a great chief of the tribe. Age, 23; height, 5.5; head, 24; chest, 36¼.

717. BLACK BUFFALO.

718. LONG KNIFE.

## 2. KEECHIES.

The Keechies, of whom there are now only a small remnant of about 90 in the Indian Territory, affiliated with the Wichitas, Wacos, and Tawacanies; were originally from Texas, and are supposed to be the Quitzies of the Spanish authorities of 1780. Even at that time they were a small tribe, numbering about 100 warriors. After the admission of Texas, were placed on a State reservation, where they remained undisturbed until 1859, when their presence became so distasteful to the settlers that it became necessary to remove them. Land was leased from the Choctaws and Chickasaws, and the Keechies settled on it, building their villages of grass houses along the Canadian River. The breaking out of the civil war set them back, just as they were beginning to prosper, compelling another remove for safety. In 1867 they were restored to their lands again, and since then have progressed rapidly in civilized pursuits. Like the Wichitas and Wacos, they are of the same stock as the Pawnees.

*List of illustrations.*

411. KNEE-WAR-WAR, (front.)

412. KNEE-WAR-WAR, (profile.)

## 3. PAWNEES.

There is but little definite knowledge of the early history of the Pawnees, although they are among the longest known to the whites west of the Mississippi. Marquette notes them in his map, 1673, as divided into various bands. They are supposed to be the Panimaha of La Salle's voyage in 1688. At the time of Lewis and Clarke's visit, in 1803, their principal village was on the south side of the Platte. Pike, in 1806, estimated the population of three of their villages at 6,233, with nearly 2,000 warriors, engaged in fierce combats with neighboring tribes. In 1820, three of the four bands into which they have been for a long time divided resided on the banks of the Platte and its tributaries, with a reservation on Loup Fork, on the ninety-eighth meridian. Were then estimated at about 10,000 souls, living in earth-covered lodges, and much devoted to the cultivation of the soil, but engaging regularly every season in a grand buffalo-hunt. The Delawares, in 1823, burnt the Great Pawnee village on the Republican, and these Pawnees, becoming much reduced in numbers by small-pox soon after, sold all their lands south of the Platte, and removed to the reservation on Lou Fork. The means were provided, and many exertions made to place them on the high road to prosperity; but their inveterate foe, the Sioux, harassed them continually; drove them repeatedly off their reservation, and despoiled their villages. This warfare and disease soon reduced them to half their former number. In 1861, they raised a company of scouts for service against the Sioux, and a much larger force under the volunteer organization, incurring in consequence an increased hostility from their enemies, who harassed them so continuously, that in 1874 the chiefs in general council determined upon removing to a new reservation in the Indian Territory, lying between the forks of the Arkansas and Cimarron, east of the ninety-seventh meridian. Their removal was almost entirely effected during the winter of 1874–'75.

The Pawnees now number in all 2,026, and yet retain the subdivision into bands, as follows: The Skeedee (Pawnee Mahas, or Loups), Kit-ka-hoct, or Republican Pawnees, Petahoweret, and the Chowee or Grand Pawnees. There are also living on the Washita, a small band of affiliated Wacos and Wichitas, sometimes called Pawnee Picts, who are undoubtedly an offshoot of the Grand Pawnees. They are under the care of the Friends; have well-organized day and industrial schools, and are well supplied with implements and means to carry forward a systematic cultivation of the soil.

*List of illustrations.*

530-2. PETA-LA-SHA-RA. *Man and Chief.* CHOWEE.
Reputed head chief of the Pawnees, though really chief only of his own band, the *Chowee*. His claim was based partly on the fact of having been the first signer of their treaty of 1857. Being a good Indian orator, and of dignified bearing, he was generally awarded the first place in their councils, and led off in speech. In 1820, it is said that he put a stop to the custom, then prevalent among the Pawnees, of offering human sacrifices, but only by a display of great courage. In 1825 he visited Washington with a delegation of his tribe, and attracted much attention by his fine presence. Has always been friendly to the whites and in favor of the advancement of his tribe in civilized habits, although very slow himself to adopt new ideas. He died in the summer of 1874 from an accidental pistol-shot. Had but one wife, and she survives him.

533. LA-TA-CUTS-LA-SHAR. *Eagle Chief.* SKEEDEE.
At present the oldest, and consequently the head chief of the tribe.

534. LA-ROO-CHUK-A-LA-SHAR. *Sun Chief.* CHOWEE.
A son of *Peta-lá-sha-ra* and head chief of the Chowee band; also a leader in the councils. Height, 5.9; head, 22; chest, 36½.

535. TUH-COD-IX-TE-CAH-WAH. *Brings Herds.* SKEEDEE.
Height, 5.10; head, 22; chest, 42.

543. TU-TUC-A-PICISH-TE-RUK. *Gives to the Poor.* SKEEDEE.
A soldier or policeman of the Skeedees. Height, 5.9; head, 22½; chest, 42.

545. SQUAW OF TU-TUC-A-PICISH-TE-RUK. SKEEDEE.

548. LA-HIC-TA-HA-LA-SHA. *Pipe Chief.* CHOWEE.
One of the signers of the treaty of 1858.

528. 
- LA-ROO-CHUK-A-LA-SHAR. *Sun Chief.* See No. 534. CHOWEE.
- ARU-SAW-LA-KIT-TOWY. *A Fine Horse.* SKEEDEE.
- SKI-AR-RA-RA-SHAR. *Lone Chief.* CHOWEE.
- SE-TED-E-ROW-WEET. *One Aimed At.* SKEEDEE.
- COT-TA-RA-TET-GOOTS. *Struck with a Tomahawk.* SKEEDEE.

66       CATALOGUE OF INDIAN PHOTOGRAPHS.

529. {

TE-RAR-A-WEET.  *Stopped with the Horses.*   KIT-KA-HOOT.
Height, 5.7; head, 21½; chest, 37.   A soldier of his band.

LA-SHARA-CHI-EKS.  *Humane Chief.*   KIT-KA-HOOT.
One of the four chiefs of his band, dresses well; is pleasant in manner, and of progressive tendencies. Height, 5.10; head, 22½; chest, 36.

AS-SON-OO-COT-TUK.  *As a Dog, but yet a High Chief.*
KIT-KA-HOOT.
One of the four chiefs of his band.  Height, 5.8; head, 22; chest, 35.

LA-SHARA-TU-RA-HA.  *Good Chief.*   KIT-KA-HOOT.
Head chief of the band.  Height, 5.7; head, 22½; chest, 39.

LA-SHAROO-TOO-ROW-OO-TOWY.  *Difficult Chief.*
KIT-KA-HOOT.
One of the soldiers and head men of this band.

552–3. GROUP OF FOUR BROTHERS OF THE KIT-KA-HOOT BAND, viz:

LA-ROO-RUTK-A-HAW-LA-SHAR.  *Night Chief.*

LA-ROO-RA-SHAR-ROO-COSH.  *A Man that left his Enemy lying in the Water.*
A noted brave.  Height, 5.10; head, 23; chest, 39.

TEC-TA-SHA-COD-DIC.  *One who strikes the Chiefs first.*
Second chief of his band, and one of four noted brothers (see No. 552), pre-eminent in their tribe for bravery in war and wisdom in council.  Height, 5.8; head, 23; chest, 39.

TE-LOW-A-LUT-LA-SHA.  *Sky Chief.*
A chief, and a brave leader of his band, taking the first place in war or peace. Was killed by the Sioux in the massacre of the Pawnees in 1873, while hunting buffalo in the valley of the Republican.

BAPTISTE BAYHYLLE, or LA-SHARA-SE-RE-TER-REK.
*One whom the Great Spirit smiles upon.*
United States interpreter, French half-breed.

550–1. NIGHT CHIEF AND THE MAN THAT LEFT HIS ENEMY LYING IN THE WATER.

554–5. BAPTISTE BAYHYLLE.

560. TE-LOW-A-LUT-LA-SHA. *Sky Chief.*
     The same as in No. 552, No. 4.

558–9. { COO-TOWY-GOOTS-OO-TER-A-OOS. *Blue Hawk.* PETAHOWERAT.
       { TUC-CA-RIX-TE-TA-RU-PE-ROW. *Coming around with the Herd.* PETAHOWERAT.

556–7. PERRUS KITTY-BUSK. *Small Boy.* SKEEDEE.

575. LOO-KIT-TO WY-HOO-RA. *On a fine Horse.* PETAHOWERAT.

576. LUH-SA-COO-RE-CULLA-HA. *Particular in the Time of Day.* KIT-KA-HOCT.

577. LA-ROO-CHUK-A-RAR-OO. *The Sun Coming in.* CHOWEE.

578. SE-RAR-WOT-COWY. *Behind the one that strikes first.* SKEEDEE.

579, 585, 607. CAW-CAW-KITTY-BUSK. *Little Raven.* SKEEDEE.

580. AS-SAU-TAW-KA. *White Horse.* PETAHOWERAT.

581. LOOTS-TOW-OOTS. *Rattlesnake.* SKEEDEE.

582. KE-WUK. *Fox.* KIT-KA-HOCT.

583. KE-WUK-O-WE-TE-RAH-ROOK. *Acting a Fox.* SKEEDEE.

584. KIT-TOOX. *Beaver.* KIT-KA-HOCT.

586. AS-SOW-WEET.

592. AS-SOW-WEET AND SAWKA. *White.* CHOWEE.

589. TER-RA-RE-CAW-WAH. PETAHOWERAT.
     Died in 1875; the oldest chief in the tribe. Very prominent in his day as a brave warrior.

591. CAW-HEEK. *An Old Man.* KIT-KA-HOCT.

593. { LOO-KIT-TOWY-HIS-SA. *On a Fine Horse.* SKEEDEE.
     { ARE-WAUKS. *A Male Calf.* CHOWEE.

594. LOOTS-TOW-OOS. *Rattlesnake,* and squaw. SKEEDEE.

595. E-RAH-COT-TA-HOT. *In the Front of Battle,* and squaw. SKEEDEE.
     Alias Jim Curoux. A steady worker, and wearing citizens' dress.

596. A-RUS-SAW-E-ROOT-COWY. *A Nice Horse.* SKEEDEE.

597. CU-ROOX-TA-RI-HA. *Good Bear.* SKEEDEE.
598. TIT-TOWY-OOT-SE. *Beginning to go to War.* SKEEDEE.
    Alias Johnson Wright. A civilized Indian.
599. KE-WUK-O-CAR-WAR-RY. *Fox on the War-Path.* SKEEDEE.
    Alias Fat George. Assistant carpenter at the agency.
600. CAW-CAW-KE-REEK. *Crow Eyes.* PETAHOWERAT.
601. KEE-WEEK-O-WAR-UXTY. *Medicine Bull.* SKEEDEE.
602. TEC-TA-SHA-COD-DIC. *One who strikes the Chiefs first.*
    KIT-KA-HOCT.
603. LE-TA-CUTS-A-WAR-UXTY. *Medicine Eagle.* SKEEDEE.
604. TA-CAW-DEEX-TAW-SEE-UX. *Driving a Herd.* SKEEDEE.
605. US-CAW-DA-WAR-UXTY. *Medicine Antelope.* KIT-KA-HOCT.
606. TER-RA-HA-TU-RIHA. *Good Buffalo.* PETAHOWERAT.
608. SIT-TE-ROW-E-HOO-RA-REEK. *Seen by All.* SKEEDEE.
609. LOO-KIT-TOWY-HIS-SA. *On a Fine Horse.* SKEEDEE.
610. PAW-HOO-CUT-TAW-WAH. *Knee-Mark on the Ground on Stooping to Drink.* SKEEDEE.
611. SQUAW AND PAPPOOSE.
523, 567-8. THE VILLAGE OF THE PAWNEES.
    Situated on the Loupe Fork of the Platte River, about 100 miles west of Omaha. It was divided into two parts, the Skeedees occupying one part by themselves, and the other three bands jointly in the other. The entire village accommodated about 2,500 people. Each lodge was capable of holding several families; they were formed by erecting several stout posts in a circle, forked at the top, into which cross-beams were laid, and against these long poles were inclined from the outside toward the centre; all was then covered with brush, and finally with earth, leaving a hole at the apex for the escape of smoke, and a long tunnel-like entrance at the base. This village is now (1876) entirely destroyed, and the Indians removed to the Indian Territory.
524, 539. A MUD LODGE.
    In the Pawnee village, showing the tunnel-like entrance. (See No. 523.)

537-9. SCHOOL BUILDING on the Pawnee reserve, on the Loupe Fork, Nebraska.
573-4. GROUPS OF THE HEAD MEN of the tribe.
525-7. GROUPS OF INDIAN CHILDREN (attending the boarding-school on the reservation).

The first shows the younger children of the primary classes, and the two latter numbers the older and more advanced scholars.

570-2. GROUPS OF CHILDREN in their every-day attire, which consists principally of the covering with which nature first clothed them.
536. A GROUP OF YOUNG SQUAWS in the village.
541-2. AGENCY BUILDINGS.
540. NATIVE PAINTING ON A BUFFALO-SKIN.

A biography, or narration of the principal events in the life of a prominent chief, by the means of picture-writing.

547-9; 561-6; 587-90; 612. MISCELLANEOUS PORTRAITS OF PAWNEES without information as to name or history.

### 4. WACOS.

742. LONG SOLDIER. (Front.)
743. LONG SOLDIER. (Profile.)

### 5. WICHITAS.

744. ASSADAWA. (Front.)
745. ASSADAWA. (Profile.)
746. ESQUITZCHEW. (Front.)
747. ESQUITZCHEW. (Profile.)
748. BLACK HORSE.
165, 167. BUFFALO GOAD. (Front.)
166, 168. BUFFALO GOAD. (Profile.)

Was one of the great delegation of chiefs from the Indian Territory in 1872, among whom were Little Raven, Little Robe, Bird Chief, &c. He impressed all as being a man of more than usual ability and dignity.

## V. SHOSHONES.

### 1. BANNACKS.

The Bannacks, Bonnacks, or Pannaques, a small, scattered tribe of Shoshone stock, roaming over the desert plains of Idaho and portions of the surrounding Territories, were first found about the Blue Mountains. In 1833 Bonneville met them on the Snake River, near the mouth of the Portneuf, "numbering about 120 lodges. They are brave and cunning warriors, and deadly foes of the Blackfeet, whom they easily overcome in battle when their forces are equal. They are not vengeful and enterprising in warfare, however, seldom sending parties to attack the Blackfeet towns, but contenting themselves with defending their own territories and houses." They frequent the headwaters of the Snake and Yellowstone countries to hunt and fish.

They have generally enjoyed a reputation for friendliness, although, in 1866, all but the Eastern Bannacks under Tahgee engaged in hostilities against the whites.

At the present time there are 600 Bannacks associated with 900 Shoshonees at the Fort Hall reservation on Snake River, where the attempt is being made to civilize them. There are 200 more at the Lemhi reservation, where there are also 340 Sheep-eaters, a band of the Bannacks living a retired life in the mountains dividing Idaho from Montana, and 500 Shoshonees.

*List of illustrations.*

46. GROUP of eight of the leading chiefs and braves; photographed at the Snake River agency in 1872, among whom are PAQUITS, or *Bannock Jim*, a prominent chief; TOTSE-CABE-NATSY, *The White-faced Boy*, and *Major Jim*.
47. GROUP of a miscellaneous crowd at the agency.
48. FAMILY GROUP.

In 1871, while returning from the exploration of the Yellowstone region, and while encamped near the head of the Medicine Lodge Creek, the camp of a family of the Sheep-eater band of Bannacks was accidentally discovered near by, almost completely hidden in a grove of willows. Their tent or tepee is made of a few boughs of willow, about which are thrown an old canvas

picked up in some of the settlements. The present of
a handful of sugar and some coffee reconciled them to
having their photographs taken. In the group are the
father and mother and five children. The Sheep-eaters
are a band of the Bannacks, running in the mountains north of the Kamas prairies, and are so shy and
timid that they are but rarely seen.

51-61. GROUPS AND SCENES about the agency.

Eleven views, showing the various operations of the
agency, some of the idlers, and a few groups of squaws
and pappooses.

## 2. COMANCHES.

A roving, warlike, and predatory tribe of Shoshone descent,
roaming over much of the great prairie country from the Platte
to Mexico. Their traditions and early history are vague, but
they claim to have come from the west. They call themselves
*Naüni* (live people), but the Spanish called them Comanches
or Camanches *(Les Serpents)*, the name adopted by the Americans. Procuring horses from the Spaniards at an early day
they became expert riders, which, united with their daring and
aggressiveness, made them noted and feared throughout the
Southwest. Engaged in long and bloody wars with the Spaniards, but were subdued by them in 1783. Were estimated
about that time at 5,000 warriors. In 1816 lost heavily by smallpox. Up to 1847 were variously estimated at from 9,000 to
12,000 in all. Were at one time on a reservation in Texas, but
were driven out of the State, and since then have been unrelenting enemies of the people of that State. The General Government has set apart a new reservation for them in the western part of the Indian Territory and are gradually drawing
them all on to it, though not without much trouble. They now
number 1,570 in all, and are divided into eight bands. Have
made a commencement in farming, and have been induced to
send a few of their children to an industrial school.

W. Blackmore, esq., in an article on the North American Indians, thus describes the Comanche:

"These fierce, untamed savages roam over an immense region,
eating the raw flesh of the buffalo, drinking its warm blood, and
plundering Mexicans, Indians, and whites with judicial impartiality. Arabs and Tartars of the desert, they remove their

villages (pitching their lodges in regular streets and squares) hundreds of miles at the shortest notice. The men are short and stout, with bright copper faces and long hair, which they ornament with glass beads and silver gewgaws."

Catlin says of them:

"In their movements they are heavy and ungraceful, and on their feet one of the most unattractive and slovenly races I have ever seen; but the moment they mount their horses they seem at once metamorphosed, and surprise the spectator with the ease and grace of their movements. A Comanche on his feet is out of his element, and comparatively almost as awkward as a monkey on the ground without a limb or branch to cling to; but the moment he lays his hand upon his horse his *face* even becomes handsome, and he gracefully flies away, a different being."

*List of illustrations.*

128. ASA HAVIE. *The Milky Way.* (Front.)    PENETATHKA.

129. ASA HAVIE. *The Milky Way.* (Profile.)

    Is one of the head men of his band, dividing the office of chief with Toshoway. (No. 134.) Has been one of the most noted raiders into Texas, leading many bands of the restless young men of his tribe, until about ten years since, when he was badly wounded in an encounter and left for dead upon the field. Is now endeavoring to live in the white man's ways, having had a comfortable log house built for himself, and a few acres of ground enclosed, which he is successfully cultivating. This portrait of *Asa havie* was made in 1872, while on a visit to Washington with a delegation of his tribe. Age, about 45; height, 5.9½; head, 23½; chest, 44½; weight, about 200 pounds.

130. WIFE OF ASA HAVIE. (Front.)
131. WIFE OF ASA HAVIE. (Profile.)

    Age, about 40; height, 5.4; head, 23; chest, 38; weight, 170 pounds.

132. TIMBER BLUFF. (Front.)
133. TIMBER BLUFF. (Profile.)
134. TO-SHO-WAY. *Silver Knife.* (Front.)    PENETATHKA.

135. TO-SHO-WAY. *Silver Knife.* (Profile.) PENETATHKA.

One of the chiefs of his band, sharing the position with *Asa havie.* Is noted for good sense and fair dealing, and has long been friendly to the whites. In youth, however, was not behind the other adventurous spirits of his tribe in predatory exploits and raids into Texas. Age, about 55; height, 5.6; head, 22¼; chest, 41; weight, 168.

136. WIFE OF TOSHOWAY. (Front.)
137. WIFE OF TOSHOWAY. (Profile.)

Age, 55; height, 4.10; head, 21; chest, 34; weight, 120.

138-9, 140. ASA-TO-YET. *Gray Leggings.* (Front.)

PENETATHKA.

One of the leading men of his tribe, taking an active interest in their advancement. Lives in a house, cultivates the ground, and has a good lot of stock. Speaks English fluently. Age, 45; height, 5.10; head, 34; chest, 42.

141-2. CHEEVERS. *He Goat.* TAMPARETHKA.

A prominent and influential man in his tribe, and chief of his band.

143-4. WIFE OF CHEEVERS. TAMPARETHKA

One of the three wives of Cheevers. She accompanied him to Washington with the delegation in 1872. None of his wives have any children.

145-6. MOTHER OF CHEÉVERS. TAMPARETAKA
147-8. QUIRTS-QUIP. *Chewing Elk.* TAMPARETHKA.

One of the chiefs of the tribe; a shrewd and able person, with considerable executive and financial ability. Age, 45; height, 5.6¾; head, 23; chest, 39.

149, 150. HO-WE-OH. *Gap in the Salt.* TAMPARETHKA.

A chief who is doing his best to lead his tribe in civilized ways, as well as to walk in that way himself. Age,—; height, 5.11½; head, 23; chest, 43.

151-2. DAUGHTER OF GAP IN THE SALT. TAMPARETHKA
153-4. PARRY-WAH-SA-MEN. *Ten Bears.* TAMPARETHKA.

Formerly head chief of the Tamparethkas band of Comanches. He died in November, 1872, just after his return from Washington with a visiting delegation from his tribe. Was friendly to the whites, and a man of influence among his people, maintaining this influence and his chieftainship to the unusual age of 80 years.

155-6. BUFFALO HUMP.     TAMPARETHKA.
157-8. JIM.     TAMPARETHKA.
178-9. NATIVE DRAWINGS.

### 3. KIOWAS.

The Kiowas, or prairie men, are one of the tribes that compose the Shoshone family. They are a wild and roving people, occupying the country about the head-waters of the Arkansas, but also formerly ranging over all of the country between the Platte and the Rio Grande. They had the reputation of being the most rapacious, cruel, and treacherous of all the Indians on the plains, and had a great deal of influence over the Comanches and other neighboring Indians. Our first knowledge of them was through Lewis and Clarke, who found them on the Paducah. They were at war with many of the northern tribes, but carried on a large trade in horses with some other tribes. Little intercourse was had with them until 1853, when they made a treaty and agreed to go on a reservation, but soon broke it and went raiding into Texas. The citizens of that State drove them out, but in revenge for the stoppage of their annuities, they retaliated upon the Texans, and until recently the warfare was kept up between them. In 1869, were placed on a reservation of over three and a half millions of acres with some Comanches and Apaches, but were restive and unsettled. In 1871, under their great chief Satanta, raided Texas again, but it resulted in the capture of himself and Big Tree, and their imprisonment soon after. Were afterwards pardoned by the governor of Texas, in whose custody they were, through interposition from Washington, and restored to their tribe; but this did not seem to lessen their hostility, and new disturbances arose, chiefly in consequence of raiding parties of whites from Texas, that led finally to the re-arrest of Satanta and his imprisonment in Texas.

*List of illustrations.*

402. LONE WOLF. (Front.)
403. LONE WOLF. (Profile.)

404. SQUAW OF LONE WOLF. (Front.)
405. SQUAW OF LONE WOLF. (Profile.)
406. SQUAW OF LONE WOLF. (Standing.)
407. SLEEPING WOLF.
408. SON OF THE SUN. (Front.)
409. SON OF THE SUN. (Profile.)
410. NATIVE DRAWING.

4. SHOSHONES.

The Shoshones, or Snakes, are a tribe inhabiting the country about the head-waters of the Green and Snake Rivers, and a part of a great family of the same name, including the Comanches, Utahs, and Kiowas. They occupy nearly all of the great Salt Lake Basin, to the eastern base of the Sierra Nevada, and extend also easterly to Texas. The Shoshonees proper are divided into many bands under various names, the most important being the Buffalo-Eaters, of Wind River; the Mountain Sheep-Eaters, of Salmon River, and the Western Shoshonees, near Boise, separated from the rest of the tribe by the kindred Bannacks, numbering in the aggregate, with some lesser tribes on the Humboldt, between five and six thousand souls. Our first knowledge of them was through Lewis and Clarke, who found them west of the Rocky Mountains on the waters of the Columbia, but are supposed to have at one time inhabited the plain-country east of the mountains. James Irwin, United States Indian agent, in his report to the Commissioner, says: "They emigrated north about 1781, and proceeded to the upper waters of Green River under a leader or chief called Shoshone, or Snake. At this point they divided, one party going over on the Oregon slope, who are now called Western Shoshones, and have an agency in common with the Bannacks at Fort Hall. The other party constitute the eastern band of Shoshones, and have roamed around the Wind River Mountains from the time mentioned until 1868, when a treaty was made at Fort Bridger, that provided a reservation for them embracing the Wind River Valley. Recently they entered into a contract with the Government by which they ceded a portion of their reservation, leaving them a district perhaps 50 miles in length, and 30 in breadth, embracing a beautiful valley on the east side of the Wind River Mountains. They now number about 1,800 souls, and must have diminished greatly since the time of Lewis and

Clarke. Their life was a continued warfare; at first with the Crows and Blackfeet, and since then with the Cheyennes, Arapahoes, and Sioux, and all this time contending almost naked with the elements and struggling for subsistence."

*List of illustrations.*

657-8. VILLAGE IN SOUTH PASS.

During the expedition of 1870, the United States Geological Survey of the Territories came across the above village of Shoshones, numbering nearly one hundred lodges, encamped among the southern foot-hills of the Wind River Mountains, where the above and some of the following views were secured. They were under the well-known chief Washakie, and were on their way to the Wind River Valley to hunt buffalo for the winter's supply of food and clothing. Although the village had all the appearance of being a permanent abiding-place, yet the following morning, before the sun was an hour high, there was not a tent in sight, and the last pack-pony with trailing lodge-poles had passed out of sight over the hills to the eastward.

659-660. WAR CHIEF'S TENT.

The war chief is generally a man of more importance in the village, especially when in the neighborhood of enemies, than the chief himself. In this instance his tent, situated in the centre of the encampment, is adorned with broad bands of black, yellow, and white, rendering it quite conspicuous. The war chief, or his lieutenant, issues forth frequently to announce, in the far-reaching voice peculiar to Indians, the orders which are to govern their actions, while within is an almost uninterrupted thumping on drums.

661-2. WASHAKIE AND HIS WARRIORS.

A group in front of the tent of the head chief Washakie. About him are gathered all the chief men of the encampment.

663-4. WASHAKIE.

This well-known chief is a man of more than ordinary ability, and his record as a steadfast friend of the white people has come down to the present time without a blemish. He is now well advanced in years, but still retains his vigor, and his influence over the tribe. One of the above portraits was made in the South Pass encampment, and the other is a copy of one made in Salt Lake City.

665-6. VIEWS IN THE VILLAGE.

667-676. GROUPS of in-door and out-door subjects, copied from small card views made in Salt Lake City, and which formed a part of the first Blackmore collection.

## 5. UTAHS.

The Utahs, Yutas, or Utes, as the name is variously written, are a large tribe belonging to the great Shoshone family, and who occupy the mountainous portion of Colorado, with portions of Utah, New Mexico, and Nevada. Those living in the mountains where game abounds have a fine physical development, are brave and hardy, and comparatively well to do; while those who inhabit the sterile plains of the Salt Lake Basin are miserably poor, and spiritless. We derive our first knowledge of the Utahs from the early Spanish explorers, who came in contact with them on the upper waters of the Rio Grande del Norte, and who gave them the reputation of being a brave and warlike tribe. Their country bordered that of the Navajos on the south (the Rio San Juan now dividing them), who formerly ranged as far north as the waters of the Grand, but were crowded back by the Utahs. A continuous warfare was kept up between the tribes, in which the Navajos were worsted. The Utahs were employed against them by the Government at the time of their expulsion from their country in 1863. The tribe is divided into many bands, which are continually changing, but as now recognized are as follows: Capotes, Weeminuches, Tabeguaches, Muaches, Grand River, Yampas, Uintahs, Peahs, Goships, and Mouaches. The tribe now numbers in the aggregate 5,260. The Pi-Utes, Pi-Edes, Timpanagos, San-pitches, and others in Utah are kindred tribes.

The Utahs have generally been friendly to the whites, although there was some fighting in 1859 and 1860 about Pike's Peak, many emigrants plundered at various times, and stray miners cut off by disaffected bands. The Capotes, Weeminuches, and others in the southern portion of the Territory have been more troublesome than those of the north.

Treaties were made in 1863 and 1868, giving them 18,320 square miles of reservation in the western part of the Territory.

The southern portion of it, known as the San Juan region, was found to be rich in precious metals, and as it was already attracting a large influx of miners, additional treaties were made in 1872 for the cession of that part of their reservation. In 1874 the tribe consented to the sale of about 6,000 square miles for $25,000 a year forever. Much dissatisfaction ensued from the failure of the Government to promptly carry out the provisions of the treaty, and from the fact that much of their most valuable agricultural lands were unwittingly included in the purchase.

"Though holding a hereditary friendship for the white people and acknowledging the supremacy of the Government, and for the most part included under agencies and receiving Government rations to a greater or less extent, no tribe in the country is more averse to manual labor, or has yielded less to civilizing influences, partly because of the abundance of game and partly because of their remoteness from settlements."

*List of illustrations.*

765-7, OURAY. *Arrow.* TABEGUACHE.

Ouray was born in 1834, in Taos, N. Mex., his father being a Ute, and his mother a Jicarilla Apache. He attended the Mexican school at Taos, under the tuition of Jesuit priests, and acquired there a perfect knowledge of the Spanish language. In 1850, he married, and joined his tribe as a warrior, it being then at war with the Navajos of New Mexico, and the Cheyennes and Arapahos of Colorado. Soon after, in a fight with the Arapahos, his only son was captured and carried off by the enemy, and since then he has never ceased, nor allowed his tribe to rest, from hostilities against these Indians. In 1856, his knowledge of the Spanish language and superior executive ability secured him the position of Government interpreter, which position he has held ever since, and through the same means he has gradually risen from a simple warrior to be the principal chief of the nation. In 1863, he accompanied, as interpreter, a delegation of his tribe to Washington, when their first treaty with the Government was made. In 1868, he again, as chief of the Tabeguaches, in company with the chiefs of the other tribes, visited Washington, and it was mainly through his influence and eloquence a treaty was made, whereby the Utes ceded a large portion of their country in Colorado. Soon after his return, the principal chief of Utes, Nevava, died, and he became the acknowledged leader. In 1873, when the discovery of rich mines upon their lands (the San Juan region) was very near involving the Utes in war with the miners, he avoided this by agreeing to a cession of the lands in dispute, and against a strong opposition from the greater portion of the nation. As a chief he is very strict with his people, punishing all crimes, and sometimes simple disobedience, with death; but he is very kind nevertheless, and has gained his influence more through moral suasion than command. He is a steadfast friend of the whites, and has never lifted his hand against any of them, though some of his people have at times been on the point of making war. Ouray is quite wealthy, owning a herd of several hundred horses, among which are some famous racers, and also large flocks of sheep. He lives at the Government agency in a comfortable house, in a somewhat civilized style, and has a carriage with driver, while his people live altogether in tents. The Government places great confidence in his ability and suggestions, and he has managed to keep the Utes at peace with the fast-encroaching people of Colorado.

768. GUERO.

Present chief of the Tabeguache Utes. Guero belongs to that class of chiefs among the Indians who generally succeed their fathers as leaders of a band which hunts and fights in a separate party. He has about 50 lodges in his band, and therefore has considerable influence. When younger he distinguished himself in the wars against the Navajos, but in later years has abandoned his warlike proclivities. He is a staunch supporter of Ouray's peace policy with the Government, and generally lives at the agency, assisting the agent in the distribution of the annuity goods and provisions.

772-3, 781. SHAVANO.  TABEGUACHE.

War chief of the Tabeguaches, and the most prominent warrior among the Utes. The Arapahoes and

Cheyennes fear and hate him; he never goes on the war-path but brings back a scalp of his enemies. Has distinguished himself often by the fierceness of his attack, generally going into a fight naked, and has been wounded several times in such encounters. In the council he is always for peace with the whites, and has used his influence to make those treaties whereby all difficulties were obviated. He is an eloquent orator, and when speaking is often applauded by his people.

751. TAPUCHE. CAPOTE.

A young chief of the Capote band of Utes, son of Sobita, their principal chief. The latter is now very old, and does not attend to the duties of his office, his son taking his place. Both are strong supporters of Ouray and his peace-policy. Tapuche was the delegate of his tribe to visit Washington and confirm the treaty of 1873.

752. MAUTCHICK. MUACHE.

A young chief of the Muache Utes, who has during the last few years gained considerable influence, and is now considered the war chief of his band in place of Curacanto. Was also delegate to Washington in 1873.

754. CO-HO. *The lame man.* MUACHE.

756–758. ANTERO. *Graceful Walker.*

759–760. WA-NE-RO. *Yellow Flower.*

761–762. TABIYUNA. *One Who Wins the Race.*

763–764. KO-MUS.

An intelligent young Indian of the Uinta band, who was brought east by Major Powell, of the Colorado exploring expedition, who educated him, and then employed him as a clerk in his office in Washington, but died suddenly a short time since.

769. JOHN. YAMPAH.

A young warrior of the Yampah Utes, well known among the people of Colorado by the soubriquet of "John," and as a particularly good friend of the white settlers. Died suddenly at the Hot Springs in Middle Park in 1873.

770. KWA-KO-NUT. *A King*, and MOSE.    MUACHE.
771. CU-RA-CAN-TE.    MUACHE.

The old war chief of his band, and in former days quite noted for his independent raids into the country of the Cheyennes and their allies. In the winter of 1868–'69 he organized a body of 100 warriors, and, as leader of these, was attached to the column under Colonel Evans, operating against the Kiowas and Comanches, which campaign ended in the surrender of these Indians. He is now quite old and has lost much of his influence, his son Maut chick succeeding him.

774. WA-RETS and SHAVANO.    TABEGUACHE.
775. GROUP representing—
OURAY.
SHAVANO.
GUERO.
ANKATOSH.
WA-RETS.
776. GROUP of seven, representing—
" JOHN."
MA-KU-TCHA-WO or SA-PE-A.
CU-RA-CAN-TE.
TO-SHI-MY, or *Black Bear*.
KWA-KO-NUT, or *A King*.
" MOSE."
MEXICANO.
777. SURIAP.    YAMPAH.

A son of Lodge Pole, a prominent chief and a warrior in his band. Was one of a delegation to visit Washington in 1868 to make the treaty with the Government. He has not, however, come up to the expectations of his people, as, although a young man, he has not distinguished himself in any way, so that he remains a simple warrior to this day.

778. CHIPPIN. *Always Riding*.
779. LITTLE SOLDIER.

780. SQUAW OF LITTLE SOLDIER.
782. LOVO. *The Wolf.*

Lovo was noted among the Utes for his ability in following the trail of man or beast, hunting, or on the war-path, and had gained the name of being the best scout. Was frequently employed as "runner" by the Government in carrying dispatches, and was noted for his promptness in executing these commissions. Is a brother of the chief Guero, and died in October, 1874, while hunting on the Republican River.

783. RAINBOW.
784. NICK-A-A-GOD. *Green Leaf.* YAMPAH.

A chief of the Yampahs and formerly a man of considerable influence, which he has lost, however, through several petty thieving excursions which he has led against the whites. He has but few followers left, and is one of the few mischievous Utes. In 1868, was delegated to go to Washington, and while there was considered to have equal influence with Ouray, both being in favor of the treaty made that year. Speaks English well, has considerable intelligence, and a good knowledge of the customs of the whites, but since his repudiation by his tribe he has not come in contact with them much.

785. PE-AH, or *Black-Tail Deer.*

A young chief of the Grand River band of Utes. As a delegate of his tribe, he helped to make the treaty of 1868 in Washington, and signed it; but since then he has never acknowledged it, and, with his band, has kept off the present reservation, camping generally near Denver. He has about 35 lodges, or 250 people, with him. He is a nephew of the late principal chief *Nevava*, who died in 1868. He is quite a young man, very adroit and ambitious, and possessed of considerable ability. Has distinguished himself as a warrior in contests with the Arapahoes. He has many enemies among the Utes on account of his overbearing disposition and pride of birth and position, but manages to gain in influence, so that the Government has been obliged to establish a special agency for his band at Denver.

SAHAPTINS—NEZ PERCÉS.

935. COLORADO.
787. SAPPIX and SON.
788. CHU.
789. KANOSH.
790-6, 965-74. Miscellaneous groups, all copies; a portion of the original Blackmore collection.
955-9. UTE ENCAMPMENT on the plains near Denver.
960-3. CAMP SCENES among the Utes at Los Pinos.
520. GROUP of Peah and his head men.

## VI. SAHAPTINS.

The Sahaptin family inhabit the country south of the Salish, between the Cascade and Bitter Root Mountains, reaching southward, in general terms, to the forty-fifth parallel, but very irregularly bounded by the Shoshone tribes of the California group. Of its nations, the Nez Percés, or Sahaptins proper, dwell on the Clearwater and its branches, and on the Snake about the forks. The Palouse occupy the region north of the Snake, about the mouth of the Palouse; the south banks of the Columbia and Snake, near their confluence, and the banks of the Lower Walla Walla, are occupied by the Walla Wallas. The Yakimas and Klikelats inhabit the region north of the Dalles, between the Cascade Range and the Columbia. The natives of Oregon, east of the Cascade Range, who have not usually been included in the Sahaptin family, are divided somewhat arbitrarily into the Wascoes, extending from the mountains eastward to John Day River, and the Cayuses from this river across the Blue Mountains to the Grande Ronde.

### 1. NEZ PERCÉS.

The Nez Percés, or the Sahaptin proper, inhabit Idaho and portions of Oregon and Washington. They style themselves Numepo, but Lewis and Clarke called them the Chopunnish. The origin of their present name is buried in obscurity. Early in the present century they were estimated to number 8,000; and in 1836, when a mission was established among them, about 4,000. In the Oregon Indian war most of the tribe remained friendly and did effective service for the whites on a number of occasions. In 1854 a treaty was made ceding part of their lands, but only a portion of the tribe recognizing it, led to a separation, one party becoming wandering hunters, while the other remained on the reservations.

"Of the 2,800 Nez Percés now living, nearly half located on the Kamiah and Lapwai reservations in northern Idaho, and a few others settled on lands outside the reserve, are prosperous farmers and stock-growers. The rest are "non-treaties," who, with other non-treaty Indians in that region, make every exertion to induce the reservation Indians to lease their farms and join them in their annual hunting and root-gathering expeditions."

Early in the summer of the present year troubles arose in regard to the occupancy of the Wallowa Valley by white settlers, it having been withdrawn in 1875 from the reservation assigned them by treaty in 1873, from a failure on their part to permanently occupy it. An Indian, belonging to a band of malcontents or non-treaties under the Chief Joseph, was killed by some settlers, when they insisted upon the removal of all the whites and the restitution of the valley to them. Upon the refusal of the Government to this demand, and further attempts to compel all the non-treaty Indians to come into the reservation at Lapwai, an outbreak occurred under the leadership of Joseph, which resulted in a number of pitched battles, with great loss of life, but were compelled to retreat, the forces under General Howard pursuing them eastwardly across the headwaters of the Snake River and through the Yellowstone National Park, where the pursuit was taken up by the forces under General Terry, resulting finally in the capture of Joseph and the remainder of his force by General Miles.

*List of illustrations.*

427–8. KAL-KAL-SHU-A-TASH, or *Jason.*
429–431. TA-MA-SON, or *Timothy.*
433–4. ENCAMPMENT ON THE YELLOWSTONE RIVER.
 The temporary camp of a small hunting party, who were visiting their friends the Crows at the old agency, near the mouth of Shields River. This and the following views were made in 1871:
435–6. LODGES IN THE VILLAGE.
437. THE CHIEF OF THE VILLAGE.

438. This man has long yellow hair and blue eyes, but is in every other respect a thorough Indian. Is said to be a son of one of the expedition under Lewis and Clarke, who visited their country early in this century.

439–441. VILLAGE VIEWS.

## 2. WARM SPRINGS.

The Warm Springs Indians, so named from their location about the thermal springs in Northern Oregon, are related to the Walla Wallas, and number 187, on a reservation of some 725 square miles, on which are also some 300 Wascoes and Teninoes. The combined tribes cultivate about 800 acres of the land. They are very well off in live stock and derive some of their income by lumbering. All wear citizen's dress, many have good comfortable houses, and support two schools, with an attendance of about 50 scholars. They assisted in the operations against the Modocs in 1872, raising a company of scouts for that purpose, who rendered good service.

*List of illustrations.*

1058. CAPPOLAS. *A Boney Man.*

Took a prominent part in the Modoc war, and distinguished himself by the capture of Captain Jack in the lava-beds. Height, $5.5\frac{1}{2}$; circumference of head, $22\frac{3}{4}$.

1061. SHAKA. *Little Beaver.*

A sergeant in the company that captured Captain Jack. Height, 5.8; circumference of head, $22\frac{5}{8}$.

1056. SKE-METZE. *Chopped up.*

Familiarly known as "Billy." Height, $5.4\frac{1}{2}$; circumference of head, $22\frac{3}{8}$.

1054. KE-HEY-A-KIN. *Crooked Stick.*

Height, $5.6\frac{1}{2}$; circumference of head, $21\frac{3}{4}$.

1063. HISTO. *Clam Fish.*

Height, $5.7\frac{3}{4}$; circumference of head, $22\frac{7}{8}$.

1059. WEY-A-TAT-HAN. *Owl.*

The married man of the party, his wife accompanying him on his travels. Was wounded in the lava-beds, and with five others were the scouts who first discovered Captain Jack's hiding-place in the cave.

1064. CHIN-CHIN-WET. *Alone.*

Wife of Weyatathan. A very comely and intelligent Indian woman, of whom but very few are found among the far western tribes. Height, 4.11½; circumference of head, 21½.

1057. SEMEO, or *Umatilla Jim.*

### 3. WASCOS.

The Wascos, like the Warm Springs Indians, are related to the Walla Wallas, and through them to the Sahaptin family. The name signifies "basin," and the tribe derives its name, traditionally, from the fact that formerly one of their chiefs, his wife having died, spent much of his time in making cavities or basins in the soft rock for his children to fill with water and pebbles, and thereby amuse themselves." They came originally from around the Dalles. Are associated with the Warm Springs and Teninoes on a reservation in Oregon just south of the Columbia. Now number 263, profess the Christian religion, and are more advanced in civilization than any tribe in the State. All the tribes of this reservation are self-supporting, deriving about half their subsistence by agriculture and the rest by fishing and hunting.

*List of illustrations.*

1062. KLE-MAT-CHOSNY. *Agate Arrow-Point.*

Is a chief and a member of the Presbyterian Church, and a zealous worker for the spiritual welfare of his people. Height, 5.6¾; circumference of head, 21¾.

1060. STAT-TLA-KA. *Pole Cat.*

Height, 5.4; circumference of head, 20⅝.

1055. OSCAR MARK, or *Little Vessel.*

Height, 5.5; circumference of head, 23¼.

### VII. KLAMATHS.

#### 1. KLAMATHS.

A comprehensive name applied to this as well as to several tribes on the Klamath River, differing in language and type. Live mainly by fishing and root-digging. By treaty in 1864 the

Klamaths and Modocs ceded all their lands, reserving a small tract on Klamath Lake, in Oregon, of 1,600 square miles, the Government to pay $8,000 in fifteen years, as well as other large sums for subsistence. Much of their reservation is mountainous, only a small portion being fit for cultivation. The Klamaths did not like the introduction of the Modocs on their reservation, and it eventually led to the Modoc war. They now number 676, and are quite prosperous. Have a large number of horses and cattle, but derive their chief support by lumbering.

*List of illustrations.*

975–6. WAL-AIKS-SKIDAT,

Known as David Hill, cousin of Captain Jack, is the war chief of the Klamaths (the parent tribe of the Modocs), and is recognized as the leader in civilization of all the Indians of the Lake country. He is 33 years of age. He distinguished himself, before the Indians were gathered into reservations, as the leader of the young braves of the Klamaths in their wars with surrounding tribes, and his military record shows that he has never known defeat. He has always been the friend of the white man. In the long-protracted fight with the Snake tribe, lasting over eight years, he was our ally as the leader of the Klamath warriors. He commanded the Klamath scouts during the war with Captain Jack. Mr. Hill is a christianized Indian, and is a member of the Methodist Episcopal Church. His father was the first chief who became friendly with the white man. This was in 1843, when he met Frémont and acted as his guide.

977. YUM-NIS-POC-TIS,

(Chief without beads), better known as Tecumseh, is the "medicine man" of the Klamaths, and is the descendant of a long line of "medicine men." He has had a Damon and Pythias friendship with David Hill since his childhood. In his native tongue he is famous as an orator. He won great distinction in the Snake war, as Hill's comrade; and, with him, is the earnest champion of civilization in his tribe. He is also a Methodist and lives a civilized life in the reservation. Both Tecumseh and Hill are covered with scars that they have received in their desperate conflicts.

## 2. MODOCS.

The Modocs were originally part of the Klamaths, but recently hostile to them. Their name is an Indian word meaning *enemies*. Their original territory was on the south side of Klamath Lake, including some 4,000 square miles. Were early known as a treacherous and cruel people, and up to 1850 had cut off more than 50 whites. Engagements followed between them and the whites in 1851—when Wright massacred 41 out of a total of 46—which were kept up until 1864, when they agreed to go on a reserve. The treaty to that effect was not ratified for seven years, and in the mean time were induced to go on the Klamath reserve. Were harassed and dissatisfied, and afterwards put on Yaniax reservation, but most of the tribe left under two rival chiefs, Schonchin and Captain Jack. The former settled peaceably near the settlements, while the latter went back to their old home and became troublesome. In 1872, were ordered back to the reserve, and upon their refusing to go troops were called on to enforce the order, the citizens joining in an attack on their entrenched camps, but were repulsed. The Modocs then retreated to the "lava-beds," a volcanic region so broken up into great caves and fissures as to serve as a natural fortification. After several engagements a commission was organized to enquire into the trouble, and while holding a conference with the leaders were attacked, and General Canby and Dr. Thomas were killed, (April 11, 1873.) After two months' further operations, the hostiles were reduced, their leaders hung, and the rest removed to the Indian Territory. About 100 who took no part in the trouble remained at the Klamath agency.

*List of illustrations.*

1008. SCAR-FACED CHARLEY.

The famous war chief of the lava-bed warriors, and the greatest of their soldiers. He was the most trusted of Captain Jack's braves, and the most desperate of his fighters. Rev. Dr. Thomas, who was slain at the peace-commission massacre, on the day before his death called Scar-Faced Charley the "Leonidas of the lava-beds." He was never known to be guilty of any act not authorized by the laws of legitimate warfare, and entered his earnest protest against the assassination of General Canby and Dr. Thomas. He led the

Modocs against Major Thomas and Colonel Wright when the United States troops were so disastrously repulsed and when two-thirds of our men were killed and wounded. Wearied of the slaughter, he shouted to the survivors, "You fellows that are not dead had better go home; we don't want to kill you all in one day." He has said since, " My heart was sick of seeing so many men killed."

1009. SHACK-NASTY JIM,

The sub-chief of the tribe and chief of the Hot Creek band of the Modocs; although hardly twenty-one years of age, is known throughout Christendom as one of the most fearless warriors that the red men ever sent to fight the pale-faces. He led the tribal forces that suffered most severely. After the massacre he quarrelled with Captain Jack; and, with "Bogus Charley," "Hooker Jim," and "Steamboat Frank," became scout for General Jeff. C. Davis—which led to the capture of the remnants of the Modoc army.

1010. STEAMBOAT FRANK,

One of the participators in the Modoc war, but after the massacre of General Canby's party, left his tribe, and as a scout under General Davis, did good service in securing the capture of the remnants of Captain Jack's forces.

1011. WI-NE-MA, or *Tobey Riddle*.

The modern Pocahontas, who, at the risk of her own life, saved the life of Col. A. B. Meacham, chairman of the Modoc peace commission, at the Modoc massacre. The Oregon Statesman truly says: "A truer heroine was never born in the American forest than the poor Indian woman, Tobey Riddle, whose exertions to save one who had befriended herself and people were no less daring and resolute than the devotion of Pocahontas. We have nowhere read of a woman, white, black, or red, performing an act of sublimer heroism than Tobey Riddle, when, under suspicions of treachery, she returned to her people in the rocks, with an almost absolute certainty of being flayed alive. The description of that event is one of the finest passages in Mr. Meacham's speech, and is a fitting tribute to the courage and fidelity of his dusky, lion-hearted friend. The gratitude, fidelity, and devotion of that poor squaw ought to forever put to silence and shame those heartless savages who, in the midst of a Christian civilization, are clamoring for the extinction of a people whom God had planted where they were found." Tobey is 28 years of age, and the wife of Frank Riddle. She is honored by all who know her.

### 3. ROGUE RIVERS.

The Rogue Rivers, so called from the stream upon which they have lived for a long time, have also been known by the names Lototen or Tototutna. As a general rule the coast tribes are inferior in physique and character to the inland tribes, but an exception must be made in favor of the Rogue Rivers. "The men are tall, muscular, and well made, the women are short and some of them quite handsome, even in the Caucasian sense of the word." They are associated with some 15 or 20 tribes or bands at the Siletz agency, the whole numbering less than 1,500 souls.

*List of illustrations.*

978. OL-HA-THE, or *George Harvey.*

Chief of the confederated tribes of Indians of Siletz reservation, Oregon, lineal descendant of a long line of Rogue River chiefs, was captured when a small boy at the Rogue River war between the United States forces and the Rogue River tribes of Southern Oregon, and carried to the Siletz reservation, where he has lived ever since. He is a fine speaker, and has acted many years as an interpreter. This office having brought him into close and constant contact with American civilization, he long ago abandoned his aboriginal habits and religion, and adopted the customs and faith of the whites. He is well known throughout Oregon, and is held in the highest esteem. He has been complimented by the judges everywhere for his integrity and intelligence, and both by his loyalty and education is a living proof of the folly and wickedness of the theory that the Indian can neither be civilized nor be made the friend of the white race.

## VIII. PIMAS.

### 1. PAPAGOS.

The Papapootans, as they style themselves, belong to the Pima family, and have long resided in the country south of the Gila. Have always been at enmity with the Apaches until within the last year, but were friendly to the Spaniards, who, with a few exceptions, have maintained missions among them continuously up to the present time. At the close of the Mexican war were Mexican citizens, and partly civilized, but were not recognized as such by the United States, and were left without an agency or reservation until 1874, when they were settled on the Santa Cruz River, a tributary of the Gila, on a tract of 70,400 acres. They now number between 5,000 and 6,000 souls. Have well-cultivated farms, and live in houses of their own construction.

650. ASCENCION RIOS. (Front.)
651. ASCENCION RIOS. (Profile.)

### 2. PIMAS.

The Pimas, calling themselves Ohotama, are a portion of a family of Indians of the same name, comprising, besides themselves, the Opates, Eudevis, and Joves, occupying much of Southern Arizona, Sonora, and Sinaloa. Missions were established among them at an early day by the Spaniards, but they revolted many times, killing several of the missionaries. They have long been divided into the Upper and Lower Pimas, the former living on the Gila, in mud-covered huts, and cultivating the soil extensively. Have been long associated with the Maricopas, the two tribes now living together as one on a reservation of 64,000 acres. The Pimas now number 4,100; are self-supporting, wear civilized dress, and are ready for the privileges of citizenship.

653. LUIG MORAGUE. (Front.)
654. LUIG MORAGUE. (Profile.)
655. ANTONIO AZUL. (Front.)
656. ANTONIO AZUL. (Profile.)

## IX. IROQUOIS.

### 1. SENECAS.

One of the Five Iroquois Nations in Western New York, comprising, originally, the Sinnekaas, as the Dutch called them, (hence the word Senecas,) Onondagas, Mohawks, Cayugas, and Oneidas. When first known to the French, were living on the south side of Lake Ontario, and engaged in a fierce war with their Algonkin neighbors. By conquest several other tribes became incorporated with them. Missions were established among them by the French as early as 1657. In 1763 the Senecas alone, of the Six Nations, joined in Pontiac's league to extirpate the English. During the Revolution sided with the English, but made a peace in 1784, and during the second war remained loyal. Early in the century part of the tribe settled in Ohio, afterwards removing to the Indian Territory, where they now are to the number of 240. The New York Senecas still occupy the Alleghany, Cattaraugus, and Tonawanda reserve of 66,000 acres, where they all live in good houses and have large, well-cultivated farms, and are in every way a civilized and well-regulated class of people.

1048. DYAR-YO-NAÄ-DAR-GA-DAH. *One who Carries Hemlock Boughs on his Back.*

  English name, Caster Redeye. Was born on the Alleghany reservation; belongs to the traditionary Bear clan. Is now President of the New York Senecas. Does not speak English, but is an eloquent speaker in his native tongue. Has been a councillor three terms. Is a farmer and lumberman, and has also been a pilot for several years on the Alleghany River. Caster is a grandson of Governor Blacksnake, the famous chief of the Senecas, who died in 1859 at the age of 120 years. Age, 46; height, 5.9; head, 22½; chest, 43.

1045. DAR-GAR-SWEN-GAR-ANT. *Dropping the Stock of the Gun.*

  Commonly known as Harrison Halftown; belongs to the Snipe clan. Was born on the Alleghany reservation. Is the clerk of the nation, which position he has held for the last eight years. Was well educated at a Quaker school adjoining the reservation, and speaks English fluently. Is a fine speaker, and is quite noted as an orator. Age, 47; height, 5.8; head, 23¼; chest, 42.

IROQUOIS—WYANDOTS. 93

1046. HOH-HO-I-YO. *Splendid Doer.*

Samuel Jimson, as he is ordinarily known, is one of a family of thirty-one children, and was born on the Alleghany reservation in 1837. Is a descendant of Mary Jimson, a white captive among the Senecas, whose descendants now number 111. Is a farmer, but also a fine orator, and of more than ordinary ability. Has been a councillor for eleven terms in succession. Height, 6.1; head, 23; chest, 43.

1047. JOHN IRVING.

President of the peacemakers' court. Is a grandson of Governor Blacksnake. Age, 50; height, 5.9½; head, 22; chest, 44.

979. MYRON SILVERHEELS.

980. GROUPS COMPRISING 1045-46-47.

715. A DAUGHTER OF GENERAL PARKER.

Copy from an old daguerreotype.

## 2. WYANDOTS.

The Wyandots, or Hurons, a western Iroquois tribe, lived originally on the shores of Lake Huron, where they raised tobacco to such an extent that they were called Petem, or Tobacco Indians. Were driven west to Wisconsin and to the shores of Lake Superior, and by the Sioux back again to the neighborhood of Detroit, where they remained up to the close of the wars between the United States and England. In 1832 ceded all their lands in Ohio to the Goverument, and 687 were removed to Kansas, where they have since resided, at the junction of the Kansas and Missouri Rivers. In 1855 many became citizens, and had their lands divided among them, the others being removed to the Indian Territory, where they now are, numbering 258 souls. Some of the Wyandots remained near Detroit, and by treaty with the English government were assigned a reservation on the Detroit River of 23,600 acres, where they yet remain, but have declined within the present century from 200 to 72. Their hereditary king remained with the Canadian band.

## List of illustrations.

**981. MATHEW MUDEATER.**

Head chief of the Wyandots, and a delegate in 1875 to Washington, with power to settle all complications between his tribe and the Government growing out of sundry treaties. Was born in 1813, in Canada.

**982. NICHOLAS COTTER.**

A councillor in his tribe, and delegate to Washington with Mudeater, 1875. Was born in Canada in 1822.

## X. MUSKOGEES.

### 1. CREEKS.

The Creeks are known in their own language as the Muskokee or Muskogee and occupied originally the greater part of Georgia, Alabama, and Florida. Their traditions say that they emigrated from the Northwest until they reached Florida, when they fell back to the country between the headwaters of the Alabama and Savannah rivers. As this was full of small rivers and creeks it was called by the early settlers the creek country, hence the name of the Creek Indians, who, when first known to the whites, were living there. Those remaining in Florida were called the Seminoles or Isti-semole (wild men). The nation became a confederacy of tribes speaking other languages, modifying somewhat the original Muskogee, but who, nevertheless, numbered seven-eighths of their whole number. Before a dominant power was established in the South they were courted by the Spanish, French, and English, and were about equally divided in their allegiance to these nations, but the final success of the English brought them entirely under their influence. "They took an active part in the war of the Revolution against the Americans, and continued their hostilities till the treaty concluded at Philadelphia in 1795. They then remained at peace eighteen years; but at the beginning of the last war with Great Britain a considerable portion of the nation, excited, it is said, by Tecumseh, and probably receiving encouragement from other sources, took arms without the slightest provocation, and at first committed great ravages in the vicinity of their western frontier. They received a severe chastisement, and the decisive victories of General Jackson at that time, and some years later over the Seminoles, who had renewed the war, have not only secured a permanent peace with the southern Indians, but, together with the progress of the settlements, have placed them all under the absolute control of the United States. The Creeks and Seminoles, after some struggles among themselves, have ceded the whole of their territory and accepted in exchange other lands beyond the Mississippi."—*Gallatin.*

Twenty-four thousand five hundred and ninety-four were removed west of the Mississippi, only 744 remaining on their old hunting-grounds. At the breaking out of the civil war the western Creeks numbered less than 15,000. The tribe divided and engaged in pitched battles against each other, the Unionists suffering badly, many fleeing to Kansas. They were brought together again after the war, and in 1872 numbered 13,000, on a reservation of over 3,000,000 acres in the Indian Territory.

By the report of the Commissioner of Indian Affairs for 1876, they were numbered at 14,000, including 3,000 mixed-bloods, and all wearing citizens' dress and living in good houses. They have 36 school buildings, with an attendance of about 750 pupils; over $24,000 was expended upon their education. There are 20 churches on the reserve, with a membership among the Creeks of over 3,000. They rank among the first of civilized tribes.

*List of illustrations.*

97. LO-CHA-HA-JO. *The Drunken Terrapin.*

Served as a first lieutenant in the Union Army during the rebellion, and was at that time and is now the leading spirit of the loyal Creeks. Is the treaty-making chief. Age, about 35.

98. TAL-WA-MI-KO. *Town King.*

Commonly known as John McGilvry. Is a brother-in-law of Oporthleyoholo, a famous chief of the last generation, and stood by him during their struggles with and flight from the rebel Creeks. Is at the present time the second leading spirit of the loyal Creeks. Age, about 30.

99. TAM-SI-PEL-MAN. *Thompson Perryman.*

First organizer of the loyal Creeks that came north during the rebellion. Was a councillor of Oporthleyoholo, and a steadfast adherent to the treaties made with the Government. Age, about 40.

100. HO-TUL-KO-MI-KO. *Chief of the Whirlwind.*

English name, Silas Jefferson; is of mixed African and Creek parentage; born in Alabama and raised among the Creeks in that State, removing with them to their present home in the Indian Territory. Is to all intents and purposes one of the tribe, taking a wife from among them, and sharing all their troubles. Was interpreter for the loyal Creeks during the war, and is now the official interpreter of the nation. Age, 45.

102. GROUP OF THE PRECEDING CHIEFS.

103. KOT-CO-CU, or *Tiger.*

Served in the Union Army as a lieutenant. Was one of the council in framing the treaty of 1866. In 1871 was a candidate for chief, but was defeated, and died shortly after.

104. OK-TA-HA-SAS-HAJO, or *Sand.*

The predecessor of Lo-cha-ha-jo as the treaty-making chief of the nation, and second chief under Oporthleyoholo. Was among the first to join the Union forces during the rebellion. Was chief of the council that framed the new constitution in 1866. Has not been educated, but has great natural ability, and is of an extremely sensitive and kindly disposition.

105–107. FAMILY OF GEORGE STEADMAN. (Half-bloods.)

108. A CREEK BRAVE.

2. SEMINOLES.

"The Isti-Semole (wild men) who inhabit the peninsula of Florida (1836) are pure Muskogees, who have gradually detached themselves from the confederacy, but were still considered members of it till the United States treated with them as with an independent nation. The name of Seminoles was given to them on account of their being principally hunters and attending but little to farming."

Were very hostile to the Americans up to the cession of Florida in 1819, but a treaty was finally made with them in 1823. Other treaties followed looking to their removal westward, in attempting to carry out which a war ensued, lasting from 1835 until 1842. Nearly 2,000 had then been removed, leaving about

300 in Florida, and 145 of these, under Billy Bowlegs, joined the western band in the Indian Territory in 1858. Had much trouble in getting settled upon a reservation, locating finally upon a tract of 200,000 acres bought of the Creeks, where they now number 2,553—a prosperous and civilized tribe.

*List of illustrations.*

714. O-LAC-TO-MI-CO. *Billy Bowlegs.*

The well-known and famous leader of the Seminoles in the Florida war, 1835–'42, but was finally compelled to remove with the remnants of his tribe to the Indian Territory.

3. CHICKASAWS.

When first known the Chickasaws were located north of Mississippi on the Cumberland and Tennessee Rivers. Were mixed up in the early French and English wars, remaining loyal to the English up to 1783. Operated with the Americans against the Creeks in 1793. Commenced to migrate west of the Mississippi early in the present century. Sold their lands to good advantage and amassed considerable wealth, and were in every way a prosperous, progressive nation. They purchased a large tract of land from the Choctaws, a tribe speaking the same language, and affiliated with them in all tribal affairs. In 1855, on payment of $150,000 to the Choctaws, they effected a political separation. Like the Choctaws, they first went south with the confederates during the civil war, but returned to the northern army afterwards. They lost very much property, besides a large number of slaves.

Their numbers have not undergone any material change, the latest census placing their numbers at 5,800. Nearly 2,000 of these are mixed bloods. Two weekly papers are supported between the Choctaws and themselves. They are also well supplied with churches, schools, and other appliances of an industrious, civilized, and prosperous people. They have intermarried to a great extent with the whites, some of the following portraits being of subjects having a large proportion of white blood in their veins.

*List of illustrations.*

73. J. D. JAMES.
74. ASH-KE-HE-NA-NIEW.

75. SHO-NI-ON.
76. ANNIE GUY.
77. A YOUNG BRAVE.

### 4. CHOCTAWS.

The Choctaws, or Chahtas, at the time of De Soto's visit in 1540, were living south of the Chickasaws, and west of the Creeks. Unlike the surrounding tribes, they were peaceably disposed, and a nation of farmers, and much farther advanced in civilization than any of their neighbors. Coming in contact with the French, Spanish, English, and Americans, they have never been at war with any of them. Commenced moving west of the Mississippi in 1801, and by 1830 had exchanged all their lands for other in the Indian Territory. By 1861 had advanced far in civilization, numbering with the Chickasaws 25,000, with 5,000 slaves. In the civil war they joined first the South and then the North, losing a great deal in property, and a reduction to 17,000 of their population. They now number 16,000, of whom two-thirds are of mixed blood. Are governed by a written constitution; elect their chief every four years; have a council, consisting of 40 members, and a judiciary, and trial by jury.

Of the following subjects, nearly all are of mixed blood.

*List of illustrations.*

88. ISRAEL FOLSOM.
89. PETER FOLSOM.
90. SAMUEL FOLSOM.
91. ―― FOLSOM.
92. FAUNCEWAY BAPTISTE.
93. B. L. LE FLORE.
94. SAMUEL GARLAND.
95. COLONEL PYTCHLYNN.
96. ALLEN WRIGHT.
936-7. SQUAWS.
938-9. YOUNG BOYS.

## XI. INDEPENDENT AND UNCLASSIFIED TRIBES.

### 1. ARAPAHOS.

"Very little is known of the early history of the Arapahos, but are supposed by some to be the Querechos of the early Spanish explorers. They called themselves Atsinas, of whom, however, they are but a branch. The early English knew them as the Fall Indians, and the French as the Gros Ventres of the south. They were then roaming over the plain country about the heads of the Platte and Arkansas. Gallatin speaks of them as a detached tribe of the Rapid Indians, which has wandered as far south as the Platte and Arkansas and formed a temporary union with the Kaskasias and some other erratic tribes. At the present time (1862) the Arapahos are divided into two portions or bands. The first portion call themselves Na-ka-si-nin, 'People of the Sage,' and number one hundred and eighty lodges. They wander about the sources of the South Platte and the region of Pike's Peak; also northward to the Red Buttes on the North Platte. Sometimes they extend their journeyings in search of buffalo along the foot of the Big Horn Mountains in the Crow country. The second band call themselves Na-wuth-i-ni-hau, the meaning of which is obscure. It implies a mixture of different kinds of people of different bands. They number 200 lodges, and range along the Arkansas River and its tributaries."—*Hayden*.

In 1820 Morse estimated them at 10,000, and speaks of them as a warlike people and often making predatory and murderous excursions on their eastern and northern neighbors.

The Arapahos affiliate with the Cheyennes, with whom they have been on friendly terms for many years. Lately, however, an antipathy seems to be growing up between the two tribes in the Indian Territory, and the Commissioner of Indian Affairs advises a separation. They are divided into two principal divisions, known respectively as the Northern and Southern Arapahos. Those of the north, numbering 1,562, affiliate with the Cheyennes and Ogalallas at the Red Cloud agency. They have been ordered to join their southern brethren, and at the present time the necessary preparations are under way. The Southern Apaches, who number 1,664, with the Southern Cheyennes and a small band of Apaches, are temporarily occupying a large reservation in the western portion of the Territory. The new reservation assigned them lies along the northern border of the Territory west of the Creek and Cherokee countries, and was purchased from them. It comprises nearly 5,000,000 acres.

But little has been done by them looking toward civilization, beyond signifying their willingness to have farms apportioned to them and in sending their children to school.

21. YELLOW BEAR.     NORTHERN ARAPAHOS.
   LITTLE WOLF.      NORTHERN ARAPAHOS.
22. POWDER FACE and SQUAW.   NORTHERN ARAPAHOS.
23. MEDICINE PIPE.     NORTHERN ARAPAHOS.
   FOOL DOG.       NORTHERN ARAPAHOS.
24. CRAZY BULL.      NORTHERN ARAPAHOS.
   FRIDAY.        NORTHERN ARAPAHOS.
25. PLENTY BEARS.     NORTHERN ARAPAHOS.
   OLD EAGLE.      NORTHERN ARAPAHOS.
32–35. BI-NAN-SET. *Big Mouth.*   SOUTHERN ARAPAHOS.
36–37. WHITE CROW.     SOUTHERN ARAPAHOS.
38–39. BLACK CROW.     SOUTHERN ARAPAHOS.
40–41. LEFT HAND.      SOUTHERN ARAPAHOS.
42–43. YELLOW HORSE.     SOUTHERN ARAPAHOS.
44–45. HEAP O' BEARS.     SOUTHERN ARAPAHOS.
62–65. OHASTE. *Little Raven.*   SOUTHERN ARAPAHOS.

   In 1865, Richardson described him as follows: "The savage, like Falstaff, is a coward on instinct; also treacherous, filthy, and cruel. But our chief, The Little Raven, was the nearest approximation I ever met to the ideal Indian. He had a fine manly form, and a human, trustworthy face."

909, 911. BIRD CHIEF. (Bust, front and profile.)
910, 912. BIRD CHIEF. (Standing, front and profile.)
984, 5. FRIDAY.

   The well-known chief of the Northern Arapahos and one who has had a prominent position for the last twenty-five years. Speaks English fluently and always acts as his own interpreter.

755. A YOUNG MAN.
Living with and brought up with the Southern Arapahos, but claimed by Ouray, chief of the Utes, to be his son, captured in battle several years since. Ouray has made an appeal to the Government for his restitution, but the young man prefers his present home.

## 2. CADDOS.

The Caddos, or Cadodaquious," at present a small remnant of a tribe that once ranged over the Red River country, where they were first met with in 1687 by Jontel and other survivors of the La Salle expedition. They are now consolidated with Wacos, Wichitas, Keechies, Tawacouies, Ionies, and Delawares, and number 552, occupying the Wichita reservation of about 1,200 square miles in extent between the branches of the—
They have now well-managed farms, and are noted for industry and general intelligence.

159–160. SHO-E-TAT. *Little Boy.*
English name, Geo. Washington. Born in Louisiana in 1816. Is probably the most progressive Indian on the reservation; has long since adopted the dress and customs of the whites; owns a trading-store, and has a well-cultivated farm of 113 acres, with good houses and improvements. Was captain during the rebellion of a company of Indian scouts and rangers in the service of the Confederate States army, and engaged in three battles, one on Cache Creek, Indian Territory, with Kiowas and Apaches; one with Cheyennes, in the Wichita Mountains; and one on the Little Washita, with renegade Caddos.

161–162. NAH-AH-SA-NAH. *Indian.* ANADARKO.
Commonly known as Warloupe; probably a corruption of Guadeloupe. Was born near Nacitoches about 1825. Is now chief of the Caddos, and considered in advance of most of his people. Is doing his utmost to elevate his tribe to the standard of the white man. Height, 5.6½; chest, inspiration, 37; expiration, 34½; circumference of head over ears, 21½; diameter of head from ear to ear, 14½.

163–4. ANTELOPE.
With the preceding was a delegate to Washington in 1872, but died shortly after his return.

## 3. CHEROKEES.

When first discovered, the Cherokees were occupying the mountainous country about the headwaters of the Tennessee River and portions of Georgia and South Carolina, up to 1830. They form a family by themselves, supposed, however, to be somewhat remotely connected with the Great Iroquois family. They call themselves in their language Tsaraghee. According to their traditions, they came to this country before the Creeks, dispossessing a people of whom there is now no record. Before and during the Revolution they were friendly to and aided the English. A treaty of peace was made with them, by which they acknowledged the sovereignty of the United States November 28, 1785, and were confirmed in the possession of their lands, occupying a considerable portion of Tennessee and parts of North Carolina, Georgia, Alabama, and Mississippi. Commenced migrating to the trans-Mississippi country as early as 1790, consequent upon the encroachments of civilization, and in 1818 3,000 more emigrated. As frequent cessions of their lands had reduced their territory to less than 8,000 square miles in extent, and also in consequence of the hostility of the Georgians, they were all removed in 1838 to their present reservation in the Indian Territory, excepting about 1,000, who remained in North Carolina. At the opening of the civil war they had progressed to a high degree of prosperity, but suffered great injury from both parties ravaging their country, and also in the emancipation of their slaves. Nearly all the Cherokees at first joined the Confederacy, but after the fight at Pea Ridge, seeing the result doubtful, 9,000, under Colonel Downing, with a majority of the nation, abandoned the southern cause and joined the Union forces; 6,500 adhered to the Confederacy to the end. At the time of their removal west the Cherokees numbered about 27,000. In 1867 they were reduced to 13,566, but since then have increased, so that they now number about 18,000. There are about 1,700 yet in North Carolina, in a prosperous condition, owning about 70,000 acres of land.

The reservation in the Indian Territory comprises about 5,000,000 acres, only one-third of it capable of cultivation, and of which they are now working some 90,000 acres. Their crops for 1875 aggregated 630,000 bushels corn, 70,000 bushels wheat, 35,000 bushels oats, 50,000 tons hay, 500,000 feet of lumber, &c. They have 63 schools, attended by nearly 2,000 children, that are supported by a fund of $1,580,000, held by the United States. Under their present constitution they are governed by a national committee and council elected for two years. The executive, or chief, is elected for four years.

The following portraits show the effects of the civilizing influences they have been living under, and also the extensive admixture of white blood among them by intermarriage:

*List of illustrations.*

66. COLONEL DOWNING.
67. RICHARDS.
68. COLONEL ADAIR.
69. SAMUEL SMITH.
70. BORUM DAVIS.
71. CAPTAIN SCRAPER.
72. BINGO.

4. MOQUIS.

A tribe of semi-civilized Indians living in seven villages on the plateau between the San Juan and Little Colorado Rivers. They were among the Pueblos visited by the expedition under Coronado in 1540, who named the region inhabited by them the Province of Tusayan. The Franciscans established missions among them, but in the general uprising of 1680 all were expelled or killed. Numerous attempts were afterward made to reduce them, but without success, and they have remained independent to this day. They have the reputation of being an extremely kind-hearted and hospitable people; are exclusively agricultural, raising maize, squashes, pumpkins, and peaches. They also have many sheep and goats. Have suffered much by depredations from the Apaches and Navajos. Their villages are perched upon the summits of mesas, from 400 to 600 feet in height. Their houses are built of stone laid in adobe-mortar, in terrace form, seldom exceeding three stories in height, and reached only by ladders. The women knit, spin, and weave, making fine blankets, women's robes, and other like articles, which they trade to the neighboring tribes.

When they first came under the jurisdiction of the United States, were estimated to number 8,000. Were almost destroyed by small-pox in 1855 and 1857, and lost many more by the famine in 1867. On both occasions their villages were aban-

104   CATALOGUE OF INDIAN PHOTOGRAPHS.

doned, and the people scattered among the mountains, or took refuge among the kindred Zuñis, and other pueblos. Are now estimated at 1,500 souls. They use no intoxicating drink; are industrious and virtuous. The men adopt the usual Mexican dress, while the women wear a woven tunic and a small blanket tacked over the shoulders. Before marriage the hair of the women is worn in two large rosettes upon each side of the head, and after marriage, is worn  ose down the back or rolled up back of the head.

Being entirely self-supporting, they have had but few agents and very little assistance from the General Government. Their remote and nearly inaccessible location has also removed them beyond the reach of most missionary enterprises. Within the last two or three years some efforts have been made to establish schools among them, supported mainly by Presbyterian enterprise.

*List of illustrations.*

416. DELEGATION TO BRIGHAM YOUNG.

Copy of a photograph of three Moqui Indians from the Pueblo of Oraybi, delegated to visit the Mormon president for the purpose of encouraging trade.

983. NUM-PAYU. *Harmless Snake.*

A comely young maiden of the pueblo of Téwa. The peculiar style in which the hair is worn, as shown in this picture, is a sign of maidenhood. After marriage the hair is allowed to hang down the back, or is gathered in a small knot at the back of the head. The Moquis dress themselves entirely in woolen goods of their own manufacture, in which they are quite expert, their women's dress and blankets forming their principal stock in trade.

1019. TÉ-WA.

1020. HOUSE OF THE CAPITAN OF TÉ-WA.

986. STREET VIEW IN TÉ-WA.

1021, 988. GUALPI or O PEE-KI.

1024. SHE-MÓ-PA-VE.

1023. MOO-SHA-NA-VE.

1022, 991. SHE-PAÚ-LA-VAY.

1025. HOUSE OF THE CAPITAN OF SHE-MO-PA-VE.

The above are four of seven towns which are collectively generally known as the Moquis Pueblos. By a census taken in the spring of 1877, they were found to contain a population of 492 men, 440 women and 672 children, 1,604 in all; of which Té-wa has 132, Gualpi 234, She-mo-pa-ve 189, and She-pau-la-vay 198. With the exception of Oraybi, all these villages are built upon the summits of sandstone mesas, 600 feet above the valleys below them, and from which has to be brought their water, wood, and everything they raise. They possess considerable flocks of goats and sheep, which are secured every night in pens along the sides and upon the summits of the mesa, as shown in No. 987. Although there is no running water within many miles, and consequently they cannot irrigate, yet they are quite successful in cultivating corn, melons, &c., usually raising much more than they consume.

### 5. PUEBLOS.

A general name applied by the Spaniards to several tribes of semi-civilized Indians in what is now New Mexico. The term *pueblo*, in Spanish, literally means the *people* and their *towns*. They were first visited by Cabeza de Vaca in 1537, who conveyed the first authentic account of their villages to Mexico, which resulted, in 1540, in the expedition of Coronado. As nearly as can be ascertained at the present time, he visited and subdued the Pueblos in the neighborhood of Zuñi, along the Rio Grande, and the Moqui of the province of Tusayan; but only occupied the country two years. Were finally subdued in 1586, and the Spanish retained uninterrupted control, with the exception of the period of the insurrection of 1680, until the cession of the territory to the United States in 1847. At the time of Coronado's visit they were as advanced as now, raising grain, vegetables, and cotton, and manufacturing fine blankets. Their houses are sometimes built of stone, but generally of adobe; are several stories in height—three to five usually—each one receding from the one below, leaving a terrace or walk. The general plan is a hollow square, although in some cases they are built in a solid mass, like a pyramid, six or eight stories in height. In each pueblo there are large rooms, sometimes under ground, for religious observances or councils, called in Spanish, *estufas*. The towns are sometimes built upon the summits of high terraces or *mesas*, extremely difficult of approach.

The Pueblos constitute several tribes, with different languages; some are now extinct; but those existing are the Zuñis; Toltos in Taos, with whom are classed the people of Picuris, the Sandia, and Isleta; the Tiguas in San Juan, Santa Clara, Nambé, San Ildefonso, Pojuaque, and Tesuque; (the Moquis of pueblo of Te'-wa are said to speak this language); the Queres in Cochité, San Domingo, San Filipe, Santa Aña, Zia, Laguna, and Acoma; the Jemez, in the pueblo of the same name. In the 19 pueblos named there are now estimated to be 8,400 people, the most populous being Zuñi, with some 1,500 souls, and the least, Pojuaque, numbering only some 30 or 40 persons. Were recognized as citizens under Mexican rule, but since the admission of New Mexico the matter has been left in doubt. In 1858, Government confirmed to them the old Spanish grants of the land the Pueblos cultivate, averaging about twelve square leagues to each pueblo. They retain their own form of government, each village electing a governor, and a council consisting of three old men. Have been under Catholic influence since the Spanish conquest; but in the division of the tribes among the religious denominations, the Pueblos were first assigned to the Baptists, and afterward to the Presbyterians, who are now actively engaged in establishing schools among them.

*List of illustrations.*

1015. NA-NA-ÁN-YE. *A al Metor de la Sierra.*
    Spanish name, Antonio José Atencio. Head chief of all the Pueblos. Can read and write Spanish. Age, 70; height, 5.4½.

1016. TSE-WA-ÁN-YE. *Tail of the Eagle Fluttering.*
    Spanish name, Antonio al Churleta. Governor of the pueblo of San Juan, and is the bearer of a cane, the badge of his office, which is marked "A. Lincoln, á San Juan, 1863." Can read and write in the Spanish language. Age, 64; height, 5.6½.

1017. WA-SÓ-TO-YÁ-MIN. *Small Feathers of the Eagle.*
    Spanish name, Juan Jesus Leo. Governor of the pueblo of Taos; which position is retained but for one year. Is the bearer of a cane marked "A. Lincol á Taos." Age, 45; height, 5.7½.

643. AMBROSIA ABEITA.

644. ALEJANDRO PADILLO.

645–6. GROUPS with ABEITA and PADILLO.

992. GROUP OF ANTONIO JOSÉ ATENCIO, ANTONIA AL CHURLETA, and JUAN JESUS LEO.
15–17. THE HERDER.
>One of the former governors of the pueblo of Taos.
20. GROUP OF CORRIDORES.
>Young men who are selected to run foot-races during the "feasts" or religious holidays.
618, 623. YOUNG MAIDEN.
>A very good-looking young woman of the pueblo of Taos, with her hair gathered over the ears, signifying her single state. This custom also obtains among the Moquis.
614–617; 620, 626–7. YOUNG GIRLS AND WOMEN OF THE PUEBLO OF TAOS.
19, 613, 625, 619, 621–2. VARIOUS INDIVIDUALS belonging to the pueblo of Taos.
628–642. VIEWS OF THE PUEBLO OF TAOS.

### 6. TAWACANIES.

A small tribe in the Indian Territory associated with the Caddos, Kiowas, and others on the Wichita agency. They are well advanced toward civilization.

738–739. DAVE.
740–741. CAW-LAC-ITS-CA. *Son of Dave.*

### 7. TEMICULSA.

A small band of Indians living in the southern portion of California, who are extensively intermarried with the Mexicans. They are a thrifty, prosperous people, fully able to take good care of themselves, and are not under the care of any agent.

993. KA-LEK. *Hanging.*
>Chief of the Temiculas, and delegate recently to Washington, to seek from the General Government the restitution of some of their land, from which this tribe had been ejected by the State government. Is a man of marked intelligence, and speaks Spanish fluently. Age, 45; height, 5.10; head, 23½; chest, 47½; weight, 245.

994. ANDREW MAGRAND.
>Temicula and Mexican half-breed. Age, 27.

995. JOHN CLIFT.
>Temicula and Mexican half-breed. Age, 25.

# NUMERICAL INDEX.

|  | Page. |
|---|---|
| 1–2. Es-kel-ta-sa-la, *Apache* | 25 |
| 3–4. Santo, *Apache* | 25 |
| 5–6. Ta-ho, *Apache* | 25 |
| 7–8. Gray Eagle, *Apache* | 25 |
| 9–10. Capitan, *Apache* | 25 |
| 11–12. Pacer, *Apache* | 25 |
| 13–14. Wife of Pacer, *Apache* | 25 |
| 15–17. The Herder, governor of Taos, *Pueblo* | 107 |
| 18. Son of Vicenti, *Apache* | 26 |
| 19. A Pueblo Indian | 107 |
| 20. Corridores, or Runners, *Pueblo* | 107 |
| 21. Yellow Bear and Little Wolf, *Arapaho* | 100 |
| 22. Powder Face and squaw, *Arapaho* | 100 |
| 23. Medicine Pipe and Fool Dog, *Arapaho* | 100 |
| 24. Crazy Bull and Friday, *Arapaho* | 100 |
| 25. Plenty Bears and Old Eagle, *Arapaho* | 100 |
| 26. Lame White Man and Wild Hog, *Cheyenne* | 7 |
| 27. Bald Bear and Cut Foot, *Cheyenne* | 7 |
| 28. Dull Knife and Little Wolf, *Cheyenne* | 7 |
| 29. Crazy Head and Spotted Wolf, *Cheyenne* | 7 |
| 30–31. Stone Calf and squaw, *Cheyenne* | 7 |
| 33–35. Big Mouth, *Cheyenne* | 7 |
| 36–37. White Crow, *Cheyenne* | 7 |
| 38–39. Black Crow, *Cheyenne* | 7 |
| 40–41. Left Hand, *Cheyenne* | 7 |
| 42–43. Yellow Horse, *Cheyenne* | 7 |
| 44–45. Heap o' Bears, *Cheyenne* | 7 |
| 46–47. Groups of Bannacks | 70 |
| 48. Family of Sheep-eater Bannacks | 70 |
| 51–61. Groups about the Bannack Agency | 70 |
| 62–65. Little Raven, *Arapaho* | 100 |
| 66. Colonel Downing, *Cherokee* | 103 |
| 67. Richards, *Cherokee* | 103 |
| 68. Colonel Adair, *Cherokee* | 103 |
| 69. Samuel Smith, *Cherokee* | 103 |
| 70. Borum Davis, *Cherokee* | 103 |
| 71. Captain Scraper, *Cherokee* | 103 |
| 72. Bingo, *Cherokee* | 103 |
| 73. J. D. James, *Chickasaw* | 97 |
| 74. Ash-ke-he-naw-niew, *Chickasaw* | 97 |

# NUMERICAL INDEX.

|   |   | Page. |
|---|---|---|
| 75. | Shonion, *Chickasaw* | 98 |
| 76. | Annie Guy, *Chickasaw* | 98 |
| 77. | A young brave, *Chickasaw* | 98 |
| 78–79. | Hole in the Day, *Chippewa* | 11 |
| 80. | Bad Boy, *Chippewa* | 11 |
| 81. | Crossing Sky, *Chippewa* | 11 |
| 82. | Standing Forward, *Chippewa* | 11 |
| 83. | Stump, *Chippewa* | 11 |
| 84. | Red Bird, *Chippewa* | 11 |
| 85. | Foremost Sitter, *Chippewa* | 11 |
| 86. | Noon-Day, *Chippewa* | 11 |
| 88. | Israel Folsom, *Choctaw* | 98 |
| 89. | Peter Folsom, *Choctaw* | 98 |
| 90. | Samuel Folsom, *Choctaw* | 98 |
| 91. | ——— Folsom, *Choctaw* | 98 |
| 92. | Faunceway Batiste, *Choctaw* | 98 |
| 93. | B. L. Le Flore, *Choctaw* | 98 |
| 94. | Samuel Garland, *Choctaw* | 98 |
| 95. | Colonel Pytchlynn, *Choctaw* | 98 |
| 96. | Allen Wright, *Choctaw* | 98 |
| 97. | The Drunken Terrapin, *Creek* | 95 |
| 98. | Town King, *Creek* | 95 |
| 99. | Thompson Perryman, *Creek* | 95 |
| 100. | Chief of the Whirlwind, *Creek* | 96 |
| 102. | Group of Creeks | 96 |
| 103. | Tiger, *Creek* | 96 |
| 104. | Sand, *Creek* | 96 |
| 105–107. | Family of George Stedman, *Creek* | 96 |
| 108. | A Creek brave | 96 |
| 109. | Little Robe, *Cheyenne* | 6 |
| 110. | Whirlwind, *Cheyenne* | 7 |
| 111. | White Shield, *Cheyenne* | 7 |
| 112. | White Horse, *Cheyenne* | 7 |
| 113. | Medicine Man, *Cheyenne* | 7 |
| 114. | Pawnee, *Cheyenne* | 7 |
| 115. | Edward Guerrer, interpreter, *Cheyenne* | 7 |
| 116. | Whilwind and Pawnee, *Cheyenne* | 7 |
| 118–121. | Little Robe, *Cheyenne* | 6 |
| 122. | High Toe, *Cheyenne* | 7 |
| 123–124. | Groups at Cheyenne Agency | 7 |
| 125–126. | Pedro Scradalicto, *Apache* | 26 |
| 127. | Eschapa, *Apache* | 26 |
| 128–129. | Asa-havie, *Comanche* | 72 |
| 130–131. | Wife of Asa-havie, *Comanche* | 72 |
| 132–133. | Timber Bluff, *Comanche* | 72 |
| 134–135. | Silver Knife, *Comanche* | 72–73 |
| 136–137. | Wife of Silver Knife, *Comanche* | 73 |
| 138–140. | Gray Leggings, *Comanche* | 73 |
| 141–142. | Cheevers, *Comanche* | 73 |

## NUMERICAL INDEX. 111

| | Page. |
|---|---|
| 143–144. Wife of Cheevers, *Comanche* | 73 |
| 145–146. Mother of Cheevers, *Comanche* | 73 |
| 147–148. Chewing Elk, *Comanche* | 73 |
| 149–150. Gap in the Salt, *Comanche* | 73 |
| 151–152. Daughter of Gap in the Salt, *Comanche* | 73 |
| 153–154. Ten Bears, *Comanche* | 73 |
| 155–156. Buffalo Hump, *Comanche* | 74 |
| 157–158. Jim, *Comanche* | 74 |
| 159–160. George Washington, *Caddo* | 101 |
| 161–162. War-loupe, *Caddo* | 101 |
| 163–164. Antelope, *Caddo* | 101 |
| 165–168. Buffalo Goad, *Wichita* | 69 |
| 170–171. Red Thunder, *Dakota* | 45 |
| 172–173. Good Hawk, *Dakota* | 45 |
| 174–175. Walking Crane, *Dakota* | 45 |
| 176–177. Yellow Eagle, *Dakota* | 45 |
| 178–179. Comanche drawings | 74 |
| 181–182. Black Beaver, *Delaware* | 12 |
| 186. Great Bear, *Delaware* | 12 |
| 187–190. Long Mandan, *Two Kettle Dakota* | 43 |
| 191. Spotted Horse, *Two Kettle Dakota* | 43 |
| 192. Little Short Horn, *Sissiton Dakota* | 43 |
| 193. Other Day, *Wahpeton Dakota* | 43 |
| 194–196. Yellow Hawk, *Sans-Arc Dakota* | 42 |
| 197–198. Little Crow, *M'dewakanton* | 38 |
| 199. Medicine Bottle, *M'dewakanton Dakota* | 38 |
| 200. Shakpe, *M'dewakanton Dakota* | 38 |
| 201–202. The Shooter, *Santee Dakota* | 42 |
| 203. Red Ensign, *Santee Dakota* | 42 |
| 204. Black Lightning, *Santee Dakota* | 42 |
| 205. Scarlet all over, *Santee Dakota* | 42 |
| 206. Flute Player, *Santee Dakota* | 42 |
| 207. Standing Soldier, *Santee Dakota* | 42 |
| 208. Walks Following the Eagle, *Santee Dakota* | 42 |
| 209. Red Ensign, *Santee Dakota* | 42 |
| 210. His Man Horse, *Santee Dakota* | 42 |
| 211. Coming Among the Clouds, *Santee Dakota* | 42 |
| 212. Blue Bird, *Santee Dakota* | 42 |
| 213. Standing Cloud, *Santee Dakota* | 42 |
| 214. Scarlet Night, *Santee Dakota* | 42 |
| 215. Red Legs, *Santee Dakota* | 42 |
| 216. Seraphin Renville, interpreter, *Santee Dakota* | 43 |
| 217. Struck by the Ree, *Yankton Dakota* | 43 |
| 218–219. Jumping Thunder, *Yankton Dakota* | 43 |
| 220. Long Foot, *Yankton Dakota* | 43 |
| 221. White Swan, *Yankton Dakota* | 43 |
| 222–224. Medicine Cow, *Yankton Dakota* | 43 |
| 225–228. Two Lance, *Yankton Dakota* | 43 |
| 229. Feather in the Ear, *Yankton Dakota* | 43 |

## NUMERICAL INDEX.

|  | Page. |
|---|---|
| 230–231. Little Bird, *Yankton Dakota* | 43 |
| 232–233. Black Eagle, *Yankton Dakota* | 43 |
| 234. Bear lying down, *Yankton Dakota* | 43 |
| 235. Running Bull, *Yankton Dakota* | 43 |
| 236. Walking Elk, *Yankton Dakota* | 43 |
| 237. Standing Elk, *Yankton Dakota* | 43 |
| 238. Smutty Bear, *Yankton Dakota* | 43 |
| 239. Struck by the Ree, *Yankton Dakota* | 43 |
| 240–241. Smutty Bear and Struck by the Ree, *Yankton Dakota* | 43 |
| 244. Yankton war-dance | 45 |
| 248. Santee brave | 43 |
| 249. Great Scalper, *Santee* | 42 |
| 250. Standing Buffalo, *Santee* | 43 |
| 251. Old Betts, *Santee* | 43 |
| 252–254. Grass, *Blackfeet Dakota* | 34 |
| 255–256. Sitting Crow, *Blackfeet Dakota* | 34 |
| 257–258. Iron Scare, *Blackfeet Dakota* | 34 |
| 259. Red Plume, *Blackfeet Dakota* | 34 |
| 260–261. Bear's Rib, *Oncpapa Dakota* | 41 |
| 262–263. Running Antelope, *Oncpapa Dakota* | 41, 42 |
| 264–265. Iron Horn, *Oncpapa Dakota* | 42 |
| 266–267. Walking Shooter, *Oncpapa Dakota* | 42 |
| 268–269. Thunder Hawk, *Oncpapa Dakota* | 42 |
| 270–271. Big Head, *Upper Yanktonais Dakota* | 44 |
| 272–273. Black Eye, *Upper Yanktonais Dakota* | 44 |
| 274–275. Big Razor, *Upper Yanktonais Dakota* | 44 |
| 276–277. Bull's Ghost, *Lower Yanktonais Dakota* | 44 |
| 278–279. Foolish Bear, *Lower Yanktonais Dakota* | 44 |
| 280–281. Two Bears, *Lower Yanktonais Dakota* | 44 |
| 282–283. Medicine Bear, *Cut Head Dakota* | 37 |
| 284–285. Afraid of the Bear, *Cut Head Dakota* | 37 |
| 286–287. Bear's Nose, *Cut Head Dakota* | 37 |
| 288–289. Skin of the Heart, *Cut Head Dakota* | 37 |
| 290–291. Red Lodge, *Cut Head Dakota* | 37 |
| 292–293. Man who packs the Eagle, *Cut Head Dakota* | 37 |
| 294–295. Squaw of the Man who packs the Eagle, *Cut Head Dakota* | 37 |
| 296–297. Red Cloud, *Ogalalla Dakota* | 38 |
| 298. Red Cloud and Mr. Blackmore, *Ogalalla Dakota* | 40 |
| 299–300. Red Dog, *Ogalalla Dakota* | 40 |
| 201–302. Lone Wolf, *Ogalalla Dakota* | 40 |
| 303–304. Ear of Corn, squaw of LoneWolf, *Ogalalla Dakota* | 40 |
| 305–306. Big Foot, *Ogalalla Dakota* | 40 |
| 307–308. White Hawk, *Ogalalla Dakota* | 40 |
| 309–310. Afraid of the Eagle, *Ogalalla Dakota* | 40 |
| 311–312. Blue Horse, *Ogalalla Dakota* | 40 |
| 313–314. Stabber, *Ogalalla Dakota* | 40 |
| 315–316. Dirt Face, *Ogalalla Dakota* | 40 |
| 317–318. Good Buffalo, *Ogalalla Dakota* | 40 |
| 319–320. Poor Elk, *Ogalalla Dakota* | 40, 41 |

## NUMERICAL INDEX.

|  | Page. |
|---|---|
| 321–322. Two Elks, *Ogalalla Dakota* | 41 |
| 323–324. High Wolf, *Ogalalla Dakota* | 41 |
| 325–326. Coyote, *Ogalalla Dakota* | 41 |
| 327–328. Hard Heart, *Ogalalla Dakota* | 41 |
| 329–330. Slow Bull, *Ogalalla Dakota* | 41 |
| 331. One Horned Elk, *Ogalalla Dakota* | 41 |
| 332. Big Rib, *Ogalalla Dakota* | 41 |
| 333. War Eagle, *Ogalalla Dakota* | 41 |
| 334. Old Man Afraid of his Horses and Chiefs, *Ogalalla Dakota* | 41 |
| 336–337. Spotted Tail, *Brulé Dakota* | 34, 35 |
| 338. Spotted Tail and squaw, *Brulé Dakota* | 36 |
| 339–340. Squaw of Spotted Tail, *Brulé Dakota* | 36 |
| 341–342. Gassy, *Brulé Dakota* | 36 |
| 343–344. Whitewash his Face, *Brulé Dakota* | 36 |
| 345–346. Charge on the Hawk, *Brulé Dakota* | 36 |
| 347–348. Two Strikes, *Brulé Dakota* | 36 |
| 349–350. Squaw of Two Strikes, *Brulé Dakota* | 36 |
| 351–352. Black Crow, *Brulé Dakota* | 36 |
| 353–354. One who runs the Tiger, *Brulé Dakota* | 36 |
| 355–356. Bald Eagle, *Brulé Dakota* | 36 |
| 357–358. Thigh, *Brulé Dakota* | 36 |
| 359–360. Squaw of Thigh, *Brulé Dakota* | 36 |
| 361–362. Black Bull, *Brulé Dakota* | 36 |
| 363–364. No Flesh, *Brulé Dakota* | 36, 37 |
| 365–367. Iron Shell, *Brulé Dakota* | 37 |
| 368–369. Wicked Bear, *Brulé Dakota* | 37 |
| 370–371. Yellow Hairs, *Brulé Dakota* | 37 |
| 372–373. White Eyes, *Brulé Dakota* | 37 |
| 374–375. Swift Bear, *Brulé Dakota* | 37 |
| 376–377. White Thunder, *Brulé Dakota* | 37 |
| 378–380. Iron Nation, *Brulé Dakota* | 37 |
| 382–384. Group of Santees with Mr. Hinman | 43 |
| 385–386. British, *Iowa* | 47 |
| 387. Black Hawk, *Iowa* | 48 |
| 388–389. Knife, *Iowa* | 47 |
| 390. Little Chief, *Iowa* | 47 |
| 391. Deer Ham, *Iowa* | 47 |
| 392–394. No Heart, *Iowa* | 48 |
| 395. Deer Ham, *Iowa* | 47 |
| 396. George Gomez, *Sac and Fox* | 18 |
| 397. Little Bear, *Kansas* | 48 |
| 398, 399. Ka-ke-ga-sha, *Kansas* | 48 |
| 400. Wahcoma, *Sac and Fox* | 18 |
| 401. Grey Eyes, *Sac and Fox* | 18 |
| 402, 403. Lone Wolf, *Kiowa* | 74 |
| 404–406. Squaw of Lone Wolf, *Kiowa* | 75 |
| 407. Sleeping Wolf, *Kiowa* | 75 |
| 408, 409. Son of the Sun, *Kiowa* | 75 |
| 410. Drawing by a Kiowa Indian | 75 |

# NUMERICAL INDEX.

|  | Page. |
|---|---|
| 411, 412. Knee-war-war, *Keechie* | 63 |
| 414, 415. José Pocati, *Apache* | 26 |
| 416. Moqui delegates | 104 |
| 419. Lum-ki-kom, *Miami* | 14 |
| 420. Thomas Miller, *Miami* | 14 |
| 421. Joe Dick, *Miami* | 14 |
| 422, 424. Roubideaux, *Miami* | 14 |
| 425. Thomas Richardwell, *Miami* | 14 |
| 426. Roubideaux and Richardwell, *Miami* | 14 |
| 427, 428. Jason, *Nez Percé* | 84 |
| 429, 431. Timothy, *Nez Percé* | 84 |
| 433, 434. A Nez Percé camp | 84 |
| 435, 436. Nez Percé lodges | 84 |
| 437. A Nez Percé chief | 84 |
| 438. A Nez Percé half-breed | 85 |
| 439–441. Views in a Nez Percé camp | 85 |
| 442. Guerito, *Apache* | 25 |
| 443. A young brave, *Apache* | 26 |
| 444. Son of Guerito, *Apache* | 26 |
| 445–446. Young braves, *Apache* | 26 |
| 447. Pah-yeh, *Apache* | 26 |
| 448. A young brave, *Apache* | 26 |
| 449. Guachinito, *Apache* | 25 |
| 450. A young brave | 26 |
| 451. Kle-zeh, *Apache* | 25 |
| 452–555. Navajos | 28 |
| 457, 458. Omaha Indian Agency buildings | 53 |
| 459, 460. View from Black Bird Hill | 53 |
| 461, 462. Omaha Indian village | 53 |
| 463. Gihiga, *Omaha* | 53 |
| 464. Gihiga's lodge, *Omaha* | 53 |
| 465, 466. Standing Hawk and squaw, *Omaha* | 53 |
| 467. Standing at the End, *Omaha* | 53 |
| 468. Standing Bent, *Omaha* | 53 |
| 469, 470. Betsy, *Omaha* | 53 |
| 471. Indian carpenters at work, *Omaha* | 54 |
| 472–476. Groups of school-children, *Omaha* | 54 |
| 447. A brave, *Omaha* | 54 |
| 478. Ebahomba's lodge, *Omaha* | 54 |
| 479. Village scene, *Omaha* | 54 |
| 480. Stand by it, *Otoe* | 56 |
| 481. True Eagle, *Missouria* | 51 |
| 482, 483. Medicine Horse, *Otoe* | 57 |
| 484–485. One who eats his Food Raw, *Missouria* | 51 |
| 486. Big Bear, *Missouria* | 52 |
| 487. Little Pipe, *Otoe* | 57 |
| 488. Little Iowa, *Otoe* | 58 |
| 489, 490. Little Pipe, *Otoe* | 57 |
| 491. Little Pipe and group, *Otoe* | 59 |

## NUMERICAL INDEX. 115

| | Page. |
|---|---|
| 492-494. Medicine Horse, *Otoe* | 57 |
| 495. Buffalo Chief, *Otoe* | 58 |
| 496. Medicine Horse, Buffalo Chief, and interpreter, *Otoe* | 59 |
| 497. Baptiste Devoin and Buffalo Chief, *Otoe* | 58 |
| 498. Black Elk, *Missouria* | 52 |
| 499. Medicine Horse and Buffalo Chief, *Otoe* | 59 |
| 500. Blue Bird and Buck Elk Walking, *Otoe* | 58 |
| 501. Group of Otoes | 59 |
| 502. Medicine Horse, *Otoe* | 57 |
| 503. The One They are Afraid of, *Missouria* | 51 |
| 504. Sucker, *Ottawa* | 15 |
| 505. Lightning, *Ottawa* | 15 |
| 506. John Wilson, *Ottawa* | 15 |
| 507. Passing Through, *Ottawa* | 15 |
| 509. The Savage, *Osage* | 56 |
| 510. The Distant Land, *Osage* | 56 |
| 511. Joseph, *Osage* | 55 |
| 512. One who reaches to the Sky, *Osage* | 56 |
| 513. Saucy Chief, *Osage* | 56 |
| 517, 518. Group of four Ponca chiefs | 59 |
| 519. Iron Whip, *Ponca* | 59 |
| 520. Peah and other Ute chiefs | 83 |
| 521. Native Ponca drawing | 59 |
| 522. Thunder coming down to the Ground, *Pottawatomie* | 16 |
| 523. Pawnee Indian village, *Nebraska* | 68 |
| 524. Pawnee mud lodge | 68 |
| 525-527. Groups of Pawnee school-children | 69 |
| 528, 529. Groups of Pawnee chiefs and headmen | 65, 66 |
| 530-532. Peta-lashara, *Pawnee* | 65 |
| 533. Eagle Chief, *Pawnee* | 65 |
| 534. Sun Chief, *Pawnee* | 65 |
| 535. One who brings Herds, *Pawnee* | 65 |
| 536. Group of Pawnee squaws | 69 |
| 537-539. Pawnee school-buildings, Nebraska | 69 |
| 540. Pawnee decorative painting on buffalo-skin | 69 |
| 541, 542. Pawnee agency buildings | 69 |
| 543. One who gives to the Poor, *Pawnee* | 65 |
| 545. Squaw of One who gives to the Poor, *Pawnee* | 65 |
| 547. A brave, *Pawnee* | 69 |
| 548. Pipe Chief, *Pawnee* | 65 |
| 549. A brave, *Pawnee* | 69 |
| 550, 551. Group of two Pawnee chiefs | 66 |
| 552, 553. Group of four Pawnee chiefs | 66 |
| 554, 555. Baptiste Babylle, *Pawnee* | 67 |
| 556, 557. Small Boy, *Pawnee* | 67 |
| 558, 559. Blue Hawk and Coming with the Herd, *Pawnee* | 67 |
| 560. Sky Chief, *Pawnee* | 67 |
| 561-566. Miscellaneous groups of Pawnees | 67 |
| 567, 568. Pawnee Indian village | 68 |

# NUMERICAL INDEX.

|  | Page. |
|---|---|
| 569. Pawnee mud lodge | 69 |
| 570, 572. Pawnee pappooses | 69 |
| 573, 574. Groups of Pawnee chiefs | 69 |
| 575. On a Fine Horse, *Pawnee* | 67 |
| 576. Particular as to Time of day, *Pawnee* | 67 |
| 577. The Sun Coming in, *Pawnee* | 67 |
| 578. Behind the One who strikes first, *Pawnee* | 67 |
| 579. Little Raven, *Pawnee* | 67 |
| 580. White Horse, *Pawnee* | 67 |
| 581. Rattlesnake, *Pawnee* | 67 |
| 582. Fox, *Pawnee* | 67 |
| 583. Acting like a Fox, *Pawnee* | 67 |
| 584. Beaver, *Pawnee* | 67 |
| 585. Little Raven, *Pawnee* | 67 |
| 586. As-sow-weet, *Pawnee* | 67 |
| 587, 588. Young braves, *Pawnee* | 69 |
| 589. Ter-rer-e-caw-wah, *Pawnee* | 67 |
| 590. Long Dog, *Pawnee* | 67 |
| 591. An old man, *Pawnee* | 67 |
| 592. As-sow-weet and Sawka, *Pawnee* | 67 |
| 593. Male Calf and On a Fine Horse, *Pawnee* | 67 |
| 594. Rattlesnake and squaw, *Pawnee* | 67 |
| 595. In the Front and squaw, *Pawnee* | 67 |
| 596. Nice Horse, *Pawnee* | 67 |
| 597. Good Bear, *Pawnee* | 68 |
| 598. Beginning to go to War, *Pawnee* | 68 |
| 599. Fox on the War-Path, *Pawnee* | 68 |
| 600. Crow's Eyes, *Pawnee* | 68 |
| 601. Medicine Bull, *Pawnee* | 68 |
| 602. One who strikes the Chiefs first, *Pawnee* | 68 |
| 603. Medicine Eagle, *Pawnee* | 68 |
| 604. Driving a Herd, *Pawnee* | 68 |
| 605. Medicine Antelope, *Pawnee* | 68 |
| 606. Good Buffalo, *Pawnee* | 68 |
| 607. Little Raven, *Pawnee* | 67 |
| 608. One Seen by All, *Pawnee* | 68 |
| 609. On a Fine Horse, *Pawnee* | 68 |
| 610. Knee-Mark on the Ground, &c., *Pawnee* | 68 |
| 611. Bad Man, *Pawnee* | 69 |
| 612. Growling Bear, *Pawnee* | 69 |
| 613. Pueblo Indian from Taos | 107 |
| 614–617. Indian girls and women from the pueblo of Taos | 107 |
| 618. A Pueblo girl | 107 |
| 619. A Pueblo man | 107 |
| 620. A Pueblo girl | 107 |
| 621, 622. Pueblo men | 107 |
| 623–624. Pueblo women | 107 |
| 625. A Pueblo man | 107 |
| 626, 627. Pueblo girls | 107 |

NUMERICAL INDEX. 117

| | Page. |
|---|---|
| 628–642. Views in the Pueblo of Taos, New Mexico | 107 |
| 643. Ambrosia Abeita, *Pueblo* | 106 |
| 644. Alejandro Padillo, *Pueblo* | 106 |
| 645, 646. Abeita and Padillo, *Pueblo* | 106 |
| 647. Ambrosia Abeita, *Pueblo* | 106 |
| 648. Alejandro Padillo, *Pueblo* | 106 |
| 649. W. F. M. Arny, Pueblo agent, *Pueblo* | 106 |
| 650–651. Ascencion Rios, *Papago* | 91 |
| 652. Eschapa, *Apache* | 26 |
| 653, 654. Luig Morague, *Pima* | 91 |
| 655, 656. Antonio Azul, *Pima* | 91 |
| 657, 658. Shoshone village in South Pass | 76 |
| 659, 660. War chief's tent, Shoshone village | 76 |
| 661, 662. Washakie and his warriors, *Shoshone* | 76 |
| 663, 664. Washakie, *Shoshone* | 76 |
| 665, 666. Views in a Shoshone village | 76 |
| 667–676. Groups and miscellaneous portraits of Shoshones | 77 |
| 677. Keokuk, sr., *Sac and Fox* | 17 |
| 678. Keokuk, jr., *Sac and Fox* | 17 |
| 679. Charles Keokuk, *Sac and Fox* | 17 |
| 680–684. Keokuk, jr., and Charles Keokuk, *Sac and Fox* | 17 |
| 685, 686. Moless, *Sac and Fox* | 17 |
| 687–688. Sacapee, *Sac and Fox* | 17 |
| 689–690. Moless and Sacapee, *Sac and Fox* | 17 |
| 691. George Gomez, *Sac and Fox* | 18 |
| 692. Dead Indian, *Sac and Fox* | 17 |
| 693. The Sea, *Sac and Fox* | 17 |
| 694. Big Bear, *Sac and Fox* | 17 |
| 695–699. Mokohoko, *Sac and Fox* | 18 |
| 700. Manotowa, *Sac and Fox* | 18 |
| 701. George Gomez, *Sac and Fox* | 18 |
| 705. Keokuk, jr., *Sac and Fox* | 17 |
| 706, 707. Group of delegates, *Sac and Fox* | 18 |
| 708. Sac chief, *Sac and Fox* | 18 |
| 709. Group of Sac and Fox chiefs, *Sac and Fox* | 18 |
| 710. Commissioner and delegates, *Sac and Fox* | 18 |
| 711. Wa-wa-si-mo, *Shawnee* | 19 |
| 712. F. A. Rogers, *Shawnee* | 19 |
| 713. Charles Tucker, *Shawnee* | 19 |
| 714. Billy Bowlegs, *Seminole* | 97 |
| 715. A daughter of General Parker, *Seneca* | 93 |
| 716. Bertram. *Shawnee* | 19 |
| 717. Black Buffalo, *Arickaree* | 63 |
| 718. Long Knife, *Arickaree* | 63 |
| 725. Light Foot, *Yankton Dakota* | 43 |
| 732, 733. Many Horns, *Dakota* | 45 |
| 734, 735. Black Eye, *Dakota* | 45 |
| 736, 737. Long Fox, *Dakota* | 45 |
| 738, 739. Dave, *Tawacanie* | 107 |

|     |     | Page. |
| --- | --- | --- |
| 740, 741. | Caw-hac-its-ca, *Tawacanie* | 107 |
| 742, 743. | Long Soldier, *Waco* | 69 |
| 744, 745. | Assadawa, *Wichita* | 69 |
| 746, 747. | Esquitzchew, *Wichita* | 69 |
| 748. | Black Horse, *Wichita* | 69 |
| 749, 750. | Charlie Arriwawa, *Apache* | 26 |
| 751. | Tapuche, *Utah* | 80 |
| 752. | Mautchick, *Utah* | 80 |
| 753. | Guerito, *Apache* | 25 |
| 754. | Coho, *Utah* | 80 |
| 755. | Utah-Arapaho | 101 |
| 756–758. | Antero, *Utah* | 80 |
| 759, 760. | Wanero, *Utah* | 80 |
| 761, 762. | Tabiyuna, *Utah* | 80 |
| 763, 764. | Komus, *Utah* | 80 |
| 765–767. | Ouray, *Utah* | 78 |
| 768. | Guero, *Utah* | 79 |
| 769. | John, *Utah* | 80 |
| 770. | Kwa-ko-nut and Mose, *Utah* | 81 |
| 771. | Cu-ra-can-te, *Utah* | 81 |
| 772, 773. | Shavano, *Utah* | 79 |
| 774. | Warets and Shavano, *Utah* | 81 |
| 775. | Group of Ouray and chiefs, *Utah* | 81 |
| 776. | Group of chiefs, *Utah* | 81 |
| 777. | Shuriap, *Utah* | 81 |
| 778. | Chippin, *Utah* | 81 |
| 779. | Little Soldier, *Utah* | 81 |
| 780. | Squaw of Little Soldier, *Utah* | 82 |
| 781. | Shavano, *Utah* | 79 |
| 782. | Lovo, *Utah* | 82 |
| 783. | Rainbow, *Utah* | 82 |
| 784. | Nick-a-a-god, *Utah* | 82 |
| 785. | Pe-ah, *Utah* | 82 |
| 786. | Barban-cito, *Navajo* | 28 |
| 787. | Sappix and son, *Utah* | 83 |
| 788. | Chu, *Utah* | 83 |
| 789. | Kanosh, *Utah* | 83 |
| 790–696. | Miscellaneous groups, *Utah* | 83 |
| 797, 798. | Bloody Mouth, *Oncpapa Dakota* | 42 |
| 799, 800. | Lost Medicine, *Oncpapa Dakota* | 42 |
| 801, 802. | Black-Horn, *Oncpapa Dakota* | 42 |
| 803, 804. | Bull-Rushes, *Oncpapa Dakota* | 42 |
| 805. | Group of Fox chiefs | 18 |
| 806. | Commissioner Bogy reading treaty | 18 |
| 808. | Group of Winnebagoes | 61 |
| 809–811. | Winnebago children | 61 |
| 812. | Wife of Martin Van Buren, *Winnebago* | 61 |
| 813. | Winnebago children | 61 |
| 814. | Blue Cloud Passing, *Winnebago* | 61 |

# NUMERICAL INDEX.

|  | Page. |
|---|---|
| 815. General Sherman and Indian commissioners at Fort Laramie, 1868 | 45 |
| 816. Commissioners in council at Laramie | 45 |
| 817. Old Man Afraid, and group | 45 |
| 818-830. Miscellaneous groups about Laramie | 45 |
| 831. Sioux burial | 46 |
| 832- 5. Groups about Laramie | 46 |
| 838. Sioux delegation at the White House | 46 |
| 839-844. Saint Mary's Mission, Kansas, (Pottawatomie school) | 46 |
| 845. The sergeant of the guard | 46 |
| 851. Little Shell and chiefs, *Chippewas* | 9 |
| 852. Moses Ladd, *Menominee* | 13 |
| 853. Eskiminzin, *Apache* | 23 |
| 854. Eskiminzin and squaw, *Apache* | 23 |
| 855. Cassadora, *Apache* | 23 |
| 856. Cassadora and squaw, *Apache* | 23 |
| 857. Eskinilay, *Apache* | 24 |
| 858. Eskinilay and squaw, *Apache* | 23 |
| 859. Group of Crow delegates | 30 |
| 860. Chiquito, *Apache* | 23 |
| 861. Chiquito and squaw, *Apache* | 23 |
| 862. Saygully, *Apache* | 23 |
| 863. Eskayela, *Apache* | 24 |
| 864. Skellegunny, *Apache* | 24 |
| 865. Cullah, *Apache* | 24 |
| 866. Hautushnehay, *Apache* | 24 |
| 867. Napashgingush, *Apache* | 24 |
| 868. Cushashado, *Apache* | 24 |
| 869. Pinal, *Apache* | 24 |
| 870. Passelah, *Apache* | 24 |
| 871. Marijildo Grijalva, interpreter | 24 |
| 872, 873. Group of Apache delegates | 26 |
| 874. Little Big Man, *Ogalalla Dakota* | 41 |
| 875. Young Man Afraid of his Horses, *Ogalalla Dakota* | 41 |
| 876. American Horse, *Ogalalla Dakota* | 41 |
| 877. Little Wound, *Ogalalla Dakota* | 41 |
| 878. He Dog, *Ogalalla Dakota* | 41 |
| 879. Yellow Bear, *Ogalalla Dakota* | 41 |
| 880. Three Bears, *Ogalalla Dakota* | 41 |
| 881. Sword, *Ogalalla Dakota* | 41 |
| 882. Garnet, interpreter, *Ogalalla Dakota* | 41 |
| 883. Group, including Nos. 874-882, *Ogalalla Dakota* | 41 |
| 884. Charles Papinea, interpreter for Mandans | 50 |
| 885. Yellow Smoke, *Omaha* | 53 |
| 886. Black Dog, *Osage* | 55 |
| 887. Group of chiefs, *Osage* | 55 |
| 888. Joseph and Black Dog, *Osage* | 56 |
| 889. Joseph, Black Dog, and others, *Osage* | 56 |
| 890. Iron Black Bird, *Yankton Dakota* | 43 |

|   |   | Page. |
|---|---|---|
| 891. | Flying Pipe, *Yankton Dakota* | 43 |
| 892. | Little Thunder, *Yankton Dakota* | 44 |
| 893. | Sacred Bull, *Yankton Dakota* | 44 |
| 894. | Flying Bird, *Yankton Dakota* | 44 |
| 895. | Chief with Big War Bonnet, *Yankton Dakota* | 45 |
| 896. | He Kills First, *Yankton Dakota* | 44 |
| 897. | Sacred Ghost, *Yankton Dakota* | 44 |
| 898, 899. | Bear with a Big Voice, *Yankton Dakota* | 44 |
| 900. | Pretty Rock, *Yankton Dakota* | 44 |
| 901. | One who Catches the Enemy, *Yankton Dakota* | 44 |
| 902. | One who Walks Home, *Yankton Dakota* | 44 |
| 903. | Bear that Walks Lying Down, *Yankton Dakota* | 44 |
| 904, 905. | The Bear that Turns Around, *Yankton Dakota* | 44 |
| 906, 907. | Long Foot, *Yankton Dakota* | 43 |
| 908. | Medicine Bull, *Yankton Dakota* | 44 |
| 909–912. | Bird Chief, *Arapaho* | 100 |
| 916. | Maza-o-zan-zan, *Dakota* | 45 |
| 917. | Iron Elk, *Dakota* | 45 |
| 920. | Goose, *Blackfeet Dakota* | 34 |
| 921. | Iowa chief | 48 |
| 922. | Group of Iowas | 48 |
| 923. | Red Owl, *Dakota* | 45 |
| 925. | Cut Nose, *Dakota* | 45 |
| 927. | Iron Shooter, *Dakota* | 45 |
| 931. | Tall Feather Joining, *Dakota* | 45 |
| 932. | Medicine Bottle, *Dakota* | 45 |
| 933. | Plenty, *Dakota* | 45 |
| 935. | Colorado, *Utah* | 83 |
| 936, 937. | Choctaw boys | 98 |
| 938, 939. | Choctaw girls | 98 |
| 940. | Blackfoot and squaw, *Crow* | 30 |
| 941. | Iron Bull and squaw, *Crow* | 30 |
| 942. | Bear Wolf and squaw, *Crow* | 30 |
| 943. | Old Crow and squaw, *Crow* | 30 |
| 944. | Blackfoot, Long Horse, and White Calf, *Crow* | 30 |
| 945. | Momukhpitche, Thin Belly, and The One that Leads the Old Dog, *Crow* | 30 |
| 946. | Blackfoot, *Crow* | 30 |
| 947. | He Shows his Face, *Crow* | 30 |
| 948. | Old Onion, *Crow* | 30 |
| 949. | Group of chiefs, *Crow* | 30 |
| 950. | Group of squaws, *Crow* | 31 |
| 951. | Inside view of a Crow lodge | 31 |
| 952. | Crow village, (adobe houses) | 31 |
| 953. | The Old Mission, or Crow Agency | 31 |
| 954. | Crow burial | 31 |
| 955–959. | Encampment of Ute Indians, near Denver | 83 |
| 960–963. | Ute Indians in camp at Los Pinos | 83 |

NUMERICAL INDEX. 121

| | Page. |
|---|---|
| 965–974. Miscellaneous groups of Ute Indians | 83 |
| 975–976. Wal-aiks-ski-dat, *Klamath* | 87 |
| 977. Yumnispoctis, *Klamath* | 87 |
| 978. Olhathe, *Rogue River* | 90 |
| 979. Myron Silverheels, *Seneca* | 93 |
| 980. Group of Senecas | 93 |
| 981. Mathew Mudeater, *Wyandot* | 94 |
| 982. Nicholas Cotter, *Wyandot* | 94 |
| 983. Num-payu, *Moqui* | 103 |
| 984–985. Friday, *Arapaho* | 100 |
| 986. Street view in Tewa, *Moqui Pueblos* | 104 |
| 988. View of Gualpi, *Moqui Pueblos* | 104 |
| 991. View in Shepaulave, *Moqui Pueblos* | 104 |
| 992. Group of Pueblo governors | 106 |
| 993. Kalek, or Oligario, *Temicula* | 107 |
| 994. Andrew Magrand, *Temicula* | 107 |
| 995. John Clift, *Temicula* | 107 |
| 1001. Little Shell, *Chippewa* | 9 |
| 1002. Little Bull, *Chippewa* | 9 |
| 1003. Something Blown up by the Wind, *Chippewa* | 9 |
| 1004. The Man who Knows how to Hunt, *Chippewa* | 9 |
| 1005. Lance, *Mandan* | 50 |
| 1006. Rushing War Eagle, *Mandan* | 50 |
| 1007. Running Face, *Mandan* | 50 |
| 1008. Scar-faced Charley, *Modoc* | 88 |
| 1009. Shacknasty Jim, *Modoc* | 88 |
| 1010. Steamboat Frank, *Modoc* | 88 |
| 1011. Win-nema, *Modoc* | 89 |
| 1015. Antonio José Atencio, *Pueblo* | 106 |
| 1016. Antonio al Churleta, *Pueblo* | 106 |
| 1017. Juan Jesus Leo, *Pueblo* | 106 |
| 1018. Group of Atencio, Churleta, and Leo, *Pueblo* | 106 |
| 1019. Téwa, *Moqui Pueblos* | 104 |
| 1020. House of the Capitan of Tewa, *Moqui Pueblos* | 104 |
| 1021. Gualpi, *Moqui Pueblos* | 104 |
| 1022. Shepaulave, *Moqui Pueblos* | 104 |
| 1023. Mooshanave, *Moqui Pueblos* | 104 |
| 1024. Shemopave, *Moqui Pueblos* | 104 |
| 1025. House of the Capitan, *Shemopave, Moqui Pueblos* | 104 |
| 1027. Manulito, *Navajo* | 27 |
| 1028. Juanita, *Navajo* | 27 |
| 1029. Manulito Segundo, *Navajo* | 27 |
| 1030. Cayatanito, *Navajo* | 27 |
| 1031. Barbas Hueros, *Navajo* | 27 |
| 1032. Cabra Negra, *Navajo* | 27 |
| 1033. Narbona Primero, *Navajo* | 28 |
| 1034. Carnero Mucho, *Navajo* | 28 |
| 1035. Granada Mucho, Tienne-su-se, and Mariáno, *Navajo* | 28 |
| 1038. Juanita and Governor Arny | 28 |

|  | Page. |
|---|---|
| 1039. Frank King, *Ottawa* | 15 |
| 1040. Joseph King, *Ottawa* | 15 |
| 1041. L. S. Dagnet, *Ottawa* | 15 |
| 1042. Rushing War Eagle, *Arickaree* | 63 |
| 1043. Black Fox, *Arickaree* | 63 |
| 1044. Bull Head, *Arickaree* | 63 |
| 1045. Harrison Halftown, *Seneca* | 92 |
| 1046. Samuel Jimson, *Seneca* | 93 |
| 1047. John Irving, *Seneca* | 93 |
| 1048. Caster Red Eye, *Seneca* | 92 |
| 1049. J. C. W. Adams, *Stockbridge* | 20 |
| 1050. Jacob Jacobs, *Stockbridge* | 20 |
| 1054. Keheyakin, *Warm Spring* | 85 |
| 1055. Oscar Mark, *Wasco* | 86 |
| 1056. Ske-metze, *Warm Spring* | 85 |
| 1057. Semeo, *Warm Spring* | 86 |
| 1058. Cappolas, *Warm Spring* | 85 |
| 1059. Wayatatkin, *Warm Spring* | 85 |
| 1060. Stat-tla-ka, *Wasco* | 86 |
| 1061. Shaka, *Warm Spring* | 85 |
| 1062. Klematchosny, *Wasco* | 86 |
| 1063. Histo, *Warm Spring* | 85 |
| 1064. Chin-chin-wet, *Warm Spring* | 86 |
| 1065. Lyman P. Fowler, *Brotherton* | 20 |
| 1068. Sour Spittle, *Chippewa* | 9 |
| 1069. Bad Boy, *Chippewa* | 10 |
| 1070. Thé Boy, *Chippewa* | 10 |
| 1071. Auguste, *Chippewa* | 10 |
| 1072. Moose's Dung, *Chippewa* | 10 |
| 1073. Something in the air falling, *Chippewa* | 10 |
| 1074. The son of Essiniwub, *Chippewa* | 11 |
| 1075. Something beginning to sail off, *Chippewa* | 11 |
| 1076. A yellow-haired one sailing along, *Chippewa* | 11 |
| 1077. Like a Bird, *Chippewa* | 11 |
| 1080. John M. St. Cyr, *Winnebago* | 61 |

# ADDENDUM.

*List of negatives taken during the printing of the catalogue.*

1081. HDE-DÁ-SKA. *White Eagle.* PONCA.
Head chief. Age, 41 years; height, 6 feet 2 inches; circumference of head, 22¼ inches; circumference of chest, 38½ inches.

1082. TA-TÁU-KA-NÚ-ZHE. *Standing Buffalo.* PONCA.
Age, 44 years; height, 5 feet 11½ inches; circumference of head, 23 inches, circumference of chest, 42½ inches.

1083. MA-CHÚ-NÚ-ZHE. *Standing Bear.* PONCA.
Age, 51 years; height, 5 feet 10¼ inches; circumference of head, 23 inches; circumference of chest, 40 inches.

1084. ÚMP-PA-TONGA. *Big Elk.* PONCA.
Age, 36 years; height, 5 feet 9¾ inches; circumference of head, 23 inches; circumference of chest, 40 inches.

1085. KHÁ-KA-SÁPA. *Black Crow.* PONCA.
Age, 52 years; height, 5 feet 8½ inches; circumference of head, 22½ inches; circumference of chest, 39½ inches.

1086. MA-GÁ-SKA. *White Swan.* PONCA.
Age, 51 years; height, 5 feet 8 inches; circumference of head, 22½ inches; circumference of chest, 39 inches.

1087. GIHEGA. *Big Chief.* PONCA.
Age, 41 years; height, 5 feet 10½ inches; circumference of head, 23½ inches; circumference of chest, 40 inches.

1088. SHÚ-DA-GÁ-KA. *Smoke Maker.* PONCA.
Age, 51 years; height, 5 feet 9¾ inches; circumference of head, 23½ inches; circumference of chest, 42½ inches.

1089. MA-CHÚ-HINKTH-TÁ. *Hairy Bear.* PONCA.
Age, 40 years; height, 5 feet 11¾ inches; circumference of head, 23½ inches; circumference of chest, 38½ inches.

1090. WASE-Á-TOÚGA. *Big Snake.* PONCA.
Age, 45 years; height, 6 feet 1¼ inches; circumference of head, 24½ inches; circumference of chest, 43 inches.

1091. CHARLES LE CLAIR. *Interpreter.*
French and Ponca half-breed.

1092. BAPTISTE BUMABY. *Interpreter.*
Mother an Iowa and father an Otoe.

1093. GROUP of four chiefs and two interpreters of the Ponca delegation.

1094. GROUP of all the members of the Ponca delegation in Washington, November 14, 1877.

DEPARTMENT OF THE INTERIOR.
UNITED STATES GEOLOGICAL SURVEY OF THE TERRITORIES.
F. V. HAYDEN, U. S. GEOLOGIST.

MISCELLANEOUS PUBLICATIONS, No. 10.

# BIBLIOGRAPHY

OF

# NORTH AMERICAN INVERTEBRATE PALEONTOLOGY,

BEING A

REPORT UPON THE PUBLICATIONS THAT HAVE HITHERTO BEEN MADE UPON THE INVERTEBRATE PALEONTOLOGY OF NORTH AMERICA, INCLUDING THE WEST INDIES AND GREENLAND.

BY

C. A. WHITE, M. D.,
PALEONTOLOGIST OF THE UNITED STATES GEOLOGICAL SURVEY,

AND

H. ALLEYNE NICHOLSON, M. D., D. Sc.,
PROFESSOR AT THE UNIVERSITY OF ST. ANDREWS, SCOTLAND.

WASHINGTON:
GOVERNMENT PRINTING OFFICE.
1878.

# PREFATORY NOTE.

U. S. GEOLOGICAL AND GEOGRAPHICAL
SURVEY OF THE TERRITORIES,
*Washington, D. C., January* 1, 1878.

This Bibliographical Record has been prepared for the purpose of conveying to the public a brief general view of the work that has hitherto been done in the Invertebrate Paleontology of North America, and also of furnishing students and investigators with a ready index to the works of all the authors who have made contributions to it.

The fundamental value of paleontological research in connection with every geological survey renders it desirable to extend all practicable facilities for its prosecution.

Part I of this work has been prepared by Dr. C. A. White, the Paleontologist of the Survey, and comprises the publications that have been made within the limits of the United States.

Part II has been prepared by Prof. H. Alleyne Nicholson, of the University of St. Andrews, Scotland, and comprises the publications that have been made upon the subject herein embraced outside the limits of the United States. Professor Nicholson's extensive acquaintance with this subject, and the important part he has taken in paleontological research in North America, render this contribution especially acceptable.

It is gratifying to note that so important a part of the paleontological research which is indicated in this record has been accomplished in connection with the Geological Survey under my direction during the few years that it has been in existence; and yet the field for future labor of this kind, in the same connection, is practically unlimited. Every year's explorations bring to light not only new specific forms, but also new and important facts bearing both upon the geological and biological history of the continent.

It is expected that additions to this work will appear annually in some of the publications of the Survey, so that a continuous record may be kept of the progress of the science in North America.

F. V. HAYDEN,
*United States Geologist.*

# BIBLIOGRAPHY OF NORTH AMERICAN INVERTEBRATE PALEONTOLOGY.

## PART I.

EMBRACING TITLES AND ABSTRACTS OF PUBLICATIONS MADE IN THE UNITED STATES.

By C. A. WHITE, M. D.

# PREFACE TO PART I.

A number of difficulties have arisen in the course of the preparation of this work, which, being common to all works of the kind, are only mentioned that the author may not seem to have been unmindful of them.

Many of the publications that have been consulted are only in part devoted to the subject in hand; but the aim has been to record every publication that contains a real contribution to the science, however slight, whether of recorded fact or philosophical discussion. Thus, all purely geological writings have been excluded; but it has not always been easy to draw the line in this regard. Local lists of fossils, and lists given in geological writings merely to characterize the formations there under discussion, have also been excluded; but classified lists involving the relations of zoological groups have been included.

Again, many of the publications consulted embrace a description or discussion of both recent and fossil forms; but a single fossil species has been thought sufficient to entitle the work containing it to a place in this record.

Furthermore, many of the genera and higher groups which include some of the fossil species are found diagnosed or discussed only or mainly in works devoted to living species. Therefore the subject has been left somewhat incomplete in this respect; but the line must be drawn somewhere, and it has been thought best to include only those publications that treat, at least in part, of fossil species.

The scope of this compilation is primarily restricted to those works which treat, either wholly or in part, of invertebrate fossils found within the limits of North America, including the West Indies and Greenland; but, for convenience, the comparatively few contributions that citizens of the United States have made to the paleontology of other countries, and published in their own, have been also included in Part I.

The compiler has not felt it necessary to make any discrimination as to the relative value of the publications recorded; but he has endeavored to include even the most obscure and rare, if they have been properly published.

The scope of each separate entry has been a matter of much consideration. It is impracticable to make an extended abstract of each publication in a report like this; and if it were not, such abstracts could not obviate the necessity of the student to consult the full original text. Therefore, only a brief indication of the character of the contents is given in each case, except that a list of the genera therein diagnosed, either originally or otherwise, is included in the entry, no distinction being made in the entry between genera and subgenera. A list of the species is also given in the case of obscure publications; but they are omitted from those that one naturally expects to find in all good libraries. A very large proportion of the publications entered consists wholly of descriptions, no abstract of which is practicable, and it has been a custom among American writers to make the titles of their publications so full as to amount to a brief abstract of their work.

The arrangement of the entries is by authors, in the alphabetical order of their names, and subordinately by dates. The year only is given, although some of the works indicate the month of their publication, and in the case of others the exact year of publication is uncertain. As a rule, the date of the title-page is given as the date of publication; but this has been varied from in a few cases, according to the personal knowledge of the compiler, or attention is called to the discrepancy in an appended note.

While no publication that would come properly within the scope of this work has been intentionally omitted, it is not unlikely that some have been overlooked; but it is expected that annual additions and corrections will be made in some of the publications of the Survey. The publications that are most likely to have been overlooked are "extra copies" or advance sheets of articles that afterward appeared in some of the scientific periodicals. Usually, exact date of publication only is involved in such cases, but sometimes the regular edition contains changes or modifications that are more or less important. However, the cases of such omission are believed to be very few that would involve the exclusion of any fact or idea that has been advanced by any author.

The compiler would esteem it a favor if those into whose hands this work may fall would promptly inform him of any error or omission, that it may be subsequently corrected.

C. A. W.

WASHINGTON, D. C., *January* 1, 1878.

# I.—PUBLICATIONS MADE IN THE UNITED STATES.

Anon. Correspondence of J. Barrande, W. E. Logan and James Hall. "On the Taconic system and the age of the fossils found in the rocks of Northern New England, and the Quebeck group of rocks." <*Am. Journ. Sci.*, vol. xxxi, 2d ser., pp. 210–226. 1861.

Anthony, J. G.  New Trilobites. <*Am. Journ. Sci.*, vol. xxxiv, 1st ser., pp. 379, 380, 1 woodcut. 1838.

*Ceratocephalus ceralepta.*

Anthony, J. G.  Description of a new fossil (Calymene bucklandi). <*Am. Journ. Sci.*, vol. xxxvi, 1st ser., pp. 106, 107, 2 woodcuts. 1839.

Anthony, J. G., U. P. James, G. Graham, and.  *See* James, U. P. 1846.

Atwater, Caleb.  On some ancient human bones, &c., with a notice of the bones of the Mastodon, or Mammoth, and of various shells found in Ohio and the West. <*Am. Journ. Sci.*, vol. ii, 1st ser., pp. 242–246, 1 plate. 1820.

*Terebratula (Spirifer) pennata* is figured and described.

Bailey, J. W.  On fossil Infusoria, discovered in peat-earth, at West Point, N. Y.; with some notices of American Diatomæ. <*Am. Journ. Sci.*, vol. xxxv, 1st ser., pp. 118–124, 1 plate. 1839.

Bailey, J. W.  Notice of American Polythalmia from the Upper Mississippi, and also from the Cretaceous formation of the Upper Missouri. <*Am. Journ. Sci.*, vol. xli, 1st ser., pp. 400, 401, 4 woodcuts. 1841.

Bailey, J. W.  A sketch of the Infusoria of the family Bacillaria, with some account of the most interesting species which have been found in a recent or fossil state in the United States. <*Am. Journ. Sci.*, vol. xlii, 1st ser., pp. 88–105, 2 plates. 1842.

Also published in *Trans. Asso. Am. Nat. & Geol.*, vol. i, pp. 112–164.

Bailey, J. W.  A sketch of the Infusoria, of the family Bacillaria, with some account of the most interesting species which have been found in a recent or fossil state in the United States. <*Trans. Assoc. Am. Nat. & Geol.*, vol. i, pp. 112–164, 1 plate. 1843.

Also published in *Am. Journ. Sci.*, vol. xlii, 1st ser. (1842), pp. 88–105, with 2 plates.

Bailey, J. W.  Infusoria. <*Mather's Report on the Geology of the First District, New York*, pp. 48–79. 1843.

This article is mainly a reproduction of those that had been previously published both in the *Am. Journ. Sci.*, and as above cited. The author presents a systematic classification of the *Infusoria*, both fossil and living.

**Bailey, J. W.** Account of some new Infusorial forms discovered in the fossil Infusoria from Petersburg, Va., and Piscataway, Md. <*Am. Journ. Sci.*, vol. xlvi, 1st ser., pp. 137-141, 1 plate. 1844.

**Bailey, J. W.** Notice of some new localities of Infusoria, fossil and recent. <*Am. Journ. Sci.*, vol. xlviii, 1st ser., pp. 321-343, 1 plate. 1845.

This article embraces much more than its title would imply. It not only includes much of the author's original investigations, but much that had been done by Ehrenberg. Among other matter, several new genera and species are described.

**Bailey, J. W.** New localities of Infusoria in the Tertiary of Maryland. <*Am. Journ. Sci.*, vol. vii, 2d ser., p. 437. 1849.

**Bailey, J. W.** Miscellaneous notices. <*Am. Journ. Sci.*, vol. xi, 2d ser., pp. 85, 86. 1851.

Among these "notices" are those of the occurrence of fossil *Infusoria* in the Southern rice-fields, in Maryland, and in Florida.

**Bailey, J. W.** On some new localities of fossil Diatomaceæ in California and Oregon. <*Am. Journ. Sci.*, vol. xvii, 2d ser., pp. 179, 180. 1854.

**Barrett, S. T.** Description of a new Trilobite. <*Am. Journ. Sci.*, vol. xi, 3d ser., p. 200. 1876.

**Billings, E.** Note on Conocephalites. Addendum to "Description of a new Trilobite from the Potsdam Sandstone," by F. H. Bradley. <*Am. Journ. Sci.*, vol. xxx, 2d ser., pp. 242, 243. 1860.

Also, an "Additional note on the Potsdam fossils" on pp. 337, 338, of the same volume.

**Billings, E.** I. On some new or little known species of Lower Silurian fossils from the Potsdam group (Primordial zone). <*Geology of Vermont*, vol. ii, pp. 942-955. II. On some new species of fossils from the Calciferous, Chazy, Black River, and Trenton formations. <*Ibid.*, pp. 955-960. 1861.

These two articles are a reprint of the first 24 pages of vol. i, *Paleozoic Fossils of the Geological Survey of Canada.*

**Billings, E.** Further observations on the age of the Red Sandrock formation (Potsdam group) of Canada and Vermont. <*Am. Journ. Sci.*, vol. xxxiii, 2d ser., pp. 100-105. 1862.

This is a continuation of the author's observations in vol. xxxii, p. 232.

**Billings, E.** On the genus Centronella, with remarks on some other genera of Brachiopoda. <*Am. Journ. Sci.*, vol. xxxvi, 2d ser., pp. 236-240. 1863.

In this paper, the author republishes the diagnoses of both *Centronella*, Billings, and *Cryptonella*, Hall.

**Billings, E.** Description of some new species of fossils, with remarks on others already known, from the Silurian and Devonian rocks of Maine. <*Proc. Portland Soc. Nat. Hist.*, vol. i, pp. 104-126. 1863.

**Billings, E.** Note on the structure of the Blastoidea. <*Am. Journ. Sci.*, vol. xlvii, 2d ser., p. 353. 1869.

In this note, the author points out the differences and similarities between the genera *Nucleocrinus, Pentremites,* and *Codaster*, especially with regard to the function of the summit openings.

## I.—PUBLICATIONS MADE IN THE UNITED STATES.

**Billings, E.** Notes on the structure of the Crinoidea, Cystidea and Blastoidea. < *Am. Journ. Sci.*, vol. xlviii, 2d ser., pp. 69-83. 1869. Continued in vol. xlix, pp. 51-58, and in vol. l, pp. 225-240. 1869.

This series of articles comprises an extended discussion of the structure and functions of different parts of those Echinoderms.

**Billings, E.** Fossils from the so-called Huronian of Newfoundland. < *Am. Journ. Sci.*, vol. iii, 3d ser., pp. 223, 224. 1872.

A brief abstract of a paper by Mr. Billings read before the Natural History Society of Montreal, January, 1872.

**Billings, E.** Fossils probably of the Chazy era in the Eolian limestone of West Rutland, Vt. < *Am. Journ. Sci.*, vol. iv, 3d ser., p. 133. 1872.

**Billings, E.** On the structure of Obolella chromatica. < *Am. Journ. Sci.*, vol. xi, 3d ser., pp. 176-178. 1876.

The author here gives more extended and complete descriptions of generic and specific characters than were allowed by the only specimens discovered at the time his original descriptions were published.

**Bigsby, J. J.** Description of a new species of Trilobite. < *Journ. Acad. Nat. Sci. Phila.*, vol. iv, 1st ser., pp. 365-368, 1 plate. 1825.

**Bouvé, T. T.** Description of Pygorhynchus gouldi, a new Echinus from the Millstone Grit of Georgia. < *Am. Journ. Sci.*, vol. iii, 2d ser., p. 437. 1846.

The rock from which this fossil comes is Tertiary, not Carboniferous. The description is also published in *Proc. Bost. Soc. Nat. Hist.*, vol. ii, pp. 192, 193.

**Bouvé, T. T.** Description of Pygorhynchus gouldii from the Millstone Grit of Georgia. < *Proc. Bost. Soc. Nat. Hist.*, vol. ii, pp. 192, 193. 1847.

The rock from which the fossil comes is Tertiary, not Carboniferous. The description is also published in the *Am. Journ. Sci.*, vol. iii, 2d ser., p. 437.

**Bouvé, T. T.** Descriptions of a number of new species of fossil Echinoderms from the Lower Tertiary rocks of Georgia. < *Proc. Bost. Soc. Nat. Hist.*, vol. iv, pp. 2-4. 1851.

**Bradley, Frank H.** Description of a new Trilobite from the Potsdam Sandstone, with a note by E. Billings. < *Am. Journ. Sci.*, vol. xxx, 2d ser., pp. 241-243. 1860. Republished, as in next entry.

**Bradley, Frank H.** Description of a new Trilobite from the Potsdam Sandstone, with a note by E. Billings. < *Proc. Am. Assoc. Adv. Sci.*, vol. xiv, pp. 161-166, 3 woodcuts. 1861.

**Bradley, Frank H.** Description of two new Land Snails from the Coal-measures. < *Am. Journ. Sci.*, vol. iv, 3d ser., pp. 87, 88, 2 woodcuts. 1872.

**Browne, Peter A.** Some notice of the fossil Cephalopodes belemnosepia, long known by the name of "Belemnite", and of the diphosphate of iron, called "Mullicite", found together at Mullica Hill. < *Proc. Am. Assoc. Adv. Sci.*, vol. i, pp. 13-16. 1849.

General and mineralogical description, and not properly paleontological.

**Burbank, L. S.** On Eozoon canadense in the Crystalline Limestones of Massachusetts. < *Proc. Am. Assoc. Adv. Sci.*, vol. xx, pp. 262-266. 1872.

**Casseday, S. A.** *See* Lyon, S. S., *and* S. A. Casseday.

**Chapman, E. J.** On the supposed fossil tracks called Protichnites and Climatichnites. <*Am. Journ. Sci.*, vol. xiv, 3d ser., p. 240. 1877.

Abstract from Canadian Journal. The author takes the view that the impressions are those of Fucoids, and not of Articulates.

**Conrad, T. A.** On the geology and organic remains of a part of the peninsula of Maryland, with an "Appendix containing descriptions of twenty-nine new species of fossil shells, noticed in the preceding paper". <*Journ. Acad. Nat. Sci. Phila.*, vol. vi, 1st ser., pp. 205–230, 2 plates. 1830.

**Conrad, T. A.** Description of fifteen new species of recent and three of fossil shells, chiefly from the coast of the United States. < *Journ. Acad. Nat. Sci. Phila.*, vol. vi, 1st ser., pp. 256–268, 1 plate. 1830.

Tertiary.

**Conrad, T. A.** Fossil shells of the Tertiary formations of North America, vol. i, pp. 56, 16 plates, 8°, Philadelphia. 1832. Also, in pamphlet form, No. 3, pp. 10, and No. 4, pp. 8, of vol. i.

This article contains a discussion of the characteristics of American Tertiaries, and comparisons with those of Europe, but it consists mainly of descriptions of species.

**Conrad, T. A.** Observations on the Tertiary and more recent formations of a portion of the Southern States. <*Journ. Acad. Nat. Sci. Phila.*, vol. vii, 1st ser., pp. 116–129; together with an "Appendix,—Descriptions of new Tertiary fossils from the Southern States", pp. 130–157. 1834.

**Conrad, T. A.** Description of five new species of fossil shells in the collection presented by Mr. Edward Miller to the Geological Society. < *Trans. Geol. Soc. Penn.*, vol. i, pt. ii, pp. 267–270, 1 plate. 1835.

*Stylifer primogenia, Turbo tabulatus, T. insectus, Productus confragosus, Pecten arungerus.* All probably Carboniferous, but neither the position nor locality is given.

**Conrad, T. A.** Observations on a portion of the Atlantic Tertiary region. < *Trans. Geol. Soc. Penn.*, vol. i, pt. ii, pp. 335–341, 1 plate. 1835.

*Panopea elongata, Modiola cretacea, Turritella humerosa, Lithodendron lineatus.*

**Conrad, T. A.** Report on the paleontological department. < *Ann. Rep. Geol. Surv. N. Y.*, vol. ii, pp. 107–119. 1838.

Contains descriptions of several species of Paleozoic fossils.

**Conrad, T. A.** Notes on American geology.—Observations on characteristic fossils, and upon a fall of temperature in different geological epochs. <*Am. Journ. Sci.*, vol. xxxv, 1st ser., pp. 237–251. 1839.

**Conrad, T. A.** Second annual report on the paleontological department. <*Ann. Rep. Geol. Surv. N. Y.*, vol. iii, pp. 57–66. 1839.

Contains descriptions of several species of Paleozoic fossils.

**Conrad, T. A.** On the Silurian system; with a table of the strata and characteristic fossils. <*Am. Journ. Sci.*, vol. xxxviii, 1st ser., pp. 86–92. 1840.

**Conrad, T. A.** New fossil shells from North Carolina. <*Am. Journ. Sci.*, vol. xxxix, 1st ser., pp. 387, 388. 1840.

Tertiary.

# I.—PUBLICATIONS MADE IN THE UNITED STATES. 13

**Conrad, T. A.** Third annual report on the paleontological department. <*Ann. Rep. Geol. Surv. N. Y.*, vol. iv, pp. 199–207. 1840.

Contains descriptions of several species of fossils.

**Conrad, T. A.** Appendix to "Observations on the Secondary and Tertiary formations of the Southern Atlantic States, by James T. Hodge". <*Am. Journ. Sci.*, vol. xli, 1st ser., pp. 332–348, 1 plate. 1841.

This appendix consists of descriptions of Tertiary shells.

**Conrad, T. A.** Descriptions of twenty-six new species of fossil shells discovered in the Medial Tertiary deposit of Calvert Cliffs, Maryland. <*Proc. Acad. Nat. Sci. Phila.*, vol. i, pp. 28–33. 1841.

One *Cardium* and one *Fusus* are from the Lower Tertiary.

**Conrad, T. A.** Fifth (fourth?) annual report on the paleontological department. <*Ann. Rep. Geol. Surv. N. Y.*, vol. v, pp. 25–57. 1841.

Contains descriptions of genera and species of Palæozoic fossils.

**Conrad, T. A.** Descriptions of new genera and species of organic remains. <*Ann. Rep. Geol. Surv. N. Y.*, pp. 48–57. 1841.

Silurian and Devonian. Genera *Dicranurus, Nuculites, Orthonota, Lyrodesma, Cypricardites.*

**Conrad, T. A.** Description of twenty-four new species of fossil shells, chiefly from the Tertiary deposits of Calvert's Cliffs, Maryland. <*Journ. Acad. Nat. Sci. Phila.*, vol. viii, 1st ser., pp. 183–190. 1842.

**Conrad, T. A.** Observations on the Silurian and Devonian systems of the United States, with descriptions of new organic remains; including descriptions of new species of organic remains belonging to the Silurian, Devonian, and Carboniferous systems of the United States. <*Journ. Acad. Nat. Sci. Phila.*, vol. viii, 1st ser., pp. 228–280, 6 plates. 1842.

Genera *Microdon, Cameroceras, Diploceras, Trocholites, Plectostylus, Platyostoma, Stephanocrinus, Ichthyocrinus, Nucleocrinus.*

**Conrad, T. A.** Observations on a portion of the Atlantic Tertiary region, with a description of new species of organic remains. <*2d Bulletin, Proc. Nat. Inst. Prom. Sci. Washington, D. C.*, pp. 171–194, 2 plates. 1842.

Publication long since discontinued. List of fossils described:—*Ostrea sellæformis, Pholadomya marylandica, Pholas petrosa, Isocardia markoëi, Pecten humphreysi, Dispotæa constricta, Scalaria expansa, Buccinum integrum, Scutella aberti.*

**Conrad, T. A.** Descriptions of a new genus, and of twenty-nine new Miocene, and one Eocene, fossil shells of the United States. <*Proc. Acad. Nat. Sci. Phila.*, vol. i, pp. 305–311. 1843.

Genus *Ecphora.*

**Conrad, T. A.** Descriptions of nineteen species of Tertiary fossils of Virginia and North Carolina. <*Proc. Acad. Nat. Sci. Phila.*, vol. i, pp. 323–329. 1843.

**Conrad, T. A.** Observations on the lead-bearing limestone of Wisconsin, and descriptions of a new genus of Trilobites and fifteen new Silurian fossils. <*Proc. Acad. Nat. Sci. Phila.*, vol. i, pp. 329–335. 1843.

Genus *Thaleops.*

**Conrad, T. A.** Descriptions of new shells, &c. An appendix to "Observations on the Secondary and Tertiary Formations of the Southern Atlantic States, by James T. Hodge". < *Trans. Assoc. Am. Geol. & Nat.*, vol. i, pp. 94-111, 1 plate. 1843.

Fossils probably all Tertiary. Localities and position not given with the descriptions.

**Conrad, T. A.** Descriptions of eight new fossil shells of the United States. < *Proc. Acad. Nat. Sci.*, vol. ii, pp. 173-175. 1844.

All Tertiary except a *Bellerophon* from Saint Genevieve (Mo. ?).

**Conrad, T. A.** Observations on the Eocene formation of the United States, with descriptions of species of shells, &c., occurring in it. < *Am. Journ. Sci.*, vol. i, 2d ser., pp. 209-221, 2 plates. 1846.

**Conrad, T. A.** Tertiary of Warren County, Mississippi. < *Am. Journ. Sci.*, vol. ii, 2d ser., pp. 124, 125. 1846.

In this article, Mr. Conrad states that all the Tertiary fossils found near Vicksburg are specifically different from those of the Eocene of Maryland, Virginia, and Alabama.

**Conrad, T. A.** Descriptions of new species of organic remains, from the Upper Eocene limestone of Tampa Bay. < *Am. Journ. Sci.*, vol. ii, 2d ser., pp. 399, 400, 9 woodcuts. 1846.

**Conrad, T. A.** Descriptions of new species of fossil and recent shells and corals. < *Proc. Acad. Nat. Sci. Phila.*, vol. ii, pp. 19-27, 1 plate. 1846.

Silurian, Devonian, Carboniferous, and Tertiary.

**Conrad, T. A.** Observations on the Eocene formation, and descriptions of one hundred and five new fossils of that period, from the vicinity of Vicksburg, Mississippi; with an appendix. < *Proc. Acad. Nat. Sci. Phila.*, vol. iii, pp. 280-299. 1847.

This article is republished in the *Journ. Acad. Nat. Sci. Phila.*, vol. i, 2d ser., pp. 111-134, and illustrated with 4 plates. (See second entry below.)

**Conrad, T. A.** Fossil shells from the Tertiary deposits on the Columbia River, near Astoria. < *Am. Journ. Sci.*, 2d ser., vol. v, pp. 432, 433, 15 woodcuts. 1848.

**Conrad, T. A.** Observations on the Eocene formation, and descriptions of one hundred and five new fossils of that period, from the vicinity of Vicksburg, Mississippi; with an appendix. (Vanuxem's fossils.) < *Journ. Acad. Nat. Sci. Phila.*, vol. i, 2d ser., pp. 111-134, 4 plates. 1848.

Genus *Scobinella*. Originally published in the *Proceedings* of the same academy, vol. ii, pp. 280-299. See second entry above.

**Conrad, T. A.** Descriptions of new fossil and recent shells of the United States. < *Journ. Acad. Nat. Sci. Phila.*, vol. i, 2d ser., pp. 207-209. 1849.

Upper Eocene.

**Conrad, T. A.** Description of Tertiary shells from Astoria. Constituting pp. 723-730 of *Dana's Paleontological Report of Wilkes's U. S. Expl. Exped.*, vol. x. 1849.

**Conrad, T. A.** Descriptions of one new Cretaceous and seven new Eocene fossils. < *Journ. Acad. Nat. Sci.*, vol. ii, 2d ser., pp. 39-41, 1 plate. 1850.

Conrad, T. A. Notes on shells, with descriptions of new species. < *Proc. Acad. Nat. Sci. Phila.*, vol. vi. 1852.
> Tertiary and Cretaceous. Genus *Schizotherus*.

Conrad, T. A. Remarks on the Tertiary strata of St. Domingo and Vicksburg (Miss.). < *Proc. Acad. Nat. Sci. Phila.*, vol. vi, pp. 198, 199. 1852.

Conrad, T. A. Description of the fossils of Syria collected in the Palestine expedition. < *Official Report of the United States Expedition to Explore the Dead Sea and the River Jordan*, by Lieut. W. F. Lynch, U. S. N. 1852.
> Cretaceous.

Conrad, T. A. Monograph of the genus Fulgur. < *Proc. Acad. Nat. Sci. Phila.*, vol. vi, pp. 316–319. 1853.

Conrad, T. A. Notes on shells. < *Proc. Acad. Nat. Sci. Phila.*, vol. vi, pp. 320, 321. 1853.
> Principally corrections of previous descriptions.

Conrad, T. A. Synopsis of the genera Cassidula, Humph., and a proposed new genus. Tertiary. < *Proc. Acad. Nat. Sci. Phila.*, vol. vi, pp. 448, 449. 1853.
> Genus *Athleta*.

Conrad, T. A. Descriptions of new fossil shells of the United States. < *Journ. Acad. Nat. Sci. Phila.*, vol. ii, 2d ser., pp. 273–276, 1 plate. 1853.
> Cretaceous and Tertiary.

Conrad, T. A. Rectification of the generic names of Tertiary fossil shells. < *Proc. Acad. Nat. Sci. Phila.*, vol. vii, pp. 29–31. 1854.

Conrad, T. A. Notes on shells; with descriptions of three recent and one fossil species. < *Proc. Acad. Nat. Sci. Phila.*, vol. vii, pp. 31, 32. 1854.
> Tertiary and Silurian. *Trigonella* Con. changed to *Pachydesma* Con.

Conrad, T. A. Observations on the Eocene deposit of Jackson, Miss., with descriptions of thirty-four new species of shells and corals. < *Proc. Acad. Nat. Sci. Phila.*, vol. vii, pp. 257–263. 1855.
> Genera *Lapparia, Fusimitra, Platyoptera, Papillina, Osteodes*.

Conrad, T. A. Descriptions of eighteen new Cretaceous and Tertiary fossils, &c. < *Proc. Acad. Nat. Sci. Phila.*, vol. vii, pp. 265–268. 1855.
> Genus *Petrophyllia*.

Conrad, T. A. Descriptions of one Tertiary and eight Cretaceous fossils from Texas, in the collection of Major Emory. < *Proc. Acad. Nat. Sci. Phila.*, vol. vii, pp. 268, 269. 1855.
> Genus *Rostellites*.

Conrad, T. A. Note on the Miocene and Post-Pliocene deposits of California, with descriptions of two new fossil corals. < *Proc. Acad. Nat. Sci. Phila.*, vol. vii, p. 441. 1855.

Conrad, T. A. Description of a new species of Pentamerus. < *Proc. Acad. Nat. Sci. Phila.*, vol. vii, p. 441. 1855.

Conrad, T. A. Description of the Tertiary fossils collected on the survey. < *Pacific Railroad Reports*, vol. vi, pp. 69–73, 4 plates. 1855.
> Genera *Schizopyga, Tamiosoma*. These descriptions accompany the geological report of Dr. J. S. Newberry.

**Conrad, T. A.** Report on the paleontology of the survey. < *Pacific Railroad Reports*, vol. vii, pp. 189-196, 10 plates. 1855.

Tertiary. This is an appendix to the geological report of Dr. Thomas Antisel.

**Conrad, T. A.** Report of Mr. T. A. Conrad on the fossil shells collected in California by W. P. Blake, geologist of the expedition under the command of Lieut. R. S. Williamson, U. S. Topographical Engineers, 1853. pp. 20, 8°. 1855.

This is an appendix to the preliminary report of Professor Blake of the Expl. and Surv. Pacific R. R., and is comprised in one of the 8° volumes published in advance of the quarto series.

**Conrad, T. A.** Descriptions of three new genera and twenty-three new species of Middle Tertiary fossils from California, and one from Texas. < *Proc. Acad. Nat. Sci. Phila.*, vol. viii, pp. 312-316. 1856.

Genus *Schizopyga, Tamiosoma, Astrodaspis.*

**Conrad, T. A.** Descriptions of two new genera of shells. < *Proc. Acad. Nat. Sci. Phila.*, vol. i, 2d ser., pp. 165, 166. 1857.

Genera *Gonidea, Calyptraphorus.*

**Conrad, T. A.** Description of a new species of Myacites. < *Proc. Acad. Nat. Sci. Phila.*, vol. i, 2d ser., p. 166. 1857.

Illustrated on pl. 1, vol. iv. (The plate is erroneously numbered 7.)

**Conrad, T. A.** Rectification of some of the generic names of American Tertiary fossils. < *Proc. Acad. Nat. Sci. Phila.*, vol. i, 2d ser, p. 166. 1857.

**Conrad, T. A.** Descriptions of Cretaceous and Tertiary fossils. < *Emory's Report on the United States and Mexican Boundary Survey*, vol. i, pt. ii, pp. 141-174, plates 1-21. 1857.

**Conrad, T. A.** Observations on a group of Cretaceous fossil shells found in Tippah County, Miss., with descriptions of fifty-six new species. < *Journ. Acad. Nat. Sci. Phila.*, 2d ser., vol. iii, p. 323, 2 plates. 1858.

Genera *Legumen, Pyrifusus, Bullopsis.*

**Conrad, T. A.** Notes on shells. < *Proc. Acad. Nat. Sci. Phila.*, vol. iv, 2d ser., pp. 231, 232. 1860.

Mainly rectifications of former descriptions.

**Conrad, T. A.** Descriptions of new species of Cretaceous and Eocene fossils of Mississippi and Alabama. < *Journ. Acad. Nat. Sci. Phila.*, vol. iv, 2d ser., pp. 275-298, 2 plates. 1860.

Genera *Linearia, Sphærella, Solenoceras, Pugnellus, Pyropsis, Gyrodes, Turbinopsis, Morea, Thylacus, Paranomia, Tornatellæa, Cerithioderma, Mazzalina, Pteropsis.*

**Conrad, T. A.** Descriptions of new genera, subgenera, and species of Tertiary and recent shells. < *Proc. Acad. Nat. Sci. Phila.*, vol. vi, 2d ser., pp. 284-291. 1862.

Genera *Pleiothyris, Carinorbis, Parastarte, Idoncarca, Trigonarca, Latiarca, Striarca, Granoarca, Pteromeris, Mytiloconcha, Lyropecten.*

**Conrad, T. A.** Catalogue of the Miocene shells of the Atlantic slope. < *Proc. Acad. Nat. Sci. Phila.*, vol. vi, 2d ser., pp. 559-582. 1862.

**Conrad, T. A.** Descriptions of new, recent and Miocene shells. < *Proc. Acad. Nat. Sci. Phila.*, vol. vi, 2d ser., pp. 583-586. 1862.

# I.—PUBLICATIONS MADE IN THE UNITED STATES.

**Conrad, T. A.** Notes on shells, with descriptions of new fossil genera and species. < *Proc. Acad. Nat. Sci. Phila.*, vol. viii, 2d ser., pp. 211-214, 2 woodcuts. 1864.

Genera *Lirosoma, Erycinella, Cyprimeria, Dosinopsis.*

**Conrad, T. A.** Observations on the Eocene Lignite formation of the United States. < *Proc. Acad. Nat. Sci. Phila.*, vol. ix, 2d ser., pp. 70-73. 1865.

In this paper, Mr. Conrad makes some comparisons of the American deposits with those of similar age in Europe.

**Conrad, T. A.** Catalogue of the Eocene Annulata, Foraminifera, Echinodermata and Cirripedia of the United States. < *Proc. Acad. Nat. Sci. Phila.*, vol. ix, 2d ser., pp. 73-75. 1865.

**Conrad, T. A.** Descriptions of new species of Echinidæ. < *Proc. Acad. Nat. Sci. Phila.*, vol. ix, 2d ser., p. 75. 1865.

Probably Tertiary, but the fact is not stated, and no definite locality is mentioned.

**Conrad, T. A.** Observations on American fossils; with descriptions of two new species. < *Proc. Acad. Nat. Sci. Phila.*, vol. ix, 2d ser., p. 184. 1865.

Tertiary.

**Conrad, T. A.** Catalogue of the Eocene and Oligocene Testacea of the United States. < *Am. Journ. Conch.*, vol. i, pp. 1-36. Corrections and additions to the same, pp. 389, 390. 1865.

**Conrad, T. A.** Descriptions of new Eocene shells from Enterprise, Mississippi. < *Am. Journ. Conch.*, vol. i, pp. 137-141, 2 plates, which also illustrate the following article in part. 1865.

Genera *Alveinus, Sphærella, Arcoperna, Eburneopecten.*

**Conrad, T. A.** Descriptions of new Eocene shells of the United States. < *Am. Journ. Conch.*, vol. i, pp. 142-149, 2 plates, which also illustrate in part the preceding article. 1865.

Genera *Cochlespira, Monilopsis, Tortoliva, Tornatellæa, Cytheriopsis, Actæonema.*

**Conrad, T. A.** Catalogue of the older Eocene shells of Oregon. < *Am. Journ. Conch.*, vol. i, pp. 150-154. 1865.

This treats of the fossils of the Wilkes's exploration expedition, which Mr. Conrad formerly referred to the Miocene, but now refers to Eocene.

**Conrad, T. A.** Descriptions of new Eocene shells and references, with figures, to published species. < *Am. Journ. Conch.*, vol. i, pp. 210-212, 2 plates, which in part illustrate the following article. 1865.

**Conrad, T. A.** Descriptions of five new species of older Eocene shells from Shark River, Monmouth County, N. J. < *Am. Journ. Conch.*, vol. i, pp. 213, 2 plates, which in part illustrate the preceding article. 1865.

**Conrad, T. A.** Illustrations of Miocene fossils, with descriptions of new species. < *Am. Journ. Conch.*, vol. ii, pp. 65-74, 2 plates. 1866.

Genera *Bulliopsis, Volutifusus.*

**Conrad, T. A.** Observations on recent and fossil shells, with proposed new genera and species. < *Am. Journ. Conch.*, vol. ii, pp. 101-103. 1866.

Genera *Hercoglossa, Cimomia, Anchura, Cyprimeria, Pseudocardia, Orthonota, Plectosolen, Venilia* (Morton).

**Conrad, T. A.** Note on the genus Gadus, with descriptions of some new genera and species of American fossil shells. <*Am. Journ. Conch.*, vol. ii, pp. 75-78. 1866.

Genera *Ecphora, Leptonotis, Diploschiza, Lacunaria, Cyclomera.*

**Conrad, T. A.** Descriptions of new species of Tertiary, Cretaceous and recent shells. <*Am. Journ. Conch.*, vol. ii, pp. 104-106, 2 plates. 1866.

**Conrad, T. A.** Check lists of the Invertebrate fossils of North America. Eocene and Oligocene. <*Smithsonian Miscellaneous Publications* (No. 200), pp. 1-41. 1866.

Subgenus *Priarchus* and other notes.

**Conrad, T. A.** Reply to Mr. Gabb on the Cretaceous rocks of California. <*Am. Journ. Sci.*, vol. xliv, 2d ser., pp. 376-377. 1867.

For Mr. Gabb's article, see page 226 of the same volume.

**Conrad, T. A.** Note on the Tertiary of North and South Carolina. <*Am. Journ. Sci.*, vol. xliii, 2d ser., p. 260. 1867.

Reference is made in this note to the occurrence of Cretaceous forms in Eocene strata of South Carolina; and the author states that the evidence is conclusive that the admixture took place by a breaking-up of the previously deposited Cretaceous strata in Eocene time.

**Conrad, T. A.** Paleontological miscellanies. <*Am. Journ. Conch.*, vol. iii, pp. 5-7. 1867.

This consists of notes on some described fossils, with a description of the new genus *Lyropecten* and the species *L. intermedius.*

**Conrad, T. A.** Description of new genera of fossil shells. <*Am. Journ. Conch.*, vol. iii, pp. 8-16. 1867.

Genera *Paranomia, Trigonarca, Prisconaia, Palæocardit1, Pleuromeris, Leptomya, Leptosolen.*

**Conrad, T. A.** Synopsis of the genera Sycotypus, Browne, and Busycon, Bolten. <*Am. Journ. Conch.*, vol. iii, pp. 182-185, 2 plates. 1867.

**Conrad, T. A.** Descriptions of new Miocene shells. <*Am. Journ. Conch.*, vol. iii, pp. 186, 187. 1867.

Genera *Fasciolina, Tortifusus.*

**Conrad, T. A.** Notes on fossil shells and descriptions of new species. <*Am. Journ. Conch.*, vol. iii, pp. 188-190. 1867.

Tertiary.

**Conrad, T. A.** Descriptions of new genera and species of Miocene shells, with notes on other fossil and recent species. <*Am. Journ. Conch.*, vol. iii, pp. 257-270, 4 plates. 1867.

Genera *Bellaspira, Sthenorhytis, Paranassa, Tritiaria, Buccinofusus, Meganema, Erysinella.*

**Conrad, T. A.** Catalogue of the family Anatinidæ. <*Am. Journ. Conch.*, vol. iv, Appendix, pp. 49-58. 1868.

**Conrad, T. A.** Descriptions of Miocene shells of the Atlantic slope. <*Am. Journ. Conch.*, vol. iv, pp. 64-68, 2 plates. 1868.

**Conrad, T. A.** Notes on recent and fossil shells, with descriptions of new genera. <*Am. Journ. Conch.*, vol. iv, pp. 246-249. 1868.

Genera *Aphrodina, Vertocardia, Mactrodesma, Hercorhynchus, Solenaia.* The article contains also "Notes on the genera *Pyrifusus* and *Athleta*, and other shells figured in the Geological Survey of India".

# I.—PUBLICATIONS MADE IN THE UNITED STATES.

Conrad, T. A. Descriptions of and references to Miocene shells of the Atlantic slope, and descriptions of two new supposed Cretaceous species. < *Am. Journ. Conch.*, vol. iv, pp. 278, 279, 2 plates. 1868.

    One of the species (*Astarte veta*) is referred to Triassic.

Conrad, T. A. Description of a new Unio and fossil Goniobasis (G. carteri). < *Am. Journ. Conch.*, vol. iv, p. 280, 1 plate. 1868.

Conrad, T. A. Notes on American fossiliferous strata. < *Am. Journ. Sci.*, vol. xlvii, 2d ser., pp. 358-364. 1869.

    Mr. Conrad here refers to the fossil Unios and other shells, published by Dr. Morton in vol. xxix, *Am. Journ. Sci.*, 1st series, and states that some of the same species of Unios are found in New Jersey. The age of the deposits containing them he regards as somewhere from Miocene to Post-Pliocene.

Conrad, T. A. Description of Miocene, Eocene, and Cretaceous shells. < *Am. Journ. Conch.*, vol. v, pp. 39-45, 2 plates. 1869.

    Genus *Goniosoma*.

Conrad, T. A. Observations on the genus Astarte, with descriptions of three other genera of Crassatellidæ. < *Am. Journ. Conch.*, vol. v, pp. 46-48. 1869.

    Genera *Lirodiscus, Radioconcha, Pachythærus, Scambula, Vetocardia*.

Conrad, T. A. Descriptions of new fossil Mollusca, principally Cretaceous. < *Am. Journ. Conch.*, vol. v, pp. 96-103. 1869.

    Genera *Pachycardium, Nemodon, Pereisqnota, Liroscapha, Cyprinopsis, Paleocorbis*.

Conrad, T. A. Notes on recent and fossil shells, with descriptions of new species. < *Am. Journ. Conch.*, vol. vi, pp. 71-78. 1870.

    Genera *Æora, Tellimera, Linearia, Æona, Veleda, Oriocardium, Solyma, Artena*.

Conrad, T. A. Description of new fossil shells of the Upper Amazon. < *Am. Journ. Conch.*, vol. vi, pp. 192-198, 1 plate. 1870.

    Genera *Isæa, Liris, Ebora, Nesis, Hemisinus, Dyris, Anisothyris*.

Conrad, T. A. Descriptions of new Tertiary fossils, with notes on two genera of Lamellibranchiata. < *Am. Journ. Conch.*, vol. vi, pp. 199-201, 2 plates, which in part illustrate "Paleontological Notes", p. 314, of the same volume. 1870.

Conrad, T. A. On the Eocene beds of Utah. < *Am. Journ. Sci.*, vol. i, 3d ser., pp. 381-383. 1871.

    These beds are those of the Laramie Group of King, and are the same as those found in the Valley of Sulphur Creek, at Mellis's Station, on the U. P. R. R.

Conrad, T. A. Paleontological notes. < *Am. Journ. Conch.*, vol. vi, pp. 314, 315, 1 plate. 1871.

    These notes contain redescriptions of *Catina bilix* and *C. arctatus*; and also "Description of a new fresh-water and a land shell of the Oregon Tertiary".

Conrad, T. A. Descriptions and illustrations of genera of shells. < *Proc. Acad. Nat. Sci. Phila.*, vol. ii, 3d ser., pp. 50-55, 1 plate. 1872.

    Genera *Pleuroconcha, Plionema, Scambula, Pteromeris, Euloxa, Alveinus, Latiarca, Idonearca, Breviarca, Vetericardia* (the latter spelling substituted for the former "*Vetocardia*").

Conrad, T. A. Descriptions of a new recent species of Glycimeris from Beaufort, North Carolina, and of Miocene shells of North Carolina. < *Proc. Acad. Nat. Sci. Phila.*, vol. ii, 3d ser., pp. 216, 217, 1 plate. 1872.

    Genus *Ostreonomia*.

**Conrad, T. A.** Remarks on the Tertiary Clay of the Upper Amazon, with descriptions of new shells. < *Proc. Acad. Nat. Sci. Phila.*, vol. vi, 3d ser., pp. 25-32, 1 plate. 1874.

Genera *Ostomya, Tozosoma, Cirrobasis, Liosoma, Cyclocheila.*

**Conrad, T. A.** Description of two new fossil shells of the Upper Amazon. < *Proc. Acad. Nat. Sci. Phila.*, vol. vi, 3d ser., pp. 32, 83, 1 plate. 1874.

Genus *Haplothærus.*

**Conrad, T. A.** Description of a new fossil shell from Peru. < *Proc. Acad. Nat. Sci. Phila.*, vol. v, 3d ser., p. 139, 1 plate. 1875.

*Ostrea callacta.*

**Conrad, T. A.** Notes on the genus Catillus, Brong. < *Proc. Acad. Nat. Sci. Phila.*, vol. v, 3d ser., pp. 466, 467. 1875.

Genus *Haploscapha* Con. proposed as a substitute for *Catillus* Brong.

**Conrad, T. A.** Descriptions of new genera and species of fossil shells of North Carolina, in the State cabinet at Raleigh. < *Kerr's Geol. Surv. North Carolina*, vol. i, Appendix A, pp. 1-28, plates 1-4. 1875.

This paper includes the two following sub-titles:—" Synopsis of the Cretaceous Mollusca of North Carolina"; and "Remarks on some genera of shells."

Genera *Trigonarca, Nemodon, Plagiarca, Polynema, Inoperna, Etea, Brachymeris, Pachythærus, Arene, Trachycardium, Cyclothyris, Œne, Liothyris, Cymella* (Meek), *Diploconcha, Callonema, Leptothyris, Pterothyris, Liopistha* (Meek). Cretaceous and Tertiary.

**Conrad, T. A.** Description of the genus Haploscapha and subgenus Cucullifera, together with the species H. grandis and. H. (C.) excentrica. < *U. S. Geol. & Geog. Surv. Terr.*, vol. iii, Cretaceous Vertebrata (Cope), pp. 23, 24, 2 plates. 1875.

**Conrad, T. A.** Note on a Cirripede of the California Miocene, with remarks on fossil shells. < *Proc. Acad. Nat. Sci. Phila.*, vol. vi, 3d ser., pp. 273-275. 1876.

**Conrad, T. A.** Note on the relations of Balanus estrellanus of the California Miocene. < *Am. Journ. Sci.*, vol. xiii, 3d ser., pp. 156, 157. 1877.

The author states his positive conviction that the fossil is a true *Balanus*, and not referable to the *Rudistæ*. In the same note, he advances the opinion that true *Cucullea* and several other genera should be excluded from the Cretaceous period, they being represented by closely allied, but not identical, genera.

**Conrad, T. A.** On certain generic names proposed by Zittel, Stoliczska and Zekeli. < *Proc. Acad. Nat. Sci. Phila.*, vol. vii, 3d ser., pp. 22, 23. 1877.

**Conrad, T. A.** Notes on shells. < *Proc. Acad. Nat. Sci. Phila.*, vol. vii, 3d ser., pp. 24, 25. 1877.

These are notes of rectification of certain genera.

**Cox, E. T.** A description of some of the most characteristic shells of the principal coal seams in the Western Basin of Kentucky. < *Kentucky Geol. Surv.* (Owen), vol. iii, pp. 566, 576, 2 plates. 1857.

The plates, together with a map, are in a fascicle separate from the volume.

**Cozzens, Isaachar.** Description of three new fossils from the Falls of the Ohio. < *Ann. N. Y. Lyceum Nat. Hist.*, vol. iv, pp. 157-159. 1846.

Genera *Pentagonia* and *Piliolites.*

# I.—PUBLICATIONS MADE IN THE UNITED STATES.

Dall, W. H. * A revision of the Terebratulidæ and Lingulidæ, with remarks on the descriptions of some recent forms. < *Am. Journ. Conch.*, vol. vi, pp. 88-168, many woodcuts and 3 plates. 1870.
    Genera *Laqueus, Megasella, Gluttidia, Gotlandia.*

Dall, W. H. Supplement to the "Revision of the Terebratulidæ", with additions, corrections, and a revision of the Craniidæ and Discinidæ. <*Am. Journ. Conch.*, vol. vii, pp. 39-85, 2 plates. 1871.

Dall, W. H. Note on the genus Anisothyris, Conrad, with a description of a new species. < *Am. Journ. Conch.*, vol. vii, pp. 89-92. 1871.

Dall, W. H. Index to the names which have been applied to the subdivisions of the class Brachiopoda, excluding the Rudistes, previous to the year 1877. < *Bulletin of the U. S. Nat. Mus.*, No. 8, pamphlet, pp. 88. 1877.
    The catalogue includes both living and fossil *Brachiopoda.*

Dana, J. D. Genera of fossil corals of the family Cyathophyllidæ. < *Am. Journ. Sci.*, vol. i, 2d ser., pp. 178-186. 1846.
    Published in advance of Professor Dana's great work on Zoophytes, comprising vol. vii of *Wilkes's U. S. Expl. Exped.*
    Genus *Calophyllum, Arachnophyllum, Clisiophyllum.*

Dana, James D. Remarks on corals. < *Am. Journ. Sci.*, vol. i, 2d ser., pp. 220, 221. 1846.
    These remarks are in the form of an appendix to an article on Eocene fossils of the United States, by T. A. Conrad.

Dana, James D. Zoophytes. < *Wilkes's U. S. Expl. Exped.*, vol. vii. 1846.
    This volume includes descriptions of several genera and species of fossil, as well as of many recent corals.

Dana, James D. Descriptions of fossil shells of the collections of the exploring expedition under the command of Charles Wilkes, U. S. N., obtained in Australia from the lower layers of the coal formation in Illawarra, and from a deposit, probably of nearly the same age, at Harper's Hill, Valley of the Hunter. <*Am. Journ. Sci.*, vol. iv, 2d ser., pp. 151-160. 1847. Continued in vol. v, pp. 433-435.
    Genus *Helicerus, Pentadia, Oleobis, Astartila, Pyramus, Myonia.* These fossils are all redescribed and illustrated in the large report of the Wilkes exploration expedition, where *Myonia* is changed to *Maonia.*

Dana, James D. Descriptions of fossils. < *Appendix to vol. x, Wilkes's U. S. Expl. Exped.*, pp. 681-730, with atlas of 21 plates, folio. 1849.
    This work contains descriptions of Invertebrate fossils from Australia, South America, and Western North America. The Tertiary fossils of Oregon are described by Conrad. The following genera and subgenera of Mollusca are proposed by Dana:—*Astartila, Maonia, Pyramis, Oleobis, Pentadia, Heliceras.*

Dana, James D. Observations in reply to Mr. Lonsdale's "Remarks". < *Am. Journ. Sci.*, vol. iv, 2d ser., pp. 359-362. 1857.
    For the "Remarks" referred to, see the same volume, p. 357.

Dana, J. D. Note on a fossil Echinoderm from the Blue Limestone (Lower Silurian) of Cincinnati, Ohio. < *Am. Journ. Sci.*, vol. xxxv, 2d ser., p. 295. 1863.
    The author changes the name of *Asterias anthonii*, in the first edition of his *Manual of Geology*, to *Palasterina* (?) *jamesii.* The latter name is adopted in the 2d edition of his *Manual*, and the fossil figured in both.

**Dana, James D.** On fossil insects from the Carboniferous formation in Illinois. < *Am. Journ. Sci.*, vol. xxxvii, 2d ser., pp. 34, 35, 2 woodcuts. 1864.

The two genera *Miamia* and *Hemeristia* are here proposed and diagnosed.

**Dana, J. D.** On the history of Eozoön canadense. < *Am. Journ. Sci.*, vol. xl, 2d ser., pp. 344–362, illustrated by woodcuts and 1 plate. 1865.

The article appears in the *Journal* without a name; *i. e.*, editorially. This history embraces a full discussion of the subject, and includes a complete description and illustration of the structure of the fossil, and the chemical composition of specimens.

**Dana, James D.** On the supposed legs of the Trilobite, Asaphus platycephalus. < *Am. Journ. Sci.*, vol. i, 3d ser., pp. 320, 321; additional note on p. 386. 1871.

See also a note by Professor Dana on the same subject in vol. iii, 3d ser., pp. 221, 222.

**Dana, J. D.** On the supposed legs of Trilobites. < *Am. Journ. Sci.*, vol. iii, 3d ser., pp. 221, 222. 1872.

The author restates his belief that the supposed legs of Trilobites are arches along the under surface, and not real legs. See his former remarks, vol. i, p. 320, of this series of the *Journal*.

**Dawson, J. W.** On the footprints of Limulus as compared with the Protichnites of the Potsdam Sandstone. (Abstract of a paper in the Canadian Naturalist.) < *Am. Journ. Sci.*, vol. xxxiv, 2d ser., pp. 416, 417. 1862.

The author agrees with Owen in supposing the impressions to have been made by some Crustacean. In a note at the close of the abstract, on page 417, Professor Dana opposes this view.

**Dawson, J. W.** Notes on fossils recently obtained from the Laurentian rocks of Canada, and on objections to the organic nature of Eozoön. < *Am. Journ. Sci.*, vol. xliv, 2d ser., pp. 367–376. 1867.

This article also contains notes by W. B. Carpenter; and "Summary" and "Conclusion" of King and Rowney on the same subject; the latter gentleman opposing, and the former advocating, the organic origin of Eozoön.

**Dawson, J. W.** On new specimens of Eozoön canadense, with a reply to Professors King and Rowney; with notes by W. B. Carpenter. < *Am. Journ. Sci.*, vol. xlvi, 2d ser., pp. 245–257, 2 plates. 1868.

The authors advocate the organic origin of Eozoön.

**Dawson, J. W.** On some new specimens of fossil Protozoa from Canada. < *Proc. Am. Assoc. Adv. Sci.*, vol. xxiv, pp. 100–105. 1876.

The author gives general description and illustration of *Eozoön canadense*, and also *Foraminifera*, from Cretaceous rocks. He advocates the organic origin of *Eozoön*.

**Dawson, J. W.** New facts relating to Eozoön canadense. < *Proc. Am. Assoc. Adv. Sci.*, vol. xxv, pp. 231–234. 1876.

The fossil nature of *Eozoön canadense* is advocated.

**DeKay, James E.** Note on the organic remains termed Bilobites; from the Kaatskill Mountains. < *Ann. N. Y. Lyc. Nat. Hist.*, vol. i, part i, pp. 45–49. 1823.

The author believes these bodies to be casts of a species of *Cardium*.

**DeKay, James E.** Observations on the structure of Trilobites, and a description of an apparently new genus. < *Ann. N. Y. Lyc. Nat. Hist.*, vol. i, part i, pp. 174–189, 2 plates. 1824.

    Genus *Isotelus*.

**DeKay, James E.** Report on several multilocular shells from Delaware; with observations on a second specimen of the genus Eurypterus. < *Ann. N. Y. Lyc. Nat. Hist.*, vol. i, pp. 273–279. 1827.

    The "multilocular shells" are Cretaceous Cephalopods, from the Delaware and Chesapeake Canal, and the *Eurypterus* is from near Lake Erie.

**Derby, O. A.** On the Carboniferous Brachiopoda of Itaituba, Rio Tapajos, Province of Pará, Brazil. < *Bull. Cornell Univ.*, vol. i, No. 2, pp. 1–63, 9 indistinct photolithograph plates. 1874.

**Derby, Orville A.** Notice of the Paleozoic fossils of Lake Titicaca. < *Bull. Mus. Comp. Zool. Cambridge, Mass.*, vol. iii, No. 12, pp. 279–286. 1876.

**Eaton, Amos.** Trilobites. < *Am. Journ. Sci.*, vol. xxii, 1st ser., pp. 165,166. 1832.

    The article is descriptive, and the genus *Brongniartia* is proposed and diagnosed.

**Eaton, Amos.** Geological text-book for aiding the study of North American geology. 8°. pp. 134. 1832.

    22 pages and 5 plates devoted to paleontology. The following genera and species are described as new :—*Bellerophon volutus* Eaton; *B. convolutus* Eaton; BRONGNIARTIA Eaton; *B. carcinoidea* Eaton; NUTTAINIA Eaton; *N. concentrica* Eaton; *N. sparsa* Eaton; *Echinus gyracanthus* Eaton; *Columnaria intermedia* Eaton; *Sarcinula microphthalma* Eaton; *S. ramosa* Eaton; *Alcyonia fungioidea* Eaton; *Flustra carbascoides* Eaton; *Terebratula spiriferoides* Eaton.

**Ehrenberg, C. G.** Fossil Infusoria of West Point, New York. < *Am. Journ. Sci.*, vol. xxxix, 1st ser., pp. 191,192. 1840. Abstract from *Proc. Royal Prussian Acad. Sci. Berlin*, Feb., 1839.

    The abstract contains determinations of specific and generic forms of *Infusoria*.

**Ehrenberg, C. G.** Notice of a memoir by C. G. Ehrenberg, "On the extent and influence of microscopic life in North and South America." < *Am. Journ. Sci.*, vol. xlvi, 1st ser., pp. 297–313. 1844.

**Ehrenberg, C. G.** "On Infusorial deposits on the river Chutes in Oregon." < *Am. Journ. Sci.*, vol. ix, 2d ser., p. 140. 1850.

    This is an editorial note giving a brief summary of an article on that subject by Ehrenberg in *Monatsb. Acad. Berlin*, Feb., 1849, p. 76.

**Eights, James.** Description of Sphæroma bumastiformis. < *Emmons's Report on the Second Geological District of New York*, pp. 433, 434. 1842.

**Emmons, Ebenezer.** Report on the geology of the second district of New York. 1842.

    In this work, Dr. Emmons gives two plates of fossils from the Post-Tertiary beds of New England and Canada, but no descriptions. Other fossils are figured and named by the author in various parts of the volume, some of which are original, but none are described in the usual manner.

**Emmons, Ebenezer.** On the identity of the Atops trilineatus and the Triarthrus beckii (Green), with remarks upon the Elliplocephalus asaphoides. < *Proc. Am. Assoc. Adv. Sci.*, vol. i, pp. 16–19. 1849.

**Emmons, Ebenezer.** On new fossil corals from North Carolina. < *Am. Journ. Sci.*, vol. xxii, 2d ser., pp. 389, 390, 5 woodcuts. 1856.

Genus *Paleotrochis*. See also note on the same, by Prof. James Hall, p. 278, vol. xxiii, 2d series.

**Emmons, Ebenezer.** Geological Report Midland Counties of North Carolina. 1856.

The following descriptions occur in the volume:—*Posidonia ovalis*, p. 323 ; *P. multicostata*, p. 337; *P. triangularis*, p. 338.

**Emmons, Ebenezer.** Report of the North Carolina geological survey. 8°. Chapters xviii and xix, pp. 245–313, 157 woodcuts. 1858.

Chapters entitled respectively "Description of the Cephalopods, Gasteropods and Lamellibranchiata", and "Descriptions of the Echinoderms—Sea Urchins—Polyparia". Two species of Cretaceous *Belemnitella* are described, but all the other species are Tertiary. A portion of both the species and genera are newly described. Genera *Microcrinus*, *Goniocypeus*.

**Evans, John,** *and* **B. F. Shumard.** On some new species of fossils from the Cretaceous formation of Nebraska Territory. < *Trans. St. Louis Acad. Sci.*, vol. i, pp. 38–42. 1857.

Descriptive.

**Ford, S. W.** Notes on the Primordial rocks in the vicinity of Troy, New York. < *Am. Journ. Sci.*, vol. ii, 3d ser., pp. 32–34. 1871.

**Ford, S. W.** Note on the discovery of the opercula of Hyolithes in New York. < *Am. Journ. Sci.*, vol. i, 3d ser., p. 472. 1871.

**Ford, S. W.** Descriptions of some new species of Primordial fossils. < *Am. Journ. Sci.*, vol. iii, 3d ser., pp. 419–422. 1872.

**Ford, S. W.** On some new species of fossils from the Primordial or Potsdam Group of Rensselaer County, N. Y. < *Am. Journ. Sci.*, vol. v, 3d ser., pp. 211–215, 3 woodcuts. 1873.

The operculum of *Hyolithes emmonsi* is here figured and described.

**Ford, S. W.** Remarks on the distribution of the fossils in the Lower Potsdam rocks at Troy, N. Y.; with descriptions of a few new species. < *Am. Journ. Sci.*, vol. vi, 3d ser., pp. 134–140. 1873.

**Ford, S. W.** Note on the discovery of a new locality of Primordial fossils in Rensselaer County, N. Y. < *Am. Journ. Sci.*, vol. ix, 3d ser., pp. 204–206. 1875.

**Ford, S. W.** On additional species of fossils from the Primordial of Troy and Lansingburg, Rensselaer County, N. Y. < *Am. Journ. Sci.*, vol. xi, 3d ser., pp. 369–371. 1876.

**Ford, S. W.** Note on Microdiscus speciosus. < *Am. Journ. Sci.*, vol. xiii, 3d ser., pp. 141, 142. 1877.

A correction of the description of that species as originally given by the author in vol. vi, p. 5.

**Ford, S. W.** New embryonic forms of Trilobites. < *Am. Journ. Sci.*, vol. xiii, 3d ser., pp. 265–273, 1 plate. 1877.

The author describes and illustrates the metamorphoses of *Olenellus* (*Elliptocephalus*) *asaphoides* Emmons.

Gabb, W. M. Descriptions of two new species of Carboniferous fossils, brought from Fort Belknap, Texas, by Dr. Moore. Illustrated on plate i, vol. iv. 1859.

The plate is erroneously numbered 7.

Gabb, W. M. Descriptions of new species of Cretaceous fossils from New Jersey. < *Proc. Acad. Nat. Sci. Phila.*, vol. iv, 2d ser., pp. 93–95, 1 plate. 1860.

Gabb, W. M. Description of a new genus and species of Amorphozoön from the Cretaceous formation of New Jersey. < *Proc. Acad. Nat. Sci. Phila.*, vol. iv, 2d ser., p. 518. 1860.

Genus *Desmatocerium*.

Gabb, W. M. Descriptions of some new species of Tertiary fossils from Chiriqui, Central America. < *Proc. Acad. Nat. Sci. Phila.*, vol. iv, 2d ser., pp. 567, 568. 1860.

Gabb, W. M. Descriptions of some new species of Cretaceous fossils. < *Journ. Acad. Nat. Sci. Phila.*, vol. iv, 2d ser., pp. 299–305, 1 plate. 1860.

One plate illustrates this and the following article also.

Gabb, W. M. Description of new species of fossils, probably Triassic, from Virginia. < *Journ. Acad. Nat. Sci. Phila.*, 2d ser., vol. iv, pp. 307, 308. 1860.

One plate illustrates this and the preceding article also.

Gabb, W. M. Descriptions of new species of American Tertiary and Cretaceous fossils. < *Journ. Acad. Nat. Sci. Phila.*, vol. iv, 2d ser., pp. 375–406, 3 plates. 1860.

Genera *Odontopolys, Eucheiloden, Leiorhinus, Acervicloesa, Heterocrisina*.

Gabb, W. M. Synopsis of American Cretaceous Brachiopoda. < *Proc. Acad. Nat. Sci. Phila.*, vol. v, 2d ser., pp. 18, 19. 1861.

Gabb, W. M. Description of new Cretaceous fossils from New Jersey, Alabama, and Mississippi. < *Proc. Acad. Nat. Sci. Phila.*, vol. v, 2d ser., pp. 318–330. 1861.

Gabb, W. M. Notes on Cretaceous fossils, with descriptions of a few additional new species. < *Proc. Acad. Nat. Sci. Phila.*, vol. v, 2d ser., pp. 363–367. 1861.

Gabb, W. M. Descriptions of new species of American Tertiary fossils, and a new Carboniferous Cephalopod from Texas. < *Proc. Acad. Nat. Sci. Phila.*, vol. v, 2d ser., pp. 367–372. 1861.

Gabb, W. M. Revision of the species of Baculites described in Dr. Morton's Synopsis of the Cretaceous group of the United States. < *Proc. Acad. Nat. Sci. Phila.*, vol. v, 2d ser., pp. 394–396, 1 plate. 1861.

Gabb, W. M. Synopsis of the Mollusca of the Cretaceous formation, including the geographical and stratigraphical range and synonymy. < *Proc. Am. Philos. Soc.*, vol. viii, pp. 57–257. 1861.

Gabb, W. M. Notes on some fossils from the Gold-bearing Slates of Mariposa, with descriptions of some new species. < *Proc. Cal. Acad. Nat. Sci.*, vol. iii, pp. 172, 173. 1864.

Gabb, W. M.  Paleontology of California.  > Vol. i, Descriptions of Triassic and Cretaceous fossils of California and the adjacent Territories, pp. 19-243, plates 3-32.  1864.

Gabb, W. M.  On the subdivisions of the Cretaceous rocks of California. < Am. Journ. Sci., vol. xliv, 2d ser., pp. 226-229.  1867.

Gabb, W. M.  An attempt at a revision of the two families Strombidæ and Aporrhaidæ.  < Am. Journ. Conch., vol. iv, pp. 137-149, 2 plates.  1868.

Gabb, W. M.  Descriptions of fossils from the Clay Deposits of the Upper Amazon.  < Am. Journ. Conch., vol. iv, pp. 197-200, 1 plate.  1868.
Tertiarys

Gabb, W. M.  Descriptions of some Secondary fossils from the Pacific States. < Am. Journ. Conch., vol. v, pp. 5-18, 5 plates.  1869.
Jurassic and Triassic.

Gabb, W. M.  Notes on the genera Alaria, Diarthema, Dicroloma, &c., being a supplement to "An attempt at a revision of the Strombidæ and Aporrhaidæ".  < Am. Journ. Conch., vol. v, pp. 19-23.  1869.

Gabb, W. M.  Descriptions of new species of South American fossils. < Am. Journ. Conch., vol. v, pp. 25-32.  1869.
Tertiary.

Gabb, W. M.  Paleontology of California.  > Vol. ii, Cretaceous and Tertiary fossils.  pp. 299, 36 plates.  1869.

Gabb, W. M.  Notes on the genus Palorthus, Gabb.  < Proc. Acad. Nat. Sci. Phila., vol. ii, 3d ser., pp. 259-262, 1 plate.  1872.

Gabb, W. M.  Notice of a collection of Cretaceous fossils from Chihuahua, Mexico.  < Proc. Acad. Nat. Sci. Phila., vol. ii, 3d ser., pp. 263-265, 2 plates. 1872.

Gabb, W. M.  Notes on American Cretaceous fossils, with descriptions of some new species.  < Proc. Acad. Nat. Sci. Phila., vol. vi, 3d ser., pp. 276-324, 1 plate.  1876.
Genera *Volutoderma, Volutomorpha, Ptychosyca, Gyrotropis, Laxispira, Endoptygma, Ataphrus, Paliurus.*

Gabb, W. M.  Note on the discovery of representatives of three orders of fossils new to the Cretaceous formation of North America.  < Proc. Acad. Nat. Sci. Phila., vol. vi, 3d ser., pp. 178-179, 1 plate.  1876.
*Pentacrinus bryani, Goniaster mammillata, Scalpellum conradi.*

Gabb, W. M., and G. H. Horn.  Descriptions of new Cretaceous Corals from New Jersey.  < Proc. Acad. Nat. Sci. Phila., vol. iv, 2d ser., pp. 366, 367.  1860.

Gabb, W. M., and G. H. Horn.  Monograph of the fossil Polyzoa of the Secondary and Tertiary formations of North America.  < Journ. Acad. Nat. Sci. Phila., vol. v, 2d ser., pp. 111-179, 3 plates.  1862.
Genera *Phidolopora, Oligotresium, Ennallipora, Multiporina, Pliophlœa, Heteractis.* All other genera used are also diagnosed, as well as some of the higher groups.

**Gill, Theodore.** On Contributions to Paleontology, published by the Smithsonian Institution. < *Am. Journ. Sci.*, vol. xliii, 2d ser., pp. 363–370. 1867.

This is not only a review of the works of Meek, of Meek and Hayden, and of Conrad, referred to, but the article also contains some philosophical discussion of important questions.

**Gill, ¶Theodore.** On the systematic position of Buccinum altile and B. escheri. < *Am. Journ. Conch.*, vol. iii, pp. 153, 154. 1867.

Genus *Ptychosalpinx*. The paper embraces a discussion of both fossil and recent shells.

**Gill, Theodore.** On the genus Fulgur and its allies. < *Am. Journ. Conch.*, vol. iii, pp. 141–152. 1867.

The paper embraces a discussion of both fossil and recent shells.

**Gill, ¶Theodore.** On the Pteroceræ of Lamarck, and their mutual relations. < *Am. Journ. Conch.*, vol. v, pp. 120–139. 1869.

Genera *Harpagodes, Ceratosiphon*. The paper embraces a discussion of both fossil and recent shells.

**Gill, Theodore.** Arrangement of the families of Mollusks. < *Smithsonian Miscellaneous Collections* (227), pp. 49. 1871.

The paper embraces a discussion of both recent and fossil *Mollusca*.

**Green, Jacob.** A monograph of the Trilobites of North America, with colored models of the species. 12°. pp. 93, 1 plate. With an appendix, pp. 24. Philadelphia. 1832.

The following genera and species are diagnosed:—CALYMENE Brong.; *C. blumenbachii* Brong.; *C. callicephala* Green; *C. selenecephala* Green; *C. platys* Green; *C. microps* Green; *C. anchiops* Green; *C. diops* Green; *C. macrophthalma* Green; *C. bufo* Green; *C. bufo* var. *rana* Green; ASAPHUS Brong.; *A. laticostatus* Green; *A. selenurus* Eaton; *A. limulurus* Green; *A. caudatus* Brunnich. (Brong.); *A. hausmanni* Brong.; *A. pleuroptyx* Green; *A. micrurus* Green; *A. wetherilli* Green; PARADOXIDES Brong.; *P. boltoni* Bigsby; ISOTELUS DeKay; *I. gigas* DeKay; *I. planus* DeKay; *I. cyclops* Green; *I. megalops* Green; *I. stegops* Green; CRYPTOLITHUS Green; *C. tessellatus* Green; DIPLEURA Green; *D. dekayi* Green; TRIMERUS Green; *T. delphinocephalus* Green; CERAURUS Green; *C. pleurexanthemus* Green; TRIARTHRUS Green; *T. beckii* Green; NUTTAINIA Eaton; *N. sparsa* Eaton; BRONGNIARTIA Eaton; *B. platycephala* Eaton; OGYGIA Brong.; AGNOSTUS Brong.; NILEUS Dalman; HEMICRUPTURUS Green; ILLÆNUS Dalman; AMPYX Dalman.

**Green, Jacob.** Description of a new Trilobite from Nova Scotia (Asaphus ! crypturus). < *Trans. Geol. Soc. Penn.*, vol. i, pt. i, pp. 37–39, 1 wood ut. 1834.

**Green, Jacob.** Description of a new Trilobite. < *Am. Journ. Sci.*, vol. xxxii, 1st ser., pp. 167–169. 1837.

The article contains descriptions of *two species*. See also note of correction on page 6 of the same volume.

**Green, Jacob.** Descriptions of several new Trilobites. < *Am. Journ. Sci.*, vol. xxxii, 1st ser., pp. 343–349, 2 woodcuts. 1837.

**Green, Jacob.** Description of two new species of Trilobites. < *Journ. Acad. Nat. Sci. Phila.*, vol. vii, 1st ser., pp. 217–226. 1837.

**Green, Jacob.** Some remarks on the genus Paradoxides of Brongniart, and on the necessity of preserving the genus Triarthrus, proposed in the Monograph of the Trilobites of North America. < *Am. Journ. Sci.*, vol. xxxiii, 1st ser., pp. 341–344. 1838.

Green, Jacob. New Trilobites. < *Am. Journ. Sci.*, 1st ser., vol. xxxiv, p. 380. 1838.
: Description of species.

Green, Jacob. Description of a new Trilobite. < *Am. Journ. Sci.*, vol. xxxiii, 1st ser., pp. 406, 407. 1838.

Green, Jacob. Remarks on the Trilobite. < *Am. Journ. Sci.*, vol. xxxvii, 1st ser., pp. 25–39. 1839.
: A general discussion of the nature of the *Trilobite*.

Green, Jacob. Description of a new Trilobite. < *Am. Journ. Sci.*, vol. xxxvii, 1st ser., p. 40. 1839.

Green, Jacob. The inferior surface of the Trilobite discovered. 12°. pp. 33. Philadelphia. 1839.
: In this small book, Dr. Green describes portions of the under surface of *Calymene bufo* Green, and suggests that the *Trilobites* were Decapodous Crustaceans, but he records no actual discovery of any appendages.

Grinnell, G. B. On a new Crinoid from the Cretaceous formation of the West. < *Am. Journ. Sci.*, vol. xii, 3d ser., pp. 81–83, 1 plate. 1876.
: Genus *Uintacrinus*.

Grinnell, G. B. Notice of a new genus of Annelids from the Lower Silurian. < *Am. Journ. Sci.*, vol. xiv, 3d ser., pp. 229–230. 1877.
: Genus *Nereidavus*.

Grote, A. R., and W. H. Pitt. Description of a new Crustacean from the Water Lime Group at Buffalo. < *Bull. Buffalo Soc. Nat. Sci.*, vol. iii, pp. 1, 2, 1 plate. 1875.
: Genus *Eusarcus*.

Grote, A. R., and W. H. Pitt. On new species of Eusarcus and Pterygotus from the Waterlime Group at Buffalo. < *Bull. Buffalo Soc. Nat. Sci.*, vol. iii, pp. 17–20. 1875.

Hall, Charles E. Contribution to Paleontology from the Museum of the Second Geological Survey of Pennsylvania. < *Proc. Am. Philos. Soc. Phila.*, vol. xvi, pp. 691, 692. 1877.
: Two species of *Eurypterus*.

Hall, James. Descriptions of two new species of Trilobites belonging to the genus Paradoxides. < *Am. Journ. Sci.*, vol. xxxiii, 1st ser., pp. 139–142, 2 woodcuts. January, 1838.

Hall, James. Geological Survey of New York; Report on the Fourth District. 4°. pp. 683. Many woodcut illustrations. 1843.
: This report contains much paleontological matter distributed throughout the volume, a part of which is there originally published; but none of the descriptions are separate from the geological text.

Hall, James. Descriptions of organic remains collected by Captain J. C. Frémont in the Geographical Survey of Oregon and North California. < *Frémont's Report of Expl. Exped. to the Rocky Mountains and to Oregon and North California*, pp. 304–310, 2 plates. 1845.
: Invertebrate fossils. Cretaceous and Tertiary.

**Hall, James.** Paleontology of New York. Vol. i. pp. 338, 98 plates. 1847.

Lower Silurian. Genera *Echino-encrinites* (H. von Meyer), *Tellinomya, Modiolopsis, Ambonychia, Holopea, Subulites* (Conrad), *Carinaropsis, Oncoceras, Cameroceras* (Conrad), *Platynotus* (Conrad), *Thaleops* (Conrad), *Sphenothallus, Favistella, Discophyllum, Heterocrinus, Glyptocrinus, Scolithus* (Hald.), *Palæophycus, Buthotrepis, Ophileta* (Vanuxem), *Streptoplasma, Raphistoma, Bucania, Phytopsis, Stromatocerium, Gonioceras, Endoceras, Escharopora, Stictopora, Stellipora, Schizocrinus, Scyphocrinus, Lyrodesma* (Conrad).

This great work, of which the fourth quarto volume has been published, and others are in course of preparation, is confined in its scope to the Paleozoic rocks. It comprises not only descriptions and profuse illustrations of a very large number of species, but a large proportion of the whole work is devoted to definitions of the higher groups and philosophic discussion of their relations. Much material is also introduced into the work, for illustration, from beyond the limits of the State of New York.

**Hall, James.** Remarks on the observations of S. S. Haldeman "On the supposed identity of Atops trilineatus with Triarthrus beckii": < *Am. Journ. Sci.*, vol. v, 2d ser., pp. 322-327. 1848.

**Hall, James.** On the trails and tracks in the Sandstones of the Clinton Group of New York; their probable origin, &c., and a comparison of some of them with Nereites and Myrianites. < *Proc. Am. Assoc. Adv. Sci.*, vol. ii, pp. 256-260. 1850.

**Hall, James.** On the Brachiopoda of the Silurian period, particularly the Leptænidæ. < *Proc. Am. Assoc. Adv. Sci.*, vol. ii, pp. 347-351. 1850.

**Hall, James.** On Graptolites; their duration in geological periods, and their value in the identification of strata. < *Proc. Am. Assoc. Adv. Sci.*, vol. ii, pp. 351, 352. 1850.

**Hall, James.** Description of new species of fossils, and observations upon some other species, previously not well known, from the Trenton Limestone. < *3d Ann. Rep. Regents Univ. N. Y. on Condition State Cabinet*, pp. 167-175. 1850.

Genera *Ægilops, Colpoceras.*

**Hall, James.** New genera of fossil Corals. < *Am. Journ. Sci.*, vol. xi, 2d ser., pp. 398-401. 1851.

Genera *Helopora, Phænopora, Rhinopora, Polydilasma, Conophyllum, Diplophyllum, Astrocerium, Cladopora, Ca'opora, Trematopora, Striatopora, Clathropora, Ceramopora, Lichenalia Sagenella, Dictyonema, Inocaulis.*

**Hall, James.** Description of new or rare species of fossils, from the Paleozoic series. < *Foster & Whitney's Report on the Geology of the Lake Superior Land District*, pp. 203-231, plates xxiii-xxxv. 1851.

Silurian and Devonian.

**Hall, James.** Notes upon some of the fossils collected on the route from the Missouri River to the Great Salt Lake, and in the vicinity of the latter place, by the expedition under the command of Captain Howard Stansbury, T. E. < *Stansbury's Expl. and Surv. of the Valley of the Great Salt Lake of Utah*, Appendix E, pp. 401-414, 4 plates. 1852.

Carboniferous.

**Hall, James.** Paleontology of New York, Vol. ii. pp. 362, 104 plates. 1852.

Upper Silurian.

Genera *Trochoceras, Arthrophycus, Rusophycus, Ichnophycus, Camaropora, Helopora, Phænopora, Rhinopora, Stropheodonta, Pyrenomæus, Cyclonema, Discosorus, Polydilasma, Conophyllum, Diplophyllum, Astrocerium, Cladopora, Callopora, Trematopora, Striatopora, Diamesopora, Megalomus, Stephanocrinus* (Conrad), *Clathropora, Ceramopora, Lichenalia, Sagenella, Dictyonema, Inocaulis, Closterocrinus, Homocrinus, Glyptaster, Thysanocrinus, Myelodactylus, Dendrocrinus, Ichthyocrinus* (Conrad), *Lyriocrinus, Lecanocrinus, Macrostylocrinus, Saccocrinus, Heterocystites, Callocystites. Hemicystites, Palæaster, Calceocrinus, Platyostoma* (Conrad).

**Hall, James.** Notes on some fossils of the so-called Taconic system, described by Dr. Emmons. < *Am. Journ. Sci.*, 2d ser., vol. xix, pp. 434, 435. 1855.

**Hall, James.** Description of new species of fossils from the Carboniferous Limestones of Indiana and Illinois. < *Trans. Albany Inst.*, vol. iv, pp. 1–36. 1856.

This paper embraces a large number of minute species of shells, mainly from the locality in Washington County, Indiana, known as "Spergen Hill". They are all from the Lower Carboniferous series, except *Terebratula millepunctata*, which is from the Coal-measures. Genera *Cypricardella, Bulimella*.

**Hall, James.** Descriptions and notices of the fossils collected on the route. < *Pacific R. R. Reports*, vol. iii, pp. 99–105, 2 plates. 1856.

Carboniferous and Cretaceous.

**Hall, James.** Descriptions of Paleozoic fossils, chiefly from those constituting the third volume of the Paleontology of New York; with others from the fourth volume, &c., &c. < *10th Ann. Report Regents Univ. N. Y. on Condition of State Cabinet*, Appendix C, pp. 41–180, many woodcuts. 1857.

**Hall, James.** On the genus Tellinomya and allied genera. < *10th Ann. Report Regents Univ. N. Y. on Condition of State Cabinet*, Appendix C, pp. 181–186. 1857.

Reprinted from the *Canadian Naturalist and Geologist*.

**Hall, James.** Observations on the genus Archimedes, or Fenestella, with description of species, &c. < *Proc. Am. Assoc. Adv. Sci.*, vol. x, pp. 176–180. 1857.

See, also, *Am. Journ. Sci.*, vol. xxiii, 2d ser., pp. 203, 204.

**Hall, James.** Remarks upon the genus Archimedes, or Fenestella, from the Carboniferous Limestones of the Mississippi Valley. < *Am. Journ. Sci.*, vol. xxiii, 2d ser., pp. 203, 204. 1857.

See, also, *Proc. Am. Assoc. Adv. Sci.*, vol. x, pp. 176–180.

**Hall, James.** Paleontology of Iowa. < *Hall's Geol. Surv. of Iowa*, vol. i, pt. ii, pp. 473–724, 29 plates. 1858.

Devonian and Carboniferous. Parts I and II of vol. i (the only one published) of this work, are each bound as separate volumes.

**Hall, James.** Notice of the genera Ambonychia, Palæarca, and Megambona. < *12th Ann. Rep. Regents Univ. N. Y. on Condition of State Cabinet*, pp. 8–14. 1859.

Also a supplementary note on *Ambonychia*, p. 110.

Hall, James. Observations on the genera Capulus, Pileopsis, Acroculia, and Platyceras. <12th Ann. Rep. Regents Univ. N. Y. on Condition of State Cabinet, pp. 15–19. 1859.

Hall, James. Observations on the genera Platyostoma and Strophostylus. <12th Ann. Rep. Regents Univ. N. Y. on Condition of State Cabinet, pp. 20–22. 1859.

Hall, James. Observations on the genus Nucleospira. <12th Ann. Rep. Regents Univ. N. Y. on Condition of State Cabinet, pp. 24–26. 1859.

Hall, James. The genus Trematospira. <12th Ann. Rep. Regents Univ. N. Y. on Condition of State Cabinet, pp. 27, 28. 1859.

Hall, James. The genus Rhynchospira. <12th Ann. Rep. Regents Univ. N. Y. on Condition of State Cabinet, pp. 29, 30. 1859.

Hall, James. The genus Tropidoleptus. <12th Ann. Rep. Regents Univ. N. Y. on Condition of State Cabinet, p. 31. 1859.

Hall, James. The genus Leptocœlia. <12th Ann. Rep. Regents Univ. N. Y. on Condition of State Cabinet, pp. 32–34. 1859.

Hall, James. Observations on the genus Eatonia. <12th Ann. Rep. Regents Univ. N. Y. on Condition of State Cabinet, pp. 34–37. 1859.

Hall, James. Observations on the genus Rensselæria. <12th Ann. Rep. Regents Univ. N. Y. on Condition of State Cabinet, pp. 38–41. 1859.

Hall, James. Observations on the genus Camarium. <12th Ann. Rep. Regents Univ. N. Y. on Condition of State Cabinet, pp. 42, 43. 1859.

Hall, James. The genus Triplesia. <12th Ann. Rep. Regents Univ. N. Y. on Condition of State Cabinet, p. 44. 1859.

Hall, James. Notes upon the genus Graptolithus, with remarks upon some of the species, their mode-of growth and manner of reproduction. <12th Ann. Rep. Regents Univ. N. Y. on Condition of State Cabinet, pp. 45–58. 1859.

Genus *Phyllograptus*.

Hall, James. The Trilobites of the Shales of the Hudson River Group. <12th Ann. Rep. Regents Univ. N. Y. on Condition of State Cabinet, pp. 59–62. 1859.

*Olenus thompsoni, O. vermontana.*

Hall, James. Catalogue of the species of fossils described in volumes i, ii, and iii of the Paleontology of New York; with corrections in nomenclature, as far as determined to the present time. <12th Ann. Rep. Regents Univ. N. Y. on Condition of State Cabinet, pp. 63–92. 1859.

Hall, James. Notices of new forms of the genus Graptolithus and allied genera. <13th Ann. Rep. Regents Univ. N. Y. on Condition of State Cabinet, pp. 55–64. 1860.

Genus *Thammnograptus*.

Hall, James. The genus Rhynchonella, with observations on the R. (Atrypa) increbscens. <13th Ann. Rep. Regents Univ. N. Y. on Condition of State Cabinet, pp. 65–68. 1860.

**Hall, James.** Observations upon Orthis insignis of the Lower Helderberg Group; Orthis pyramidalis of the Niagara Group, and a similar species from Tennessee. <13th *Ann. Rep. Regents Univ. N. Y. on Condition of State Cabinet*, pp. 69, 70. 1860.

Genus *Skenidium.*

**Hall, James.** Observations on the genus Ambocœlia. <13th *Ann. Rep. Regents Univ. N. Y. on Condition of State Cabinet*, pp. 71–72. 1860.

**Hall, James.** The genus Vitulina. <13th *Ann. Rep. Regents Univ. N. Y. on Condition of State Cabinet*, p. 72. 1860.

**Hall, James.** Observations on the genera Athyris (Spirigera), Merista (= Camarium), Meristella, and Leiorhynchus. <13th *Ann. Rep. Regents Univ. N. Y. on Condition of State Cabinet*, pp. 73–75. 1860.

See also observations in 15th *Ann. Report,* pp. 178–181.

**Hall, James.** Descriptions of new species of fossils from the Hamilton Group of Western New York, with notices of others from the same horizon in Iowa and Indiana. <13th *Ann. Rep. Regents Univ. N. Y. on Condition of State Cabinet*, pp. 76–94. 1860.

**Hall, James.** Notes and observations upon the fossils of the Goniatite Limestone in the Marcellus Shale of the Hamilton Group, in the eastern and central parts of the State of New York; and those of the Goniatite beds of Rockford, Indiana; with some analogous forms from the Hamilton Group proper. <13th *Ann. Rep. Regents Univ. N. Y. on Condition of State Cabinet*, pp. 95–112. 1860.

Also a supplementary note on page 125.

**Hall, James.** Note upon the Trilobites of the Shales of the Quebec Group, in the town of Georgia, Vermont. <13th *Ann. Rep. Regents Univ. N. Y. on Condition of State Cabinet*, pp. 113–118. 1860.

Genera *Barrandia, Bathynotus.* The generic name *Barrandia* is changed by Professor Hall to *Olenellus,* on page 114, 15th *Ann. Rep. Regents Univ. N. Y. on Condition of State Cabinet.* See note on p. 196 of 15th *Ann. Rep.*

**Hall, James.** New species of fossils from the Hudson River Group of Ohio and other Western States. <13th *Ann. Rep. Regents Univ. N. Y. on Condition of State Cabinet*, pp. 119–121. 1860.

**Hall, James.** Observations on a new genus of Crinoidea, Cheirocrinus. <13th *Ann. Rep. Regents Univ. N. Y. on Condition of State Cabinet*, pp. 121–124. 1860.

Professor Hall abandons the name *Cheirocrinus,* as here proposed, for *Calceocrinus,* which was proposed by him in vol. ii, *Pal. of N. Y.,* p. 352, both forms being congeneric. See 26th *Ann. Rep. Regents Univ. N. Y. on Condition of State Cabinet,* explanatory page of plate 19.

**Hall, James.** Contributions to the Paleontology of Iowa, being descriptions of new species of Crinoidea and other fossils. (Subcarboniferous.) <*Supplement to vol.* i, *part* ii, *Hall's Geological Survey of Iowa.* 1860.

Genus *Trematocrinus.* This supplement was published by Professor Hall after the publication of the principal work.

**Hall, James.** Observations upon some new and other species of fossils from the rocks of the Hudson River Group of Ohio and the Western States, with descriptions. <14th *Ann. Rep. Regents Univ. N. Y. on Condition of State Cabinet*, pp. 89–92. 1861.

I.—PUBLICATIONS MADE IN THE UNITED STATES. 33

**Hall, James.** Note on the genera Bellerophon, Bucania, Carinopsis, and Cyrtolites. <14th Ann. Rep. Regents Univ. N. Y. on Condition of State Cabinet, pp. 91–98. 1861.

<small>Genera Phragmosoma, Oleioderma.</small>

**Hall, James.** Descriptions of new species of fossils from the Upper Helderberg, Hamilton, and Chemung Groups; with observations upon previously described species. <14th Ann. Rep. Regents Univ. N. Y. on Condition of State Cabinet, pp. 99–109. 1861.

<small>Genus Cryptonella.</small>

**Hall, James.** Contributions to Paleontology, comprising descriptions of new species of fossils from the Upper Helderberg, Hamilton, and Chemung Groups. <15th Ann. Rep. Regents Univ. N. Y. on Condition of State Cabinet, pp. 29–80. 1861.

<small>The 15th Report contains 9 woodcut plates, illustrating the fossils that are described in this and preceding reports.</small>

**Hall, James.** Preliminary notice of the Trilobites and other Crustacea of the Upper Helderberg, Hamilton, and Chemung Groups. <15th Ann. Rep. Regents Univ. N. Y. on Condition of State Cabinet, pp. 82–113. 1861.

**Hall, James.** Preliminary notice of some of the species of Crinoidea known in the Upper Helderberg and Hamilton Groups of New York. <15th Ann. Rep. Regents Univ. N. Y. on Condition of State Cabinet, pp. 115–153, 1 plate. 1861.

<small>Genera Ancyrocrinus, Nucleocrinus (Conrad), Cacabocrinus (Troost).</small>

**Hall, James.** Observations on a new genus of Brachiopoda (Zygospira). <15th Ann. Rep. Regents Univ. N. Y. on Condition of State Cabinet, pp. 154, 155. 1861.

**Hall, James.** Observations on the genera Athyris (=Spirigera), Merista, Camarium, and Meristella. <15th Ann. Rep. Regents Univ. N. Y. on Condition of State Cabinet, pp. 178–181. 1861.

<small>See also observations in 13th Ann. Report, pp. 73–75.</small>

**Hall, James.** Descriptions of new species of fossils, chiefly from the Hamilton Group of Western New York. <15th Ann. Rep. Regents Univ. N. Y. on Condition of State Cabinet, pp. 181–191. 1861.

**Hall, James.** Note on the genus Cypricardites. <15th Ann. Rep. Regents Univ. N. Y. on Condition of State Cabinet, pp. 192, 193. 1861.

**Hall, James.** Plate (No. 11) of illustrations of certain of Conrad's genera and species, but no descriptions. <15th Ann. Rep. Regents Univ. N. Y. on Condition of State Cabinet, facing p. 194. 1861.

**Hall, James.** Notes and corrections. <15th Ann. Rep. Regents Univ. N. Y. on Condition of State Cabinet, pp. 195–197. 1861.

<small>In these notes, the genus Pholadops is amended, the horizon of Goniatites pattersoni, as given on page 99 of the 13th Ann. Rep., corrected, and an explanation given concerning the title of an article on page 113 of 13th Ann. Rep.</small>

**Hall, James.** Descriptions of new species of Crinoidea from the Carboniferous rocks of the Mississippi Valley. <Journ. Bost. Soc. Nat. Hist., vol. vii, pp. 261–328. 1861.

**Hall, James.** Descriptions of new species of Crinoidea. From Investigations of the Iowa Geological Survey. Preliminary notice. Albany, February 25, 1861.

> The first ten pages of this pamphlet are a reprint of the preceding article. The nine following pages of the pamphlet are new, and contain descriptions of the following species, besides the genus *Heterocidaris* and subgenus *Lepidechinus:—Actinocrinus cariea, A. ovatus, A. multibrachiatus, A. lucina, A. thetis, A. thoas, A. quoternarius, A. themis, A. remibrachiatus, A. tenuiradiatus, A. eryx, A. erodus, A. insculptus, A. althea, A. lagena, A. thallia, A. matuta, A. attenuata, A. tenuidissus, A. securus, A. infrequens, A. laura, A. locellus, A. doris, Platycrinus olla, P. regalis, P. glyptus, P. calyculus, P. nodobrachiatus, P. parvinodus, P. eminulus, P. aqualis, Synbathocrinus papillatus, Rhodocrinus Wachsmuthi, Lepidechinus imbricatus, Protaster ? Barrisi, Heterocidaris Keokuk, H. lævispinus.*

**Hall, James.** Paleontology of New York. vol. 3. pp. 532, 141 plates, in a separate volume. 1861.

> Upper Silurian. Genera *Cypricardinia, Mariacrinus, Edriocrinus, Aspidocrinus, Coronocrinus, Lepadocrinus* (Conrad), *Sphærocystites, Anomalocystites, Dictyocrinus* (Conrad), *Technocrinus, Trematospira, Rhyncospira, Nucleospira, Eatonia, Leptocœlia, Rensselæria, Megambonin, Palæarca, Platyostoma* (Conrad), *Strophostylus, Platyceras* (Conrad), *Camarium, Pholidops, Phyllograptus, Thamnograpius, Triplesia*. Pages 149–152 contain a synopsis of the *Cystidea*, comprising diagnoses of eighteen genera.

**Hall, James.** Descriptions of new species of fossils. < *Report of the Superintendent of the Geological Survey (of Wisconsin)*, pamphlet, pp. 52, 8°. 1861.

> Silurian.

**Hall, James.** Notice of some new species of fossils from a locality of the Niagara Group in Indiana, with a list of identified species from the same place. < *Trans. Albany Inst.*, vol. iv, pp. 195–228. 1862.

> This locality is in Shelby County, Indiana. The 28th *Ann. Rep. Regents Univ. N. Y.* contains 32 plates of illustrations of these fossils, but the descriptions are not there repeated.

**Hall, James.** Preliminary notice of the fauna of the Potsdam Sandstone; with remarks upon the previously known species of fossils, and descriptions of some new ones, from the Sandstones of the Upper Mississippi Valley. < *Trans. Albany Inst.*, vol. v, pp. 93–196. 1862.

> This article, illustrated, was also published in the 16th *Ann. Rep. Regents Univ. N.Y. on Condition of State Cabinet.*

**Hall, James.** Remarks upon the condition of the fossils in the rocks of the several formations; catalogue of the fossils known in the Paleozoic formations of Wisconsin, with observations upon some of the known species, and descriptions of several new forms. < *Rep. Geol. Surv. Wisconsin (Hall & Whitney)*, vol. i, pp. 425–448. 1862.

**Hall, James.** Descriptions of new species of Brachiopoda, from the Upper Helderberg, Hamilton, and Chemung Groups. < 16th *Ann. Rep. Regents Univ. N. Y. on Condition of State Cabinet*, Appendix D, pp. 19–37. 1863.

**Hall, James.** Observations on some of the Brachiopoda, with reference to the characters of the genera Cryptonella, Centronella, Meristella, Trematospira, Rhynchospira, Retzia, Leptocœlia, and allied forms. < 16th *Ann. Rep. Regents Univ. N. Y. on Condition of State Cabinet*, pp. 38–59. 1863.

**Hall, James.** Note on the genus Leptocœlia. < 16th *Ann. Rep. Regents Univ. N. Y. on Condition of State Cabinet*, pp. 59–61. 1863.

> The genus *Cœliospira* is here proposed.

# I.—PUBLICATIONS MADE IN THE UNITED STATES. 35

**Hall, James.** Observations upon the genus Streptorhynchus, with remarks upon some species heretofore referred to the genera Strophomena and Orthis. < 16*th Ann. Rep. Regents Univ. N. Y. on Condition of State Cabinet*, pp. 61–66. 1863.

**Hall, James.** Note on the geological range of the genus Receptaculites in American Paleozoic strata. < 16*th Ann. Rep. Regents Univ. N. Y. on Condition of State Cabinet*, pp. 67–69. 1863.

**Hall, James.** Note on the occurrence of Astylospongia in the Lower Helderberg rocks. < 16*th Ann. Rep. Regents Univ. N. Y. on Condition of State Cabinet*, pp. 69, 70. 1863.

**Hall, James.** On the occurrence of Crustacean remains of the genera Ceratiocaris and Dithyrocaris, with a notice of some new species from the Hamilton Group and Genesee Slate. < 16*th Ann. Rep. Regents Univ. N. Y. on Condition of State Cabinet*, pp. 71–75, 1 plate. 1863.

**Hall, James.** Observations upon some spiral growing Fucoidal remains of the Paleozoic rocks of New York. < 16*th Ann. Rep. Regents Univ. N. Y. on Condition of State Cabinet*, pp. 76–83. 1863.

**Hall, James.** Observations upon the genera Uphantænia and Dictyophyton; with notices of some species from the Chemung Group of New York and the Waverly Sandstone of Ohio. < 16*th Ann. Rep. Regents Univ. N. Y. on Condition of State Cabinet*, pp. 84–91. 1863.

12 plates of illustrations accompany this and the following articles.

**Hall, James.** Preliminary notice of the fauna of the Potsdam Sandstone, with remarks upon the previously known species of fossils, and descriptions of some new ones, from the Sandstone of the Upper Mississippi Valley. < 16*th Ann. Rep. Regents Univ. N. Y. on Condition of State Cabinet*, pp. 119–225, including "Supplementary note on the Potsdam Sandstone". 1863.

12 plates of illustrations accompany this and the preceding articles. The following genera are here proposed:—*Lingulepis, Ptychaspis, Chariocephalus, Illænurus, Triarthrella, Aglaspis.*

**Hall, James.** On a new Crustacean from the Potsdam Sandstone. < *Am. Journ. Sci.*, vol. xxxv, 2d ser., p. 295. 1863.

This is a very brief abstract of a paper on that subject in the *Canadian Naturalist and Geologist*, Dec., 1862, vii, p. 443.

**Hall, James.** Observations upon some of the Brachiopoda, with reference to the genera Cryptonella, Centronella, Meristella, and allied forms. < *Am. Journ. Sci.*, vol. xxxv, 2d ser., pp. 396–406. 1863. Many woodcut illustrations.

This article is an extended abstract from *Trans. Albany Institute* of the same year, with corrections and additions by the author. It is continued in vol. xxxvi of the same series, pp. 11–15.

**Hall, James.** Preliminary notice of some species of Ciinoidea from the Waverly Sandstone series of Summit County, Ohio, supposed to be of the age of the Chemung Group of New York. < 17*th Ann. Rep. Regents Univ. N. Y. on Condition of State Cabinet*, pp. 50–60. 1864.

See, also, *Paleontology of Ohio (Newberry)*, vol. ii, pp. 162–179.

**Hall, James.** On the occurrence of a convoluted plate within the body of certain species of Crinoidea. < *Proc. Boston Soc. Nat. Hist.*, vol. x, pp. 33, 34. 1865.

**Hall, James.** Observations upon some species of Spirifera, being the concluding remarks of the chapter on the descriptions of species of that genus from the Upper Helderberg, Hamilton, and Chemung Groups. (From the *Paleontology of New York*, vol. iv, pp. 252–257; unpublished.) < *Proc. Am. Philos. Soc.*, vol. x, pp. 246–254. 1866.

Vol. iv has since been published.

**Hall, James.** Paleontology of New York. Vol. iv. pp. 428, 69 plates. 1867.

Devonian. Genera *Productella*, *Meristella*, *Cœlospira*, *Stenocisma* (Conrad), *Leiorhynchus*, *Pentamerella*, *Gypidula* (Dalman), *Amphigenia*, *Cryptonella*, *Tropidoleptus*, *Vitulina*.

**Hall, James.** Notice of vol. iv of the Paleontology of New York; with an enumeration of the species described, and observations on their relation to Carboniferous forms. < *20th Ann. Rep. Regents Univ. N. Y. on Condition of State Cabinet*, pp. 145–168. 1868.

Genera *Gypidula* (Dalman), *Anastrophia*, *Amphigenia*, *Pentamerella*, *Stricklandinia* (Billings).

**Hall, James.** Introduction to the study of the Graptolitidæ. < *20th Ann. Rep. Regents Univ. N. Y. on Condition of State Cabinet*, pp. 169–240, 4 plates. 1868.

**Hall, James.** The genus Chonetes (Fischer). < *20th Ann. Rep. Regents Univ. N. Y. on Condition of State Cabinet*, pp. 242–244. 1868.

**Hall, James.** Remarks on the genera Productus, Strophalosia, Aulosteges, and Productella. < *20th Ann. Rep. Regents Univ. N. Y. on Condition of State Cabinet*, pp. 245–250. 1868.

**Hall, James.** On the genera Spirifera, Cyrtinia, and allied genera. < *20th Ann. Rep. Regents Univ. N. Y. on Condition of State Cabinet*, pp. 251–257. 1868.

**Hall, James.** On the genera Athyris, Merista, and Meristella. < *20th Ann. Rep. Regents Univ. N. Y. on Condition of State Cabinet*, pp. 258–266. 1868.

**Hall, James.** Note on the genus Zygospira, and its relations to Atrypa. < *20th Ann. Rep. Regents Univ. N. Y. on Condition of State Cabinet*, pp. 267, 268. 1868.

**Hall, James.** Remarks upon the genera Rhynchonella and Leiorhynchus. < *20th Ann. Rep. Regents Univ. N. Y. on Condition of State Cabinet*, pp. 269–273. 1868.

**Hall, James.** Note on the genus Eichwaldia (Billings). < *20th Ann. Rep. Regents Univ. N. Y. on Condition of State Cabinet*, pp. 274–278. 1868.

**Hall, James.** On the genus Tropidoleptus. < *20th Ann. Rep. Regents Univ. N. Y. on Condition of State Cabinet*, pp. 279–281. 1868.

**Hall, James.** Note on the genus Palæaster, with descriptions of some new species and observations upon those previously described. < *20th Ann. Rep. Regents Univ. N. Y. on Condition of State Cabinet*, pp. 282–301, 1 plate. 1868.

To this is added notes on the genera *Urasterella* (McCoy), *Protaster* (Forbes), *Petraster* Billings, *Lepidechinus* Hall, *Eocidaris* (Desor), *Agelacrinus* (Vanuxem), *Tæniaster* Billings, *Eugaster* Hall, *Ptilonaster* Hall. The last two genera are new.

# I.—PUBLICATIONS MADE IN THE UNITED STATES. 37

**Hall, James.** Account of some new or little known species of fossils from rocks of the age of the Niagara Group. <20th Ann. Rep. Regents Univ. N. Y. on Condition of State Cabinet, pp. 305-401, 14 plates. 1868.

Genera *Gomphocystites, Holocystites, Echinocystites, Crinocystites.*

**Hall, James.** Description of new species of Crinoidea and other fossils from strata of the age of the Hudson River Group and Trenton Limestone. <24th Ann. Rep. Regents Univ. N. Y. on Condition of State Museum, pp. 205-224. 1872.

Genus *Lichenocrinus.* 4 plates illustrate this and the following articles.

**Hall, James.** Description of new species of fossils from the Hudson River Group in the vicinity of Cincinnati, Ohio. <24th Ann. Rep. Regents Univ. N. Y. on Condition of State Cabinet, pp. 225-232. 1872.

Genus *Leptobolus.* 4 plates illustrate this and the preceding articles.

**Hall, James.** Notice of three new species of fossil shells from the Devonian of Ohio. <23d Ann. Rep. Regents Univ. N. Y. on Condition of State Cabinet, pp. 240, 241. 1873.

There are some unfortunate discrepancies of date on the title-pages of some of these reports. The 23d is dated 1873, while the 24th is dated 1872. See remarks in preface to part I, and also in relation to the *28th Regents Report* on a following page.

**Hall, James.** Notice of two new species of fossil shells from the Potsdam Sandstone of New York. <23d Ann. Rep. Regents Univ. N. Y. on Condition of State Cabinet, pp. 241, 242. 1873.

Genus *Palæacmæa.*

**Hall, James.** Description of Trematis punctostriata and T. rudis. <23d Ann. Rep. Regents Univ. N. Y. on Condition of State Cabinet, p. 243. 1873.

**Hall, James.** Notes on some new or imperfectly known forms among the Brachiopoda, &c. <23d Ann. Rep. Regents Univ. N. Y. on Condition of State Cabinet, pp. 244-247, 1 plate. 1873.

Genera *Lingulops, Discinella, Dicellomus, Dinobolus, Rhynobolus.*

**Hall, James.** Descriptions of Bryozoa and Corals of the Lower Helderberg Group. <26th Ann. Rep. Regents Univ. N. Y. on Condition of State Museum, pp. 93-115. 1874.

Genera *Paleschara, Vermipora.*

**Hall, James.** Descriptions of new species of Goniatitidæ, with a list of previously described species. <27th Ann. Rep. Regents Univ. N. Y. on Condition of State Cabinet, pp. 132-136. 1875.

**Hall, James.** 32 lithogr. plates, illustrating a paper in vol. iv, Trans. Albany Inst., pp. 195-208, 1862, entitled "Notice of some new species of fossils from a locality of the Niagara Group in Indiana, with a list of identified species from the same place". <28th Ann. Rep. Regents Univ. N. Y. on Condition of State Museum. 1877.

This report bears date 1875 on its title-page, but it was not issued until 1877, and then only in very small number of copies. See *Am. Journ. Sci.*, vol. xiv, p. 494; also dates of text.

**Hall, James.** Paleontology of New York. Illustrations of Devonian fossils, Gasteropoda, Pteropoda, Cephalopoda, Crustacea, and Corals of the Upper Helderberg, Hamilton, and Chemung Groups. 1877.

This work is reviewed on page 493, vol. xiv, 3d series, *Am. Journ. Sci.*, but it has not been seen by me (C. A. W.), search for it in the libraries of Washington and Philadelphia having been unsuccessful. Only 100 copies are reported to have been published.

**Hall, James, and F. B. Meek.** Descriptions of new species of fossils from the Cretaceous formations of Nebraska; with observations on Baculites ovatus and B. compressus, and the progressive development of the septa in Baculites, Ammonites, and Scaphites. < *Mem. Am. Acad. Arts and Sci.*, vol. v, new ser., pp. 379–411, 8 plates. 1856.

**Hall, James, and R. P. Whitfield.** Description of new species of fossils from the vicinity of Louisville, Kentucky, and the Falls of the Ohio. < 24th *Ann. Rep. Regents Univ. N. Y. on Condition of State Museum*, pp. 181–200ª. 1872.

Genus *Ptychodesma*. The 27th *Report* contains 5 plates illustrating this article.

**Hall, James, and R. P. Whitfield.** Remarks on some peculiar impressions in the Sandstones of the Chemung Group of New York. < 24th *Ann. Rep. Regents Univ. N. Y. on Condition of State Museum*, pp. 201–204. 1872.

Genus *Hippodophycus*.

**Hall, James, and R. P. Whitfield.** Descriptions of new species of fossils from the Devonian of Iowa. < 23d *Ann. Rep. Regents Univ. N. Y. on Condition of State Cabinet*, pp. 223–239, 5 plates. 1873.

**Hall, James, and R. P. Whitfield.** Descriptions of invertebrate fossils, mainly from the Silurian system. < *Paleontology of Ohio (Newberry)*, vol. ii, pp. 67–161, plates i–ix. 1875.

**Hall, James, and R. P. Whitfield.** Descriptions of Crinoidea from the Waverly Group. < *Paleontology of Ohio (Newberry)*, vol. ii, pp. 162–179, plates xi–xiii. 1875.

**Hall, James, and R. P. Whitfield.** Paleontology. < *U. S. Geol. Expl. 40th Parallel (King)*, part ii, pp. 197–302, 7 plates. 1877.

Silurian, Devonian, Carboniferous, Triassic, Jurassic. Genus *Septocardia*.

**Harlan, Richard.** Critical notices of various organic remains hitherto discovered in North America. < *Trans. Geol. Soc. Penn.*, vol. i, part i. 1834.

The portion referring to invertebrate paleontology is embraced in pp. 95–109, and contains the original description of *Eurypterus lacustris* Harlan, and diagnosis of the genus.

**Harlan, Richard.** Notice of nondescript Trilobites from the State of New York, with some observations on the genus Triarthrus. < *Trans. Geol. Soc. Penn.*, vol. i, part ii, pp. 263–266, 1 plate. 1835.

*Paradoxides triarthrus* and *P. arcuatus*. The author takes the ground that the genus *Triarthrus* was not correctly established, and is therefore obsolete.

**Harger, O.** Notice of a new fossil Spider from the Coalmeasures of Illinois. < *Am. Journ. Sci.*, vol. vii, 3d ser., pp. 219–223. 1874.

Genus *Arthrolycosa*.

**Harper, L.** Description of Ceratites americanus. < *Proc. Acad. Nat. Sci. Phila.*, vol. viii, pp. 126–128, 4 woodcuts. 1856.

**Hartt, C. F., *and* Richard Rathbun.** On the Devonian Trilobites and Mollusks of Ereré, Province of Pará, Brazil. < *Ann. N. Y. Lyceum. Nat. Hist.*, vol. xi, pp. 110–127. 1875.

**Hayden, F. V.** *See* **Meek, F. B.,** *and* **F. V. Hayden.**

**Hitchcock, C. H.** A catalogue of the fossils of the Potsdam Group in North America. < *Proc. Portland Soc. Nat. Hist.*, vol. i, pp. 87–90. 1862.

**Hitchcock, C. H.** Helderberg Corals in New Hampshire. < *Am. Journ. Sci.*, vol. ii, 3d ser., pp. 148, 149. 1871.

The fossils are obscure, but the genera *Favosites* and *Zaphrentis* have been identified by Mr. Billings.

**Hitchcock, E., Jr.** A new fossil shell in the Connecticut River Sandstone. < *Am. Journ. Sci.*, vol. xxii, 2d ser., pp. 239, 240, 1 woodcut. 1856.

The author refers the supposed shell to the *Rudistæ*, and suggests that it belongs to the genus *Sphærulites*.

**Hitchcock, E., *Sen*.** Report on the Geology of Vermont. Vol. i. Part 2. pp. 251–451. 1861.

In the discussion of Hypozoic and Paleozoic strata, Dr. Hitchcock gives figures and descriptions of many Silurian fossils, none of which were new, and also reprints some valuable matter from the publications of Prof. James Hall. Several genera of *Trilobites* and other fossils are here redescribed.

**Holmes, F. S.** *See* **Tuomey, M.,** *and* **F. S. Holmes.**

**Horn, G. H.** *See* **Gabb, W. M.,** *and* **G. H. Horn.**

**Hunt, T. Sterry.** Crinoids injected by silicates. < *Am. Naturalist*, vol. v, pp. 445–447. 1871.

This is an abstract of a communication made by Dr. Hunt to the Montreal Natural History Society, and has important bearing on the question of the animal origin of *Eozoön canadense*.

**Hyatt, Alpheus.** Remarks on the Beatricæ, a new division of Mollusca. < *Am. Journ. Sci.*, vol. xxxix, 2d ser., pp. 261–266. 1865.

Professor Hyatt then regarded the Beatriceæ as Cephalopods, but Professor Shaler states (*Am. Naturalist*, vol. xi, p. 628) that Professor Hyatt has abandoned that view.

**Hyatt, Alpheus.** On the parallelism between the different stages of life in the individual and those in the entire group of the Molluscous order Tetrabranchiata. < *Mem. Bost. Soc. Nat. Hist.*, vol. i, pp. 193–209. 1866.

**Hyatt, Alpheus.** The fossil Cephalopods of the Museum of Comparative Zoölogy, Cambridge, Mass. Vol. i. No. 5. pp. 71–102. 1867.

Professor Hyatt proposes material changes in the classification of the fossil *Cephalopoda*, and in the division of the genera he has made, the following new ones are proposed:—*Ammatoceras, Androgynoceras, Arnioceras, Astroceras, Cæloceras, Coroniceras, Cycloceras, Dactyloceras, Deroceras, Discoceras, Grammoceras, Hildoceras, Hammatoceras, Leioceras, Liparoceras, Microceras, Ophioceras, Pelecoceras, Peronoceras, Phymatoceras, Platypleuroceras, Pleuroceras, Psiloceras, Thysanoceras, Tropidoceras, Rhacoceras.*

**Hyatt, Alpheus.** On reversions among the Ammonites. < *Proc. Boston Soc. Nat. Hist.*, vol. xiv, pp. 22–43. 1870.

Professor Hyatt announces the discovery of a series of reversionary characteristics among the *Ammonitidæ*, which he discusses at some length in connection with several genera.

**Hyatt, Alpheus.** Embryology and development of the shells of Ammonitoids and Nautiloids.  < *Proc. Boston Soc. Nat. Hist.*, vol. xiv, pp. 396–399. 1871.

This paper contains a brief summary of the subject, which the author so fully elaborated afterward in *Bull. Mus. Comp. Zool.*, vol. iii, No. 5.

**Hyatt, Alpheus.** The non-reversionary series of the Liparoceratidæ, and remarks upon the series of the allied family Dactyloidæ.  < *Proc. Boston Soc. Nat. Hist.*, vol. xv, pp. 4–21. 1872.

The author contrasts this series with those discussed in the preceding article.

**Hyatt, Alpheus.** Fossil Cephalopods of the Museum of Comparative Zoology. Embryology.  < *Bull. Mus. Comp. Zool. Cambridge, Mass.*, vol. iii, No. 5, pp. 59–111, 4 double plates. 1872.

Professor Hyatt describes and illustrates embryological features in *Deroceras, Goniatites, Arnioceras, Asteroceras, Nautilus,* and *Argonauta.*

**Hyatt, Alpheus.** Evolution of the Arietidæ.  < *Proc. Boston Soc. Nat. Hist.*, vol. xvi, pp. 166–170. 1873.

The author takes the genus *Arietes* of Von Buch as the "parent form" of the family, and traces the differences and similarities that characterize the species composing the family.

**Hyatt, Alpheus.** Genetic relations of the Angulatidæ.  < *Proc. Boston Soc. Nat. Hist.*, vol. xvii, pp. 15–23. 1874.

This family is one of those into which the *Ammonites* have been divided by the author.

**Hyatt, Alpheus.** Appendix to communications on reversions among the Ammonites.  < *Proc. Boston Soc. Nat. Hist.*, vol. xvii, pp. 23–28. 1874.

See *Proc.*, vol. xiv, p. 22.

**Hyatt, Alpheus.** Appendix to communication on "The non-reversionary series of the Liparoceratidæ, &c."  < *Proc. Boston Soc. Nat. Hist.*, vol. xvii, pp. 29–33. 1874.

See *Proc.*, vol. xv, p. 4.

**Hyatt, Alpheus.** Abstract of a "Memoir on the biological relations of the Jurassic Ammonites".  < *Proc. Boston Soc. Nat. Hist.*, vol. xvii, pp. 236–241. 1874.

**Hyatt, Alpheus.** Remarks on two new genera of Ammonites, Agassiziceras and Oxynoticeras.  < *Proc. Boston Soc. Nat. Hist.*, vol. xvii, pp. 225–234. 1875.

**Hyatt, Alpheus.** Jurassic and Cretaceous Ammonites collected in South America by Prof. James Orton, with an appendix upon the Cretaceous Ammonites of Professor Hartt's collection.  < *Proc. Boston Soc. Nat. Hist.*, vol. xvii, pp. 365–372. 1875.

The author identifies a considerable proportion of these fossils with European species, and describes the new genus *Buchiceras.*

**Hyatt, Alpheus.** Genetic relations of Stephanoceras.  < *Proc. Boston Soc. Nat. Hist.*, vol. xviii, pp. 360–400. 1876.

Professor Hyatt divides the genus *Stephanoceras* of Waagen into ten "series", or sections, besides one doubtful series, to which he refers the *Ammonites refractus* of D'Orb.

# I.—PUBLICATIONS MADE IN THE UNITED STATES. 41

**James, U. P.** On a new species of fossil from the Lower Silurian (Cyrtolites costatus). <*Am. Journ. Sci.*, vol. iii, 3d ser., pp. 26. 1872.

**James, U. P.** Descriptions of new species of Brachiopods, from the Lower Silurian Rocks, Cincinnati Group. < *Cin. Quart. Journ. of Sci.*, pp. 19–22. 1874.

    The *Cincinnati Quarterly Journal of Science* was published by S. A. Miller at Cincinnati, Ohio, for the years 1874 and 1875 only, making vols. I and II complete.

**James, U. P.** Descriptions of one new species of Leptæna and two species of Cyclonema, from the Lower Silurian Rocks,—Cincinnati Group. < *Cin. Quart. Journ. Sci.*, pp. 151–154. 1874.

**James, U. P.** Descriptions of new species of fossils from the Lower Silurian Formation,—Cincinnati Group. < *Cin. Quart. Journ. Sci.*, pp. 239–242. 1874.

**James, U. P.** Descriptions of new species of Brachiopoda, from the Lower Silurian formation,—Cincinnati Group. < *Cin. Quart. Journ. Sci.*, pp. 333–335. 1874.

**James, U. P.** Catalogue of Lower Silurian fossils at Cincinnati, Ohio, and vicinity, with descriptions of some new species of Corals and Polyzoa. Cincinnati, Ohio. Pamphlet. pp. 8. 1875.

    *Chætetes ? calycula, Chætetes clavacoides, Chætetes cincinnatiensis, Chætetes ? o'nealli, Alveolites ? granulosa, Ceramopora nicholsoni, Ptylodictya acuminata, Alecto nezilis.* A previous edition of this catalogue was published, but without any description of species.

**James, U. P., G. Graham,** *and* **J. G. Anthony.** Two species of fossil Asterias in the Blue Limestone of Cincinnati. <*Am. Journ. Sci.*, vol. i, 2d ser., pp. 441, 442. Illustrated. 1846.

    See note by Professor Dana on page 295, vol. xxxv, same series; and also both editions of *Dana's Manual of Geology*.

**Johnson, Alexander S.** Notice of some undescribed Infusorial shells. <*Am. Journ. Sci.*, vol. xiii, 2d ser., p. 33. 1852.

    Genus *Asterodiscus*.

**Lea, Henry Carey.** Descriptions of some new species of fossil shells from the Eocene of Claiborne, Alabama. <*Am. Journ. Sci.*, vol. xl, 1st ser., pp. 92–103, 1 plate. 1841.

**Lea, Henry Carey.** Description of some new fossil shells from the Tertiary of Petersburg, Virginia. < *Trans. Am. Philos. Soc.*, 2d ser., vol. ix, pp. 229–274, 4 plates. 1843.

**Lea, Isaac.** Contributions to Geology. 8°. pp. 227 and 6 plates. 1833.

    The subdivisions of this work are:—1. Tertiary formation of Alabama. 2. Supplement to the same. 3. Tertiary fossil shells from Maryland and New Jersey. 4. New genus of fossil shells from New Jersey (*Palmula*; Cretaceous).

**Lea, Isaac.** On some new fossil Mollusks in the Carboniferous Slates of the Anthracite seams of the Wilkesbarre Coal formation. < *Journ. Acad. Nat. Sci. Phila.*, vol. ii, 2d ser., pp. 203–206, 1 plate. 1853.

**Lea, Isaac.** Descriptions of new fossil Mollusca, from the Cretaceous formation at Haddonfield, New Jersey. < *Proc. Acad. Nat. Sci. Phila.*, vol. v, 2d ser., pp. 148–150. 1861.

**Lea, Isaac.** Descriptions of Unionidæ, from the Lower Cretaceous formation of New Jersey. < *Proc. Acad. Nat. Sci. Phila.*, vol. xii, 2d ser., pp. 162–164. 1868.

**Le Sueur, C. A.** Observations on a new genus of fossil shells. < *Journ. Acad. Nat. Sci. Phila.*, 1st ser., vol. i, pp. 312, 313, 1 plate. 1818.

<small>Genus *Maclurite*. Since changed by common consent and custom to *Maclurea*.</small>

**Locke, John.** On a new species of Trilobite of very large size. < *Am. Journ. Sci.*, vol. xlii, 1st ser., pp. 366–368, 1 plate. 1842.

<small>*Isotelus megistos*. Also published in *Trans. Assoc. Am. Geol. & Nat.*, vol. i, pp. 221–224.</small>

**Locke, John.** On the fossil Cryptolithus tesselatus. < *Proc. Acad. Nat. Sci. Phila.*, vol. i, pp. 196, 197. 1842.

<small>Further observations on the same, with one woodcut, p. 236. (1843.) This *Trilobite* is from the Lower Silurian strata at Cincinnati, Ohio.</small>

**Locke, John.** Notice of a new Trilobite. < *Am. Journ. Sci.*, vol. xliv, 1st ser., p. 346, 1 woodcut. 1843.

<small>*Ceraurus crosotus*.</small>

**Locke, John.** On a new species of Trilobite of very large size < *Trans. Assoc. Am. Geol. & Nat.*, vol. i, pp. 221–224, 1 plate. 1843.

<small>*Isotelus megistos*. Also published in *Am. Journ. Sci.*, vol. xlii, 1st ser., pp. 366–368.</small>

**Logan, W. E.** On organic remains in the Laurentian rocks of Canada. < *Am. Journ. Sci.*, vol. xxxvii, 2d ser., pp. 272, 273. 1864.

<small>This is one of the earlier announcements of the existence of the fossil now known as *Eozoön canadense*.</small>

**Logan, W. E.,** *and* **T. S. Hunt.** On the composition of recent and fossil Lingulæ and some other shells. < *Am. Journ. Sci.*, vol. xvii, 2d ser., pp. 235–239. 1854.

**Lonsdale, W.** Remarks on the characters of several species of Tertiary Corals from the United States, in reply to Mr. Dana. < *Am. Journ. Sci.*, vol. iv, 2d ser., pp. 357–359. 1847.

<small>For the article replied to see *Am. Journ. Sci.*, vol. i, 2d ser., p. 220.</small>

**Lyell, Charles.** On the discovery of some Reptilian remains, and a land shell in the interior of an erect fossil tree in the Coal Measures of Nova Scotia, with remarks on the origin of coal-fields, and the time required for their formation. < *Am. Journ. Sci.*, vol. xvi, 2d ser., pp. 33–41. 1853.

<small>Reprinted from *Proc. Royal Soc. of Great Britain.*</small>

**Lyon, Sidney S.** Description of new species of organic remains. < *Kentucky Geological Survey (Owen)*, vol. iii, pp. 467–498, 5 plates. 1857.

<small>The plates are in a fascicle separate from the volume. Genera *Asterocrinus*, *Dolatocrinus*, *Vasocrinus*. Devonian and Carboniferous.</small>

**Lyon, Sidney S.** Descriptions of four new species of Blastoidea, from the Subcarboniferous rocks of Kentucky. < *Trans. St. Louis Acad. Sci.*, vol. i, pp. 628–634, 1 plate. 1860.

**Lyon, Sidney S.** Descriptions of new Paleozoic fossils from Kentucky and Indiana. < *Proc. Acad. Nat. Sci. Phila.*, vol. v, 2d ser., pp. 409–414, 1 plate. 1861.

**Lyon, Sidney S.** Remarks on thirteen new species of Crinoidea from the Paleozoic Rocks of Indiana, Kentucky, and Ohio, and a description of certain peculiarities in the structure of the columns of Dolatocrinus, and their attachment to the body of the animal. < *Trans. Am. Philos. Soc.,* vol. xviii, pp. 443-466, 2 plates. 1869.

Genera *Hadrocrinus, Ataxiacrinus.*

**Lyon, Sidney S.**, *and* **S. A. Casseday.** Description of nine new species of Crinoidea from the Subcarboniferous rocks of Indiana and Kentucky. < *Am. Journ. Sci.,* vol. xxviii, 2d ser., pp. 233-246. 1859.

Genera *Goniasteroidocrinus, Eretmocrinus.* Vol. xxix contains an article by these authors having the same title, but the article is wholly different.

**Lyon, Sidney S.**, *and* **S. A. Casseday.** Description of nine new species of Crinoidea, from the Subcarboniferous rocks of Indiana and Kentucky. < *Am. Journ. Sci.,* vol. xxix, 2d ser., pp. 68-79. 1860.

Genus *Onychocrinus.* Vol. xxviii contains an article by these authors having the same title, but the article is entirely different.

**Lyon, Sidney S.**, *and* **S. A. Casseday.** A synonymic list of the Echinodermata of the Paleozoic Rocks of North America. < *Proc. Am. Acad. Arts & Sci. Boston,* vol. iv, pp. 282-304. 1859.

**Lyon, Sidney S.**, *and* **S. A. Casseday.** Description of two new genera and eight new species of fossil Crinoidea. < *Proc. Am. Acad. Arts & Sci. Boston,* vol. v, pp. 16-31. 1860.

Genera *Cotyledonocrinus, Alloprosallocrinus.*

**Marsh, O. C.** On the Palæotrochis of Emmons, from North Carolina. < *Am. Journ. Sci.,* vol. xlv, 2d ser., pp. 217-219. 1868.

Professor Marsh takes the view that these bodies are wholly of mineral, and not of organic origin.

**Marsh, O. C.** Description of a new species of Protichnites, from the Potsdam Sandstone of New York. < *Am. Journ. Sci.,* vol. xlviii, 2d ser., pp. 46-49, 1 plate. 1869.

**Marsh, O. C.** Description of a new species of Protichnites from the Potsdam Sandstone of New York. < *Proc. Am. Assoc. Adv. Sci.,* vol. xvii, pp. 322-324. 1869.

**Marsh, O. C.** On the preservation of color in fossils from Paleozoic formations. < *Proc. Am. Assoc. Adv. Sci.,* vol. xvii, pp. 325, 326. 1869.

**McChesney, J. H.** Descriptions of fossils from the Paleozoic Rocks of the Western States, with illustrations. < *Trans. Chicago Acad. Sci.,* vol. i, pp. 1-57, plates 1-9. 1869.

This work was published as a separate paper, under the auspices of the academy, in 1859, and afterward revised by the author and F. B. Meek, and republished as above.

**Meek, F. B.** Description of new organic remains from the Cretaceous rocks of Vancouver's Island. < *Trans. Albany Inst.,* vol. iv, pp. 37-49. 1856.

The fossils here described were collected by Dr. J. S. Newberry, geologist of Lieutenant Williamson's North California and Oregon Exploring Expedition.

**Meek, F. B.** Descriptions of new fossil remains collected in Nebraska and Utah by the exploring expeditions under the command of Capt. J. H. Simpson, of the U. S. Topographical Engineers. (Extracted from that officer's forthcoming report.) < *Proc. Acad. Nat. Sci. Phila.*, vol. iv, 2d ser., pp. 308–315. 1860.

Devonian, Carboniferous, Jurassic, Cretaceous, and Tertiary. Republished with illustrations in a quarto volume of Captain Simpson's Reports, in 1876.

**Meek, F. B.** Descriptions of new Cretaceous fossils collected by the Northwestern Boundary Commission on Vancouver's and Sucia Islands. < *Proc. Acad. Nat. Sci. Phila.*, vol. v, 2d ser., pp. 314–318. 1861.

**Meek, F. B.** Remarks on the family Actæonidæ, with descriptions of some new genera and subgenera. < *Am. Journ. Sci.*, vol. xxxv, 2d ser., pp. 84–94. 1863.

Genera *Trochactæon, Euconactæon, Aptycha.* The author makes two divisions of the family, namely, *Acteoninæ* and *Ringiculinæ.*

**Meek, F. B.** Remarks on the family Pteriidæ (= Aviculidæ), with descriptions of some new fossil genera. < *Am. Journ. Sci.*, vol. xxxvii, 2d ser., pp. 212–220. 1864.

Genera *Gryphorhynchus, Eumicrotis.*

**Meek, F. B.** Check lists of the Invertebrate fossils of North America. Cretaceous and Jurassic. < *Smithsonian Miscellaneous Publications* (No. 177), pp. 1–40. 1864.

Contains, besides list, "Notes and explanations" of generic and specific characters, of much importance.

**Meek, F. B.** Check lists of the Invertebrate fossils of North America. Miocene. < *Smithsonian Miscellaneous Publications* (No. 183), pp. 1–32. 1864.

Contains, besides the list, "Notes and explanations" of generic and specific characters.

**Meek, F. B.** Description of Carboniferous and Jurassic fossils. < *Paleontology of California* (*Whitney*), vol. i, pp. 1–16, 2 plates. 1864.

Genus *Omphalotrochus.*

**Meek, F. B.** Preliminary notice of a small collection of fossils found by Dr. Hays (Hayes) on the west shore of Kennedy Channel, at the highest northern localities ever explored. < *Am. Journ. Sci.*, vol. xl, 2d ser., pp. 31–34. 1865.

Upper Silurian.

**Meek, F. B.** Note on the genus Gilbertsocrinus, Phillips. < *Proc. Acad. Nat. Sci. Phila.*, vol. ix, 2d ser., pp. 166–167. 1865.

The author takes the ground that the difference between *Gilbertsocrinus* Phillips, *Goniasteroidocrinus* Lyon & Casseday, and *Trematocrinus* Hall is at most not more than subgeneric.

**Meek, F. B.** Observations on the microscopic shell structure of Spirifer cuspidatus, Sowerby, and some similar American forms. < *Proc. Acad. Nat. Sci. Phila.*, vol. ix, 2d ser., pp. 275–277. 1865.

**Meek, F. B.** Note on the affinities of the Bellerophontidæ. < *Proc. Chicago Acad. of Sci.*, pp. 9–11. 1866.

The author places this family near *Fissurellida, Haliotida,* and *Pleurotomariida.*

# I.—PUBLICATIONS MADE IN THE UNITED STATES.

**Meek, F. B.** Note on Bellinurus danæ, from the Illinois Coal-measures. <*Am. Journ. Sci.*, vol. xliii, 2d ser., pp. 257, 258. 1867.

> In this note, the author expresses the opinion that *Bellinurus danæ* Meek and Worthen properly belongs to the recently proposed genus *Prestwichia* Woodward.

**Meek, F. B.** Note on a new genus of Crustacea. <*Am. Journ. Sci.*, vol. xliii, 2d ser., pp. 394, 395. 1867.

> Genus *Euproöps*. This genus was afterward fully described and illustrated in vol. III of *Worthen's Illinois Geological Reports*.

**Meek, F. B.** Note on the punctate shell-structure of Syringothyris. <*Am. Journ. Sci.*, vol. xliii, 2d ser., pp. 407, 408. 1867.

**Meek, F. B.** Remarks on Professor Geinitz's views respecting Upper Paleozoic rocks and fossils of Southeastern Nebraska. <*Am. Journ. Sci.*, vol. xliv, 2d ser., pp. 170–187; continued, pp. 327–339; note to the same, pp. 282, 283. 1867.

> This is an extended discussion and criticism of Dr. Geinitz's "Carbonformation und Dyas in Nebraska".

**Meek, F. B.** Note on the genus Palæacis, Haime, 1860 (= Sphenopoterium, M. & W., 1866). <*Am. Journ. Sci.*, vol. xliv, 2d ser., pp. 419, 420. 1867.

> The author here takes the view that *Sphenopoterium*, originally published in the *Illinois Geol. Reports*, is identical with *Palæacis*.

**Meek, F. B.** Preliminary notice of a remarkable new genus of Corals, probably typical of a new family; forwarded for study by Prof. J. D. Whitney, from the Silurian Rocks of Nevada Territory. <*Am. Journ. Sci.*, vol. xlv, 2d ser., pp. 62–64. 1868.

> Genus *Ethmophyllum*.

**Meek, F. B.** Note on Ethmophyllum and Archeocyathus. <*Am. Journ. Sci.*, vol. xlvi, 2d ser., p. 144. 1868.

> The author abandons his formerly proposed genus *Ethmophyllum*, believing it to be identical with *Archeocyathus* of Billings.

**Meek, F. B.** Note on the shell-structure and family affinities of the genus Aviculopecten. <*Am. Journ. Sci.*, vol. xlv, 2d ser., pp. 64, 65. 1868.

> The author shows that by the shell-structure the Aviculopectens are allied to *Avicula* rather than to *Pecten*.

**Meek, F. B.** Remarks on the geology of the Valley of Mackenzie River, with figures and descriptions of fossils from that region, in the Museum of the Smithsonian Institution, chiefly collected by the late Robert Kennicott, esq. <*Trans. Chicago Acad. of Sci.*, vol. i, pp. 61–114, plates xi–xv. 1869.

> Devonian.

**Meek, F. B.** Descriptions of fossils collected by the U. S. Geological Survey, under the charge of Clarence King, esq. <*Proc. Acad. Nat. Sci. Phila.*, vol. xiv, 2d ser., pp. 56–64. 1870.

> Silurian, Devonian, and Tertiary. Afterward republished and illustrated in vol. iv of Mr. King's series of final reports, 1877.

**Meek, F. B.** A preliminary list of fossils collected by Dr. Hayden in Colorado, New Mexico, and California, with brief descriptions of a few new species. <*Proc. Am. Philos. Soc.*, vol. xi, pp. 425–431. 1870.

> Silurian, Carboniferous, Jurassic, Cretaceous, and Tertiary.

46   BIBLIOGRAPHY OF INVERTEBRATE PALEONTOLOGY.

**Meek, F. B.**   Preliminary notice of a new species of Trimerella from Ohio.
< *Am. Journ. Sci.*, vol. i, 3d ser., pp. 305, 306.   1871.

*Trimerella ohioensis.*   Republished and illustrated in *Paleontology of Ohio (Newberry).*

**Meek, F. B.**   On some new Silurian Crinoids and Shells.   < *Am. Journ. Sci.*, vol. ii, 3d ser., pp. 295-302.   1871.

This article consists of descriptions of species, together with some extended remarks on the genus *Lichenocrinus* of Hall.

**Meek, F. B.**   Descriptions of new species of Invertebrate fossils, from the Carboniferous and Devonian of Ohio.   < *Proc. Acad. Nat. Sci. Phila.*, vol. i, 3d ser., pp. 57-93.   1871.

Afterward republished and illustrated in the *Paleontology of Ohio (Newberry).*

**Meek, F. B.**   Descriptions of new species of fossils from Ohio and other Western States and Territories.   < *Proc. Acad. Nat. Sci. Phila.*, vol. i, 3d ser., pp. 159-184.   1871.

This paper contains descriptions of fossils, mostly Carboniferous, from Ohio, Illinois, and Texas, with a *Melantho* and *Viviparus* from Wyoming.

**Meek, F. B.**   Notice of a new Brachiopod, from the lead-bearing rocks at Mine La Motte, Missouri.   < *Proc. Acad. Nat. Sci. Phila.*, vol. i, 3d ser., pp. 185-187, 4 woodcuts.   1871.

*Lingulella lamborni.*

**Meek, F. B.**   Descriptions of new Western Paleozoic fossils, mainly from the Cincinnati Group of the Lower Silurian series of Ohio.   < *Proc. Acad. Nat. Sci. Phila.*, vol. i, 3d ser., pp. 308-336.   1871.

Afterward redescribed and illustrated in the *Paleontology of Ohio (Newberry).*

**Meek, F. B.**   Descriptions of some new types of Paleozoic shells.   < *Am. Journ. Conch.*, vol. vii, pp. 4-10, 1 plate.   1871.

Carboniferous and Cretaceous?   Genera *Promacrus, Prothyris.*

**Meek, F. B.**   List of Carboniferous fossils from West Virginia, with descriptions of new species.   < *Appendix "B", Report of Regents of West Virginia University for* 1870, pp. 68-70.   1871.

New species:—*Macrodon obsoletus, Nucula ? anodontoides, Yoldia stevensoni, Yoldia carbonaria, Phillipsia stevensoni.*

**Meek, F. B.**   Supplementary note on the genus Lichenocrinus.   < *Am. Journ. Sci.*, vol. iii, 3d ser., pp. 15-17.   1872.

This is supplementary to the article at page 299 of vol. ii.

**Meek, F. B.**   Descriptions of two new Starfishes and a Crinoid from the Cincinnati Group of Ohio and Indiana.   < *Am. Journ. Sci.*, vol. iii, 3d ser., pp. 257-262.   1872.

These descriptions, with illustrations, are republished in the *Paleontology of Ohio (Newberry).*

**Meek, F. B.**   Descriptions of new species of fossils from the Cincinnati Group of Ohio.   < *Am. Journ. Sci.*, vol. iii, 3d ser., pp. 423-428.   1872.

These are since redescribed and figured in the *Paleontology of Ohio (Newberry).*

**Meek, F. B.** Descriptions of a few new species and one new genus of Silurian fossils from Ohio. < *Am. Journ. Sci.*, vol. iv, 3d ser., pp. 274-281. 1872.

    Genus *Dicraniscus*. Afterward fully described and illustrated in the *Paleontology of Ohio* (*Newberry*).

**Meek, F. B.** Preliminary Paleontological report, consisting of lists of fossils, with descriptions of some new types, &c. < *Hayden's Prelim. Rep. U. S. Geol. Surv. of Wyom. and Portions of Contig. Terr.*, pp. 287-318. 1872.

    Silurian, Carboniferous, Jurassic, Cretaceous, and Tertiary. Genera *Arcopagella, Crassatellina, Leptesthes, Pyrgulifera*. The latter is only named here. The genus is described in vol. iv of *Geological Expl. of the 40th Parallel* (*Clarence King*).

**Meek, F. B.** Preliminary list of fossils collected by Dr. Hayden's Exploring Expedition of 1871 in Utah and Wyoming Territories, with descriptions of a few new species. < *U. S. Geol. Surv. of Montana and Adjacent Terr., Report for* 1871, pp. 373-377. 1872.

    Silurian, Carboniferous, Jurassic, Cretaceous, and Tertiary.

**Meek, F. B.** Report on the Paleontology of Eastern Nebraska; with some remarks on the Carboniferous rocks of that district. < *Hayden's Final Rep. of the U. S. Geol. Surv. of Nebraska*, pp. 83-264, 11 plates. 1872.

    Carboniferous fossils only. Genera *Rhombopora, Entolium*.

**Meek, F. B.** Spergen Hill fossils identified among specimens from Idaho. < *Am. Journ. Sci.*, vol. v, 3d ser., pp. 383, 384. 1873.

    The author identifies, among some collections made by Prof. F. H. Bradley, some of the minute species of *Mollusca*, for which the locality in Washington County, Indiana, known as "Spergen Hill", is noted.

**Meek, F. B.** Preliminary Paleontological report; consisting of lists of fossils, with remarks on the ages of the rocks in which they were found, &c., &c. < *Hayden's Sixth Ann. Report of the U. S. Geol. Survey of the Terr.*, pp. 431-518. 1873.

    Silurian, Carboniferous, Jurassic, Cretaceous, and Tertiary. Genera *Admetopsis, Velatella*.

**Meek, F. B.** Descriptions of Invertebrate fossils of the Silurian and Devonian systems. < *Paleontology of Ohio* (*Newberry*), vol. i, pp. 1-243, plates 1-22, and 3 plates of diagrams of Crinoids. 1873.

**Meek, F. B.** Notes on some of the fossils figured in the recently issued fifth volume of the Illinois State Geological Report. < *Am. Journ. Sci.*, vol. vii, 3d ser., pp. 189-193 ; continued on pp. 369-376, and 484-490, and 580-584. 1874.

    In this series of articles, Mr. Meek revises and extends the descriptions of a large number of the species embraced in the fifth volume of *Ill. Geol. Rep.*, and also presents some very important philosophical discussions of the relations of the species and of the higher groups.

**Meek, F. B.** The new genus Euchondria. < *Am. Journ. Sci.*, vol. vii, 2d ser., p. 445. 1874.

    Mr. Meek, in a brief note, proposes the generic name *Euchondria*, of which the *Pecten æglectus* of Geinitz is the type.

**Meek, F. B.** Description of Pleurotomaria taggerti. < *Hayden's Ann. Rep. U. S. Geol. and Geog. Survey of the Terr. for* 1873, p. 231, foot-note. 1874.

Carboniferous.

**Meek, F. B.** Notes on some fossils from near the eastern base of the Rocky Mountains, west of Greeley and Evans, Colorado, and others from about 200 miles further eastward; with descriptions of a few new species. < *Bulletin U. S. Geol. and Geog. Surv. of the Terr.*, 2d ser., No. 1, pp. 39–47. 1875.

These fossils are from the Fox Hills and Laramie (Lignitic) Groups.

**Meek, F. B.** Description of Unios, supposed to be of Triassic age. < *Wheeler's Ann. Rep. Expl. and Surv. West of the 100th Merid.*, pp. 83, 84. 1875.

**Meek, F. B.** Description of Olenellus gilberti and O. howelli. < *Wheeler's Expl. and Surv. West of the 100th Merid.*, vol. iii, *Geology*, pp. 182, 183. 1875.

These two species are fully described and illustrated in *White's Report on Invertebrate Paleontology*, part 1, vol. iv, *Wheeler's Expl. and Surv. West of the 100th Meridian*.

**Meek, F. B.** Descriptions of the Invertebrate fossils from the Carboniferous System. < *Paleontology of Ohio (Newberry),* vol. ii, pp. 269–347, plates 10, 14, 15, 16, 17, 18, 19, and 20. 1875.

**Meek, F. B.** Notice of a very large Goniatite from Eastern Kansas. (Carboniferous.) < *Bulletin U. S. Geol. and Geog. Surv. of the Terr.*, No. 6, 2d ser., vol. i, p. 445. 1876.

The author regards it as at most only a variety of *G. globosus* Meek & Worthen, although attaining so great size.

**Meek, F. B.** Descriptions and illustrations of fossils from Vancouver's and Sucia Islands, and other Northwestern localities. < *Bulletin U. S. Geol. and Geog. Surv. of the Terr.*, vol. ii, No. 4, pp. 351–374, 6 plates. 1876.

Carboniferous, Cretaceous, and Tertiary; mostly Cretaceous. A large part of the species embraced in this paper were originally described by the author in 1856, in vol. iv of *Trans. Albany Institute*, and are here redescribed with others, and illustrated.

**Meek, F. B.** Note on the new genus Uintacrinus, Grinnell. < *Bulletin U. S. Geol. and Geog. Surv. of the Terr.*, vol. ii, No. 4, pp. 375–378, 2 woodcuts. 1876.

This paper consists largely of a redescription and rectification of the genus.

**Meek, F. B.** Descriptions of Cretaceous fossils. < *Report of Capt. Macomb's Expl. Exped. from Santa Fé to the Junction of the Grand and Green Rivers*, pp. 121–133, 2 plates. 1876.

The exploration was made in 1859, but the report was not published until 1876, when Mr. Meek revised the work, in accordance with his views at the time of publication.

**Meek, F. B.** Report on the Paleontological collections. < *Capt. Simpson's Report Expl. Great Basin of the Terr. of Utah*, Appendix J, pp. 339–373, plates 1–5. 1876.

Devonian, Carboniferous, Jurassic, Cretaceous, and Tertiary. The explorations were made and the fossils collected nearly eighteen years before the publication of this report; but the paleontology was corrected in accordance with the views of the author at the time of publication.

# I.—PUBLICATIONS MADE IN THE UNITED STATES. 49

**Meek, F. B.** A report on the Invertebrate Cretaceous and Tertiary Fossils of the Upper Missouri country. <*Hayden's U. S. Geol. Surv. of the Terr.*, vol. ix, pp. i–lxiv, 1–629, 45 plates, 45 ll. 4°. Washington: Government Printing Office. 1876.

This great work contains descriptions and illustrations of nearly 300 species; more than 200 genera and subgenera are fully diagnosed; besides which full diagnoses of the families which embrace them are given. Also philosophical discussion of many important questions. The greater part of the species embraced in this volume were previously, from time to time, described and published, mainly in the publications of the *Acad. Nat. Sci. Phila.*

**Meek, F. B.** Paleontology. <*U. S. Geol. Expl. 40th Parallel (King)*, part i, pp. 1–197, 17 plates. 1877.

Silurian, Devonian, Carboniferous, Triassic, Jurassic, Cretaceous, Tertiary. Genera *Entomoceras* (Hyatt), *Eudiscoceras* (Hyatt), *Polyrhytis*, *Rhytophorus*, *Pyrgulifera*.

**Meek, F. B.,** *and* **F. V. Hayden.** Descriptions of new species of Gasteropoda, from the Cretaceous formations of Nebraska Territory. <*Proc. Acad. Nat. Sci. Phila.*, vol. viii, pp. 63–69. 1856.

**Meek, F. B.,** *and* **F. V. Hayden.** Descriptions of new species of Gasteropoda and Cephalopoda, from the Cretaceous formations of Nebraska Territory. <*Proc. Acad. Nat. Sci. Phila.*, vol. viii, pp. 70–72. 1856.

**Meek, F. B.,** *and* **F. V. Hayden.** Descriptions of twenty-eight new species of Acephala and one Gasteropod, from the Cretaceous formations of Nebraska Territory. <*Proc. Acad. Nat. Sci. Phila.*, vol. viii, pp. 81–87. 1856.

**Meek, F. B.,** *and* **F. V. Hayden.** Descriptions of new species of Acephala and Gasteropoda, from the Tertiary formations of Nebraska Territory; with some general remarks on the geology of the country about the sources of the Missouri River. <*Proc. Acad. Nat. Sci. Phila.*, vol. viii, pp. 111–126. 1856.

**Meek, F. B.,** *and* **F. V. Hayden.** Descriptions of new fossil species of Mollusca, collected by Dr. F. V. Hayden in Nebraska Territory, together with a complete catalogue of all the remains of Invertebrata hitherto described and identified from the Cretaceous and Tertiary formations of that region. <*Proc. Acad. Nat. Sci. Phila.*, vol. viii, pp. 265–286. 1856.

**Meek, F. B.,** *and* **F. V. Hayden.** Descriptions of new species and genera of fossils collected by Dr. F. V. Hayden in Nebraska Territory, under the direction of Lieut. G. K. Warren, U. S. Topographical Engineers; with some remarks on the Tertiary and Cretaceous formations of the Northwest, and the parallelism of the latter with those of other portions of the United States and Territories. <*Proc. Acad. Nat. Sci. Phila.*, 2d ser., vol. i, pp. 117–148. 1857.

Genera *Pseudobuccinum*, *Corbulamella*.

**Meek, F. B.,** *and* **F. V. Hayden.** Note on fossils of Nebraska. (Letter to Lieut. G. K. Warren.) <*Am. Journ. Sci.*, vol. xxv, 2d ser., pp. 439–442. 1858.

This article is mainly geological, but the fossils which characterize the formations that are discussed are enumerated.

**Meek, F. B., and F. V. Hayden.** Descriptions of new organic remains collected in Nebraska Territory in the year 1857 by Dr. F. V. Hayden, geologist to the Exploring Expedition under the command of Lieut. G. K. Warren, Topographical Engineer, U. S. Army; together with some remarks on the geology of the Black Hills and portions of the surrounding country. < *Proc. Acad. Nat. Sci. Phila.*, vol. ii, 2d ser., pp. 41–59. 1858.

Jurassic. Afterward republished and illustrated, in 1865, in *Paleontology of the Upper Missouri, Smithsonian Contributions to Knowledge*.

**Meek, F. B., and F. V. Hayden.** Remarks on the Lower Cretaceous beds of Kansas and Nebraska, together with descriptions of Carboniferous fossils from the Valley of Kansas River. < *Proc. Acad. Nat. Sci. Phila.*, vol. ii, 2d ser., pp. 256–264. 1858.

**Meek, F. B., and F. V. Hayden.** Descriptions of new organic remains from North Eastern Kansas, indicating the existence of Permian rocks in that Territory. < *Trans. Albany Institute*, vol. iv, pp. 73–88. 1858.

This includes a note in relation to the priority of discovery of these fossils of Permian type

**Meek, F. B., and F. V. Hayden.** Geological explorations in Kansas Territory, including "List of the species mentioned in this paper, with some remarks on the synonymy, and references to the works in which they are described". < *Proc. Acad. Nat. Sci. Phila.*, vol. iii, 2d ser., pp. 8–30. 1859.

**Meek, F. B., and F. V. Hayden.** On a new genus of Patelliform shells from the Cretaceous rocks of Nebraska. < *Am. Journ. Sci.*, vol. xxix, 2d ser., pp. 33–35, 1 plate. 1860.

Genus *Anisomyon*.

**Meek, F. B., and F. V. Hayden.** Descriptions of new organic remains from the Tertiary, Cretaceous, and Jurassic rocks of Nebraska. < *Proc. Acad. Nat. Sci. Phila.*, vol. iv, 2d ser., pp. 175–184. 1860.

A description of the Carboniferous species *Myalina aviculoides* is also added; also a corrected list of fossils.

**Meek, F. B., and F. V. Hayden.** Systematic catalogue, with synonyma, &c., of Jurassic, Cretaceous, and Tertiary fossils collected in Nebraska by the Exploring Expeditions under the command of Lieut. G. K. Warren, of U. S. Topographical Engineers. < *Proc. Acad. Nat. Sci. Phila.*, vol. iv, 2d ser., pp. 417–432. 1860.

**Meek, F. B., and F. V. Hayden.** Descriptions of new Lower Silurian (Primodial), Jurassic, Cretaceous, and Tertiary fossils, collected in Nebraska by the Exploring Expedition under the command of Capt. Wm. F. Raynolds, U. S. Topographical Engineers, with some remarks on the rocks from which they were obtained. < *Proc. Acad. Nat. Sci. Phila.*, vol. v, 2d ser., pp. 415–447. 1861.

**Meek, F. B., and F. V. Hayden.** Descriptions of new Cretaceous fossils from Nebraska Territory, collected by the expedition sent out by the government under the command of Lieut. John Mullan, U. S. Topographical Engineers, for the location of a wagon-road from the sources of the Missouri to the Pacific Ocean. < *Proc. Acad. Nat. Sci. Phila.*, vol. vi, 2d ser., pp. 21–28. 1862.

## I.—PUBLICATIONS MADE IN THE UNITED STATES.

**Meek, F. B.,** and **F. V. Hayden.** Paleontology of the Upper Missouri. <*Smithsonian Contributions to Knowledge* (172), pp. 1-135, 5 plates. 1864.

Primordial, Carboniferous, Permian, and Jurassic. Genera *Camptonectes, Lioplacodes, Eumicrotis, Chænomya*. This work contains descriptions of new *fresh-water* Jurassic species, the first of that age discovered in North America. The work has additional importance in consequence of the philosophical discussion of important questions.

**Meek, F. B.,** and **A. H. Worthen.** Descriptions of new Carboniferous fossils from Illinois and other Western States. < *Proc. Acad. Nat. Sci. Phila.*, vol. iv, 2d ser., pp. 447-472. 1860.

Genera *Sphenopoterium, Soleniscus.* Afterward republished in the *Illinois Geological Reports*, vol. II.

**Meek, F. B.,** and **A. H. Worthen.** Descriptions of new species of Crinoidea and Echinoidea, from the Carboniferous rocks of Illinois and other Western States. < *Proc. Acad. Nat. Sci. Phila.*, vol. iv, 2d ser., pp. 379-397. 1860.

Afterward republished in the *Illinois Geological Reports*, vol. II.

**Meek, F. B.,** and **A. H. Worthen.** Remarks on the age of the Goniatite Limestone at Rockford, Indiana, and its relation to the "Black Slate" of the Western States, and to some of the succeeding rocks above the latter. < *Am. Journ. Sci.*, vol. xxxii, 2d ser., pp. 167-177. 1861.

**Meek, F. B.,** and **A. H. Worthen.** Descriptions of new Paleozoic fossils from Illinois and Iowa. < *Proc. Acad. Nat. Sci. Phila.*, vol. v, 2d ser., pp. 128-148. 1861.

Genera *Bursacrinus, Cardiopsis, Orthonema.* Afterward republished in the *Illinois Geological Reports*, vol. II.

**Meek, F. B.,** and **A. H. Worthen.** Note in relation to a genus of Crinoids from the Coalmeasures of Illinois and Nebraska, proposed on page 174 of this volume of the Journal. < *Am. Journ. Sci.*, vol. xxxix, 2d ser., p. 350. 1865.

The authors regard their genus *Erisocrinus* as identical with *Philocrinus* de Koninck.

**Meek, F. B.,** and **A. H. Worthen.** Notice of some new types of organic remains, from the Coal Measures of Illinois. < *Proc. Acad. Nat. Sci. Phila.*, vol. ix, 2d ser., pp. 41-53. 1865.

Genera *Acanthotelson, Palæocaris, Anthracerpes, Palæocampa.* Afterward republished and illustrated in vol. III of the *Illinois Geological Reports.*

**Meek, F. B.,** and **A. H. Worthen.** Remarks on the genus Taxocrinus (Phillips) McCoy, 1844; and its relations to Forbesocrinus, de Koninck and Le Hon, 1854, with descriptions of new species. < *Proc. Acad. Nat. Sci. Phila.*, vol. ix, 2d ser., pp. 138-143. 1865.

Republished in vol. II of the *Illinois Geological Reports.*

**Meek, F. B.,** and **A. H. Worthen.** Descriptions of new species of Crinoidea, &c., from the Paleozoic rocks of Illinois and some of the adjoining States. < *Proc. Acad. Nat. Sci. Phila.*, vol. ix, 2d ser., pp. 143-155. 1865.

A "note in regard to the name 'Cincinnati Group', used in the foregoing paper" is appended on p. 155. The descriptions are republished and the views restated in the *Illinois Geological Reports*, vol. I.

**Meek, F. B., and A. H. Worthen.** Contributions to the Paleontology of Illinois and other Western States. < *Proc. Acad. Nat. Sci. Phila.,* vol. ix, 2d ser., pp. 245-273. 1865.

> Silurian, Devonian, and Carboniferous. Genus *Endolobus*. Afterward republished in the *Illinois Geological Reports,* vol. ii.

**Meek, F. B., and A. H. Worthen.** Contributions to the Paleontology of Illinois and other Western States. < *Proc. Acad. Nat. Sci. Phila.,* vol. x, 2d ser., pp. 251-275. 1866.

> Carboniferous. Genera *Steganocrinus, Strotocrinus, Anomphalus*. Afterward republished and illustrated in the *Illinois Geological Reports*.

**Meek, F. B., and A. H. Worthen.** Descriptions of Paleozoic fossils from the Silurian, Devonian, and Carboniferous Rocks of Illinois and other Western States. < *Proc. Chicago Acad. Sci.,* pp. 11, 23. 1866.

> Genera *Monopteria, Megaptera*. Afterward republished in the *Illinois Geological Reports,* vol. ii.

**Meek, F. B., and A. H. Worthen.** Descriptions of Invertebrates from the Carboniferous System. < *Worthen's Geological Survey of Illinois,* vol. ii, pp. 145-411, plates 14-20, and 23-32. 1866.

> Genera *Sphenopoterium, Cardiopsis, Trematodiscus, Strotocrinus, Steganocrinus, Calocrinus, Oligoporus, Erisocrinus, Syntrielasma, Eumicrotis, Trachydomia, Orthonema, Soleniscus, Acanthotelson, Palæocaris, Anthracerpes, Palæocampa, Shænaster.* Volumes ii, iii, v; and vi of these *Reports* all comprise very important works on Invertebrate. Paleontology, in which are not only species and genera described, but higher groups are defined, and many important questions are philosophically discussed.

**Meek, F. B., and A. H. Worthen.** Preliminary notice of a Scorpion, a Eurypterus ? and other fossils, from the Coal-measures of Illinois. < *Am. Journ. Sci.,* vol. xlv, 2d ser., pp. 19-28. 1868.

> Afterward fully described and illustrated in one of the *Illinois Geological Reports*, vol. iii.

**Meek, F. B., and A. H. Worthen.** Notes on some points in the structure and habits of the Paleozoic Crinoidea. < *Proc. Acad. Nat. Sci. Phila.,* vol. xii, 2d ser., pp. 323-334. 1868.

> Afterward republished in the *Illinois Geological Reports,* vol. v.

**Meek, F. B., and A. H. Worthen.** Remarks on some types of Carboniferous Crinoidea, with descriptions of new genera and species of the same, and of one Echinoid. < *Proc. Acad. Nat. Sci. Phila.,* vol. xii, 2d ser., pp. 335-359. 1868.

> Genera *Barycrinus, Nipterocrinus*. Afterward republished in the *Illinois Geological Reports*, vol. v.

**Meek, F. B., and A. H. Worthen.** Paleontology of Illinois. < *Worthen's Geological Survey of Illinois,* vol. iii, pp. 291-565, plates 1-20. 1868.

> Silurian, Devonian, and Carboniferous. Genera *Anomalocrinus, Isonema, Eractinopora, Lepidesthes, Onychaster, Mazonia*.

**Meek, F. B., and A. H. Worthen.** Notes on some points in the structure and habits of the Paleozoic Crinoidea. < *Am. Journ. Sci.,* vol. xlviii, 2d ser., pp. 23-40. 1869.

> Afterward republished in the *Illinois Geological Reports,* vol. v.

# I.—PUBLICATIONS MADE IN THE UNITED STATES.

**Meek, F. B., and A. H. Worthen.** Descriptions of new Crinoidea and Echinoidea from the Carboniferous rocks of the Western States, with a note on the genus Onychaster. < *Proc. Acad. Nat. Sci. Phila.*, vol. xiii, 2d ser., pp. 67–83. 1869.
Afterward republished in the *Illinois Geological Reports*, vol. v.

**Meek, F. B., and A. H. Worthen.** Remarks on the Blastoidea, with descriptions of new species. < *Proc. Acad. Nat. Sci. Phila.*, vol. xiii, 2d ser., pp. 83–91. 1869.
Afterward republished in the *Illinois Geological Reports*, vol. v.

**Meek, F. B., and A. H. Worthen.** Note on the relations of Synocladia, King, 1849, to the proposed genus Septopora, Prout, 1858. < *Proc. Acad. Nat. Sci. Phila.*, vol. xiv, 2d ser., pp. 15–18. 1870.
The author regards these forms as congeneric.

**Meek, F. B., and A. H. Worthen.** Descriptions of new species and genera of fossils from the Paleozoic rocks of the Western States. < *Proc. Acad Nat. Sci. Phila.*, vol. xiv, 2d ser., pp. 22–56. 1870.
Silurian and Carboniferous. Genera *Codonites, Carbonarca, Clinopistha, Solenocheilus, Temnocheilus*. Afterward republished and illustrated in the *Illinois Geological Reports*, vol. vi.

**Meek, F. B., and A. H. Worthen.** Paleontology of Illinois. Descriptions of Invertebrates from the Carboniferous System. < *Worthen's Geological Survey of Illinois*, vol. v, pp. 323–619, plates 1–32. 1873.
Genera *Physetocrinus, Nipterocrinus, Codonites.*

**Meek, F. B., and A. H. Worthen.** Paleontology of Illinois. Descriptions of Invertebrates. < *Worthen's Geological Survey of Illinois*, vol. vi, pp. 491–532, plates 23–32. 1875.
Genus *Carbonarca*. A portion of these descriptions are by Mr. Worthen alone.

**Miller, S. A.** Cincinnati Quarterly Journal of Science. 1874.
This journal existed only two years, 1874 and 1875. The first year it was conducted by Mr. Miller as editor and proprietor, and the second year by the same in connection with L. M. Hosea, when it was discontinued, making volumes i and ii complete. Mr. Miller contributed descriptions of quite a number of species and two genera, which are distributed throughout the pages of both volumes. As this publication is likely to be seldom found in libraries, a list of these species and genera is here given. All are of Lower Silurian age.
ANOMALODONTA. *A. gigantea. Bellerophon mohri. Beyrichia duryi. B. chambersi. B. richardsoni. B. striatomarginatus. Buthotrepis ramulosus. Cyclora* hoffmani. *Cyrtoceras vallandighami. Cypricardites* hainesi. *Cyrtolites elegans. C. carinata. Glyptocrinus* fornshelli. *Leperditia byrnesi. Lichenocrinus tuberculatus.* MEGALOGRAPTUS. *M. welchi. Modiolopsis versaillesensis. Pascolus darwini. P. claudei. Pleurotomaria halli. Streptorhynchus ? halli. Tentaculites richmondensis. Trematis dyeri. Acidaspis anchoralis. A. o'nealli. Arthraria biclava. Beyrichia cincinnatiensis. Orania dyeri. C. multipunctata. Cyrtoceras obscura. C. ventricosum. Glyptocrinus shafferi. Heterocrinus isodactylus. Lingula van hornei. Orthis meeki. Orthoceras byrnesi. O. dyeri. O. cincinnatiensis. O. halli. O. harperi. O. fosteri. O. meeki. O. mohri. O. transversa. Trematospira (?) quadriplicata.*

**Miller, S. A.** The American Paleozoic fossils: a catalogue of the genera and species. Cincinnati, Ohio, published by the author. 1877.

**Morton, S. G.** Synopsis of the organic remains of the Ferruginous Sands. Formation of the United States; with geological remarks. < *Am. Journ. Sci.*, vol. xvii, 1st ser., pp. 274–295 ; continued in vol. xviii, pp. 243–250. 1829.

Cretaceous.

**Morton, S. G.** Description of the fossil shells which characterize the Atlantic Secondary Formation, including four new species. < *Journ. Acad. Nat. Sci. Phila.*, vol. vi, 1st ser., pp. 72–100, 4 plates. 1829.

**Morton, S. G.** Description of a new species of Ostrea, with some remarks on the O. convexa, Say. < *Journ. Acad. Nat. Sci. Phila.*, vol. vi, 1st ser., pp. 50, 51, 1 fig. on plate i. 1829.

**Morton, S. G.** Description of two new species of shells of the genera Scaphites and Crepidula; with some observations on the Ferruginous Sand, Plastic Clay, and Upper Marine formations of the United States. < *Journ. Acad. Nat. Sci. Phila.*, vol. vi, 1st ser., pp. 107–119, 1 plate. 1829.

To which is added a "Note, containing a notice of some fossils recently discovered in New Jersey", pp. 120–129.

**Morton, S. G.** Additional observations on the geology and organic remains of New Jersey and Delaware. < *Journ. Acad. Nat. Sci. Phila.*, vol. vi, 1st ser., pp. 189–204, 1 plate. 1830.

Mostly corrected descriptions of species formerly published in a previous part of the same volume.

**Morton, S. G.** Synopsis of the organic remains of the Ferruginous Sand formation of the United States, with geological remarks. < *Am. Journ. Sci.*, vol. xviii, 1st ser., pp. 243–250, 3 plates. 1830.

Continued from vol. xvii, pp. 274–295.

**Morton, S. G.** Synopsis of the organic remains of the Cretaceous Group of the United States; illustrated by nineteen plates; to which is added an appendix containing a tabular view of the Tertiary fossils hitherto discovered in North America. 8°. pp. 88 + 8 + 23. 1834.

Genera *Venilia, Hamulus.* The "appendix" was originally published in vol. viii, *Journ. Acad. Nat. Sci. Phila.*, but the body of the work is an independent publication, and contains many original descriptions of Cretaceous fossil species.

**Morton, S. G.** Notice and description of the organic remains embraced in a paper entitled "Observations on the Bituminous Coal deposits of the Valley of the Ohio, and the accompanying rock strata; with notices of the fossil organic remains and the relics of vegetable and animal bodies, illustrated by a geological map, by numerous drawings of plants and shells, and by views of interesting scenery; by Dr. S. P. Hildreth of Marietta, Ohio". < *Am. Journ. Sci.*, vol. xxix, 1st ser., pp. 149–154. 1836.

30 woodcut plates, mostly plants; but 6 of them contain figures of Invertebrate fossils. Dr. Hildreth's paper occupies the 148 pages immediately preceding that of Dr. Morton.

**Morton, S. G.** Description of several new species of fossil shells from the Cretaceous deposits of the United States. < *Proc. Acad. Nat. Sci. Phila.*, vol. i, pp. 106–110. 1841.

From New Jersey and the Upper Missouri River region.

**Morton, S. G.** Description of two new species of fossils from the Lower Cretaceous strata of New Jersey. < *Proc. Acad. Nat. Sci. Phila.*, vol. i, pp. 132, 133. 1841.

**Morton, S. G.** Description of some new species of organic remains of the Cretaceous group of the United States, with a tabular view of the fossils hitherto discovered in this formation. < *Journ. Acad. Nat. Sci. Phila.*, vol. viii, 1st ser., pp. 207–227, 2 plates. 1842.

This article also embraces a "Tabular view of the organic remains hitherto discovered in the Cretaceous strata of the United States".

**Nelson, Edward T.** On the Molluscan fauna of the later Tertiary of Peru. < *Trans. Conn. Acad. Arts and Sci.*, vol. ii, pp. 186–206, 2 plates. 1871.

Wholly a description of species.

**Newberry, J. S.** Paleontology. < *Chapter xi of Lieut. Ives's Report on the Colorado River of the West*, pp. 116–129, plates 1 and 2. 1861.

Carboniferous.

**Newberry, J. S.** Descriptions of fossils. < *Capt. Macomb's Exploring Exped.*, pp. 139–148, plate 3. 1876.

The invertebrate fossils are Carboniferous only. The same article also embraces descriptions of plants and fish remains.

**Nicholson, H. Alleyne.** On the genera Cornulites and Tentaculites, and on a new genus, Conchiolites. < *Am. Journ. Sci.*, vol. iii, 3d ser., pp. 202–206. 1872.

**Nicholson, H. Alleyne.** On the genera Conchiolites and Ortonia. < *Cincinnati Quarterly Journal of Science*, vol. i, pp. 236–238. 1874.

In this note, Professor Nicholson replies to some criticisms of the editor questioning the validity of the genera named.

**Nicholson, H. Alleyne.** Description of the Corals of the Silurian and Devonian systems. < *Paleontology of Ohio (Newberry)*, vol. ii, pp. 181–242. 1875.

This and the two succeeding articles in the same volume are illustrated on plates 21, 22, 23, 24, and 25.

**Nicholson, H. Alleyne.** Descriptions of the Amorphozoa, from the Silurian and Devonian formations. < *Paleontology of Ohio (Newberry)*, vol. ii, pp. 243–255. 1875.

For reference to illustrations, see preceding entry. Genera *Syringostroma*, *Dictyostroma*.

**Nicholson, H. Alleyne.** Descriptions of Polyzoa, from the Silurian formation. < *Paleontology of Ohio (Newberry)*, vol. ii, pp. 257–268. 1875.

For reference to illustrations, see two preceding entries.

**Norwood, J. G., and Henry Pratten.** Notice of the Producti found in the Western States and Territories, with descriptions of twelve new species. < *Journ. Acad. Nat. Sci. Phila.*, vol. iii, 2d ser., pp. 5–22, 1 plate. 1855.

Carboniferous.

**Norwood, J. G., and Henry Pratten.** Notice of the genus Chonetes, as found in the Western States and Territories; with descriptions of eleven new species. < *Journ. Acad. Nat. Sci. Phila.*, vol. iii, 2d ser., pp. 23–31, 1 plate. 1855.

**Norwood, J. G., and Henry Pratten.** Notice of fossils from the Carboniferous series of the Western States, belonging to the genera Spirifer, Bellerophon, Pleurotomaria, Macrocheilus, Natica, and Loxonema, with descriptions of eight new characteristic species. < *Journ. Acad. Nat. Sci. Phila.*, vol. iii, 2d ser., pp. 71-77, 1 plate. 1855.

**Owen, D. D.** Descriptions and figures of some organic remains supposed to be new. .< *Report of a Geol. Expl. of part of Iowa, Wisconsin, and Illinois*, Appendix, pp. 69-86. 8°. Plates xi-xviii. 1844.

Silurian, Devonian, and Carboniferous. This work is mainly reproduced in Dr. Owen's large report, subsequently published.

**Owen, D. D.** Description of new and imperfectly known genera and species of organic remains, collected during the geological surveys of Wisconsin, Iowa, and Minnesota. < *Owen's Geol. Rep. of Wisconsin, Iowa, and Minnesota*, pp. 573-587, 15 plates. 1852.

Genera *Menocephalus, Crepicephalus, Lonchocephalus, Dikelocephalus, Selenoides*. Silurian, Devonian, Carboniferous, and Cretaceous.

**Owen, D. D.** Geological reconnoissance of Arkansas. > Vol. ii (Owen). 1860.

3 plates of Cretaceous fossils, with names accompanying, but no text.

**Owen, D. D., and B. F. Shumard.** Descriptions of fifteen new species of Crinoidea from the Subcarboniferous Limestones of Iowa, collected during the U. S. Geological Survey of Iowa, Wisconsin, and Minnesota, in the years 1848-49 < *Journ. Acad. Nat. Sci. Phila.*, 2d ser., vol. ii, pp. 57-70, 1 plate. 1850.

This article was afterward republished in Owen's *U. S. Geol. Rep. of Iowa, Wisconsin, and Minnesota*, with some modifications.

**Owen D. D., and B. F. Shumard.** On the number and distribution of fossil species in the Paleozoic rocks of Iowa, Wisconsin, and Minnesota. < *Proc. Am. Assoc. Adv. Sci.*, vol. v, pp. 235-239. 1851.

**Owen, D. D., and B. F. Shumard.** Descriptions of seven new species of Crinoidea from the Subcarboniferous Limestone of Iowa and Illinois. < *Journ. Acad. Nat. Sci. Phila.*, vol. ii, 2d ser., pp. 89-94, 1 plate. 1852.

This article was afterward republished in Owen's *U. S. Geol. Rep. of Iowa, Wisconsin, and Minnesota.*

**Owen, D. D., and B. F. Shumard.** Descriptions of one new genus and twenty-two new species of Crinoidea, from the Subcarboniferous Limestones of Iowa. < *Owen's Geol. Rep. of Wisconsin, Iowa, and Minnesota*, pp. 587-598, 2 plates. 1852.

Genera *Agassizocrinus, Megistocrinus.*

**Owen, Richard.** Description of fossils. < *Geological Reconnoissance of Indiana (D. D. & R. Owen)*, pp. 362-365, 11 woodcuts. 1862.

*Siphonaria digitata, Halysites sexto-catenatus, Bucania euomphaloides, Gyroceras rhombolinearis, Oripora tricarinata, Pileopsis pablocrinus, Conularia crawfordsvillensis.* Silurian and Carboniferous.

Perry, J. B. On the "Eozoön" Limestone of Eastern Massachusetts. < *Proc. Am. Assoc. Adv. Sci.*, vol. xx, pp. 270–276. 1872.

Mr. Perry corroborates the statement of Mr. Burbank as to the existence of *Eozoön* in the crystalline limestones of Eastern Massachusetts.

Pitt, W. H. *See* Grote, A. R., *and* W. H. Pitt.

Pratten, Henry. *See* Norwood, J. G., *and* Henry Pratten.

Prime, Temple. Synonymy of the Cyclades, a family of Acephalous Mollusks. Part 1. < *Proc. Acad. Nat. Sci. Phila.*, vol. iv, 2d ser., pp. 267–301. 1860.

The list contains fossil as well as recent species. Part 2 is published in vol. v, pp. 25–33.

Prime, Temple. Synonymy of the Cyclades, a family of Acephalous Mollusca. Part 2. < *Proc. Acad. Nat. Sci. Phila.*, vol. v, 2d ser., pp. 25–33. 1861.

The list contains fossil as well as recent species. Part 1 is published in vol. iv, pp. 267–301.

Prout, Hiram A. Description of a new Graptolite in the Lower Silurian rocks near the Falls of the St. Croix River. < *Am. Journ. Sci.*, vol. xi, 2d ser., pp. 187–191, 2 woodcuts. 1851.

Prout, Hiram A. Description of a new species of Productus (P. marginicinctus) from the Carboniferous Limestone of St. Louis. < *Trans. St. Louis Acad. Sci.*, vol. i, pp. 43–45, 1 plate. 1857.

Prout, Hiram A. Description of new species of Bryozoa from Texas and New Mexico, collected by Dr. George G. Shumard, Geologist of the U. S. Expedition for boring Artesian Wells along the 32d Parallel, under the direction of Capt. John Pope, U. S. Corps Topographical Engineers. < *Trans. St. Louis Acad. Sci.*, vol. i, pp. 228–235. 1858.

Prout, Hiram A. First of a series of descriptions of Carboniferous Bryozoa. < *Trans. St. Louis Acad. Sci.*, vol. i, pp. 235–237. 1858.

Genus *Fenestralia*.

Prout, Hiram A. Second series of descriptions of Bryozoa; from the Paleozoic Rocks of the Western States and Territories. < *Trans. St. Louis Acad. Sci.*, vol. i, pp. 266–273. 1858.

Prout, Hiram A. Third series of descriptions of Bryozoa from the Paleozoic Rocks of the Western States and Territories. < *Trans. St. Louis Acad. Sci.*, vol. i, pp. 443–452, 3 plates. 1859.

Genera *Septopora, Semicoscinium*.

Prout, Hiram A. Fourth series of descriptions of Bryozoa from the Paleozoic Rocks of the Western States and Territories. < *Trans. St. Louis Acad. Sci.*, vol. i, pp. 571–581. 1860.

• Genus *Cyclopora*.

Prout, Hiram A. Descriptions of new species of Bryozoa. < *Trans. St. Louis Acad. Sci.*, vol. ii, pp. 410–413. 1866.

Prout, Hiram A. Descriptions of Polyzoa from the Paleozoic Rocks. < *Worthen's Geological Survey of Illinois*, vol. ii, pp. 412–423, plates 21 and 22. 1866.

Rafinesque, C. F. Description of a fossil Medusa, forming a new genus, Trianisites cliffordi. <*Am. Journ. Sci.*, vol. iii, 1st ser., pp. 285-287, Illustrated. 1821.

Rathbun, Richard. Preliminary report on the Cretaceous Lamellibranch collected in the vicinity of Pernambuco, Brazil, on the Morgan Expedition of 1870, Ch. Fred. Hartt in charge. <*Proc. Boston Soc. Nat. Hist.*, vol. xvii, pp. 241-256. 1874.

Rathbun, Richard. *See* Hartt, C. F., *and* Richard Rathbun.

Ravenel, Edmund. Description of two new species of fossil Scutella from South Carolina. <*Journ. Acad. Nat. Sci. Phila.*, vol. viii, 1st ser., pp. 333-336, 2 woodcuts. 1842.

Ravenel, Edmund. Description of some new species of organic remains from the Eocene of South Carolina. <*Proc. Acad. Nat. Sci. Phila.*, vol. ii, pp. 96-98. 1844.

Rogers, Wm. B., *and* Henry D. Contributions to the Geology of the Tertiary formations of Virginia,—second series—continued: being a description of several species of Meiocene and Eocene shells not before described. <*Trans. Am. Philos. Soc.*, vol. vi, new series, pp. 371-377, 5 plates. 1837.

Rominger, Carl. Description of Calamaporæ found in Gravel deposits near Ann Arbor, Michigan, with some introductory remarks. <*Am. Journ. Sci.*, vol. xxxiv, 2d ser., pp. 389-400. 1862.

Rominger, Carl. Exposition of the true nature of Pleurodyctium problematicum. <*Am. Journ. Sci.*, vol. xxxv, 2d ser., pp. 82-84. 1863.

The author regards this fossil as only the cap, or mould, of a species of *Michelinia*.

Rominger, Carl. Note on the structure of the loop in Leptocœlia concava, Hall. <*Am. Journ. Sci.*, vol. xxxv, 2d ser., p. 84, 1 woodcut. 1863.

Rominger, Carl. Observations on Chætetes and some related genera, in regard to their systematic position; with an appended description of some new species. <*Proc. Acad. Nat. Sci. Phila.*, vol. x, 2d ser., pp. 113-120. 1866.

Rominger, Carl. Fossil Corals. <*Rominger's Geological Survey of Michigan, Lower Peninsula*, vol. iii, part ii, pp. 161, 55 plates. 1876.

Silurian and Devonian. Genera *Houghtonia, Quenstedtia, Vescicularia.*

Safford, J. M. Remarks on the genus Tetradium, with notices of the species found in Middle Tennessee. <*Am. Journ. Sci.*, vol. xxii, 2d ser., pp. 236-238. 1856.

Safford, J. M. On the species of Calceola found in Tennessee:—Calceola americana. <*Am. Journ. Sci.*, vol. xxix, 2d ser., pp. 248, 249. 1860.

Safford, J. M. The Upper Silurian beds of Western Tennessee; and Dr. F. Rœmer's monograph. <*Am. Journ. Sci.*, vol. xxxi, 2d ser., pp. 205-209. 1861.

The monograph referred to is *Die Silurische Fauna des westlichen Tennessee*, and the author's object is "to point out the fact that the fauna illustrated in that work is not the only one occurring upon the glades".

## I.—PUBLICATIONS MADE IN THE UNITED STATES.

**Safford, J. M.** Geology of Tennessee. 1869.

*This report contains tables of the fossils of the various formations and 9 plates of figures, mostly of new species, which are named but not described by Dr. Safford. Silurian and Devonian.*

**Salter, J. W.** Note on the fossils in the Crystalline rocks of the North Highlands of Scotland. < *Proc. Am. Assoc. Adv. Sci.*, vol. xi, pp. 62, 63. 1858.

**Salter, J. W.** On Graptopora, a new genus of Polyzoa, allied to the Graptolites. < *Proc. Am. Assoc. Adv. Sci.*, vol. xi, pp. 63–66. 1858.

**Say, Thomas.** Observations on some species of Zoophytes, Shells, &c., principally fossil. < *Am. Journ. Sci.*, vol. i, 1st ser., pp. 381–387; continued in vol. ii, pp. 34–45. 1819.

*Genera Pentremite, Exogyra.*

**Say, Thomas.** Fossil shells found in a shell-mass from Anastasia Island. Appendix to "Description of a Testaceous formation at Anastasia Island, extracted from notes made on a journey to the southern part of the United States, during the winter of 1822 and 1823. By R. Dietz." < *Journ. Acad. Nat. Sci. Phila.*, vol. iv, 1st ser., pp. 73–80. 1824.

*This species all appear to belong to recent forms, although they were there fossilized.*

**Say, Thomas.** An account of some of the fossil Shells of Maryland. < *Journ. Acad. Nat. Sci.*, vol. iv, 1st ser., pp. 124–155, 7 plates. 1824.

*Genus Dispotea.*

**Say, Thomas.** On two genera and several new species of Crinoidea. < *Journ. Acad. Nat. Sci.*, vol. iv, 1st ser., pp. 289–296. 1825.

*Genera Caryocrinites, Pentremite (corrected).*

**Scudder, S. H.** On Devonian Insects from New Brunswick. < *Am. Journ. Sci.*, vol. xxxix, 2d ser., pp. 357, 358. 1865.

**Scudder, S. H.** On the fossil Insects from Illinois, the Miamia and Hemeristia. (Described in vol. xxxvii, *Am. Journ. Sci.*, 2d ser., p. 34.) < *Am. Journ. Sci.*, vol. xl, 2d ser., pp. 268–271. 1865.

**Scudder, S. H.** An inquiry into the Zoological relations of the first discovered traces of fossil Neuropterous Insects in North America; with remarks on the difference of structure in the wings of living Neuroptera. < *Mem. Boston Soc. Nat. Hist.*, vol. i, pp. 173–192, plate 6. 1865.

**Scudder, S. H.** The Insects of Ancient America. < *Am. Naturalist*, vol. i, pp. 225–231, 1 plate. 1868.

**Scudder, S. H.** Descriptions of fossil Insects found on Mazon Creek, and near Morris, Grundy County, Illinois. < *Worthen's Geol. Surv. of Illinois*, vol. iii, pp. 566–572, 10 woodcuts. 1868.

*Carboniferous.*

**Scudder, S. H.** On the Carboniferous Myriapods preserved in the Sigillarian stumps of Nova Scotia. < *Mem. Boston Soc. Nat. Hist.*, vol. ii, part ii, No. iii, pp. 231–239. 1873.

**Scudder, S. H.** Tertiary Physopoda of Colorada. <*Bulletin U. S. Geol. and Geog. Surv. of the Territories,* vol. i, No. 4, 2d ser., pp. 221–223. 1875.

Genera *Lithadothrips, Paleothrips.*

**Scudder, S. H.** The fossil Butterflies. <*Mem. Am. Assoc. Adv. Sci.,* i, pp. 99, 3 plates. 1875.

This is a memoir of all the fossil Butterflies known to science at the date of publication.

**Scudder, S. H.** Fossil Coleoptera, from the Rocky Mountain Tertiaries. <*Bulletin U. S. Geol. and Geog. Surv. of the Territories,* vol. ii, No. 1, pp. 77–87. 1876.

Genus *Oryctoscirtetes.*

**Scudder, S. H.** Brief synopsis of North American Earwigs, with an appendix on the fossil species. <*Bulletin U. S. Geol. and Geog. Surv. of the Territories,* vol. ii, No. 3, pp. 249–260. 1876.

**Scudder, S. H.** New and interesting Insects from the Carboniferous of Cape Breton. <*Proc. Am. Assoc. Adv. Sci.,* vol. xxiv, pp. 110, 111. 1876.

**Scudder, S. H.** The first discovered traces of fossil Insects in the American Tertiaries. <*Bulletin U. S. Geol. and Geog. Surv. of the Territories,* vol. iii, No. 4, pp. 741–762. 1877.

Genera *Lithomyza, Spiladomyia, Pronophlebia, Cyttaromyia, Sackenia.*

**Scudder, S. H.** Description of two species of Carabidæ found in the Interglacial deposits of Scarboro' Heights, near Toronto, Canada. <*Bulletin U. S. Geol. and Geog. Surv. of the Territories,* vol. iii, No. 4, pp. 763, 764. 1877.

**Shaler, N. S.** Lateral symmetry in Brachiopoda. <*Proc. Boston Soc. Nat. Hist.,* vol. viii, pp. 274–279. 1862.

**Shaler, N. S.** List of the Brachiopoda from the island of Anticosti, sent by the Museum of Comparative Zoölogy to different institutions in exchange for other specimens, with annotations. <*Bull. Comp. Zoöl. Cambridge, Mass.,* vol. i, No. 4, pp. 61–70. 1865.

This paper is wholly descriptive of Paleozoic *Brachiopoda.* Genera *Brachyprion, Brachymeris.*

**Shaler, N. S.** Memoirs of the Geological Survey of Kentucky. 1877.

On page 226, vol. xiii, 3d series, of *Am. Journ. Sci.,* a work with the above title is reviewed; in which review it is stated that the third memoir treats of the Brachiopods of the Ohio Valley. Search in the principal libraries of the country has failed to find the work, and application both to the State authorities and the author has failed to elicit any information.

**Shaler, N. S.** On the occurrence of the genus Beatricea in Kentucky. <*Am. Nat.,* vol. xi, p. 628. 1877.

Prof. Shaler adopts the suggestion that the *Beatriceæ* are related to the Sponges, and states that he is authorized by Prof. Hyatt to say that he has abandoned his former view, that they are Cephalopods.

**Shumard, B. F.** Description of the species of Carboniferous and Cretaceous fossils collected. <*Marcey's Report of the U. S. Exploration of the Red River of Louisiana,* Appendix E, pp. 186–199, 6 plates. 1854.

# I.—PUBLICATIONS MADE IN THE UNITED STATES. 61

**Shumard, B. F.** Descriptions of new species of organic remains. < *Swallow's Geological Survey of Missouri*, part ii, pp. 185–208, 3 plates. 1855.
*Upper Silurian and Carboniferous.*

**Shumard, B. F.** Description of new fossil Crinoidea from the Paleozoic Rocks of the western and southern portions of the United States. < *Trans. St. Louis Acad. Sci.*, vol. i, pp. 71–80, 1 plate. 1857.

**Shumard, B. F.** Descriptions of new fossils from the Tertiary formation of Oregon and Washington Territories, and the Cretaceous of Vancouver's Island, collected by Dr. John Evans, U. S. Geologist, under instructions from the Department of the Interior. < *Trans. St. Louis Acad. Sci.*, vol. i, pp. 120–125. 1858.

**Shumard, B. F.** Descriptions of new species of Blastoidea from the Paleozoic Rocks of the Western States, with some observations on the structure of the summit of the genus Pentremites. < *Trans. St. Louis Acad. Sci.*, vol. i, pp. 238–248, 1 plate. 1858.

**Shumard, B. F.** Notice of new fossils from the Permian strata of New Mexico and Texas, collected by Dr. George G. Shumard, geologist of the United States Government expedition for obtaining water by means of artesian wells along the 32d Parallel, under the direction of Capt. John Pope, U. S. Corps Top. Eng. < *Trans. St. Louis Acad. Sci.*, vol. i, pp. 290–297. 1858.
*Descriptions of species.*

**Shumard, B. F.** Notice of fossils from the Permian strata of Texas and New Mexico, obtained by the United States expedition under Capt. John Pope for boring artesian wells along the 32d Parallel; with descriptions of new species from these strata and the Coal Measures of that region. < *Trans. St. Louis Acad. Sci.*, vol. i, pp. 387–402, 1 plate. 1859.

**Shumard, B. F.** Descriptions of new Cretaceous fossils from Texas. < *Trans. St. Louis Acad. Sci.*, vol. i, pp. 590–610. 1860.
Drawings of a part of this important collection of fossils were made, but never published. Photograph copies of them exist in private hands, and have been referred to by Mr. Meek for identification of other collections.

**Shumard, B. F.** Descriptions of five new species of Gasteropoda from the Coal-measures, and a Brachiopod from the Potsdam Sandstone of Texas. < *Trans. St. Louis Acad. Sci.*, vol. i, pp. 624–627. 1860.

**Shumard, B. F.** The Primordial zone of Texas, with descriptions of new fossils. < *Am. Journ. Sci.*, vol. xxxii, 2d ser., pp. 213–221. 1861.

**Shumard, B. F.** Descriptions of new Cretaceous fossils from Texas. < *Proc. Boston Soc. Nat. Hist.*, vol. viii, pp. 188–205. 1861.

**Shumard, B. F.** Notice of some new and imperfectly known fossils from the Primordial zone (Potsdam Sandstone and Calciferous Sand Group) of Wisconsin and Missouri. < *Trans. St. Louis Acad. Sci.*, vol. ii, pp. 101–107. 1863.
*Description of species.*

**Shumard, B. F.** Descriptions of new Paleozoic fossils. < *Trans. St. Louis Acad. Sci.*, vol. ii, pp. 108–113. 1863.

> The fossils described are mostly from the strata of the Carboniferous system west of the Mississippi River. The propriety of separating *Elæacrinus* Rœmer is discussed and advocated.

**Shumard, B. F.** Catalogue of the Paleozoic fossils of North America. Part 1. Paleozoic Echinodermata. A chronological list of works which contain descriptions or notices of North American Echinodermata. < *Trans. St. Louis Acad. Sci.*, vol. ii, pp. 335–407. 1866.

**Shumard, B. F., Owen, D. D., and.** *See* **Owen, D. D., *and* B. F. Shumard.**

**Shumard, B. F., Yandell, L. P., and.** *See* **Yandell, L. P., *and* B. F. Shumard.**

**Shumard, B. F., *and* G. C. Swallow.** Descriptions of new fossils from the Coal Measures of Missouri and Kansas. < *Trans. St. Louis Acad. Sci.*, vol. i, pp. 198–227. 1858.

> This paper is not one of true joint authorship, but only of collaboration. Each author attaches his own name to the species he describes, thus indicating his own respective portion of the work.

**Shumard, B. F., *and* L. P. Yandell.** Notice of a new fossil genus belonging to the family Blastoidea (Eleutherocrinus). < *Am. Journ. Sci.*, vol. xxii, 2d ser., pp. 120–122. 1856.

> Also published in *Proc. Acad. Nat. Sci. Phila.*, vol. viii, pp. 73–75.

**Shumard, B. F., *and* L. P. Yandell.** Notice of a new fossil genus belonging to the family Blastoidea, from the Devonian strata near Louisville, Kentucky. < *Proc. Acad. Nat. Sci. Phila.*, vol. viii, pp. 73–75, 1 plate. 1856.

> Genus *Eleutherocrinus*. Also published in *Am. Journ. Sci.*, vol. xxii, 2d ser., pp. 120–122.

**Smith, Sidney I.** Notice of a fossil Insect from the Carboniferous formation of Indiana. < *Am. Journ. Sci.*, vol. i, 3d ser., pp. 44–46. 1871.

> Genus *Paolia*.

**Springer, Frank.** *See* **Wachsmuth, Charles, *and* Frank Springer.**

**Stevens, R. P.** Descriptions of new Carboniferous fossils from the Appalachian, Illinois, and Michigan Coalfields. < *Am. Journ. Sci.*, vol. xxv, 2d ser., pp. 258–265. 1858.

**Stevens, R. P.** Report on the Geological and Mineralogical specimens collected by Mr. C. F. Hall in Frobisher Bay. < *Am. Journ. Sci.*, vol. xxxv, 2d ser., pp. 293, 294. 1863.

> The author refers all the species to Lower Silurian age, three species of which he regards as new, but does not name or describe them.

**St. John, O. H.** *See* **White, C. A., *and* O. H. St. John.**

**Stimpson, Wm.** Description of a new Cardium from the Pleistocene of Hudson's Bay. < *Proc. Acad. Nat. Sci. Phila.*, vol. vi, 2d ser., pp. 58, 59, 1 woodcut. 1862.

**Stimpson, Wm.** On the fossil Crab of Gay Head (Mass.). < *Journ. Boston Soc. Nat. Hist.*, vol. vii, pp. 583-589. 1863.
  Genus *Archæoplax*.

**Stodder, Charles.** A contribution to Micro-geology. The "Infusorial Deposit" of Richmond and other Virginian localities. < *Proc. Boston Soc. Nat. Hist.*, vol. xviii, pp. 206-209. 1876.

**Swallow, G. C.** Descriptions of new fossils from the Carboniferous and Devonian rocks of Missouri. < *Trans. St. Louis Acad. Sci.*, vol. i, pp. 635-659. 1860.

**Swallow, G. C.** Descriptions of some new fossils from the Carboniferous and Devonian rocks of Missouri. < *Trans. St. Louis Acad. Sci.*, vol. ii, pp. 81-100. 1863.

**Swallow, G. C.** Some new varieties of Spirifer lineatus, Martin; Spirifer cameratus, Morton; Spirifer kentuckensis, Shumard; Spirifer leidyi, Norwood & Pratten; Spirifer increbescens, Hall; and Spirifer keokuk. < *Trans. St. Louis Acad. Sci.*, vol. ii, pp. 408-410. 1866.

**Swallow, G. C., and F. Hawn.** The rocks of Kansas. < *Trans. St. Louis Acad. Sci.*, vol. i, pp. 173-197. 1853.

  Under a subtitle of this article "Fossils of the Permian Rocks of Kansas" are descriptions of a number of new species, to each of which the name "Swallow" is attached, but his exclusive authorship is not mentioned in the title.

**Swallow, G. C., B. F. Shumard, and.** *See* **Shumard, B. F., and G. C. Swallow.**

**Trask, John B.** Description of a new species of Ammonite and Baculite, from the Tertiary rocks of Chico Creek. < *Proc. Cal. Acad. Nat. Sci.*, vol. i, pp. 85, 86, 1 plate. 1856.

**Trask, John B.** Description of three new species of the genus Plagiostoma, from the Cretaceous rocks of Los Angeles. < *Proc. Cal. Acad. Nat. Sci.*, vol. i, p. 86, 1 plate. 1856.

**Troost, Gerard.** On Pentremites rheinwardtii, a new fossil; with remarks on the genus Pentremites (Say), and its geognostic position in the States of Tennessee, Alabama, and Kentucky. < *Trans. Geol. Soc. Penn.*, vol. i, part ii, pp. 224-229, 1 plate. 1835.

**Troost, Gerard.** Description of a new species of fossil Asterias. (A. antiqua.) < *Trans. Geol. Soc. Penn.*, vol. i, part ii, pp. 232-235. 1835.

**Troost, Gerard.** Description of some organic remains characterizing the strata of the Upper Transition, which composes Middle Tennessee. < *Trans. Geol. Soc. Penn.*, vol. i, part ii, pp. 244-247. 1835.

  *Hamites haanii* is here described.

**Troost, Gerard.** Organic remains discovered in the strata of Tennessee. < *Troost's 5th Geological Report of Tennessee*, pp. 45-76. 1840.

  This has become known as "*Troost's Catalogue*", and is an important publication from the fact that subsequent authors have adopted some of the new specific and generic names he there proposed, although no descriptions were given.

**Troost, Gerard.** Sixth Geological Report of Tennessee. 1841.

The first 25 pages of this pamphlet contain a catalogue, partially descriptive, of Tennessee fossils. The following species are described:—*Euomphalus maclurii, Lituites murchisoni, Orthoceratites regularis, Spirula mortonii, Limaria tennesea.*

**Troost, Gerard.** Seventh Geological Report of Tennessee. 1844.

This pamphlet contains a description of *Favosites flabelliformis* on page 5.

**Troost, Gerard.** List of the fossil Crinoids of Tennessee. Also remarks of Professors Hall and Agassiz upon the same. < *Proc. Am. Assoc. Adv. Sci.*, vol. ii, pp. 59–64. 1850.

This is merely a list of names of genera and species, some of them new, without descriptions. The list is important from the fact that some of its genera and species have been adopted by subsequent authors. Like the one published in the author's 5*th Geological Report of Tennessee,* this also is known as *Troost's Catalogue.*

**Tuomey, M.** Discovery of a chambered univalve fossil in the Eocene Tertiary of James River, Virginia.' < *Am. Journ. Sci.*, vol. xliii, 2d ser., p. 187. 1842.

**Tuomey, M.** Description of some new fossils from the Cretaceous rocks of the Southern States. < *Proc. Acad. Nat. Sci. Phila.*, vol. vii, pp. 167–172. 1854.

**Tuomey, M., and F. S. Holmes.** Pliocene fossils of South Carolina, containing descriptions and figures of the Polyparia, Echinodermata, and Mollusca. Charleston, S. C. 4°. pp. 152, 30 plates. 1857.

**Van Rensselaer, Jer.** Notice of fossil Crustacea, from New Jersey. < *Ann. N. Y. Lyceum Nat. Hist.*, vol. i, pp. 195–198, 1 plate. Supplementary note to same, p. 249. 1825.

**Vanuxem, Lardner.** Geology of New York, part iii; comprising the survey of the third geological district. 4°. pp. 306. 1842.

Contains woodcut illustrations of fossils distributed throughout the text; and also a number of descriptions of species and genera, mingled with the text of descriptive geology, part of which are original. Silurian and Devonian.

**Verneuil, Ed. de.** On the parallelism of the Paleozoic deposits of North America with those of Europe; followed by a table of the species of fossils common to the two continents, with indication of the positions in which they occur, and terminated by a critical examination of each of these species. (Translated and condensed from the Bulletin of the Geological Society of France, 2d ser., vol. iv, by James Hall.) < *Am. Journ. Sci.*, vol. v, 2d ser., pp. 176–183 and 359–370; also vol. vi, pp. 45–51 and 218–231. 1848.

**Verrill, A. E.** On the affinities of Paleozoic Tabulate Corals with existing species. < *Am. Journ. Sci.*, vol. iii, 3d ser., pp. 187–194. 1872.

**Vogdes, A. W.** A monograph of American Trilobites. Part i. Pamphlet. 8°. pp. 16. Tampa, Florida. No illustrations. 1876.

Contains bibliography, 1698–1874, and synopses of the families ASAPHUS and AGRAULOS; arranging the genera *Ogygia, Dikelocephalus, Niobe, Asaphus, Isotelus, Proetus, Odontopleura,* and *Bathyurellus* as group-types under the former; and *Agraulos, Ptychoparia, Cheirurus, Crepicephalus, Calymene,* and *Homalonotus,* under the latter.

**Vodges, A. W.** Notes on the genera Acidaspis Murchison; Odontopleura Emmerich; and Ceratocephala Warder. < *Proc. Acad. Nat. Sci. Phila.*, vol. vii, 3d ser., pp. 138-141. 1877.

**Wachsmuth, Charles.** Notes on the internal and external structure of Paleozoic Crinoids. < *Am. Journ. Sci.*, vol. xiv, 3d ser., pp. 115-127 and 181-191. 1877.

**Wachsmuth, Charles,** *and* **Frank Springer.** Revision of the genus Belemnocrinus, and description of two new species. < *Am. Journ. Sci.*, vol. xiii, 3d ser., pp. 253-259. 1877.

**Wagner, Wm.** Description of five new fossils, of the older Pliocene formation of Maryland and North Carolina. < *Journ. Acad. Nat. Sci. Phila.*, vol. viii, 1st ser., pp. 51-53, 1 plate. 1839.

**Walcott, C. D.** Description of a new species of Trilobite. < *Cincinnati Quarterly Journal of Science,* vol. ii, pp. 273, 274, 1 woodcut. 1875.

*Sphærocoryphe robustus.* Lower Silurian.

**Walcott, C. D.** New species of Trilobite from the Trenton Limestone, at Trenton Falls, N. Y. < *Cincinnati Quarterly Journ. Sci.*, vol. ii, pp. 347-349, 1 woodcut. 1875.

*Remopleurides striatulus.*

**Walcott, C. D.** The Trilobite, Ceraurus pleurexanthemus, of Trenton Falls, New York. < *Ann. N. Y. Lyceum Nat. Hist.*, vol. xi, pp. 155-159. 1876.

The author explains the mode of occurrence of the remains in the layers of limestone.

**Walcott, C. D.** Preliminary notice of the discovery of the remains of the natatory and branchial appendages of Trilobites. < *28th Ann. Rep. Regents Univ. N. Y. on Condition of the State Museum,* pp. 89-92. 1877.

**Walcott, C. D.** Descriptions of new species of fossils from the Trenton Limestone. < *29th Ann. Rep. Regents Univ. N. Y. on Condition of State Museum,* pp. 93-97. 1877.

Genus *Conchopeltis.*

This report bears date on its title-page 1875, but it was not issued until 1877, and then only a very small number of copies were published. See *Am. Journ. Sci.* for December, 1877. That the title-page date is wrong is manifest from the later dates that two of the authors have appended to their articles, which no doubt correctly represent the dates of their preparation.

**Walcott, C. D.** Notes on some sections of Trilobites, from the Trenton Limestone. 7 pp. and 1 plate. 8°. 1877.

Published in advance of *Report of New York State Museum of Natural History.* In this paper, Mr. Walcott announces further discoveries concerning the ventral portion and appendages of Trilobites, and draws some important conclusions as to their homologies.

**Walcott, C. D.** Note upon the eggs of the Trilobite. 3 pp. 8°. 1877.

Published with the preceding article in advance of *Report of New York State Museum of Natural History.* In this article, the author announces his discovery of the eggs of *Ceraurus pleurexanthemus.*

**Walcott, C. D.** Descriptions of new species of fossils from the Chazy and Trenton Limestones. 7 pp. 8°. 1877.

Published with the two foregoing articles in advance of a *Report of New York State Museum of Natural History.*

**Wagner, John A.** New Trilobites. < *Am. Journ. Sci.*, 1st ser., vol. xxxiv, pp. 377–379, 1 woodcut. 1838.

Genus *Ceratocephala, C. goniata*.

**White, C. A.** Observations upon the Geology and Paleontolegy of Burlington, Iowa, and its vicinity. < *Journ. Boston Soc. Nat. Hist.*, vol. vii, pp. 209–235. 1860.

Descriptions of several species of fossils from the Lower Carboniferous rocks are appended.

**White, C. A.** Description of new species of fossils from the Devonian and Carboniferous rocks of the Mississippi Valley. < *Proc. Boston Soc. Nat. Hist.*, vol. ix, pp. 8–33. 1862.

Genera *Belemnocrinus, Acambona*.

**White, C. A.** Observations on the summit structure of Pentremites, the structure and arrangement of certain parts of Crinoids, and descriptions of new species, from the Carboniferous rocks at Burlington, Iowa. < *Journ. Boston Soc. Nat. Hist.*, vol. vii, pp. 481–506. 1862.

Genus *Cœliocrinus*.

**White, C. A.** Observations on the genus Belemnocrinus. < *Proc. Boston Soc. Nat. Hist.*, vol. x, p. 180. 1865.

Rectification of the generic formula of *Belemnocrinus*.

**White, C. A.** [Description of Smithia woodmani.] < *Geology of Iowa* (*White's Report*), vol. i, p. 188 (foot-note). 1870.

**White, C. A.** The proposed genus Anomalodonta of Miller identical with the earlier Megaptera of Meek. < *Am. Journ. Sci.*, vol. viii, 3d ser., pp. 218, 219. 1874.

**White, C. A.** Preliminary report upon Invertebrate fossils, with descriptions of new species. < *Wheeler's Geog. and Geol. Expl. and Surv. west of the 100th Merid.*, pamphlet, pp. 27. 1874.

These species were afterward republished and illustrated in vol. iv, part i, *Wheeler's U. S. Expl. and Surv. west of the 100th Merid.*

**White, C. A.** Report upon the Invertebrate fossils collected in portions of Nevada, Utah, Colorado, New Mexico, and Arizona by parties of the expeditions of 1871–1874. < *Wheeler's Expl. and Surv. west of the 100th Merid.*, vol. iv, part i. 1875.

Silurian, Carboniferous, Jurassic, Cretaceous, and Tertiary. Genus *Lispodesthes*. The full volume, with part ii by Professor Cope, was published in 1877.

**White, C. A.** Invertebrate Paleontology of the Plateau Province. < *Powell's Report on the Geology of the Uinta Mountains*, chap. iii, pp. 74–135. 1876.

Carboniferous, Jurassic, Cretaceous, and Tertiary.

**White, C. A.** Descriptions of new species of fossils from Paleozoic rocks of Iowa. < *Proc. Acad. Nat. Sci. Phila.*, vol. vi, 3d ser., pp. 27–34. 1876.

Silurian, Devonian, and Carboniferous. Genus *Strobilocystites*.

**White, C. A.** Paleontological papers No. 1: Descriptions of Unionidæ and Physidæ, collected by Prof. E. D. Cope, from the Judith River Group of Montana, during the summer of 1876. < *Bulletin U. S. Geol. and Geog. Surv. of the Territories*, vol. iii, pp. 599–602. 1877.

# I.—PUBLICATIONS MADE IN THE UNITED STATES. 67

**White, C. A.** Paleontological Papers No. 2: Descriptions of new species of Uniones, and a new genus of fresh-water Gasteropoda, from the Tertiary strata of Wyoming and Utah. < *Bulletin U. S. Geol. and Geog. Surv. of the Territories*, vol. iii, pp. 603–606. 1877.

Genus *Cassiopella*.

**White, C. A.** Paleontological Papers No. 3: Catalogue of the Invertebrate fossils hitherto published from the Fresh- and Brackish-water deposits of the western portion of North America. < *Bulletin U. S. Geol. and Geog. Surv. of the Territories*, vol. iii, pp. 607–614. 1877.

**White, C. A.** Paleontological Papers No. 4: Comparison of the North American Mesozoic and Cenozoic Unionidæ and associated Mollusks with living species. < *Bulletin U. S. Geol. and Geog. Surv. of the Territories*, vol. iii, pp. 615–624. 1877.

**White, C. A.** Paleontological Papers No. 5: Remarks on the Paleontological characteristics of the Mesozoic and Cenozoic Groups, as developed in the Green River region. < *Bulletin U. S. Geol. and Geog. Surv. of the Territories*, vol. iii, pp. 625–629. 1877.

**White, C. A.,** and **O. H. St. John.** Descriptions of new Subcarboniferous and Coal Measure fossils collected upon the geological survey of Iowa; together with a notice of new generic characters observed in two species of Brachiopods. < *Trans. Chicago Acad. Sci.*, vol. i, pp. 115–127, 10 woodcuts. 1869.

Genera *Meekella, Cryptacanthia, Tomoceras.*

**White, C. A.,** and **R. P. Whitfield.** Observations upon the rocks of the Mississippi Valley which have been referred to the Chemung Group of New York, together with descriptions of new species of fossils from the same horizon at Burlington, Iowa. < *Proc. Boston Soc. Nat. Hist.*, pp. 289–306. 1862.

**White, M. C.** Discovery of microscopic organisms in the siliceous nodules of the Paleozoic rocks of New York. < *Am. Journ. Sci.*, vol. xxxiii, 2d ser., pp. 385, 386. 1862.

**Whitfield, R. P.** Descriptions of new species of Eocene fossils. < *Am. Journ. Conch.*, vol. i, pp. 259–268, 1 plate. 1865.

**Whitfield, R. P.** Observations on the internal appendages of the genus Atrypa, with a notice of discovery of a loop connecting the spiral cones. < *20th Ann. Rep. Regents Univ. N. Y. on Condition of State Cabinet*, pp. 141–144, 1 plate. 1868.

**Whitfield, R. P.** Descriptions of new fossils. < *Captain Ludlow's Report on the Black Hills of Dakota*, pp. 103, 104, 1 plate. 1875.

These descriptions and figures are repeated in the *Report of the Chief of Engineers U. S. Army* for 1875, part ii. *Obolus pectinoides*, Primordial; *Terebratula helena*, Cretaceous.

**Whitfield, R. P.** Preliminary report on the Paleontology of the Black Hills. < *Powell's Geol. and Geog. Survey of the Rocky Mountain Region*, pamphlet, pp. 49. 1877.

Primordial, Jurassic, and Cretaceous. The final report on these fossils, illustrated, is in course of preparation.

**Whitfield, R. P.** *See* **Hall, James**, *and* **R. P. Whitfield**; *also*, **White, C. A.**, *and* **R. P. Whitfield.**

**Winchell, Alexander.** Descriptions of Cephalopods from the Marshall and Huron Groups of Michigan. < *Am. Journ. Sci.*, vol. xxxiii, 2d ser., pp. 354-366. 1862.

Carboniferous.

**Winchell, Alexander.** Descriptions of fossils from the Marshall and Huron Groups of Michigan. < *Proc. Acad. Nat. Sci. Phila.*, vol. vi, 2d ser., pp. 405-430. 1862.

Carboniferous.

**Winchell, Alexander.** Descriptions of fossils from the Yellow Sandstones lying beneath the "Burlington Limestone" at Burlington, Iowa. (Carboniferous.) < *Proc. Acad. Nat. Sci. Phila.*, vol. vii, 2d ser., pp. 2-25. 1863.

Genera *Leptopora, Syringothyris, Dexiobia.*

**Winchell, Alexander.** Notice of a small collection of fossils from the Potsdam Sandstone of Wisconsin and the Lake Superior Sandstone of Michigan. < *Am. Journ. Sci.*, vol. xxxvii, 2d ser., pp. 226-232. 1864.

**Winchell, Alexander.** Descriptions of new species of fossils from the Marshall Group of Michigan, and its supposed equivalent in other States; with notes on some fossils of the same age previously described. < *Proc. Acad. Nat. Sci. Phila.*, vol. ix, 2d ser., pp. 109-133. 1865.

Genera *Conopoterium, Pernopecten.*

**Winchell, Alexander.** On the geological age and equivalents of the Marshall Group. < *Proc. Am. Philos. Soc.*, vol. xi, pp. 57-82 and (1870) 385-418. 1869.

This article contains no descriptive paleontology, but systematic lists and other valuable matter is given.

**Winchell, Alexander.** Notes on fossils from Tennessee, collected from the strata immediately overlying the Black Shale, and transmitted for examination by Dr. J. M. Safford. < *Safford's Geology of Tennessee*, pp 440-446. 1869.

Contains descriptions of four new species of Subcarboniferous fossils.

**Winchell, Alexander.** Notices and descriptions of fossils, from the Marshall Group of the Western States, with notes on fossils from other formations. < *Proc. Am. Philos. Soc.*, vol. xi, pp. 245-260. 1870.

Carboniferous.

**Winchell, Alexander,** *and* **Oliver Marcy.** Enumeration of fossils collected in the Niagara Limestone at Chicago, Illinois; with descriptions of several new species. < *Mem. Boston Soc. Nat. Hist.*, vol. i, pp. 81-113, plates 2 and 3. 1865.

**Worthen, A. H.** Notice of a new species of Platycrinus and other fossils from the Mountain Limestone of Illinois and Iowa; being an extract from the Second Annual Report of the Illinois Geological Survey. < *Trans. St. Louis Acad. Sci.*, vol. i, pp. 569-571. 1860.

**Worthen, A. H.** 1875.

A considerable proportion of the Invertebrate fossils of vol. vi, *Worthen's Geological Survey of Illinois*, are described by Mr. Worthen alone, although the general title gives his name jointly with that of Mr. Meek.

**Yandell, Lunsford P.** On the distribution of the Crinoidea in the Western States. < *Proc. Am. Assoc. Adv. Sci.*, vol. v, pp. 229–235. 1851.

**Yandell, Lunsford P.** Description of a new genus of Crinoidea. < *Am. Journ. Sci.*, vol. xx, 2d ser., pp. 135–137. 1855.

Genus *Acrocrinus*.

**Yandell, Lunsford P.**, and **B. F. Shumard.** Contributions to the geology of Kentucky. Published at Louisville by Prentice and Weisinger. 1847.

This is a small publication of 36 pages, 8°, and one plate of illustrations of Crinoids. It contains an enumeration of fossils from the vicinity of Louisville, and from Grayson County, Kentucky, but no specific descriptions of fossils, although a few new species are named, some of which names have been adopted by subsequent authors.

**Yandell, Lunsford P.** *See* **Shumard, B. F.**, *and* **L. P. Yandell.**

# BIBLIOGRAPHY OF NORTH AMERICAN INVERTEBRATE PALEONTOLOGY.

# PART II.

EMBRACING TITLES AND ABSTRACTS OF PUBLICATIONS MADE IN BRITISH NORTH AMERICA, IN THE WEST INDIES, AND IN EUROPE.

By H. ALLEYNE NICHOLSON, M. D., D. Sc.

# PREFACE TO PART II.

The following report comprises the titles and places of publication of all works and memoirs relating to North American Invertebrate Palæontology which have been published in British North America, in the West Indies, in Britain, and on the Continent of Europe, so far as the writer has been able to discover. That this report is imperfect, and that omissions of a more or less serious character are certain to be found in it, may be taken for granted, since there are some serial publications to parts of which the author has found it impossible to obtain access, and since Palæontological papers are occasionally published in journals or works of a generally unscientific character. To ensure, therefore, anything like absolute completeness, it would have been necessary to have surveyed almost the entire range of published scientific literature, a task for which the writer's leisure would have been insufficient; especially as notices of American fossils are often to be found in memoirs which, to judge from their titles, would be supposed to deal with subjects of an entirely different nature. It is hoped, however, that such omissions as may be found will not prove to be of great importance, and that they may be excused on the ground that the writer's place of residence is one which renders it difficult for him to consult the large public libraries of London except at distant intervals.

In conclusion, the writer would wish to use this opportunity of returning his best thanks to those of his fellow-workers who have been kind enough to assist him in the preparation of this report, among whom he must mention with special gratitude Prof. H. Milne-Edwards, Prof. De Koninck, Prof. Ferdinand Roemer, M. Barrande, Dr. Gustav Lindström, M. De Loriol, Principal Dawson, Robert Etheridge, Esq., Jun., R. J. Lechmere Guppy, Esq., Prof. Martin Duncan, and J. F. Whiteaves, Esq. H. A. N.

UNITED COLLEGE, ST. ANDREWS, SCOTLAND,
*November* 19, 1877.

# II.—PUBLICATIONS MADE IN BRITISH NORTH AMERICA, WEST INDIES, AND EUROPE.

**Agassiz, Louis.** Monographies d'Echinodermes vivants et fossiles. Neuchâtel. 1838.
   Describes some North American fossil Echinoids.

**Anon.** Correspondence of Joachim Barrande, Sir William Logan and James Hall, on the Taconic System, and on the age of the fossils found in the Rocks of Northern New England, and the Quebec Group of Rocks. < *Canad. Nat.*, vol. vi, pp. 106-120. [Reprinted from the *Am. Journ. Sci. and Arts*, No. 92, 1861.] 1861.
   The correspondence deals chiefly with the characters of the fossils and the stratigraphical conclusions deducible therefrom.

**Anon.** Discovery of microscopic organisms in the Siliceous Nodules of the Palæozoic Rocks of New York. < *Canad. Nat.*, vol. vii, pp. 281-283. 1862.
   Records the discovery by Dr. M. C. White in hornstone nodules from the Carboniferous, Devonian, and Silurian Rocks of numerous *Microphytes* and *Microzoa*.

**Anthony, J. G.** Letter to C. Lyell, Esq., V. P. G. S., on an impression of the soft parts of an Orthoceras. < *Quart. Journ. Geol. Soc.*, vol. iii, pp. 255-257 (with woodcut). 1847.
   Notices the occurrence in the Cincinnati Group of Ohio of specimens of *Orthoceras*, apparently preserving impressions of the soft parts.

**Bailey, J. W.** Infusorial deposits in America. < *Ann. and Mag. Nat. Hist.*, ser. 1, vol. xv, pp. 214, 215. 1845.
   A reprint from *Silliman's American Journal*, January, 1845.

**Bailey, J. W.** On the origin of Greensand, and its formation in the oceans of the present epoch. < *Ann. and Mag. Nat. Hist.*, ser. 2, vol. xviii, pp. 425-428. 1856.
   Reprinted from *Proc. Boston Soc. Nat. Hist.*, vol. v, p. 364.

**Bailey, L. W.,** *and* **G. F. Matthew.** Preliminary report on the geology of Southern New Brunswick. < *Geological Survey of Canada: Report of Progress for* 1870-71, pp. 13-240. Ottawa, 1872.
   Contains lists of, and occasional notes on, the fossils.

**Barker, Arthur E.** Latest observations on Eozoön canadense by Prof. Max Schultze. < *Ann. and Mag. Nat. Hist.*, ser. 4, vol. xiii, pp. 379, 380. 1874.
   Publishing a letter from Prof. Max Schultze, in which he expresses the opinion that the "proper wall" of *Eozoön* is of inorganic origin.

**Barrande, Joachim.** Système Silurien du Centre de la Bohême. 4°. 1852-74.
   Describes or discusses critically a number of species of American fossils.

**Barrande, Joachim.** Observations sur quelques genres de Cephalopodes Siluriens. < *Bull. de la Soc. Géol. de France*, ser. 2, t. xiv, pp. 428-437. 1857.

> The author discusses the characters of various genera of Silurian Cephalopods, with special reference to the types which occur in North America.

**Barrande, Joachim.** Documents anciens et nouveaux sur la faune primordiale et le système Taconique en Amérique. < *Bull. de la Soc. Géol. de France*, ser. 2, vol. xviii, pp. 203-321, plates iv, v. 1861.

> The following are the principal subjects discussed in this elaborate memoir:—(1) The characters of three primordial *Trilobites* discovered at Georgia (Vermont). The characters and affinities of these are fully treated of. (2) The new fauna discovered in 1860 in the Point Lévis beds, near Quebec, and the primordial character of the *Trilobites*. (3) The extension of the primordial fauna to Texas. (4) The recognition of the primordial fauna in Tennessee in 1856 and in Nebraska in 1858. (5) The Taconic System of Dr. Emmons. Under this head, M. Barrande considers the system of deposits, so-called, both geologically and palæontologically, in great detail; and he describes and figures the *Trilobites* quoted by Emmons. (6) The remainder of the memoir is occupied with discussing the views of Hall, Marcou, and Logan on various points bearing on the above subjects.

**Barrett, L.** On some Cretaceous Rocks in the south-eastern portion of Jamaica. < *Quart. Journ. Geol. Soc. Lond.*, vol. xvi, pp. 324-326. 1860.

> A stratigraphical paper, noting, however, the occurrence of *Hippurites*, *Inocerami*, and other Cretaceous fossils in limestones underlying the Tertiary series of Jamaica.

**Bayfield, *Capt.*** On the junction of the Transition and Primary Rocks of Canada and Labrador. < *Quart. Journ. Geol. Soc. Lond.*, vol. i, pp. 450-459. 1845.

> Contains lists of the fossils.

**Bell, Robert.** On the occurrence of Fresh-water Shells in some of our Post-Tertiary deposits. < *Canad. Nat.*, vol. vi, pp. 42-51. 1861.

> Describes the occurrence of various fresh-water shells in the Post-Tertiary deposits of Lower Canada, of the Lake Ontario region, of the Niagara River, and of the country round the Georgian Bay.

**Bessels, Emil.** Notes on Polaris Bay. < *Bull. de la Soc. de Géographie*, Paris, pp. 291-299. 1875.

> Contains notes on the Silurian and Post-Pliocene fossils.

**Deyiluh, E.** Ueber Leaia leidyi. < *Zeitschrift d. deutsch. geol. Ges.*, Bd. xvi, pp. 363, 364. 1864.

> A note on the characters of *Leaia leidyi*.

**Bigsby, John J.** Notes on the Geography and Geology of Lake Huron. < *Trans. Geol. Soc. Lond.*, ser. 2, vol. i, pp. 175-209, plates xxv-xxx. 1823.

> This memoir contains various notes on the fossils, and especially on the *Orthoceratites* and Corals. In an appendix is a note by Mr. Stokes on a *Trilobite*, to which he gives the name of *Asaphus platycephalus*, from the Trenton Limestone of St. Joseph Island. One of the figures in pl. xxvii exhibits the labrum. In the explanations to the plates, various descriptive notes on the fossils are given, and Mr. Stokes appends a description of his new genus *Huronia* (which he here regards as a Coral), and names five species of the same.

**Bigsby, John J.** On the Erratics of Canada. < *Quart. Journ. Geol. Soc. Lond.*, vol. vii, pp. 215-238. 1851.

> A geological paper, but notes the occurrence of Post-Tertiary strata with numerous fossil *Uniones* on the banks of the Nottawasauga River, Georgian Bay, Ontario, along with other fresh-water shells.

**Bigsby, John J.** On the Geology of the Lake of the Woods, South Hudson's Bay. < *Quart. Journ. Geol. Soc. Lond.*, vol. viii, pp. 400–406. 1852.

Notes the occurrence of several Upper Silurian fossils in limestone at Sandhill Lake, near Lake of the Woods.

**Bigsby, John J.** On the Geology of Quebec and its environs. < *Quart. Journ. Geol. Soc. Lond.*, vol. ix, pp. 82–101, with map and 4 engravings. 1853.

Contains lists of fossils collected by the author from the Lower Silurian rocks of the neighbourhood of Quebec, and from the Quebec Group of Point Levis. A description and figure of a new species of Graptolite (*Didymograpsus caduceus*) are supplied by Mr. Salter, the specimens being from the Quebec Group.

**Bigsby, John J.** On the Palæozoic Basin of the State of New York. Part i. A synoptical view of the mineralogical and fossil characters of the Palæozoic strata of the State of New York. < *Quart. Journ. Geol. Soc. Lond.*, vol. xiv, pp. 305, 306, and 335–427. 1858.

In the first portion of this memoir, the author gives an account of the Palæozoic strata of the State of New York, from the Catskill Formation to the Potsdam Sandstone inclusive, each formation being treated of as regards its lithological characters, its geological position and stratigraphical relations, and its fossils, these last being divided into "typical", "recurrent in Europe", and "recurrent in New York". A short section is devoted to geological and palæontological "inferences and conclusions", based on the preceding synoptical view of the strata; and the memoir is concluded with elaborate tables of fossils. These tables are as follows:—I. The Silurian fossils of the State of New York; II. The group-relations of the Silurian fossils of the State of New York; III. The recurrent fossils of the Trenton Limestone; IV. The fossils escaped from Lower to Upper Silurian, into and across the Middle or Transitional Period; V. The fossils common to Europe and the Niagara Group of the State of New York; VI. The group-relations of the fossils of the four Lower Helderberg Limestones; VII. The group-relations of the Devonian fossils of the State of New York; VIII. The recurrent fossils of the Devonian System of the State of New York, including the species which enter from the Silurian; IX. The recurrency of the fossils of the Corniferous Limestone; X. Hamilton fossils common to the State of New York and Europe; and XI. European fossils in the Chemung Group of the State of New York.

**Bigsby, John J.** On the Palæozoic Basin of the State of New York. Part ii. Classification of the Palæozoic strata of the State of New York. < *Quart. Journ. Geol. Soc. Lond.*, vol. xiv, pp. 427–452. 1858.

In this portion of his memoir, the author indicates what he believes to be the natural classification and arrangement of the Palæozoic Rocks of the State of New York, as shown both by palæontological and physical evidence.

**Bigsby, John J.** On the Palæozoic Basin of the State of New York. Part iii. An enquiry into the sedimentary and other external relations of the Palæozoic fossils of the State of New York. < *Quart. Journ. Geol. Soc. Lond.*, vol. xv, pp. 251–335. 1859.

The chief subjects treated of in this part of Dr. Bigsby's memoir are the characters and conditions of sediments generally, and of the Palæozoic sediments in particular; the distribution and immediate relations of Palæozoic animal life in Wales and in the State of New York; the groupings of fossils and their order of precedence; the increment and decrement of Palæozoic genera and species; the duration of invertebrate life; the epochal and geographical diffusion of species; the recurrence of organic forms; and the resemblances between the Palæozoic basins of Wales and New York. The paper is concluded by elaborate tables showing the distribution of the Silurian and Devonian fossils of the State of New York, and the different sedimentary habitats of the former.

**Bigsby, John J.** On the Laurentian Formation: its mineral constitution, its geographical distribution, and its residuary elements of life. < *Geological Magazine*, Dec. 1, vol. i, pp. 154–158, 200–206. 1864.

Contains remarks on the distribution of phosphate of lime and carbon in the Laurentian Rocks, and on the occurrence of *Eozoön*.

**Bigsby, John J.** Thesaurus Siluricus. The Flora and Fauna of the Silurian Period. With addenda (from recent acquisitions). 1 vol. 4°. pp. 214. London, 1868.

In this well-known catalogue of Silurian fossils, all the species of Invertebrate fossils known to the author at the date of his work are recorded, with the names of their authors and their geological and geographical positions.

**[Billings, E.]** Fossils of the Potsdam Sandstone; sea-weeds, shells, and foot-prints on the rock at Beauharnois. < *Canad. Nat.*, vol. i, pp. 32-39, with 2 woodcuts. 1856.

Notes on the fossils of the Potsdam Sandstone.

**[Billings, E.]** On some of the characteristic fossils of the Lower Silurian Rocks of Canada. < *Canad. Nat.*, vol. i, pp. 39-47, with 11 woodcuts. 1856.

**[Billings, E.]** On the Crinoidea or Stone-Lilies of the Trenton Limestone; with a description of a new species. < *Canad. Nat.*, vol. i, pp. 48-57, with 4 woodcuts. 1856.

The new species described is *Glyptocrinus ramulosus*.

**[Billings, E.]** Fossils of the Upper Silurian Rocks, Niagara and Clinton Groups. < *Canad. Nat.*, vol. i, pp. 57-60, plate i. 1856.

Describes some characteristic Niagara and Clinton fossils.

**[Billings, E.]** On the fossil corals of the Lower Silurian Rocks of Canada. < *Canad. Nat.*, vol. i, pp. 115-128, with 15 woodcuts. 1856.

Describes some characteristic species.

**[Billings, E.]** On some of the technical terms used in the description of fossil shells. < *Canad. Nat.*, vol. i, pp. 128-131, with 7 woodcuts. 1856.

Describes the structure of the shell of the *Brachiopoda*.

**[Billings, E.]** On some of the fossil shells of the Niagara and Clinton formations. < *Canad. Nat.*, vol. i, pp. 131-139, plate ii. 1856.

Describes some of the characteristic Brachiopods of the above-mentioned formations.

**[Billings, E.]** On some of the Lower Silurian fossils of Canada. < *Canad. Nat.*, vol. i, pp. 203-208, with 23 woodcuts. 1856.

Describes a number of Brachiopods from the Trenton and Hudson River formations.

**[Billings, E.]** Description of fossils occurring in the Silurian Rocks of Canada. < *Canad. Nat.*, vol. i, pp. 312-320, with 10 woodcuts. 1856.

Describes a number of characteristic Silurian fossils.

**[Billings, E.]** On the Tertiary Rocks of Canada, with some account of their fossils. < *Canad. Nat.*, vol. i, pp. 321-346, with 13 woodcuts. 1856.

Describes a number of Post-Pliocene fossils from Canada.

**[Billings, E.]** Fossils of the Hamilton Group. < *Canad. Nat.*, vol. i, pp. 471-479, with 18 woodcuts. 1856.

Descriptions of common Hamilton fossils, quoted for the most part from the *Geology of New York*, by Prof. Hall.

**[Billings, E.]** On the genera of fossil Cephalopoda occurring in Canada. < *Canad. Nat.*, vol. ii, pp. 135-138, plate ii. 1857.

Describes nine genera of fossil Cephalopods as known to occur in Canada.

**Billings, E.** Notes on some of the more remarkable genera of Silurian and Devonian fossils. < *Canad. Nat.*, new ser., vol. ii, pp. 184-198, with 14 woodcuts, and pp. 405-409, with 3 woodcuts. 1857.

Discusses the structure and affinities of *Receptaculites, Pasceolus*, and *Beatricea*.

**Billings, E.** New genera and species of fossils from the Silurian and Devonian formations of Canada. < *Canad. Nat.*, vol. iii, pp. 419-444, with 24 woodcuts. 1858.

Descriptions of numerous new fossils, from the *Report of Progress of the Geological Survey of Canada for* 1857.

**Billings, E.** Report for the year 1857. < *Geological Survey of Canada: Report of Progress for the year* 1857. Toronto, 1858. pp. 147-192, with 24 engravings.

In the first part of this report, amongst other matters, is an essay on the fauna of the Black River and Trenton Limestones of Canada, as compared with that of the equivalent formations in the United States. The remainder of the report is occupied with descriptions of new genera and species of fossils. Amongst the Corals twenty new species are described from the Lower and Upper Silurian and the Devonian formations; the genus *Palæophyllum* being described as new. Thirteen new species of Lamellibranchs are described, allocated amongst the three newly defined groups of *Cyrtodonta, Vanuxemia,* and *Matheria.* Lastly, the remarkable *Obolus [Dinobolus] canadensis* is described and figured, and the new genus *Eichwaldia* is proposed for a single new Brachiopod (*E. subtrigonalis*) from the Trenton Limestone.

**Billings, E.** On the Asteriadæ of the Lower Silurian Rocks of Canada. < *Figures and Descriptions of Canadian Organic Remains: Decade III.* Montreal, 1858. pp. 75-85, plates viii-x, with 2 woodcuts.

This memoir describes 9 Echinoderms, which the author refers to the *Asteriadæ*. One of these, however, belongs to *Agelacrinites*, and another is referable to the abnormal sessile genus *Edrioaster* (here proposed by the author in lieu of the name *Cyclaster*, which he had previously brought forward, but which is preoccupied). All the species are from the Trenton Limestone or Hudson River Group. *Stenaster, Petraster,* and *Tæniaster* are defined as new genera.

**Billings, E.** On the Cystideæ of the Lower Silurian Rocks of Canada. < *Figures and Descriptions of Canadian Organic Remains: Decade III.* Montreal, 1858. pp. 9-74, plates i-vii, with 22 engravings.

In the first portion of this work, the author treats of the geological position, structure, and classification of the Cystideans, including such subjects as the general form and external skeleton of these organisms; the mouth, ambulacral orifice, and anus; the arms, ambulacral grooves, and pinnulæ; the pectinated rhombs, and the column. The second section deals with the ambulacral orifices of the Cystideans and Crinoids, and adduces a large body of evidence on this head. The third section comprises descriptions of the species of Cystideans found in the Lower Silurian of Canada, 19 species being described, belonging to the genera *Pleurocystites, Glyptocystites, Comarocystites, Amygdalocystites, Malocystites, Palæocystites,* and *Atelecystites,* of which the last three are now for the first time founded.

[**Billings, E.**] Geological Survey of Canada. Report of progress for the years 1853-54-55-56. Printed by order of the legislative assembly, 1858.

The Palæontological portion of this report is by Mr. Billings, and the first section reviews the palæontological relations of the Anticosti Rocks. In the second section the author gives detailed descriptions (unaccompanied by figures) of numerous new species of fossils from the Silurian Rocks of Canada, comprising 36 Echinoderms, 4 Brachiopods, 14 Gasteropods, 34 Cephalopods, 3 Trilobites, 2 species of *Pasceolus* (of uncertain affinities), and 2 of *Beatricea* (here referred to the vegetable kingdom). There are also descriptions of 10 species of Cystideans, which the author had previously published in the *Canadian Journal* (ser. 1, vol. ii, 1854). The new genera described are *Hybocrinus, Carabocrinus, Cleiocrinus, Porocrinus, Pasceolus,* and *Beatricea.* The *Huronia* of Stokes are referred to the genus *Orthoceras*.

**Billings, E.** On some new genera and species of Brachiopoda from the Silurian and Devonian Rocks of Canada. < *Canad. Nat.*, vol. iv, pp. 131-135, with 10 figures. [From the *Report of the Geological Survey of Canada for 1858.*] 1859.

Founds the genera *Centronella* and *Stricklandia* (subsequently altered to *Stricklandinia*), and describes three new species of the latter.

**Billings, E.** Description of a new genus of Brachiopoda, and on the genus Cyrtodonta. < *Canad. Nat.*, vol. iv, pp. 301-303. [Published in advance from the *Report of the Geological Survey of Canada*, 1858-59.] 1859.

Founds the genus *Camerella*, with three new species, and amends the characters of *Cyrtodonta*.

**Billings, E.** Fossils of the Calciferous Sandrock, including those of a deposit of White Limestone at Mingan, supposed to belong to the formation. < *Canad. Nat.*, vol. iv, pp. 345-367, with 12 engravings. [From the *Report of the Geological Survey of Canada for 1858-59.*] 1859.

Describes 41 species from the Calciferous Sandstone, of which 24 are new.

**Billings, E.** Description of a new Palæozoic Starfish of the genus Palæaster, from Nova Scotia. < *Canad. Nat.*, vol. iv, pp. 69, 70, with a woodcut. 1859.

Describes, under the name of *Palæaster parviusculus*, a new Starfish from the Lower Arisaig Group (Middle Silurian) of Arisaig, Nova Scotia.

**Billings, E.** Descriptions of some new species of Trilobites from the Lower and Middle Silurian Rocks of Canada. < *Canad. Nat.*, vol. iv, pp. 367-383, with 12 engravings. [Extracted from the *Report of the Geological Survey of Canada for 1858-59.*] 1859.

Describes 12 new species of *Trilobites* (9 of *Illænus*, 1 of *Amphion*, and 1 of *Triarthrus*).

**Billings, E.** Fossils of the Chazy Limestone, with descriptions of new species. < *Canad. Nat.*, vol. iv, pp. 426-470, with 33 engravings. [Extracted from the *Report of the Geological Survey of Canada for 1858-59.*] 1859.

Contains notices or descriptions of 129 species of fossils from the Chazy Limestone, being the total number at that time known as occurring in this formation in Canada. Thirty-four species are described as new.

[**Billings, E.**] Atrypa hemiplicata. < *Canad. Journ.*, new ser., vol. iv, p. 316. 1859.

A note stating that *Atrypa hemiplicata*, Hall, is a *Pentamerus*, and that *Pentamerus reversus*, Bill., is only a large variety of it.

**Billings, E.** On the Crinoideæ of the Lower Silurian Rocks of Canada. < *Figures and Descriptions of Canadian Organic Remains: Decade IV.* Montreal, 1859. pp. 72, plates i-x, with 24 woodcuts.

In the first portion of this work, the author gives an account of the history and structure of the Crinoids, and in the second portion he describes all the Lower Silurian Crinoids of Canada which are in such a state of preservation as to allow of characterisation. In all, 43 species are recognized, belonging to 13 genera, and 18 species of the above number are described for the first time. The new generic types described are *Blastoidocrinus*, *Pachyocrinus*, *Palæocrinus*, *Rhæocrinus*, and *Syringocrinus*. Of these, *Blastoidocrinus*, *Pachyocrinus*, and *Syringocrinus*, being based on incomplete examples, are not fully defined; and the most remarkable of them is the first, which forms in many respects a transitional between the *Blastoidea* and the true Crinoids.

## II.—PUBLICATIONS MADE IN BRITISH AMERICA, ETC. 81

**Billings, E.** On the Fossil Corals of the Devonian Rocks of Canada West. < *Canad. Journ.*, new ser., vol. iv, pp. 97-140, with 29 woodcuts. 1859.

This memoir contains descriptions of 45 species of fossil Corals from the Corniferous and Hamilton formations of Ontario. The new genera *Blothrophyllum* and *Haimeophyllum* are founded, and the new species are distributed as follows :—*Alveolites labiosa, A. cryptodens, Syringopora laxata, Aulopora cornuta, A. filiformis, A. umbellifera, Heliophyllum eriense, H. cayugaense, H. canadense, H. tenuiseptatum, H. colligatum, Clisiophyllum oneidaense, Blothrophyllum decorticatum, Eridophyllum simcoense, Diphyphyllum stramineum, D. arundinaceum, Oystiphyllum aggregatum, C. senecaense, C. grandis ?,* and *Haimeophyllum ordinatum.*

**Billings, E.** Notes on the structure of the Crinoidea, Cystidea, and Blastoidea. < *Canad. Nat.*, new ser., vol. iv, pp. 277-293, with 16 woodcuts, and pp. 426-433, with 7 woodcuts; also, *ibid.*, vol. v, pp. 180-198, with 14 woodcuts. 1859 and 1860.

**Billings, E.** On some new species of fossils from the Limestone near Point Levis opposite Quebec. < *Canad. Nat.*, vol. v, pp. 301-324, with 30 engravings. 1860.

This memoir deals with the fossils found in four limestones which are exposed at Point Levis, near Quebec, 64 species being known, but only the *Trilobites* being here described. The new species described are 3 of *Agnostus*, 1 of *Conocephalites*, 6 of *Dikellocephalus*, 2 of *Arionellus*, 2 of *Menocephalus*, 8 of *Bathyurus*, 2 of *Cheirurus*, and 2 of *Asaphus.*

**Billings, E.** Description of some new species of fossils from the Lower and Middle Silurian Rocks of Canada. < *Canad. Nat.*, vol. v, pp. 49-69, with 12 engravings. [Extracted from the *Report of the Geological Survey of Canada for* 1860.] 1860.

Describes 7 species of *Strophomena*, of which 6 are new, and 5 new species of *Trilobites.*

**Billings, E.** New species of fossils from the Lower Silurian Rocks of Canada. < *Canad. Nat.*, vol. v, pp. 161-177, with 20 engravings. [Extracted from *Report of the Geological Survey of Canada for* 1860.] 1860.

Sixteen new species are described in this memoir, 10 of these being Gasteropods and 6 Cephalopods.

**Billings, E.** On the Devonian fossils of Canada West. < *Canad. Journ.*, new ser., vol. v, pp. 249-232, and vol. vi, pp. 138-143, 253-274, and 329-363, plate i, and 133 woodcuts. 1860.

This is really a continuation of the memoir just noticed. Eleven additional species of Corals are described, belonging to the genera *Striatopora* (2 sp.), *Trachypora* (1 sp.), *Alveolites* (4 sp.), *Diphyphyllum* (1 sp.), *Heliophyllum* (1 sp.), *Chonophyllum* (1 sp.), and *Cyathophyllum* (1 sp.). The *Brachiopoda* of the Corniferous and Hamilton formations are next treated of with great fulness; the characters of many of the genera being minutely discussed. Forty-three species of Brachiopods are determined, of which 30 are previously recorded forms, whilst 13 are described as new species. In the class of the *Lamellibranchiata*, the characters of the genus *Cyrtodonta* and its synonymy are treated at length, and a new Corniferous Bivalve of the subgenus *Vanuxemia* is described under the name of *V. tompkinsi.* Three new species of Gasteropods are recorded, and, amongst Cephalopods, two new forms of *Cyrtoceras.* The occurrence of 9 species of *Trilobites* and 2 of *Leperditia* in these deposits is finally noted.

**Billings, E.** On some of the rocks and fossils occurring near Philipsburg, Canada East. < *Canad. Nat.*, vol. vi, pp. 310-328, with 6 engravings. 1861.

Describes the rocks near Philipsburg, and the fossils contained in them. From strata of the age of the Calciferous a number of fossils were obtained, of which *Camerella calcifera Eccullomphalus canadensis, E. intortus, E. spiralis,* and *Amphion salteri* are described as new species.

Mis. Pub. No. 10——6

**Billings, E.** On the occurrence of Graptolites in the base of the Lower Silurian. < *Canad. Nat.*, vol. vi, pp. 344-348. 1861.

Deals with the different forms of *Graptolites* found in the different members of the Silurian System in various parts of the world, with especial reference to the bearing of these fossils on the question as to the age of the Quebec Group.

**Billings, E.** New species of Lower Silurian fossils. Montreal, 1861. pp. 24, with 25 engravings.

In this pamphlet (subsequently republished in the same author's *Palæozoic Fossils*, vol. I, 1865), Mr. Billings describes a number of fossils from the Potsdam Sandstone, Calciferous, Chazy, Black River, and Trenton formations. The genus *Archæocyathus* (doubtfully referred to the Sponges) is proposed for some singular fossils from limestones at Anse au Loup, of the age of the Potsdam Group, the new genus *Obolella* for Brachiopods from the same formation, and the genus *Salterella* for Tubicolar *Annelides*, discovered in the same beds. Some Sponges from the Chazy Limestone are grouped together under the new generic title of *Eospongia*.

**Billings, E.** Remarks upon Prof. Hall's recent publication, entitled "Contributions to Palæontology". < *Canad. Nat.*, vol. vii, pp. 389-393. 1862.

Chiefly a controversial paper, dealing with questions of priority. The last portion of the paper is a critical notice of certain points in which Mr. Billings considers that Mr. Hall's determinations and conclusions are not correct.

[**Billings, E.**] Geological Survey of Canada. Report of progress from its commencement to 1863. pp. 983, with 498 wood-engravings. Montreal, 1863.

The greater portion of this classical work is occupied with the exposition of the geological structure of Canada; but numerous details are introduced by Mr. Billings as to the organic remains of each successive rock-formation. The fossils occurring in the typical sections of each formation are enumerated, and, though not described, very numerous illustrations are introduced for their elucidation. In an appendix, Mr. Billings gives a detailed catalogue of the Lower Silurian fossils of Canada (exclusive of those of the Quebec Group), the authority, reference, and geological range of each species being given. There is also a list of the *Graptolites* of the Quebec Group.

**Billings, E.** On the parallelism of the Quebec Group with the Llandeilo of England and Australia, and with the Chazy and Calciferous formations. < *Canad. Nat.*, vol. viii, pp. 19-30, with 4 engravings. 1863.

The object of this paper is to prove that the "Quebec Group" is truly referable to the Lower Silurian, and not to the "Primordial" formation. The evidence brought forward is mainly palæontological, though to some extent physical also. In conclusion, the author describes and figures a new species of *Harpes* (*H. dentoni*) from the Trenton Limestone of Ottawa, and a new *Cyrtina* (*C. euphemia*) from the Corniferous Limestone. The discovery of the calcareous spires of *Cyrtina* is also recorded.

**Billings, E.** Description of a new species of Phillipsia, from the Lower Carboniferous Rocks of Nova Scotia. < *Canad. Nat.*, vol. viii, pp. 209, 210, with woodcut. 1863.

The species is described under the name of *Phillipsia howi*.

**Billings, E.** On the genus Stricklandia;—proposed alteration of the name. < *Canad. Nat.*, vol. viii, p. 370. 1863.

The name *Stricklandia* being appropriated in fossil botany, the author changes the name of his genus to *Stricklandinia*.

**Billings, E.** Notice of some new genera and species of Palæozoic fossils. < *Canad. Nat.*, new ser., vol. ii, pp. 425-432. 1865.

Describes a number of species of Corals of the genera *Calapœcia, Heliolites, Favosites, Stenopora, Petraia, Zaphrentis, Eridophyllum,* and *Chonophyllum,* from the Middle Silurian of Anticosti and the Clinton Formation of Manitoulin Island. The genus *Calapœcia* is founded for Corals resembling *Heliolites*, but with twice as many septa and with mural pores.

**Billings, E.** Palæozoic fossils. Volume i. Containing descriptions and figures of new or little known species of organic remains from the Silurian Rocks. 1861-65. < *Geological Survey of Canada.* Montreal, 1865. 8°. pp. 426, with 401 engravings.

The first portion of this report (pp. 1-24) was published in 1861, and the principal changes that it has been subjected to in reprinting are that the discovery of spicules in *Archæocyathus* is noted, *A. profundus* is founded for specimens originally referred to *A. minganensis, Olenellus* is adopted instead of *Paradoxides*, and *Kutorgina* is inserted in the name of *Obolella cingulata*.

The second portion (pp. 25-56) was originally published in January, 1862, and deals with new species of fossils, mostly Gasteropods, Lamellibranchs, and Brachiopods, from the Calciferous, Chazy, Black River, and Trenton formations. The new genus *Arthroclema* is proposed for a branched *Polyzoön* (?) from the Trenton Limestone.

The third portion (pp. 57-168) was originally published in June, 1862; but pp. 57-66 are here added to the reissue, and embrace a Palæontological analysis of the fossils of the Quebec Group or Lévis Formation, as bearing on the stratigraphical relations of this deposit. The remaining portion (pp. 67-168) is occupied with descriptions of new species of fossils from the Quebec Group (pp. 67-96), and from different parts of the Lower, Middle, and Upper Silurian Rocks of Canada (pp. 96-168).

The fourth portion of the work (pp. 169-344) was originally issued in February, 1865, and the remainder (pp. 345-420) was issued with the complete work in October, 1865. These two sections of the report are occupied with detailed descriptions of the new species of fossils collected by the officers of the Geological Survey of Canada in the Lower Palæozoic formations of that country, from the Quebec Group to the Guelph Limestones, inclusive; but it would not be possible here to give any detailed analysis of the varied matter contained in the pages of this important work. It may be noted, however, that a large amount of space is devoted to the description of the fossils of the Quebec Group, and that a considerable number of species are characterised from this formation in Newfoundland.

**Billings, E.** Catalogue of the Silurian fossils of the Island of Anticosti, with descriptions of some new genera and species. pp. 93, with 28 engravings. < *Geological Survey of Canada.* Montreal, 1866.

In the first portion of this report (pp. 5-28), the author catalogues the Lower Silurian (Hudson River Group) fossils of the Island of Anticosti. The list comprises 118 species, including 28 forms which are now described for the first time. The second portion of the report (pp. 29-72) deals with the fossils of the "Anticosti Group" of rocks (Middle Silurian), enumerating 182 species; the new species, to the number of 76, being described at length. In an appendix (pp. 72, 73), some additional fossils from the Hudson River Group are considered, the new genus *Sœrichnites* being proposed for some curious tracks. An additional section (pp. 75-82) gives a general review of the palæontological relations of the Silurian deposits of Anticosti, and their relations to the Silurian formations of other regions in North America and Europe. Finally, a section is devoted to the description (pp. 82-93) of some new Cephalopods, Cystideans, and Corals from the Clinton and Niagara formations. Twenty-four new species are described, and the generic name of *Streptoceras* is proposed for Cephalopods with the form of *Oncoceras* combined with the trilobed aperture of *Phragmoceras*.

**Billings, E.** On the classification of the sub-divisions of McCoy's genus Athyris, as determined by the laws of zoological nomenclature. < *Ann. and Mag. Nat. Hist.*, ser. 3, vol. xx, pp. 233-247. 1867.

Reprinted from *Amer. Journ. Sci. and Arts*, July, 1867.

**Billings, E.** Description of two new species of Stricklandinia. < *Geological Magazine*, Dec. 1, vol. v, pp. 59–64, pl. iv. 1868.

The new species described are *Stricklandinia davidsoni* and *S. salterii*, both from the "Anticosti Group".

**Billings, E.** Note on the structure of the Blastoidea. < *Ann. and Mag. Nat. Hist.*, ser. 4, vol. iv, p. 76, 1869.

Reprinted from *Silliman's Amer. Journ.*, May, 1869.

[**Billings, E.**] Note on the Blastoidea. < *Canad. Nat.*, new ser., vol. iv, pp. 89, 90. 1869.

**Billings, E.** Notes on some specimens of Lower Silurian Trilobites. < *Quart. Journ. Geol. Soc. Lond.*, vol. xxvi, pp. 479–486, plates xxxi and xxxii. 1870.

The author describes (1) a specimen of *Asaphus platycephalus*, from the Trenton Limestone of Canada, showing the under side of the body, together with what appear to be the bases of eight pairs of legs; (2) specimens of several American species of *Asaphus*, showing "Panderian organs"; (3) a rolled-up specimen of *Calymene senaria* filled with small ovate bodies. The author also discusses the nature of *Protichnites* and *Climactichnites*, and concludes that these tracks have really been produced by *Trilobites*.

**Billings, E.** Notes on the structure of the Crinoidea, Cystidea, and Blastoidea. < *Ann. and Mag. Nat. Hist.*, ser. 4, vol. v, pp. 251–266 and 409–416, and vol. vii, pp. 142–158, with numerous engravings. 1870-71.

An elaborate paper on the above subject. Amongst the special points treated of are the position of the mouth in relation to the ambulacral system; the nature of the pectinated rhombs and calicine pores of the *Cystoidea*; the structure of *Codaster* McCoy, and of *Pentremites*; the homologies of the respiratory organs of the Palæozoic and recent Echinoderms; the "convoluted plate" of the *Crinoidea*; the structure of the calyx in *Pentremites* and *Nucleocrinus*; the resemblances between the Cystoids, Blastoids, and Crinoids on the one hand and the larvæ of the Asteroids on the other hand; and the nature and relations of the oral, anal, ovarian, and ambulacral openings. The forms upon which the author has founded his observations are American.

**Billings, E.** Note on Trimerella acuta. < *Ann. and Mag. Nat. Hist.*, ser. 4, vol. viii, pp. 140, 141. 1871.

Reprinted from *Amer. Journ. Sci. and Arts*, June, 1871.

**Billings, E.** On some new species of Palæozoic fossils. < *Canad. Nat.*, new ser., vol. vi, pp. 213–222, with 2 engravings. 1871.

Describes three new species of *Hyolithes* (*Theca*) from the Silurian of Canada, and changes *Theca triangularis*, Hall, to *Hyolithes americanus*. Defines the genus *Obolella*, and describes as new species *O. gemma* and *O. circe*. Also founds the genus *Monomerella*, and characterises two species.

**Billings, E.** Remarks on the Taconic controversy. < *Canad. Nat.*, new ser., vol. vi, pp. 313–325. 1871.

A discussion of the position of the "Taconic Rocks" of Emmons, chiefly from a palæontological point of view, and as connected with questions of priority.

**Billings, E.** On the genus Obolellina. < *Canad. Nat.*, new ser., vol. vi, pp. 326–331, with 7 woodcuts. 1871.

Gives an extended definition of *Obolellina*, and describes *O. magnifica*, from the Black River Limestone, as new.

**Billings, E.** Additional notes on the Taconic controversy. < *Canad. Nat.*, new ser., vol. vi, pp. 460–465. 1871.

**Billings, E.** On some fossils from the Primordial Rocks of Newfoundland. < *Canad. Nat.*, new ser., vol. vi, pp. 465-479, with 14 engravings. 1871.

From rocks of Primordial age in Great Bell Island, *Lingula murrayi*, *Lingulella? affinis*, L. (?) *spissa*, and *Cruziana similis* are described as new. From Menevian strata *Obolella ? miser*, *Straparollina remota*, *Hyolithes excellens*, *Agraulos socialis*, *A. affinis*, *Solenopleura communis*, *Anopolenus venustus*, *Paradoxides tenellus*, *P. decorus*, *Iphidea bella*, *Stenotheca pauper*, and *Scenella reticulata* are described as new. *Iphidea* is proposed as a new genus for small Brachiopods allied to *Acrotreta* and *Kutorgina*; and *Scenella* for Gasteropods allied to *Metoptoma*. *Aspidella terranovica* is the name given to some curious fossils from the Huronian of St. John's, associated with *Arenicolites spiralis*.

**Billings, E.** Note on the discovery of fossils in the "Winooski Marble" at Swanton, Vt. < *Canad. Nat.*, new ser., vol. vi, p. 351. 1871.

Notes the discovery of *Salterella* in the "Winooski Marble", showing this rock to be of the age of the Belle Isle Limestone.

**Billings, E.** On the Mesozoic fossils from British Columbia. < *Geological Survey of Canada: Report of Progress for 1872-73*. Appendix ii, pp. 71-75. 1873.

This memoir contains notes on the Mesozoic fossils collected by Mr. James Richardson in British Columbia in 1872. There is also a table showing the geological horizons of the Mesozoic Rocks of British Columbia as compared with those of England, Nebraska, and California.

**Billings, E.** Palæozoic fossils. Vol. ii, part i. pp. 144, with 85 woodcuts and 9 plates. < *Memoirs of the Geological Survey of Canada*. Montreal, 1874.

The first section of this work contains descriptions of the fossils of the "Gaspé Series", some of the beds of which are Upper Silurian and some Devonian, with an intermediate group that may be regarded as passage-beds. The new species determined from this series comprise 5 species of Corals, 3 of Polyzoa, 18 of Brachiopods, 10 of Lamellibranchs, 8 of Gasteropods, and 1 Trilobite. The next section gives descriptions of fossils obtained from the Primordial Rocks of Bell Island, Newfoundland, the exact position of these deposits being somewhat uncertain. Descriptions of some of these forms had been previously published (*Canad. Nat.*, 1872); but six are new species. From beds inferior to those of Bell Island, and thought to be referable to the Lower Lingula Flags or Menevian Group, eleven new species of fossils are described. From the Huronian Rocks of St. John's, Newfoundland, the author describes *Aspidella terranovica*, *Stenotheca pauper*, and *Scenella reticulata*—the last two being small patelliform Gasteropods, whilst the affinities of the first are uncertain.

The author next discusses the characters of the genus *Stricklandinia*, describing five previously recorded species and a single new form (*S. melissa*). The next portion of the work is occupied with a discussion of the structure of the *Crinoidea*, *Cystoidea*, and *Blastoidea*. This section was originally published in the *Amer. Journ. Sci. and Arts*, 1869-70, and the *Ann. and Mag. Nat. Hist.*, 1870-71. and it is reproduced here with some corrections and additions. Finally, the author describes 18 new species of *Lamellibranchiata* from the Arisaig series (Upper Silurian) of Nova Scotia. The new genus *Pteronitella* is proposed for forms like *Pterinea retroflexa*, and 3 species are referred to it.

**Billings, E.** On some new or little known fossils from the Silurian and Devonian Rocks of Canada. < *Canad. Nat.*, new ser., vol. vii, pp. 230-240, with 2 figures. 1874.

Describes *Aulocopina granti*, a new genus and species of fossil sponges from the Niagara formation. The genus *Heterophrentis* is proposed for Corals of the type of *Zaphrentis prolifica* Bill. Species of *Amplexus*, *Zaphrentis*, *Gyroceras*, *Orthoceras*, and *Lichas* are described from the Devonian of Ontario. Finally, some changes of nomenclature are noted.

**Billings, E.** On some new genera and species of Palæozoic Mollusca. < *Canad. Nat.*, new ser., vol. vii, pp. 301, 302, with 2 figures. 1875.

Founds the new genus *Illionia* for *Tellina prisca* His., *Anatina sinuata* Hall, and the new *I. canadensis* from the Upper Silurian of the Bay of Chaleurs. The genus *Pteronitella* is proposed for forms of the type of *Pterinea retroflexa.*

**Bouvé, M.** Pygorhynchus gouldii, a new Echinus from the Millstone Grit of Georgia. < *Ann. and Mag. Nat. Hist.*, ser. 1, vol. xix, p. 142. 1847.

A reprint from *Silliman's Journal*, May, 1847, p. 437.

**Bradley, Frank H.** Description of a new Trilobite from the Potsdam Sandstone, with a note by E. Billings. < *Canad. Nat.*, vol. v, pp. 420–425, with 4 engravings. 1860.

This paper by Mr. Bradley is reprinted from *Silliman's Journal*, 2d ser., vol. xxx, p. 241, and describes and figures a new *Trilobite* from the Potsdam Sandstone of Keeseville, N. Y., under the name of *Conocephalites minutus.* Mr. Billings adds a note discussing the characters of this species, and noting the other forms of the genus known to occur in Canada. Mr. Billings also appends an additional note (reprinted from *Silliman's Journal*, November, 1870), describing some new specimens of *Conocephalites minutus*, in which fresh characters are exhibited.

**Brady, G. S., and H. W. Crosskey.** Notes on fossil Ostracoda from the Post-Tertiary deposits of Canada and New England. < *Geological Magazine*, Decade I, vol. viii, pp. 60–65, plate ii. 1871.

The authors notice 33 species of *Ostracoda* from the above-mentioned deposits, of which *Cythere cuspidata, C. macchesneyi, C. logani, Oytherura granulosa, C. cristata,* and *Oytheropteron complanatum* are described for the first time.

**Brady, Henry B.** A monograph of Carboniferous and Permian Foraminifera (the genus Fusulina excepted). < *Palæontographical Society*, 1876, pp. 1–166, plates i–xii.

This work is necessarily principally concerned with British forms, but not exclusively so. At page 47 is a summary of geological localities in North America which have yielded Carboniferous or Permian *Foraminifera.* The following forms are described from the Carboniferous Rocks of North America:—*Valvulina palæotrochus* Ehrb., *V. decurrens, V. plicata* Brady, *V. bulloides,* n. sp., *V. rudis,* n. sp., *Nodosinella priscilla* Dawson, *Calcarina ambigua,* n. sp., and *Endothyra bowmani* Phill. The last is shown to be the subsequently described *Rotalia baileyi* Hall, from the Spergen Hill Limestone of Indiana.

**Brongniart, Adolphe.** Histoire des Végétaux Fossiles. Tom. i. Pl. vi, pp. 70, 71. 1824–48.

The fossils described by Brongniart under the names *Fucoides dentatus* and *Fucoides serra,* from the Quebec Group of Point Lévis, are really *Graptolites*; the former being the *Graptolithus* [*Diplograptus*] *pristiniformis* of Hall, and the latter the *G.* [*Tetragraptus*] *bryonoides* of the same author.

**Bronn, H. G.** Lethæa Geognostica, oder Abbildung und Beschreibung der für die Gebirgsformationen bezeichnendsten Versteinerungen. [Figures and descriptions of the characteristic fossils of the great formations.] 1st ed., 1835; 3d ed. (Bronn & Roemer), 1851–56. 3 vols. 8°. With atlas.

Describes many species of American fossils.

**Buckland, William.** "Geology", in "Voyage, &c., to the Pacific and Behring's Straits, performed in H. M. S. 'Blossom'", by Captain Beechey. 4°. London, 1839. p. 157.

In the geological appendix to Capt. Beechey's work, Prof. Buckland notices the resemblance of the Carboniferous Limestone of Cape Thomson, northwest of America, lat. 67° 6′ N. long. 163° 45′ W., to that of Derbyshire, and refers to its fossil contents.

**Burmeister, Hermann.** The organisation of Trilobites, deduced from their living affinities, with a systematic review of the species hitherto described. Edited from the German by Professors Bell and Forbes. *Ray Society*, 1846. pp. 136, with 6 plates.

<small>Describes several species of North American *Trilobites* and two species of *Eurypterus*.</small>

**Carpenter, Philip P.** On the Pleistocene fossils collected by Col. E. Jewett at Sta. Barbara (California); with descriptions of new species. <*Ann. and Mag. Nat. Hist.*, ser. 3, vol. xvii, pp. 274-278. 1866.

<small>The new species described are *Turritella jewettii, Bittium ? asperum, B. armillatum, Opalia (? crenatoides*, var.) *insculpta, Trophon tenuisculptus,* and *Pisania fortis.*</small>

**Carpenter, W. B.** Additional note on the structure and affinities of Eozoön canadense. <*Quart. Journ. Geol. Soc. Lond.*, vol. xxi, pp. 59-66, plates viii, ix, and woodcut. 1865.

<small>The author in this memoir gives a full description of the structure of *Eozoön canadense* as elucidated by him, and in support of the views expressed by Principal Dawson (*Quart. Journ. Geol. Soc.*, vol. xxi, p. 51). The affinities of *Eozoön* with recent *Foraminifera* are also fully discussed.</small>

**Carpenter, W. B.** Eozoön canadense. <*Intellectual Observer*, No. xl, p. 300. 1865.

<small>[Not seen by the writer.]</small>

**Carpenter, W. B.** Notes on the structure and affinities of Eozoön canadense. <*Canad. Nat.*, new ser., vol. ii, pp. 111-119. 1867.

<small>A reprint from *Quart. Journ. Geol. Soc. Lond.*, 1865.</small>

**Carpenter, W. B.** Further observations on the structure and affinities of Eozoön canadense. In a letter to the president. <*Proc. Roy. Soc. Lond.*, vol. xv, pp. 503-508. 1867.

<small>A *résumé* of the state of the Eozoön controversy at the time (1867).</small>

**Carpenter, W. B.** New observations on Eozoön canadense. <*Ann. and Mag. Nat. Hist.*, ser. 4, vol. xiii, pp. 456-470, with 2 engravings. 1874.

<small>The author treats more especially of the nummuline layer and the canal-system of the "intermediate skeleton", and concludes by summarising the *general* evidence in favour of the organic origin of *Eozoön*.</small>

**Carpenter, W. B.** Final note on Eozoön canadense. <*Ann. and Mag. Nat. Hist.*, ser. 4, vol. xiv, pp. 371, 372. 1874.

**Carpenter, W. B.** Remarks on Mr. H. J. Carter's letter to Prof. King on the structure of the so-called Eozoön canadense. <*Ann. and Mag. Nat. Hist.*, ser. 4, vol. xiii, pp. 277-284, with 2 engravings. 1874.

<small>A recapitulation of the principal facts in support of the belief that *Eozoön canadense* is a *Foraminifer*.</small>

**Carpenter, W. B.** Further researches on Eozoön canadense. <*Rep. Brit. Assoc. for* 1874, *Sections*, pp. 136, 137. 1875.

**Carpenter, W. B.** Notes on Otto Hahn's "Microgeological Investigation of Eozoön canadense". <*Ann. and Mag. Nat. Hist.*, ser. 4, vol. xvii, pp. 417-422. 1876.

**Carter, H. J.** On the structure called Eozoön canadense in the Laurentian Limestone of Canada. (A letter to Prof. W. King.) < *Ann. and Mag. Nat. Hist.*, ser. 4, vol. xiii, pp. 189-193. 1874.

> Gives reasons for believing that *Eozoön* is not of organic origin.

**Carter, H. J.** On the structure called Eozoön canadense in the Laurentian Limestone of Canada. < *Ann. and Mag. Nat. Hist.*, ser. 4, vol. xiii, pp. 376-378, with 1 engraving. 1874.

**Carter, H. J.** Relation of the Canal-system to the Tubulation in the Foraminifera, with reference to Dr. Dawson's 'Dawn of Life'. < *Ann. and Mag. Nat. Hist.*, ser. 4, vol. xvi, pp. 420-424. 1875.

> Discusses the minute structure of the test of recent *Foraminifera*, as bearing on the nature of *Eozoön canadense*.

**Casseday, S. A.** Beschreibung eines neuen Crinoiden-Geschlechtes aus dem Kohlenkalkstein Nord-Amerikas. < *Zeitschrift d. Deutsch. Geol. Ges.*, Bd. vi, pp. 237-242, plate ii. 1854.

> The author proposes and defines the genus *Batocrinus* for two new species (*B. icosadactylus* and *B. irregularis*) from the Carboniferous Limestone of Indiana.

**Castelnau, F. de.** Essai sur le Système Silurien de l'Amérique Septentrionale. Paris, 1843. pp. 56. With 17 plates.

> In this work, the author describes a number of Crustaceans, Cephalopods, Gasteropods, Brachiopods, Conchifera, Corals, Crinoids, &c., from the Silurian of North America. A large number of species are described as new, but many of these have been subsequently identified with previously recorded forms.

**C[hapman], E. J.** Asaphus canadensis. < *Canad. Journ.*, new ser., vol. i, pp. 482, 483. 1856.

> Confers the name of *Asaphus canadensis* on a new *Trilobite* from the Utica Slate.

**Chapman, E. J.** A review of the Trilobites: their characters and classification. < *Canad. Journ.*, new ser., vol. i, pp. 271-286. 1856.

> A general review of the order *Trilobita*.

**C[hapman], E. J.** Asaphus latimarginatus. < *Canad. Journ.*, new ser., vol. ii, pp. 47, 48. 1857.

> Discusses a question raised by Prof. Hall as to the identity of the author's *Asaphus canadensis* with the previously described *A. latimarginatus* Hall, and fully describes the characters of the former.

**Chapman, E. J.** On the occurrence of the genus Cryptoceras in Silurian Rocks. < *Canad. Journ.*, new ser., vol. ii, pp. 264-268. 1857.

> Notes the occurrence of the genus *Cryptoceras* in the Black River Limestone of Lorette in Eastern Canada.

**Chapman, E. J.** On the occurrence of the genus Cryptoceras in Silurian Rocks. < *Ann. and Mag. Nat. Hist.*, ser. 2, vol. xx, pp. 114-117. 1857.

> Notes the occurrence in the Lower Silurian Rocks of Canada of a species of *Cryptoceras* [*Lituites*].

**C[hapman], E. J.** Trinucleus concentricus. < *Canad. Journ.*, new ser., vol. iii, pp. 414, 415, with woodcut. 1858.

> Describes the glabella of a specimen of the above *Trilobite* from the Trenton Limestone near Quebec, which shows peculiar basal and central tubercles.

**Chapman, E. J.** On some new Trilobites from Canadian Rocks. < *Ann. and Mag. Nat. Hist.*, ser. 3, vol. ii, pp. 9–16, with 2 woodcuts. 1858.

Maintains the distinctness of *Asaphus canadensis* Chapm., which the author had previously described, by an analysis of the other known species of the genus. The name *Asaphus halli* is proposed for a second form, from the Trenton Limestone of Peterborough, Ontario.

**Chapman, E. J.** On some new Trilobites from Canadian Rocks. < *Canad. Journ.*, new ser., vol. iii, pp. 230–238, with 2 woodcuts. 1858.

Describes and figures as new species *Asaphus canadensis* from the Utica Slate and *A. halli* from the Trenton Limestone.

**Chapman, E. J.** On the Hypostoma of Asaphus canadensis, and on a third new species of Asaphus from the Canadian Rocks. < *Canad. Journ.*, new ser., vol. iv, pp. 1–4, with 2 woodcuts. 1859.

The new species is from the Utica Slate, and is named *Asaphus hincksii*.

**Chapman, E. J.** Presence of Columnaria alveolata and Stromatocerium rugosum in Trenton Limestone. < *Canad. Journ.*, new ser., vol. iv, p. 493. 1859.

Notes the discovery of the above-mentioned species in the Trenton Limestone of the neighbourhood of Belleville, Ont.

**Chapman, E. J.** On a new species of Agelacrinites, and on the structural relations of that genus. < *Ann. and Mag. Nat. Hist.*, ser. 3, vol. vi, pp. 157–162, with woodcut. 1860.

Describes *Agelacrinites billingsii*, from the Trenton Limestone of Peterborough, Canada West.

**Chapman, E. J.** Notes on the Geology of the Blue Mountain Escarpment in Collingwood Township, Canada West. < *Canad. Journ.*, new ser., vol. v, pp. 304, 305. 1860.

Contains notes on the fossils (Utica Slate and Hudson River Group).

**Chapman, E. J.** On the geology of Belleville and the surrounding district. < *Canad. Journ.*, new ser., vol. v, pp. 41–48. 1860.

Gives lists of, and notes on, the fossils of the Trenton Limestone of Belleville, Ont.

**Chapman, E. J.** Agelacrinites billingsii: a new species: preliminary notice. < *Canad. Journ.*, new ser., vol. v, pp. 204, 205. 1860.

**Chapman, E. J.** On a new species of Agelacrinites, and on the structural relations of that genus. < *Canad. Journ.*, new ser., vol. v, pp. 358–365, with woodcut. 1860.

The author describes a new species of *Agelacrinites* from the Trenton Limestone of Peterborough, Ont., under the name of *A. billingsii*. The structure and systematic relations of the genus are discussed, and the author proposes to found for its reception, along with *Edrioaster*, a new order, which he terms *Thyroida*.

**Chapman, E. J.** A popular exposition of the Minerals and Geology of Canada. < *Canad. Journ.*, new ser., vols. v, vi, vii, and viii, with 243 engravings. 1860–63.

Part iv of this series of papers (*loc. cit.*, vol. vi, pp. 500–518, vol. vii, pp. 108–121, and vol. viii, pp. 17–33) gives a general account of the fossils of Canada; and part v (vol. viii, pp. 111–127, 185–216, and 437–462) gives a review of the successive stratified formations of Canada and their characteristic organic remains.

**Chapman, E. J.** An outline of the Geology of Canada, based on a subdivision of the provinces into natural areas. 8°. pp. 104, with 12 plates and maps. Toronto, 1876.

Contains notes on the organic remains of the different geological formations of Canada, with six plates illustrating the more characteristic fossils.

**Chapman, E. J.** On the probable nature of the supposed fossil tracks known as Protichnites and Climactichnites. < *Canad. Journ.*, new ser., vol. xvi, pp. 7. 1877.

The author gives reasons for believing *Protichnites* and *Climactichnites*, from the Potsdam Sandstone, are not the tracks of Crustaceans, but the impressions of large Fucoids.

**Cleve, P. T.** On the geology of the North-eastern West India Islands. < *Kongl. Svenska Vetenskaps-Akad. Handl.*, Bd. ix, No. 12, pp. 48, with 2 plates. 1870.

Contains numerous notes on the fossils.

**Cotteau, G.** Sur les Oursins des Antilles suédoises. < *Bull. de la Soc. Géol. de France*, sér. 3, t. ii, pp. 125, 126. 1875.

A preliminary note, drawing attention to the fact that the Miocene Echinoids of the Antilles have a close resemblance to those derived from the same beds in Malta and other Mediterranean islands.

**Cotteau, —.** Echinids of the West Indies. < *Kongl. Svenska Vetenskaps-Akad. Handl.*, Bd. xiii, No. 6. 1875.

[Not seen by the writer.]

**Credner, G. R.** Ceratites fastigiatus and Salenia texana. < *Zeitschrift für d. gesammten Naturwiss.*, Bd. xii, pp. 105–116, pl. v. 1875.

Describes *Salenia texana* from the Cretaceous (?) deposits of Texas.

**Credner, Hermann.** Die vor-silurischen Gebilde der oberen Halb-Insel von Michigan. < *Zeitschr. der Deutsch. Geol. Ges.*, Bd. xxi, pp. 516–559. 1869.

**Credner, Hermann.** Die Kreide von New Jersey. < *Zeitschr. der Deutsch. Geol. Ges.*, vol. xxii, pp. 191–251, pl. iv. 1870.

A considerable section of this memoir is devoted to the description of the fossils met with in the Cretaceous deposits of New Jersey, and another deals with their vertical extension and stratigraphical relations.

**Dana, J. D.** On the supposed legs of the Trilobite, Asaphus platycephalus. < *Ann. and Mag. Nat. Hist.*, ser. 4, vol. vii, pp. 366–368. 1871.

An advance copy of an article published in the *Amer. Journ. Sci. and Arts*, May, 1871.

**D'Archiac, —.** Note sur l'existence des restes organiques dans les Roches Laurentiennes du Canada. < *Comptes Rendus*, vol. liii, pp. 192–194. 1865.

A note presented by M. D'Archiac on the part of Dr. W. B. Carpenter as to the discovery of *Eozoön canadense*.

**D'Archiac,** *Viscount, and* **Édouard de Verneuil.** On the fossils of the older deposits in the Rhenish Provinces; preceded by a general survey of the fauna of the Palæozoic Rocks, and followed by a tabular list of the organic remains of the Devonian System in Europe. < *Trans. Geol. Soc. Lond.*, ser. 2, vol. vi, part ii, pp. 303–310. 4°. 1842.

In the classified list supplied by the authors of the fossils of the older deposits of the Rhenish Provinces, and of the Devonian system of Europe generally, many species are determined as occurring in corresponding deposits in North America.

**Davidson, Thomas.** On the Lower Carboniferous Brachiopoda of Nova Scotia. < *Quart. Journ. Geol. Soc. Lond.*, vol. xix, pp. 158-175, pl. ix. 1863.

Fourteen species are described and figured, the following being new:—*Rhynchonella dawsoniana* and *R. acadiensis* (n. sp. 1).

**Davidson, Thomas,** *and* **William King.** Remarks on the genera Trimerella, Dinobolus, and Monomerella. < *Geological Magazine,* Decade I, vol. ix, pp. 442-445; also, *Ann. and Mag. Nat. Hist.,* ser. 4, vol. x, pp. 243-252. 1872.

This memoir, in which the authors found and define the family *Trimerellidæ,* is largely based upon American material.

**Davidson, Thomas,** *and* **William King.** On the Trimerellidæ, a Palæozoic family of the Palliobranchs or Brachiopoda. < *Quart. Journ. Geol. Soc. Lond.,* vol. xxx, pp. 124-172, pls. xii-xix. 1874.

This memoir treats exhaustively of the *Trimerellidæ,* and is principally founded upon American material. The following American species are fully described:—*Trimerella grandis, T. acuminata, T. billingsii, T.* (?) *galtensis, T. ohioensis, T. dalli, Monomerella prisca, M. orbicularis, Dinobolus conradi, D. canadensis,* and *D. magnificus.*

**Dawson, G. M.** Report on the Tertiary Lignite Formation in the vicinity of the 49th Parallel. < *British North American Boundary Commission, Geological Report of Progress for the year* 1873. 8°. Montreal, 1874. pp. 31, pls. i and ii.

The fossils of this formation are noticed. The Invertebrates are fresh-water and brackish-water in type.

**Dawson, G. M.** Note on the occurrence of Foraminifera, Coccoliths, &c., in the Cretaceous Rocks of Manitoba. < *Canad. Nat.,* new ser., vol. vii, pp. 252-257. 1874.

The author examined the Cretaceous Rocks of Pembina Mountain, some of which resembled the "chalk" of Nebraska in appearance and texture. The earthy base of this deposit consisted principally of *Foraminifera,* Coccoliths, and allied organisms. The author describes and figures *Textularia globulosa, T. pygmæa, Discorbina globularis, Planorbulina ariminensis,* and forms of Coccoliths and Rhabdoliths.

**Dawson, G. M.** Report on the geology and resources of the region in the vicinity of the Forty-ninth Parallel, from the Lake of the Woods to the Rocky Mountains; with lists of plants and animals collected, and notes on the fossils. pp. 379, with 18 plates and 3 maps. 1875.

There are notes on the fossils collected (mostly plants and vertebrates), and amongst these may be mentioned the microscopic organisms (*Foraminifera,* &c.) detected by the author in the Cretaceous Rocks of the Pembina escarpment and other localities.

**Dawson, J. W.** On the Coal-Measures of the South Joggins, Nova Scotia. < *Quart. Journ. Geol. Soc. Lond.,* vol. x, pp. 1-42. 1854.

The invertebrate fossils are noticed at p. 39, and some of the Lamellibranchs are figured (figs. 22-25).

**Dawson, J. W.** Acadian Geology. The geological structure, organic remains, and mineral resources of Nova Scotia, New Brunswick, and Prince Edward Island. 1st ed. 1854; 2d ed. 1868. 8°. pp. 694, with 231 engravings.

Considerable portions of this work are devoted to the invertebrate fossils of the region treated of. In Chapter V, the author gives an account of the Post-Pliocene deposits and their fossils. In Chapter XII (pp. 202-209), the *Mollusca, Annelida,* and *Crustacea* of the

Coal-Measures are treated of. In Chapter XVI (pp. 287–314), the author gives an account of the fossils of the Carboniferous Limestone, describing as new *Lithostrotion pictoense*, *Zaphrentis minus*, *Cyathophyllum billingsi*, *Stenopora exilis*, *Fenestella lyelli*, *Rhynchonella ida* Hartt, *R. evangelina* Hartt, *Centronella anna* Hartt, *Modiola poolei*, *M. avonia*, *Pteronites gayensis*, *Macrodon hardingi*, *M. curtus*, *M. ? shubenacadiensis*, *Edmondia hartii*, *E. anomala*. *Cypricardia insecta*, *Pleurophorus quadricostatus*, *Cardinia subangulata*, *C. antigonensis*, *Arca punctifer*, *Aviculopecten lyelli*, *A. reticulatus*, *A. simplex*, *A. cora*, *A. hebertianus*, *Conularia planicostata*, *Euomphalus exortivus*, *Naticopsis dispassa*, *Platyschisma dubia*, *Lozonema acutula*, *Murchisonia gypsea*, *M. tricingulata*, *Pleurotomaria dispersa*, *P. ignobilis*, *Nautilus avonensis*, *Gyroceras harttii*, *Orthoceras dilatum*, *O. vindobonense*, *O. perstrictum*, *Spirorbis angulatus*, *Serpulites hortonensis*, *S. annulatus*, *S. inelegans*, and *Beyrichia jonesii*. In Chapter XVII (pp. 383–388), the Pulmonate Mollusca, Myriapods, and Insects of the Nova Scotia Coal-Formation are described. At pp. 523–526 is an account of the Crustaceans and Insects of the Devonian, the latter (like the Insects of the Carboniferous) being described by Mr. Scudder. In Chapter XXIII are notices and lists of the Upper Silurian fossils, *Dictyonema websteri* being figured as new. Descriptions of the Upper Silurian fossils (pp. 594–610) are given, principally as published by Prof. Hall in 1860, but some new forms are described. Finally, the author gives descriptions (pp. 611–657) of the Primordial fossils of the Acadian Group from MS. notes by Mr. Hartt, a number of new forms being characterised and figured.

Dawson, J. W. Supplement to the second edition of Acadian Geology, containing additional facts as to the geological structure, fossil remains, and mineral resources of Nova Scotia, New Brunswick, and Prince Edward Island. pp. 102, with 18 engravings. Montreal, 1878.

This supplement contains all the new matter in the 3d edition of the "Acadian Geology". There are various notes on, and figures of, invertebrate fossils from the Carboniferous and Silurian.

Dawson, J. W. Supplementary chapter to Acadian Geology. 12°. pp. 70. Edinburgh, 1860. With engravings.

Notices and figures fossils from the Carboniferous, Devonian, and Silurian formations.

Dawson, J. W. On the newer Pliocene and Post-Pliocene deposits of the vicinity of Montreal, with notices of fossils recently discovered in them. < *Canad. Nat.*, vol. ii, pp. 401–426, plate vii. 1857.

Contains a descriptive list of the Post-Pliocene deposits in the neighbourhood of Montreal.

Dawson, J. W. On the Lower Coal Measures as developed in British America. < *Quart. Journ. Geol. Soc. Lond.*, vol. xv, pp. 62–76. 1859.

Part III of this memoir treats of the fauna of the Lower Coal-Measures. The Invertebrate remains noticed comprise *Entomostraca*, Annelide burrows and tracks (figs. 6 and 7), supposed Crustacean tracks (fig. 8), and a small Unio-like Bivalve.

Dawson, J. W. On a Terrestrial Mollusc, a Chilognathous Myriapod, and some new species of Reptiles, from the Coal-Formation of Nova Scotia. < *Quart. Journ. Geol. Soc. Lond.*, vol. xvi, pp. 268–277. 1860.

Having obtained numerous specimens, the author is here enabled to fully describe *Pupa vetusta* (figs. 1-3), previously characterised from a single specimen by Sir Charles Lyell (*Quart. Journ. Geol. Soc.*, vol. ix). *Xylobius sigillariæ* is also fully described and figured (figs. 4-9).

Dawson, J. W. On the structure of certain organic remains in the Laurentian Limestones of Canada. < *Quart. Journ. Geol. Soc. Lond.*, vol. xxi, pp. 51–59, pls. vi, vii. 1865.

The author gives a detailed description of the structure of the bodies described by Sir William Logan as being organic and as occurring in the Lower Laurentian Limestones

## II.—PUBLICATIONS MADE IN BRITISH AMERICA, ETC. 93

(*Quart. Journ. Geol. Soc.*, vol. xxi, p. 45). The generic name of *Eozoön* is proposed for these, and the single form described is discussed under the name of *Eozoön canadense*. The author further concludes that *Eozoön* is probably to be regarded as an ancient type of the Foraminifera.

**Dawson, J. W.** On the fossils of the genus Rusophycus. < *Canad. Nat.*, new ser., vol. i, pp. 363–367, and p. 458, with 4 woodcuts. 1866.

The author describes the general appearance and mode of occurrence of the fossils known as *Rusophycus*, and concludes that they are really casts of the burrows of *Trilobites*, on which view he proposes for them the generic name of *Rusichnites*. A new species is described and figured under the name of *R. acadicus*.

**Dawson, J. W.** On the discovery of a new Pulmonate Mollusc [Zonites (Conulus) priscus Cpr.] in the Coal-Formation of Nova Scotia, with a description of the species by Philip P. Carpenter, M. D. < *Quart. Journ. Geol. Soc. Lond.*, vol. xxiii, pp. 330–333, with woodcut. 1867.

Dr. Dawson gives an account of the precise position in the Joggins section of the bed containing the *Zonites*, which is fully described and figured by Dr. Philip Carpenter.

**Dawson, J. W.** Notes on Post-Pliocene deposits at Rivière du Loup and Tadousac. < *Canad. Nat.*, new ser., vol. ii, pp. 81–88. 1867.

Contains lists of and notes on the fossils.

**Dawson, J. W.** On certain organic remains in the Laurentian Limestones of Canada. < *Canad. Nat.*, new ser., vol. ii, pp. 99–111. 1867.

A reprint from the *Quart. Journ. Geol. Soc. Lond.*, 1865, with some additional notes. A short appendix to the paper follows at pp. 127, 128.

**Dawson, J. W.** Notes on fossils recently obtained from the Laurentian Rocks of Canada, and on objections to the organic nature of Eozoön, with notes by W. B. Carpenter, M. D., F. R. S. < *Quart. Journ. Geol. Soc. Lond.*, vol. xxiii, pp. 257–265, pls. xi, xii. 1867.

In the first part of this memoir, Dr. Dawson gives an account of the general appearance and microscopic structure of a specimen of *Eozoön canadense*, found in the Laurentian Rocks at Tudor, in which the chambers of the skeleton are filled with a dark-coloured coarse limestone. The author next deals with certain specimens from Long Lake and Wentworth, and also from Madoc, and concludes by reviewing the objections brought forward by Professors King and Rowney to the organic nature of *Eozoön*. Dr. W. B. Carpenter adds a note on the appearances presented by thin slices of specimens of *Eozoön* in which the canal-system has been infiltrated with transparent carbonate of lime.

**Dawson, J. W.** On some remains of Palæozoic Insects recently discovered in Nova Scotia and New Brunswick. < *Geological Magazine*, Decade I, vol. iv, pp. 385–388, pl. xvii, figs. 1–5. 1867.

The author notes the occurrence of one Carboniferous and four Devonian insects, and appends descriptions of them by Mr. Scudder.

**Dawson, J. W.** On some remains of Palæozoic insects, recently discovered in Nova Scotia and New Brunswick. < *Canad. Nat.*, new ser., vol. iii, pp. 202–206, with 5 woodcuts. 1868.

The author notes the discovery of insect-remains in the Carboniferous and Devonian formations. The species described by Mr. Scudder are *Haplophlebium barnesi* (Carboniferous), and *Platephemera antiqua*, *Homothetus fossilis*, *Lithentomum harttii*, and *Xenoneura antiquorum*, from the Devonian.

**Dawson, J. W.** Additional notes on the Post-Pliocene deposits of the St. Lawrence Valley. < *Canad. Nat.*, vol. iv, 1859, pp. 23–39, with 16 engravings. 1869.

> The author describes and figures the *Foraminifera* and *Bryozoa* [*Polyzoa*] of the Post-Pliocene deposits of Lower Canada. Of the former 8 species, and of the latter 6 species are enumerated, of which *Lepralia quadricornuta* is described as new. The occurrence of fresh-water shells apparently really belonging to the same deposits is further noted.

**Dawson, J. W.** On the microscopic structure of some Canadian Limestones. < *Canad. Nat*, vol. iv, pp. 161–169, with 6 woodcuts. 1869.

> Treats of the microscopic constitution of the Trenton, Black River, and Chazy Limestones, showing that all of these are essentially of organic origin.

**Dawson, J. W.** Note on some new animal remains from the Carboniferous and Devonian of Canada. < *Quart. Journ. Geol. Soc. Lond.*, vol. xxvi, p. 166. [Abstract.] 1870.

> Deals chiefly with vertebrates, but notices some insect-remains from the Coal-Measures.

**Dawson, J. W.** On the Silurian and Devonian Rocks of Nova Scotia. < *Canad. Nat.*, vol. v, pp. 133–143. 1870.

> This paper is principally a geological one, but the fossils of the various rock-groups are noted, and one new species, viz, *Dictyonema websteri* Hall, is figured.

**Dawson, J. W.** Notice of Tertiary fossils from Labrador, Maine, &c., and remarks on the climate of Canada in the newer Pliocene or Pleistocene period. < *Canad. Nat.*, vol. v, pp. 188–200, with 5 engravings. 1870.

> Notices a collection of fossils from the Post-Pliocene deposits of Tertiary Bay on the coast of Labrador, amongst which are several *Foraminifera*. The only new species is *Nonionina labradorica*. A collection of Post-Pliocene deposits from Portland, Maine, is also noticed, and the author likewise notices the occurrence of fresh-water shells in certain Post-Pliocene deposits.

**Dawson, J. W.** Notes on the Geology of Murray Bay, Lower St. Lawrence. < *Canad. Nat.*, vol. vi, pp. 138–151. 1871.

> Contains lists of the fossils discovered. In a note at the end, Mr. Billings describes and figures as a new species *Lingula eva*, from rocks of the age of the Black River Limestone.

**Dawson, J. W.** Post-Pliocene Geology of Canada. < *Canad. Nat.*, new ser., vol. vi, pp. 19–42, 166–187, 241–259, 369–416. 1871.

> A series of papers descriptive of the geological and palæontological features of the Post-Pliocene deposits of Canada, subsequently published in a collected form (Montreal, 1872).

**Dawson, J. W.** Notes on the Post-Pliocene Geology of Canada, with especial reference to the conditions of accumulation of the deposits and the marine life of the period. 8°. pp. 112, with 7 plates. Montreal, 1872.

> Most of the matter of this work was originally published in the form of a series of papers in the *Canadian Naturalist* between 1857 and 1866, in Sir William Logan's *Report on the Geology of Canada* for 1863, and in the author's *Acadian Geology*. The present work summarises the facts and conclusions of the previous papers, adding a number of fresh facts, and correcting the formerly published lists of fossils, and thus presenting as complete a view as possible of the geology and palæontology of the superficial deposits of Canada. The second portion of the work (pp. 59–102) is occupied with a catalogue, often of a critical character, of the fossils of the Post-Pliocene deposits of Canada; and the third part (pp. 103–112) is largely concerned with the relations of the Post-Pliocene fossils to questions as to the derivation of species.

## II.—PUBLICATIONS MADE IN BRITISH AMERICA, ETC. 95

**Dawson, J. W.** The Story of the Earth and Man. 8°. pp. 403. London, 1873.

A popular account of the succession of life upon the globe, chiefly based upon American data.

**Dawson, J. W.** On the footprints of Limulus as compared with the Protichnites of the Potsdam Sandstone. < *Canad. Nat.*, vol. vii, pp. 271-277, with 4 engravings. 1874.

Describes fully and figures the tracks and markings made by the recent *Limuli* in walking over the surface of the sand of the sea-shore, and the appearances produced by these Crustaceans burying themselves in the sand. The author concludes that *Protichnites* and *Climactichnites* have been in all probability produced by large Crustaceans, most likely by *Trilobites*.

**Dawson, J. W.** Impressions and foot-prints of aquatic animals and imitative markings, on Carboniferous Rocks. < *Canad. Nat.*, new ser., vol. vii, pp. 65-74, with 5 figures. 1874.

Reprinted from the *Amer. Journ. Sci. and Arts*.

**Dawson, J. W.** Origin and history of life on our planet. An address before the American Association for the Advancement of Science, at Detroit, Michigan. pp. 26. Montreal, 1875.

In this address, the author deals with the bearings of Palæontology upon the questions connected with the origin and history of life upon the earth, and upon the doctrine of descent with modification.

**Dawson, J. W.** The Dawn of Life; being the history of the oldest-known fossil remains, and their relations to geological time and to the development of the animal kingdom. pp. 239, with 8 plates and 49 woodcuts. London, 1875.

This work deals principally with the history of the discovery of *Eozoön canadense*, and with all the known facts bearing on its structure and nature. The author first gives a descriptive sketch of the Laurentian formation, accompanied by sections, and a coloured map showing the distribution of the Laurentian Limestones in the counties of Ottawa and Argenteuil. Next, a history is given of the various steps which led to the discovery of *Eozoön*, and a record of its interpretation by Carpenter and the author. Thirdly, a chapter is devoted to a consideration of the minute structure exhibited by *Eozoön*; and this is compared with the structure of recent *Foraminifera*. The fifth chapter is concerned with the manner in which *Eozoön* has been preserved, and with a consideration of the processes of fossilisation by infiltration in general. In the sixth chapter, the author deals with the successors and contemporaries of *Eozoön*, with special reference to *Archæosphærina, Stromatopora, Caunopora,* and *Receptaculites*. Another chapter is devoted to a consideration of the various objections which have been urged against the organic nature of *Eozoön*; and a final chapter treats of certain speculative considerations which may be drawn from the study of this fossil.

**Dawson, J. W.** Note on the phosphates of the Laurentian and Cambrian Rocks of Canada. < *Quart. Journ. Geol. Soc. Lond.*, vol. xxxii, pp. 285-291. 1876.

Concludes that the phosphatic material found in these rocks in Canada is of organic origin, and has been produced by the agency of marine invertebrates.

**Dawson, J. W.** On Mr. Carter's objections to Eozoön. < *Ann. and Mag. Nat. Hist.*, ser. 4, vol. xvii, pp. 118, 119. 1876.

**Dawson, J. W.** Notes on the occurrence of Eozoön canadense at Côte St. Pierre. < *Quart. Journ. Geol. Soc. Lond.*, vol. xxxii, pp. 66-74, pl. x, with 4 woodcuts. 1876.

The author gives an account of the nature and arrangement of the strata at Côte St. Pierre, with special reference to the appearances presented by *Eozoön* as occurring *in situ.* Numerous chrysotile veins pass through the limestone, but the author concludes that they are altogether subsequent to the fossil in origin. The close resemblance of weathered specimens to *Stromatopora* is insisted upon ; and two new forms of *Eozoön canadense* are described as var. *minor* and var. *acervulina.* The limestone sometimes contains numerous little globose casts of chamberlets, single or attached in groups, each of which possesses the structure of the " proper wall " of *Eozoön*. For these, the author proposes the name of *Archæospharina.*

**Dawson, J. W.** Eozoön canadense according to Hahn. < *Ann. and Mag. Nat. Hist.*, ser. 4, vol. xviii, pp. 29–38. 1877.

A critical notice of a memoir by Hahn (see *post.*), in which the latter endeavours to show that *Eozoön* is a purely mineral structure.

**Dawson, J. W.** Note on two Palæozoic Crustaceans from Nova Scotia. < *Geological Magazine*, Decade II, vol. iv, pp. 56–58, with 2 engravings. 1877.

Gives description and figures of *Anthrapalæmon (Palæocarabus) hilliana* Dawson and *Homalonotus dawsoni* Hall.

**De Cew, J.** Notes on the Geology of the townships of Windham and Middleton, county of Norfolk, C. W. < *Canad. Journ.*, new ser., vol. vi, pp. 275–277. 1861.

Contains lists of fossils discovered in the Oriskany and Corniferous formations.

**De La Beche, [*Sir*] H. T.** Remarks on the Geology of Jamaica. < *Trans. Geol. Soc. Lond.*, ser. 2, vol. ii, pp. 143–194. 1829.

Contains a few notes on the fossils.

**Desor, E.** Synopsis des Échinides fossiles. Paris, 1858. pp. 490, with atlas of plates.

Describes various fossil Echinoids from the American province.

**Desor, M. E.,** *and* **Edward C. Cabot.** On the Tertiary and more recent deposits in the Island of Nantucket. (In a letter to Sir Charles Lyell.) < *Quart. Journ. Geol. Soc. Lond.*, vol. v, pp. 340–344. 1849.

Contains lists of Post-Pliocene fossils (principally *Mollusca*) from Nantucket.

**Devine, T.** Description of a new Trilobite from the Quebec Group. < *Canad. Nat.*, vol. viii, pp. 95–98, figs. 1 and 2. 1863.

The species is described as *Olenus ? logani.* Mr. Billings adds a note on its affinities.

**Devine, T.** Description of a new Trilobite from the Quebec Group. < *Canad. Nat.*, vol. viii, pp. 210, 211, with woodcut. 1863.

The species is described as *Menocephalus salteri.*

**D'Orbigny, Alcide.** Paléontologie de Cuba. In RAMON DE LA SAGRA'S *Histoire Physique, Politique et Naturelle de l'Île de Cuba.* Paris, 1839.

[Describes the *Foraminifera* and *Mollusca.* Not seen by the writer.]

**D'Orbigny, Alcide.** Prodrome de Paléontologie stratigraphique universelle des Animaux Mollusques et Rayonnés. 3 vols. Paris, 1850–52.

Defines a few species of American fossils, and enumerates many others.

**Duchassaing, P.** Essai sur la constitution géologique de la partie basse de la Guadeloupe, dite la Grande-Terre. < *Bull. de la Soc. Géol. de France*, sér. 2, vol. iv, pp. 1093–1100. 1847.

This memoir is principally geological, but the author notes some of the fossils.

II.—PUBLICATIONS MADE IN BRITISH AMERICA, ETC. 97

**Duchassaing, P.** Observations sur les formations modernes de l'île de la Guadeloupe. <*Bull. de la Soc. Géol. de France*, sér. 2, vol. xii, pp. 753-759. 1855.

This memoir contains notes on the fossils, and is terminated by a table of the fossil and recent Echinoids of the Antilles and Gulf of Mexico.

**Duchassaing, P., and J. Michelotti.** Mémoire sur les Coralliaires des Antilles. <*Memorie della Reale Accad. delle Scienze di Torino*, ser. 2, vol. xix, pp. 279-363, with 10 plates. 1867.

This memoir treats principally of the recent Corals of the Antilles, but notices also some of the fossil forms from the same region.

**Duchassaing, P., and J. Michelotti.** Supplément au Mémoire sur les Coralliaires des Antilles. <*Memorie della Reale Accad. delle Scienze di Torino*, ser. 2, vol. xxiii, pp. 97-206, with 11 plates. 1871.

Like the preceding, this memoir is concerned principally with the recent Corals of the Antilles; but the authors also discuss some of the Tertiary forms.

**Duncan, P. Martin.** On the fossil Corals of the West Indian Islands. Part I, <*Quart. Journ. Geol. Soc. Lond.*, vol. xix, pp. 406-456, pls. xiii-xvi; Part II, <*ibid.*, vol. xx, pp. 20-44, pls. ii-v; Part III, <*ibid.*, vol. xx, pp. 358-374; Part IV, <*ibid.*, vol. xxiv, pp. 9-33, pls. i and ii. 1863-68.

Enumerates and describes a large number of new and of previously recorded species of fossil Corals from the West Indies, principally from Antigua and San Domingo, but also from Jamaica, Barbadoes, Guadeloupe, Trinidad, &c. The author also makes a number of general observations on the genera and species, and states his conclusions as to the age of the deposits in which these fossils occur.

In Part II, the author describes 28 species of fossil Corals from the Miocene formations of San Domingo, 15 species being new ones. The specimens were forwarded to the Geological Society by Mr. Lonsdale, along with a descriptive memoir written ten years before. *Antillia* and *Teleiophyllia* are founded by Dr. Duncan as new genera of *Astraida*.

In Part III, the author deals in an elaborate manner with the changes undergone by fossil Corals in general, and by those of the West Indies in particular, both prior to mineralisation and during the process of fossilisation.

In Part IV, Dr. Duncan treats principally of the fossil Corals of the Tertiary deposits of San Domingo, 6 species being described as new. Some further notes on the San Domingo Corals are added, 2 species being defined for the first time; and the Antiguan Corals, with 5 new species, are described. The new genera *Lamellastræa* and *Diplocœnia* are founded. The memoir concludes with a table of the synonyms and localities of the Cretaceous, Eocene, and Miocene Corals of the West Indies, and with a discussion as to the nature and alliances of the Coral-faunæ of this region.

**Duncan, P. Martin.** On the correlation of the Miocene beds of the West Indian Islands; and on the synchronism of the Chert-formation of Antigua with the lowest Limestone of Malta. <*Geological Magazine*, Decade I, vol. i, pp. 97-102. 1864.

From a study of the fossil Corals, the author concludes that the general correlation of the West Indian and European Mid-Tertiary strata can be asserted, and also that the Antiguan Chert-formation and the lowest of the Maltese Limestones are approximately contemporaneous.

**Duncan, P. Martin.** On the anatomy of the test of Amphidetus (Echinocardium) virginianus, Forbes, and on the genus Breynia. <*Quart. Journ. Geol. Soc. Lond.*, vol. xxv, p. 16. 1865.

Treats of the *Amphidetus virginianus* of the Miocene Tertiary of Virginia, which the author believes to be specifically identical with a recent form.

**Duncan, P. Martin,** *and* **G. P. Wall.** A notice of the Geology of Jamaica, especially with reference to the District of Clarendon, with descriptions of the Cretaceous, Eocene, and Miocene Corals of the islands. <*Quart. Journ. Geol. Soc. Lond.,* vol. xxi, pp. 1–15, pls. i, ii. 1865.

<small>The palæontological portion of this memoir contains notices or descriptions of 27 species of Corals, of which 8 are described as new. The paper concludes with remarks on the affinities of the species, and on the correlation of the Cretaceous, Eocene, and Miocene strata of Jamaica with those of Europe.</small>

**Dybowski, W. N.** Monographie der Zoantharia Sclerodermata aus der Silurformation Estlands, Nord Livlands, und der Insel Gotland, nebst einer Synopsis aller palaeozoischen Gattungen dieser Abtheilung und einer Synonymik der dazu gehörigen bereits bekannten Arten. [Monograph of the Rugose Corals of the Silurian formation of Esthonia, Northern Livonia, and the Island of Gotland, together with a synopsis of all the Palæozoic genera of this group, and a synonymy of the hitherto recorded species.] 8°. pp. 276, with 5 plates. Dorpat, 1873 and 1874.

<small>Defines several genera of North American Rugose Corals, and gives a synonymy of the recorded species in each genus.</small>

**Ehrenberg, Christian Gottfried.** Ueber die mikroscopischen kieselschaligen Polycystinen als mächtige Gebirgsmasse von Barbados. [On the microscopic siliceous Polycystina as forming whole mountain-masses in Barbadoes.] <*Monatsbericht d. K. K. Akad. d. Wiss. Berlin,* 1847.

<small>On the Polycystina of the Barbadoes earth.</small>

**Ehrenberg, Christian Gottfried.** Mikrogeologie. Leipzig, 1854. pp. 374 and pp. 88, with 40 plates.

<small>This work contains descriptions and figures of numerous American *Microzoa* and *Microphyta.* The second portion of the work is exclusively devoted to the description of the minute fossil organisms of this region.</small>

**Ehrenberg, Christian Gottfried.** Erläuterungen über den Grünsand im Zeuglodon-Kalke Alabama's in Nord-Amerika. [Investigations into the Greensand of the Zeuglodon-Limestone of North America.] <*Monatsbericht d. K. K. Akad. d. Wiss. Berlin,* 1855, pp. 86–90.

<small>The author shows that the grains of greensand interspersed in the Zeuglodon-limestone of Alabama are really of the nature of casts of the shells of Polythalamous *Foraminifera.* At least thirty different forms were recognized by the author.</small>

**Ehrenberg, Christian Gottfried.** Die weitere Entwickelung der Kenntniss des Grünsandes als grüne Polythalamien-Steinkerne, über braunrothe und corall-rothe Steinkerne der Polythalamien-Kreide in Nord-America, und über den Meeresgrund aus 12,900 Fuss Tiefe. [The further development of the discovery that the Greensand is composed of green casts of Polythalamia; also on the brownish-red or bright-red casts of Polythalamia in the Chalk of North America, and on the sea bottom at depths of 12,900 feet.] <*Monatsbericht d. K. K. Akad. d. Wiss. Berlin,* 1855, pp. 172–178.

<small>The chief point in this paper is that the brown or reddish "chalk" of Alabama owes its colour to numerous shells of *Foraminifera* filled with a similarly coloured silicate of iron.</small>

**Ehrenberg, Christian Gottfried.** Fortsetzung der mikrogeologischen Studien als Gesammt-Uebersicht der mikroscopischen Palaeontologie gleichartig analysirter Gebirgsarten der Erde, mit specieller Rücksicht auf dem Polycystinen-Mergel von Barbados. [Continuation of Microgeological studies, a general review of the microscopic Palæontology of formations which have been similarly analysed, with special reference to the Polycystina Marls of Barbadoes.] < *Abhandl. d. K. Akad. d. Wiss.*, 1875, pp. 225, with 30 plates.

A considerable portion of this work is devoted to the consideration of the *Microzoa* of the "Barbadoes earth", a large number of new species being briefly described in the explanations which accompany the beautifully executed plates.

**Emmerich, H. F.** De Trilobitis dissertatio petrefactis. Berolini, 1839.

Describes some American Trilobites.

**[Etheridge, Robert.]** On the occurrence of animal fossils, with a list of genera. < *Appendix J* in "*Report on the Geology of Trinidad*", *Part I of the West Indian Geological Survey*, by P. Wall and J. G. Sawkins. pp. 161-166. 1860.

Contains lists of notes on the Post-Pliocene, Miocene, and Cretaceous fossils of Trinidad.

**Etheridge, Robert.** Notes on some rock-specimens from the Arctic-American Archipelago. In the "Whaling cruise to Baffin's Bay and the Gulf of Boothia, and an account of the rescue of the crew of the 'Polaris' ", by Albert Hastings Markham, R. N. 8°. London, 1874.

Contains a list of rock-specimens, including some Upper Silurian fossils.

**Etheridge, R.,** *jun'r.* On the relationship existing between the Echinothuridæ, Wyville Thomson, and the Perischoechinidæ, McCoy. < *Quart. Journ. Geol. Soc. Lond.*, vol. xxx, pp. 307-315, pl. xxiv. 1874.

Defines the genera *Lepidechinus* Hall, *Melonites* D. D. Owen, and *Oligoporus* Meek and Worthen, and discusses their affinities.

**Fischer, M. P.** Sur quelques fossiles d'Alaska, rapportés par M. Pinart. [On some fossils from Alaska, collected by M. Pinart.] < *Comptes Rend.*, 1872, vol. lxv, pp. 1784-1786.

The author describes the fossils collected by M. Pinart in a visit to Alaska. Amongst these is *Monotis salinaria*, indicating the occurrence of strata of Triassic age. From another locality are *Pholadomya* and *Aucella*, indicating deposits of Jurassic, or possibly Cretaceous, age. Lastly, in the Islands of Pribyloff is found a *Cardium* of Quaternary o
· Tertiary *facies*, of the group of *C. grænlandicum* Gmelin.

**Fitton, W. K.** Geological notice of the country passed over in Captain Back's Expedition. In "Narrative of the Arctic Land Expedition to the Mouth of the Great Fish River and along the Shores of the Arctic Ocean, in the years 1833, 1834, and 1835; by Captain Back". 1 vol. 8°. pp. 543-562. London, 1836.

Contains notes by Mr. Stokes on some fossils obtained from limestone at Lake Winnipeg.

**Forbes, Edward.** On the Fossil Shells collected by Mr. Lyell, from the Cretaceous Formations of New Jersey. < *Quart. Journ. Geol. Soc. Lond.*, vol. i, pp. 61-64, with 7 engravings. 1845.

This paper is an appendix to one by Sir Charles Lyell describing the Cretaceous strata of New Jersey, &c. (*Quart. Journ. Geol. Soc.*, vol. i, p. 55). The species of shells collected by Sir Charles amounted to 60 in number, and of these the following four are described as new:—*Ostrea subspatulata, Lima reticulata, Terebratula vanuxemiana,* and *Bulla mortoni.* A note is added by Sir Charles Lyell on two *Foraminifera* from the same beds.

[Forbes, Edward.] Description of some new Fossil Shells from Bissex Hill and Springfield in Barbados Communicated by Sir Robert H. Schomburgk, Ph. D., member of the Imperial Academy Nat. Curios., &c. < *Ann. and Mag. Nat. Hist.*, ser. 2, vol. i, pp. 347-349, with 5 woodcuts. 1848.

>An excerpt from Sir Robert Schomburgk's "History of Barbados", comprising descriptions by Prof. E. Forbes and figures of *Scalaria ehrenbergi, Nucula packeri,* and *N. schomburgkii.*

Fromentel, E. D. Introduction à l'étude des Éponges Fossiles. [Introduction to the study of Fossil Sponges.] 4°. pp. 50, with 4 plates. Caen, 1859.

>The only American form described in this work is *Palæochonia* (*Palæospongia*) *cyathiformis* (= *Porites cyathiformis* Hall) from the Trenton Limestone of the State of New York.

Gabb, W. M. Notes on West Indian Fossils. < *Geological Magazine*, Decade II, vol. ii, pp. 544, 545. 1875.

>The author notes that certain fossil shells which he had previously described had been redescribed by Mr. Guppy (*Geol. Mag.*, Decade II, vol. i, pp. 404-433). Count Pourtales also adds a list of the fossil corals collected by Mr. Gabb from the Cretaceous, Miocene, and Post-Pliocene deposits of San Domingo.

Geinitz, Hans Bruno. Die Graptolithen, ein monographischer Versuch zur Beurtheilung der Grauwackenformation in Sachsen und den angrenzenden Länder-Abtheilungen, sowie der silurischen Formation überhaupt. 4°. pp. 58, with 6 plates. Leipzic, 1852.

>Though specially devoted to German *Graptolites*, some American forms are noticed. *Nemapodia* Emmons is referred to the *Graptolitida*, and the genus *Nereograptus* founded for the reception of this and of *Nereites, Nemertites,* and *Myrianites. Graptolithus gracilis* Hall and *G.* (*Dendrograptus*) *hallianus* Prout and *G. arundinaceus* Hall are referred to the Sertularians.

Geinitz, Hans Bruno. Carbonformation und Dyas in Nebraska. < *Verhandl. der Kaiserlichen Leopoldino-Carolinischen Deutschen Akademie der Naturforscher*, Bd. xxxiii, pp. i-xii and 1-91, with 5 plates. 1867.

>The palæontological portion of this important memoir is occupied with the description of 97 species of invertebrate fossils from the Carboniferous and Permian rocks of Nebraska. The paper concludes with a tabular list of the fossils collected by M. Marcou in these formations in Nebraska.

Geinitz, Hans Bruno. Carbon-Formation und Dyas in Nebraska. < *Neues Jahrb. für Min., Geogn., Geol. und Petrefaktenkunde*, Jahrg. 1867, pp. 1-9.

>A general review of the Carboniferous and Permian deposits of Nebraska, with notes on the fossils.

Gesner, Abraham. Remarks on the Geology and Mineralogy of Nova Scotia. Halifax, 1836. pp. 265.

>Contains notes on the fossils.

Gesner, Abraham. First report on the Geological Survey of the Province of New Brunswick, St. John's, 1839, pp. 87. Second report on the same, 1840, pp. 76. Third report on the same, 1841, pp. 88. Fourth report on the same, 1842, pp. 101.

>These reports are primarily concerned with the geological structure of the province of New Brunswick; but they also contain scattered notices of the fossils met with.

**Gibson, John.** Geological features of Huron County, Ontario. < *Canad. Nat.*, new ser., vol. vii, pp. 34–40. 1874.
<small>Contains notes on the fossils.</small>

**Goldfuss, August.** Petrefacta Germaniæ. 1826.
<small>Describes some North American fossils (e. g. *Favosites favosa, Columnaria alveolata*, &c.).</small>

**Grewingk, C.** Die an der Westküste Nord-Amerikas und auf den aleutischen Inseln bisher gefundenen fossilen Thier- und Pflanzen-Reste. [The hitherto discovered animal and vegetable fossils of the west coast of North America and the Aleutian Islands.] < *Verhandl. der Russ. Kaiserlichen Gesellschaft, St. Petersburg*, Jahrgang 1848–49, Petersb., 1850, pp. 343–366, with 3 plates.
<small>Contains a complete list of the organic remains known at the above date as occurring in Northwestern America and in the Aleutian Islands. The fossils are from the Carboniferous, Jurassic, Tertiary, and Post-Tertiary.</small>

**Grewingk, C.** Beitrag zur Kenntniss der orographischen und geognostischen Beschaffenheit der Nordwestküste Americas, mit den anliegenden Inseln. [On the orography and geognosy of the northwest coast of North America, and the outlying islands.] 8°. pp. 351. St. Petersburg, 1850. With 4 plates of fossils.
<small>Notices and describes collections of fossils made by M. Ilia Wosnessensky in the extreme northwestern regions of North America. The fossils are principally Tertiary and Post-Tertiary.</small>

**Gümbel, C. W.** Beiträge zur Kenntniss der Organisation und systematischen Stellung von Receptaculites. < *Abhandl. math.-phys. Classe K. Bay. Akad. d. Wiss.*, ii, Bd. xii, Abth. i, pp. 170–215, pl. A. 1876.
<small>Deals with the organisation and systematic position of *Receptaculites*, with various references to the structure of American specimens and the views of American palæontologists on this subject.</small>

**Guppy, R. J. Lechmere.** On the older Parian Formation in Trinidad. < *The Geologist*, vol. vii, pp. 204–207. 1863.
<small>Contains notes on the fossils.</small>

**Guppy, R. J. Lechmere.** The Older Parian in Trinidad. < *Geologist*, vol. vii, pp. 363, 364. 1863.
<small>A letter on the age of the Older Parian Formation, as determined by its fossils.</small>

**Guppy, R. J. Lechmere.** On the occurrence of Foraminifera in the Tertiary beds of San Fernando, Trinidad. < *Trans. Sci. Assoc. Trinidad*, 1863, p. 11. [*Geologist*, 1864, p. 159.]

**Guppy, R. J. Lechmere.** On some deposits of late Tertiary age at Matura, on the east coast of Trinidad. < *Trans. Sci. Assoc. of Trinidad*, 1864, p. 33. [*Geological Magazine*, Decade I, vol. ii, pp. 256–261. 1865.]
<small>The author enumerates more than ninety species of fossils from this deposit, mostly *Mollusca*, and makes remarks on their characters.</small>

**Guppy, R. J. Lechmere.** On the Tertiary Mollusca of Jamaica. < *Quart. Journ. Geol. Soc. Lond.*, vol. xxii, pp. 281–294, pls. xvi–xviii. 1866.
<small>After discussing the relationships of the Miocene deposits of Jamaica, the author gives a list of 61 species of Lamellibranchs and Gasteropods therefrom. Of these, 27 species are new, and are fully described and figured; references, with descriptive remarks, and in some cases figures, being made to the others.</small>

**Guppy, R. J. Lechmere.** On Tertiary Brachiopoda from Trinidad. < *Quart. Journ. Geol. Soc. Lond.*, vol. xxii, pp. 295–297, pl. xix, figs. 1–3. 1866.

Describes and figures *Terebratula trinitatensis*, *T. carneoides*, and *T. lecta* as new species. In a note subjoined to the paper, Mr. Davidson draws attention to the resemblance of *T. carneoides* Guppy to *T. carnea* of the Cretaceous on the one hand and the living *T. vitrea* on the other hand.

**Guppy, R. J. Lechmere.** On Tertiary Echinoderms from the West Indies. < *Quart. Journ. Geol. Soc. Lond.*, vol. xxii, pp. 297–301, pl. xix, figs. 4–8. 1866.

Notes nine species of Echinoids, of which *Echinolampas semiorbis*, *E. lycopersicus*, and *E. ovum-serpentis* are described as new.

**Guppy, R. J. Lechmere.** On the relations of the Tertiary formations of the West Indies, with a note on a new species of Ranina, by Henry Woodward, Esq., F. G. S.; and on the Orbitoides and Nummulinæ, by Prof. T. Rupert Jones, F. G. S. < *Quart. Journ. Geol. Soc. Lond.*, vol. xxii, pp. 570–593, pl. xxvi. 1866.

In the first portion of this memoir, the author gives a general review of our knowledge of the Tertiary formations of the West Indies. In a second section, the author describes 18 new species of fossils, of which 16 are Mollusca, one is a *Spirorbis*, and another is doubtfully referred to the Sponges under the name of *Cisseis* (gen. nov.) *asteriscus*. The paper concludes with observations on the relations of the fauna of the Caribbean Miocene, and a table showing the affinities of some of the fossils from this formation. In an appended note, Mr. Henry Woodward gives the name of *Ranina porifera* to a new Crustacean from the Tertiary of Trinidad; and in a second note, Prof. Rupert Jones discusses the *Orbitoides* and *Nummulinæ* of the Tertiary Asphaltic Bed of Trinidad.

**Guppy, R. J. Lechmere.** Notes on West Indian Geology, with remarks on the existence of an Atlantis in the early Tertiary period; and descriptions of some new fossils from the Caribbean Miocene. < *Geological Magazine*, Decade I, vol. iv, pp. 496–501, with 1 engraving. 1867.

The new species described are *Leda incognita*, *L. bisulcata*, *Tornatina coix-lacryma*, *Stomatia eidolon*, *Nucula schomburgki*, and *Mactra subovaltha*. The new genus *Crepitacella* is proposed for *C. cepula* Guppy, a Buccinoid shell from the Miocene Tertiary.

**Guppy, R. J. Lechmere.** On the Tertiary fossils of the West-Indies, with especial reference to the classification of the Kainozoic Rocks of Trinidad. < *Proc. Sci. Assoc. of Trinidad*, 1867, pp. 145–176.

After a general introduction, the author discusses the Atlantis theory, and the classification of the Tertiary deposits of Trinidad. A list of the fossil Mollusca, Echinoderms, Articulates, and Protozoa recorded up to this date from the Tertiary rocks of the Caribbean area (excluding Post-Pliocene forms) is next given. Lastly, the author describes a number of new species of *Mollusca* and two new forms of *Pentacrinus*.

**Guppy, R. J. Lechmere.** Notes on a visit to Dominica. < *Proc. Sci. Assoc. of Trinidad*, 1869, pp. 379–392. [See also *Geol. Magazine*, Decade I, vol. ix, pp. 75, 76.]

Contains notes on the geology of Dominica, with lists of Mollusca and Corals from the Pliocene formation of this island.

**Guppy, R. J. Lechmere.** On Foraminifera from the Tertiaries of San Fernando, Trinidad. < *Proc. Sci. Assoc. Trinidad*, 1872, pp. 13–16. [See also *Geol. Magazine*, Decade I, vol. x, pp. 362, 363.]

Records the discovery of *Foraminifera* in the Lower Miocene beds of San Fernando, Trinidad, and gives a list of the recognized species, 18 in number.

**Guppy, R. J. Lechmere.** On some new Tertiary fossils from Jamaica. < *Proc. Sci. Assoc. of Trinidad,* 1873, pp. 72–88, pls. i–iii.

Describes a large number of new species of fossils from the Miocene formation of Jamaica, whilst previously recorded forms are enumerated or briefly alluded to. The new forms described and figured are all *Mollusca*, with the exception of *Ditrupa dentalina*.

**Guppy, R. J. Lechmere.** On the West Indian Tertiary Fossils. < *Geological Magazine,* Decade II, vol. i, pp. 404–412, 433–446, pls. xvi–xviii. 1874.

The author describes and figures a number of *Mollusca* from the Eocene, Miocene, and Pliocene deposits of the West Indies, including 17 new species. The paper concludes with a list of the *Mollusca, Articulata, Echinodermata,* and *Protozoa* found in the above-mentioned deposits.

**Guppy, R. J. Lechmere.** Supplement to the paper on West Indian Tertiary Fossils. < *Geological Magazine,* Decade II, vol. ii, pp. 41, 42. 1875.

This is a supplement to the preceding paper, in which the author describes as new *Leda clava* and *Ditrupa dentalinum,* and proposes the name of *Crassinella* for that of *Gouldia,* pre-occupied for a genus of birds.

**Guppy, R. J. Lechmere.** On the Miocene fossils of Haiti. < *Quart. Journ. Geol. Soc. Lond.,* vol. xxxii, pp. 516–532, pls. xxviii, xxix. 1876.

A critical memoir, dealing principally with a communication by Prof. Gabb on "The Topography and Geology of San Domingo". Remarks are made upon the characters of 122 species, all but one belonging to the *Mollusca*. Twenty-one species are figured, of which 6 are new.

**Guppy, R. J. Lechmere.** On the physical geography and fossils of the older rocks of Trinidad. < *Proc. Sci. Assoc. of Trinidad,* 1877.

In the palæontological portion of this paper, the author records *Eozoön* (?) *caribbæum, Favosites fenestralis,* and species of *Pseudocrinites* and *Petraia* from the "Caribbean" series, and of undetermined species of *Murchisonia* and *Lozonema* (?) from the "Blue Limestone" series.

**Guppy, R. J. Lechmere.** On the discovery of organic remains in the Caribbean series of Trinidad. < *Quart. Journ. Geol. Soc. Lond.,* vol. xxvi, pp. 413, 414. [Abstract.]

The author described the so-called "Caribbean series" of Trinidad, which he suggested would ultimately prove to be pre-Silurian. The organic remains which he had detected consisted of fragments of corals, plants, and stems of Echinoderms, and a peculiar structure which the author regarded as most nearly related to *Eozoön,* and for which he proposed the name of *Eozoön caribbæum.*

**Hahn, Otto.** Is there such a thing as Eozoön canadense? A microgeological investigation. < *Ann. and Mag. Nat. Hist.,* ser. 4, vol. xvii, pp. 265–282. (Translated from the *Württembergische naturwissenschaftliche Jahreshefte,* 1876.)

After an examination of serpentinous limestones from Canada and Europe, the author concludes that *Eozoön canadense* is of inorganic origin.

**Hall, James.** On the supposed impression in Shale of the soft parts of an Orthoceras. (Communicated by Sir Roderick I. Murchison.) < *Quart. Journ. Geol. Soc. Lond.,* vol. v, pp. 108–111, with woodcut. 1849.

Gives reasons for concluding that the specimens of *Orthoceras* previously described by Mr. J. G. Anthony, from the Cincinnati formation, as exhibiting indications of the soft parts of the animal, are really due to concretionary action.

**Hall, James.** On the genus Tellinomya and allied genera. < *Canad. Nat.*, vol. i, pp. 390–395, with 7 woodcuts. 1856.

Fully characterises *Tellinomya*, and discusses the characters of *Nuculites* Conr., *Cucullella* McCoy, and *Lyrodesma* Conr.

**Hall, James.** Descriptions of Canadian Graptolites. < *Geological Survey of Canada: Report of Progress for the year* 1857. Toronto, 1858. pp. 109–145.

In this report, the author describes the *Graptolites* found in the "Quebec Formation" at Point Levis; a fuller description, accompanied by engravings, being subsequently given in Decade II of the publications of the Canadian Survey. Twenty-one new species of the genus "*Graptolithus*" are described and 4 new species of the new genus *Phyllograptus*.

**Hall, James.** Note upon the genus Graptolithus and description of some remarkable new forms from the shales of the Hudson River Group, discovered in the investigations of the Geological Survey of Canada, under the direction of Sir W. E. Logan, F. R. S. < *Canad. Nat.*, vol. iii, pp. 139–150 and 161–177, pls. i and ii. 1858.

Descriptions of *Graptolites* from the Quebec Group, from the "Report of Progress of the Canadian Geological Survey" for 1857.

**Hall, James.** Descriptions of new species of fossils from the Silurian Rocks of Nova Scotia. < *Canad. Nat.*, vol. v, pp. 144–159, with 20 engravings. 1860.

Describes 8 new species of Brachiopods, 15 new species of Lamellibranchs, 2 of Gasteropods, 1 new form of Orthoceras, 2 of Trilobites, and 3 of Ostracoda. Several forms are described as new varieties, and some previously known species are also noticed. All the species are from the "Arisaig Series".

**Hall, James.** On a new Crustacean from the Potsdam Sandstone. A letter addressed to Principal Dawson, dated Albany, 31st October, 1862. < *Canad. Nat.*, vol. vii, pp. 443–445, with an engraving. 1862.

Describes and figures from the Potsdam Sandstone of Wisconsin a singular Crustacean (*Aglaspis*), which appears to have possessed a caudal spine, and to have otherwise resembled the recent *Limulus*. The author suggests that it may have been this animal which produced the tracks of *Protichnites* in the Potsdam Sandstone of Canada.

**Hall, James.** Graptolites of the Quebec Group. < *Figures and Descriptions of Canadian Organic Remains*, Decade II, pp. 151, pls. i–xxiii, with 35 woodcuts. Montreal, 1865.

The first portion of this work (pp. 5–64) is of the nature of a general introduction, dealing with the nature, form, and structure of *Graptolites*, their mode of reproduction and development, their classification, geological and geographical range in America, bibliography, &c. The second section of the report is occupied with descriptions of the species which have been found in the Quebec rocks at Point Levis. Altogether, 52 species are described and figured, under the genera *Graptolithus*, *Diplograptus*, *Climacograptus*, *Retiolites*, *Retiograptus*, *Phyllograptus*, *Dendrograptus*, *Callograptus*, *Dictyonema*, *Ptilograptus*, and *Thamnograptus*. Descriptions of most of the species had been previously published in the "Report of Progress of the Geological Survey of Canada" for 1857, but without illustrations. In the concluding portion of his work, the author describes two species of *Graptolites* from the Utica Slates of the United States, introduced for comparison and illustration.

**Hall, James.** On the occurrence of an internal convoluted plate within the body of certain species of Crinoidea. < *Ann. and Mag. Nat. Hist.*, ser. 3, vol. xvii, pp. 398, 399. 1866.

A note reprinted from the Proc. Bost. Soc. Nat. Hist., x, 33.

**Hartt, C. Frederick.** On a subdivision of the Acadian Carboniferous Limestones, with a description of a section across these rocks at Windsor, N. S. < *Canad. Nat.*, new ser., vol. iii, pp. 212-224. 1868.

Contains numerous descriptive notes on the fossils.

**[Hartt, C. Frederick.]** Palæontological appendices (A and B) in "Observations on the Geology of Southern New Brunswick", by L. W. Bailey. Fredericton, 1865. pp. 131.

The palæontological appendices to the above-mentioned work deal with the fossils of New Brunswick, from the Post-Pliocene to the Primordial. Mr. Scudder also gives a letter relating to the insect-remains found in the Devonian.

**[Haughton, Samuel.]** Geological notes and illustrations, in "Reminiscences of Arctic ice-travel in search of Sir John Franklin and his companions", by Captain F. L. McClintock, R. N. < *Journ. Roy. Dublin Soc.*, vol. i, pp. 183-250, pls. v-xi, and vol. iii, pp. 53-58. 1857.

In the palæontological portion of this memoir, Professor Haughton describes numerous Palæozoic fossils, the new species being *Orthoceras griffithi, Loxonema mcclintocki, L. rossi, Cromus arcticus, Cardiola salteri, Spirifer arcticus, Monotis septentrionalis*, and *Chætetes arcticus*.

**Haughton, Samuel.** Geological account of the Arctic Archipelago, drawn up principally from the specimens collected by Captain F. L. McClintock, R. N., from 1849 to 1859. Appendix to "The Voyage of the 'Fox' in the Arctic Seas", by Capt. F. L. McClintock. London, 1859. pp. 322-399. [Reprinted in *Journ. Geol. Soc. Dublin*, vol. vii, pp. 196-213.]

This memoir contains lists of the fossils collected from the Silurian, Carboniferous, Jurassic, and Post-Pliocene deposits of the Arctic regions. *Ammonites mcclintocki* is defined as a new species.

**Hébert, E.** Documents sur la Géologie du bassin du Mackenzie, recueillis par le Père Petitot. < *Bull. de la Soc. Géol. de France*, 3e sér., t. iii, pp. 87-93. 1877.

Gives a list of nine species of Devonian fossils collected by Père Petitot in the basin of the Mackenzie River, and identified by MM: Hébert and Munier-Chalmas.

**Hector, James.** On the geology of the country between Lake Superior and the Pacific Ocean (between the 48th and 54th parallels of latitude), visited by the government exploring expedition under Captain J. Palliser (1857-60). < *Quart. Journ. Geol. Soc. Lond.*, vol. xvii, pp. 388-445. 1866.

This memoir is a geological one; but the author gives short lists of the fossils obtained from the Cretaceous rocks, and from the Palæozoic deposits which he had examined in the region in question.

**Heer, Oswald.** Flora fossilis Arctica. 1868-71.

In vol. i, pp. 129, 130, the author describes some remains of insects from the Miocene of Greenland.

**Heer, Oswald.** Flora fossilis Alaskana. [The fossil flora of Alaska.] < *Kong. Svenska Vetenskaps-Akad. Handlingar*, new series, vol. viii, Stockholm, 1869.

Though especially devoted to fossil botany, a few fossil insects are described by the author (p. 39); and M. Charles Mayer, of Zurich, gives a description of the *Mollusca* of the plant-beds (pp. 40, 41, pl. x, figs. 7-13).

**Heer, Oswald.** Contributions to the Fossil Flora of North Greenland, being a description of the plants collected by Mr. Edmund Whymper during the summer of 1867. < *Phil. Trans.*, 1869, pp. 445-488.

At pp. 484, 485, the author describes two new insects (*Clstelites punctulatus* and *Cercopidium rugulosum*) and an undetermined species of *Cyclas*, from deposits of Miocene age.

**Heer, Oswald.** Die Kreideflora der arctischen Zone, gegründet auf die von den swedischen Expeditionen von 1870 und 1872 in Grönland und Spitzbergen gesammelten Pflanzen. < *Kong. Svenska Vetenskaps-Akad. Handlingar*, new ser., vol. xii, Stockholm, 1874.

This memoir is botanical, but the author describes, under the name of *Iulopsis cretaceus*, a fossil Myriapod from Atanekerdluk in Greenland (p. 120, pl. xxxiii, fig. 7), and also two Rhynchophorous insects (pp. 91, 92).

**Heer, Oswald.** Nachträge zur miocenen Flora Grönlands, enthaltend die von der schwedischen Expedition im Sommer 1870 gesammelten miocenen Pflanzen. < *Kong. Svenska Vetenskaps-Akad. Handlingar*, vol. xiii, Stockholm, 1874.

In addition to the plant-remains, the author describes two species of *Coleoptera* (p. 25, pl. v, figs. 12 and 13).

**Helland, —.** Om de is fyldte Fjorde. < *Nyt-Tidsskrift for Mathematik og Naturkundskab*, Christiania, 1875.

Contains lists of shells by Sars.

**Heneken, T. S.** On some Tertiary deposits in San Domingo, with notes on the Fossil Shells, by J. C. Moore, Esq., F. G. S., and on the Fossil Corals, by W. Lonsdale, Esq., F. G. S. < *Quart. Journ. Geol. Soc. Lond.*, vol. ix, pp. 115-134. 1853.

The note by Mr. Moore supplies lists of and remarks on the fossil *Mollusca* collected by Colonel Heneken in San Domingo, and Mr. Lonsdale performs a corresponding service as regards the Corals.

**Hind, Henry Youle.** The North-west Territory: reports of progress, together with a general report of the Assiniboine and Saskatchewan Exploring Expedition. 4°. Toronto, 1859.

[Not seen by the writer.]

**Hind, Henry Youle.** Narrative of the Canadian Red River Exploring Expedition of 1857, and of the Assiniboine and Saskatchewan Exploring Expedition of 1858. 2 vols. 8°. London, 1860.

In vol. ii, pp. 239-350, the author gives an account of the geology of the district explored by him, along with notes and descriptions of the fossils met with. From rocks of Silurian age, *Modiolopsis parviuscula* and *Orthoceras simpsoni* are described as new. *Lucina occidentalis* from the Devonian and *Ammonites barnstoni* and *A. billingsi* from Jurassic strata are also described as new, the two latter being determined by Mr. Meek. From the Cretaceous formation a number of fossils are recognized; *Anomia flemingi*, *Inoceramus canadensis*, and *Leda hindi* being determined as new. No Tertiary fossils were obtained.

**Hinde, George Jennings.** Description of a new genus of Tabulate Coral. < *Proc. Geol. Soc. Lond.*, vol. xxxi, p. lxxxvii. 1875.

Gives the name of *Sphærolites* to a massive free corallum belonging to the *Favositidæ*, resembling *Chætetes* in general character, but having perforated walls and incomplete tabulæ. The single species *S. nicholsoni* is described from the Lower Helderberg formation (Ludlow) of New Brunswick.

**Hinde, George Jennings.** The Glacial and Interglacial strata of Scarboro' Heights and other localities near Toronto, Ontario. < *Canad. Journ.*, new ser., vol. xvi, with map. 1878.

> The author records the discovery of fresh-water and land shells (*Planorbis* and *Zonites*) in stratified sands and clays of Interglacial date, underlaid and overlaid by true "till", at Scarboro' Heights, near Toronto. These remains are accompanied by numerous fragments of plants.

**Honeyman, D.** On new localities of Fossiliferous Silurian Rocks in Eastern Nova Scotia. < *Canad. Nat.*, vol. v, pp. 293–299, with 1 engraving. [With a note by Principal Dawson on the fossils.] 1860.

> Dr. Honeyman's paper is chiefly geological, though the fossils are incidentally noticed. In an appended note, Dr. Dawson discusses several of the fossils, figuring the head of *Homalonotus dawsoni* Hall, and describing *Orthoceras exornatum* as a new species.

**Honeyman, D.** On the Geology of Arisaig, Nova Scotia. < *Quart. Journ. Geol. Soc. Lond.*, vol. xx, pp. 333–345. 1864.

> A geological paper, but contains lists of the fossils, all belonging to the Silurian series, and corresponding with the Lower Helderberg and Clinton of the State of New York.

**Honeyman, D.** Notes on the Geology of Arisaig, Nova Scotia; with a note by Prof. T. Rupert Jones, F. G. S. < *Quart. Journ. Geol. Soc. Lond.*, vol. xxvi, pp. 490–492. 1870.

> This paper is geological, but the note added by Prof. Rupert Jones deals with the Entomostraca, four species of which, of Upper Silurian type, are noted.

**Honeyman, D.** Geology of Antigonish County, N. S. < *Trans. Nova Scotia Inst. Nat. Sci.*, vol. i, part i, pp. 106–120. 1863.

> The author notes the fossils collected in the region in question.

**How, —.** Notice of the occurrence of a Trilobite in the Lower Carboniferous Limestone of Hants Co. < *Trans. Nova Scotia Inst. Nat. Sci.*, vol. i, part i, pp. 87, 88.

> The author notices the occurrence of a species of *Phillipsia*.

**[Howley, James P.]** Geological survey of Newfoundland. < *Report of Progress for the year* 1874, pp. 27–74. St. John's, 1875.

> Contains notes on the fossils.

**Hunt, T. Sterry.** Report for the year 1857. < *Geological Survey of Canada: Report of Progress for the year* 1857, pp. 193–217. Toronto, 1858.

> The first part of this report deals with the structure, composition, and mode of origin of dolomites and magnesian limestones, and contains many observations and theories of great interest to the palæontologist.

**Hunt, T. Sterry.** On the mineralogy of certain organic remains from the Laurentian Rocks of Canada. < *Quart. Journ. Geol. Soc.*, vol. xxi, pp. 67–71. 1865.

> Gives a detailed account, accompanied with analyses, of the mineral nature and structure of *Eozoön canadense*.

**Hunt, T. Sterry.** Geology and mineralogy of the Laurentian Limestones. < *Geological Survey of Canada: Report of Progress from* 1863 *to* 1866, pp. 181–233. Ottawa, 1866.

> Though essentially mineralogical, this report contains many interesting observations bearing on the nature and mode of preservation of *Eozoön canadense*.

**Hunt, T Sterry.** Notes on the silicification of fossils. < *Canad. Nat.*, new ser., vol. i, pp. 46-50. 1866.

**Isbister, A. K.** On the geology of the Hudson's Bay territories and of portions of the Arctic and North-western regions of America; with a coloured geological map. < *Quart. Journ. Geol. Soc.*, vol. xi, pp. 497-520. 1855.

This memoir is essentially geological, but contains general notices of the fossils of the districts treated of. The fossils of the Carboniferous formation, of the Jurassic strata, of the Tertiary and Post-Tertiary deposits, and of the Miocene beds of Oregon Territory, are specially alluded to.

**Jackson, C. J.** Sur un moule du Paradoxides harlani. < *Comptes Rendus*, vol. xlvi, pp. 254, 255. 1858.

Announces the discovery of a cast of *Paradoxides harlani* at Braintree, sent to M. Élie de Beaumont.

**Jackson, C. J.** Sur l'identité du Paradoxides harlani et du Paradoxides terra-novæ. < *Comptes Rendus*, vol. xlvii, p. 859. 1859.

**Jameson, Robert.** Notes on the geology of the countries discovered during Captain Parry's second expedition, A. D. 1821-22-23. In "Journal of a Third Voyage for the Discovery of a North West Passage from the Atlantic to the Pacific; performed in the years 1824-25, in His Majesty's ships Hecla and Fury, under the orders of Captain William Edward Parry". Appendix, pp. 132-151. London, 1826.

Contains various notes on the fossils observed during the expedition. Mr. Stokes communicates a note on a fossil from limestone of the island of Igloolik, which is clearly a species of *Receptaculites*.

**Jameson, Robert.** Arctic geology. In "Discovery and Adventure in the Polar Seas and Regions". 1 vol. 12°. < *Edinburgh Cabinet Library*. 1830.

The chapter on Arctic geology contains notices of the fossils discovered in the Arctic regions.

**Jeffreys, J. Gwyn.** The Post-Tertiary fossils procured in the late Arctic Expedition; with notes on some of the recent and living Mollusca from the same expedition. < *Ann. and Mag. Nat. Hist.*, ser. 4, vol. xx, pp. 229-242. 1877.

The fossils described in this communication were collected by the naturalists of the Arctic Expedition of 1875-1876 in Post-Tertiary sands and clays at heights of from 10 to 600 feet above the present sea-level. Eighteen species of Mollusca, one Cœlenterate (*Pennatula*), and one Foraminifer are noted, all now living.

**Jones, T. Rupert.** Notes on Palæozoic Bivalved Entomostraca. No. II. Some British and foreign species of Beyrichia. < *Ann. and Mag. Nat. Hist.*, ser. 2, vol. xvi, pp. 163-176, pl. vi. 1855.

The only American species described is *Beyrichia lata* Vanuxem (*Agnostus latus* Van.).

**Jones, T. Rupert.** Notes on the Palæozoic Bivalved Entomostraca. No. III. Some species of Leperditia. < *Ann. and Mag. Nat. Hist.*, ser. 2, vol. xvii, pp. 81-99, pls. vi and vii. 1856.

Amongst the American species described are *Leperditia arctica* Jones (Arctic regions, Upper Silurian), *L. alta* Conrad, and *L. gibbera*, n. sp., Upper Silurian, Beechey Island.

**Jones, T. Rupert.** On the Palæozoic Bivalve Entomostraca of Canada. < *Figures and Descriptions of Canadian Organic Remains*, Decade III, Montreal, 1858. pp. 91–101, pl. xi.

Nine species of *Ostracoda* are described in this memoir. Five new varieties of *Leperditia canadensis* are defined, and *Isochilina* (with two species) is proposed as a subgenus of *Leperditia.*

**Jones, T. Rupert.** Notes on the Palæozoic Bivalved Entomostraca. No. IV. Some North American species. < *Ann. and Mag. Nat. Hist.*, ser. 3, vol. i, pp. 241–257, pls. ix, x. 1858.

The new species described are *Beyrichia rugulifera, B. sigillata, B. clathrata*, and *B. plagosa* (from Beechey's Island); *B. logani* and *Leperditia canadensis* from the Calciferous, and the latter from the Trenton also; *L. anna* and *L. (Isochilina) ottawa* (Calciferous); *L. (Isochilina) gracilis, Oytheropsis concinna, O. siliqua*, and *O. rugosa* (Trenton); *Leperditia pennsylvanica* (Clinton); *L. ovata* (Trenton); and *Beyrichia pennsylvanica* (Onondaga Salt Group). There are also notes on several previously described forms, and a table of the genera and species of *Ostracoda* known at this date as occurring in Arctic America, Canada, and the United States.

**Jones, T. Rupert.** On some additional Palæozoic Bivalved Entomostraca. from Canada. < *Ann. and Mag. Nat. Hist.*, ser. 3, vol. i, pp. 340–342. 1858.

Occupied chiefly with giving new localities and horizons for previously described forms.

**Jones, T. Rupert.** A monograph of the fossil Estheriæ. 4°. pp. 134, with 5 plates. < *Palæontographical Society*. 1862.

Describes *Estheria ovata* from specimens collected in Pennsylvania, Virginia, and North Carolina (pp. 84–99, pl. ii, figs. 26–38). Also describes and figures *Leaia leidyi* from specimens obtained from the Lower Carboniferous Sandstones of Pennsylvania. Lastly, the author describes and figures two Ostracodes from the Trias of North America as new species, under the names *Candona ? rogersii* and *C. ? emmonsii.*

**Jones, T. Rupert.** On fossil Estheriæ and their distribution. < *Quart. Journ. Geol. Soc. Lond.*, vol. xix, pp. 140–157. 1863.

Refers especially to *Estheria ovata* Lea, from North and South Carolina, Virginia, and Pennsylvania, noticing in particular the geological horizon at which they occur.

**Jones, T. Rupert.** The relationship of certain West-Indian and Maltese strata, as shewn by some Orbitoides and other Foraminifera. < *Geological Magazine*, Decade I, vol. i, pp. 102–106. 1864.

The author remarks on some examples of *Orbitoides* from Antigua and Jamaica, and on some *Nummulinæ* from the former island, and shows that there is thus established a strong relationship between the Mid-Tertiary fauna of Malta and that of the West Indies.

**Jones, T. Rupert.** On the oldest-known fossil, Eozoön canadense of the Laurentian Rocks of Canada; its place, structure, and significance. < *Popular Science Review*, 1867, pp. 343–352, with plate xv and 2 woodcuts.

A semi-popular account of *Eozoön canadense.*

**Jones, T. Rupert.** Manual of the Natural History, Geology, and Physics of Greenland and the neighbouring regions; prepared for the use of the Arctic Expedition of 1875, under the direction of the Arctic Committee of the Royal Society. 8°. pp. 783. London, 1875.

The portion of this work relating to geology (pp. 531–553) contains a summary of all that is known on Arctic geology, with reprints or abstracts of papers on this subject by different authors, and lists of fossils.

Jones, T. Rupert, *and* H. B. Holl. Notes on the Palæozoic Bivalved Entomostraca. No. VI. Some Silurian species (Primitia). < *Ann. and Mag. Nat. Hist.*, ser. 3, vol. xvi, pp. 414–425, pl. xiii. 1865.

> Amongst the American forms noticed are *Beyrichia logani* Jones and *Cytheropsis concinna* Jones, both of which are removed to *Primitia*.

Jones, T. Rupert, *and* H. B. Holl. Notes on the Palæozoic Bivalved Entomostraca. No. VIII. Some Lower Silurian species from the Chair of Kildare, Ireland. < *Ann. and Mag. Nat. Hist.*, ser. 4, vol. ii, pp. 54–62, pl. vii. 1868.

> In a note (p. 55), the authors point out that *Cytheropsis rugosa* Jones, from the Trenton Limestone of Canada, is a *Primitia* (see *Ann. and Mag. Nat. Hist.*, ser. 3, vol. i, p. 249, pl. x, fig. 5) figured upside down.

Jones, T. Rupert, *and* H. B. Holl. Notes on the Palæozoic Bivalved Entomostraca. No. IX. < *Ann. and Mag. Nat. Hist.*, ser. 4, vol. iii, pp. 211–223, pls. xiv and xv. 1869.

> A paper descriptive of European species. At the end, however, the authors give a list of the known Silurian *Primitiæ*, noting various species from North America.

Jones, T. Rupert, *and* W. Kitchen Parker. On the Foraminifera of the family Rotalinæ (Carpenter) found in the Cretaceous formations; with notes on their Tertiary and recent representatives. < *Quart. Journ. Geol. Soc. Lond.*, vol. xxviii, pp. 103–130. 1872.

> The American forms treated of in this communication are the Cretaceous Rotalines described by Ehrenberg, from the Missouri and Mississippi (*Mikrogeologie*), and those described by Reuss from the Greensand of New Jersey (*see* REUSS).

Kalm, Peter. Travels. 1750.

> [Not seen by the writer.] Describes various fossils which he saw in limestone at Fort St. Frederick, or Crown Point, on Lake Champlain.

Kent, W. Saville. On an existing Coral closely allied to the Palæozoic genus Favosites; with remarks on the affinities of the Tabulata. < *Ann. and Mag. Nat. Hist.*, ser. 4, vol. vi, pp. 384–387, pls. xvii, xviii. 1870.

> Founds the genus *Favositipora* for a recent Coral related to *Alveopora*; and describes a fossil form of the same, believed to be from the Devonian of North America, under the name of *Favositipora palæozoica*.

King, W., *and* T. H. Rowney. On the so-called Eozoönal Rock. < *Quart. Journ. Geol. Soc. Lond.*, vol. xxii, pp. 185–218, pls. xiv and xv. 1866.

> The authors describe in this memoir the results of a careful chemical and microscopical examination of the Grenville "Eozoönal" Ophite, from which they arrive at the conclusion that *Eozoön canadense* is truly of inorganic origin.

King, W., *and* T. H. Rowney. On the so-called "Eozoönal" Rock. < *Quart. Journ. Geol. Soc. Lond.*, vol. xxv, pp. 116, 117. [Abstract.] 1869.

> The authors adduce further evidence that their views as to the mineral nature of *Eozoön* are correct.

King, W., *and* T. H. Rowney. On the mineral origin of the so-called "Eozoön canadense". < *Proc. Roy. Irish Acad.*, ser. 2, vol. i, pp. 140–153. 1871.

> A reply to papers by Drs. J. W. Dawson and T. Sterry Hunt on the zoological and chemical aspects of the question respectively. The paper concludes with a recapitulation of the various points detailed in the formerly published papers of the authors.

**King, W.,** *and* **T. H. Rowney.** Eozoön, examined principally from a Foraminiferal standpoint. < *Ann. and Mag. Nat. Hist.,* ser. 4, vol. xiv, pp. 274-289, pl. xix. 1874.

*A controversial paper, in which evidence is brought forward to show that Eozoön canadense is inorganic in its nature.*

**King, W.,** *and* **T. H. Rowney.** Remarks on the subject of Eozoön. < *Ann. and Mag. Nat. Hist.,* ser. 4, vol. xiii, pp. 390-396. 1874.

*A summary of the chief points in favour of the mineral nature of Eozoön canadense.*

**King, W.,** *and* **T. H. Rowney.** Remarks on the 'Dawn of Life' by Dr. Dawson; to which is added a supplementary note. < *Ann. and Mag. Nat. Hist.,* ser. 4, vol. xvii, pp. 360-377. 1876.

*A critical memoir, stating the objections held by the authors as to the supposed organic origin of Eozoön.*

**König, Charles.** Rock-specimens. Supplement to the "Appendix of Captain Parry's Voyage for the Discovery of a North-west Passage, in the years 1819-20", pp. ccxlvii-cclvii. London, 1824.

*Contains some notices of fossils, and defines as new Catenipora parryi, from a limestone discovered in Prince Regent's Inlet.*

**Koninck, L. de.** Description des animaux fossiles que se trouvent dans le terrain Carbonifère de la Belgique. Avec supplément. 1842-44.

*The author cites various species of Productus, Strophomena, Orthis, Spirifer, Euomphalus, and Goniatites as occurring in the Palæozoic rocks of North America.*

**Koninck, L. de.** Recherches sur les animaux fossiles. Première partie. Monographie des genres Productus et Chonetes. 4°. pp. 246, with 20 plates. Liége, 1847.

*Describes Chonetes shumardiana De Kon. from the Carboniferous of Kentucky, and cites 7 species of Productus and 5 species of Chonetes as occurring in North America.*

**Koninck, L. de.** Recherches sur les animaux fossiles. Deuxième partie. Monographie des fossiles Carbonifères de la Carinthie. 1872.

*Cites a number of Brachiopods and Bellerophon levii as occurring in the Carboniferous strata of North America.*

**Koninck, L. de.** Nouvelles recherches sur les animaux fossiles du Terrain Carbonifère de la Belgique. Première partie. Bruxelles, 1872.

*The author cites several Corals as occurring in the Carboniferous rocks of North America. He identifies the Lithostrotion ? californiense of Meek with Lonsdaleia rugosa Martin, and he shows that the Sphenopoterium of Meek and Worthen is identical with the previously described Palæacis of Jules Haime.*

**Koninck, L. de,** *and* **H. Le Hon.** Monographie des Crinoïdes Carbonifères de la Belgique. 1854.

*Cites Platycrinus planus Owen and Shumard.*

**Laspeyres, H.** Das fossile Phyllopoden-Genus Leaia, R. Jones. < *Zeitschr. der Deutsch. Geol. Ges.,* vol. xxii, pp. 733-746. 1870.

*The author describes and figures Leaia leidyi, and examines into the structure and relations of Leaia and its known species.*

**Lesueur, C. A.** Description de plusieurs animales appartenant aux Polypiers lamellifères de M. le Chevalier de Lamarck. < *Mém. du Muséum,* vol. vi, pp. 271-299, pls. xv, xvi, 1820.

*This memoir deals principally with the living Corals of the West Indies. In an appendix, however, the author treats of the "Caryophyllites fossiles que l'on trouve aux États-Unis d'Amérique", and describes three Devonian forms of Zaphrentis, under the names of Caryophyllia gigantea, C. pulmonea, and C. cornicula.*

**Lindström, Gustav.** On the affinities of the Anthozoa tabulata. <*Ann. and Mag. Nat. Hist.*, ser. 4, vol. xviii, pp. 1-17. 1876. [Translated from *Öfversigt af Kongl. Vetenskaps-Akad. Förhandl. Stockholm*, 1873.]

    Amongst American forms of Tabulate Corals specially noticed by the author may be mentioned *Ceramopora imbricata* Hall and *Trematopora ostiolata* Hall, and critical remarks are also made upon the affinities of *Callopora* Hall, *Cladopora* Hall, *Constellaria* Dana, *Cyathophora* Dale Owen, *Tetradium* Dana, &c.

**Logan, W. E.** On the packing of the ice in the river St. Lawrence; the occurrence of landslips in the modern deposits of its valley; and the existence of Marine Shells in them and on the mountain of Montreal. < *Quart. Journ. Geol. Soc. Lond.*, vol. ii, pp. 422-432. 1846.

    At the close of this memoir, the author considers the Post-Pliocene deposits of the neighbourhood of Montreal, indicating their extension to a height of 460 feet above the level of the sea, and giving a list of five shells found therein.

**Logan, W. E.** On the occurrence of a track and footprints of an animal in the Potsdam Sandstone of Lower Canada. < *Quart. Journ. Geol. Soc. Lond.*, vol. vii, pp. 247-250, with section. 1851.

    This paper deals principally with the geological horizon of the strata containing the footprints in question (*Protichnites*).

**Logan, W. E.** On the footprints occurring in the Potsdam Sandstone of Canada. < *Quart. Journ. Geol. Soc. Lond.*, vol. viii, pls. vi-viii. 1852.

    Gives a full account of the geology of the district where the footprints (*Protichnites*) occur, with lists of the fossils found in the associated strata.

**Logan, W. E.** On the track of an animal lately found in the Potsdam Formation. < *Canad. Nat.*, vol. v, pp. 279-285, with 5 engravings. 1860.

    Describes and figures *Climactichnites wilsoni*, and gives details as to the geological features and position of the beds in which these remarkable tracks occur.

**Logan, W. E.** Remarks on the Fauna of the Quebec Group of Rocks, and the Primordial Zone of Canada, addressed to Mr. Joachim Barrande. < *Canad. Nat.*, vol. v, pp. 472-477, 1860; and < *Canad. Journ.*, new ser., vol. vi, pp. 40-46, 1861.

    Discusses the characters of the fossils of the Quebec Group, with special reference to the stratigraphical position of this series of deposits.

**Logan, W. E.** On the Rocks of the Quebec Group at Point Lévis. [In a letter addressed to M. Barrande.] < *Canad. Nat.*, vol. viii, pp. 183-194. 1863.

    Contains lists of the fossils, and notes thereon.

**Logan, W. E.** On the occurrence of organic remains in the Laurentian Rocks of Canada. < *Quart. Journ. Geol. Soc. Lond.*, vol. xxi, pp. 45-50. 1865.

    This memoir is a geological one, occupied with a general description of the Laurentian Rocks of Canada, illustrated by sections. The author, however, gives an account of the discovery of *Eozoön* in the Lower Laurentian Limestone, and describes the general mode of occurrence of, and the appearance presented by, the specimens.

**Logan, W. E.** On the occurrence of organic remains in the Laurentian Rocks of Canada. < *Canad. Nat.*, new ser., vol. ii, pp. 92-99. 1867.

    A reprint from the *Quart. Journ. Geol. Soc. Lond.*, 1865, with some additional notes.

## II.—PUBLICATIONS MADE IN BRITISH AMERICA, ETC. 113

**Logan, W. E.** On new specimens of Eozoön. < *Quart. Journ. Geol. Soc. Lond.*, vol. xxiii, pp. 253–257. 1867.

This is a geological memoir, but it is of interest to the palæontologist as giving a detailed account of the precise geological position of the bed from which was obtained the least altered example of *Eozoön canadense* (the "Tudor specimen") as yet known to science.

**Lonsdale, William.** Account of twenty-six species of Polyparia, obtained from the Eocene Tertiary Formation of North America. < *Quart. Journ. Geol. Soc. London,* vol. i, pp. 509–533, with 17 engravings. 1845.

The specimens described in this memoir were collected by Sir Charles Lyell, and consist partly of true Corals and partly of *Polyzoa*. Five species of Corals and 11 of *Polyzoa* are described as new.

**Lonsdale, William.** Account of six species of Polyparia obtained from Timber Creek, New Jersey. < *Quart. Journ. Geol. Soc. Lond.*, vol. i, pp. 65–75, with 6 engravings. 1845.

This paper is an appendix to a memoir by Sir Charles Lyell describing the Cretaceous strata of New Jersey, &c. (*Quart. Journ. Geol. Soc.*, vol. I, p. 55). The species described and figured are *Montlivaltia atlantica* Morton, and, amongst Polyzoans, *Idmonea contortilis* Lonsd., *Tubulipora megæra* Lonsd., *Cellepora tubulata* Lonsd., *Escharina sagena* Morton, and *Eschara digitata* Morton.

**Lonsdale, William.** Account of ten species of Polyparia obtained from the Miocene Tertiary Formations of North America. < *Quart. Journ. Geol. Soc. Lond.*, vol. i, pp. 495–509, with 10 engravings. 1845.

The fossils here described were collected by Sir Charles Lyell, and seven of the ten species which form the subject of the paper are Polyzoans. Seven species are described as new.

**Lyell, [Sir] Charles.** Remarks on some fossil and recent shells, collected by Captain Bayfield, R. N. < *Proc. Geol. Soc. Lond.*, vol. iii, pp. 119–120. 1839.

The author describes a collection of shells obtained from the Post-Pliocene deposits of Beauport, near Quebec. The resemblance of these shells to those of the shells of Uddevalla in Sweden is noticed, and they are further compared with the species living in the Gulf of St. Lawrence.

**Lyell, [Sir] Charles.** On the Tertiary Formations and their connection with the Chalk in Virginia and other parts of the United States. < *Proc. Geol. Soc. Lond.*, vol. iii, pp. 735–742. 1839.

Contains notes upon the fossils, together with lists of the species collected.

**Lyell, [Sir] Charles.** On the Tertiary strata of the Island of Martha's Vineyard in Massachusetts. < *Proc. Geol. Soc. Lond.*, vol. iv, pp. 31–33. 1840.

Contains notes on the fossils.

**Lyell, [Sir] Charles.** Remarks on some fossil and recent shells, collected by Captain Bayfield, R. N., in Canada. < *Trans. Geol. Soc. Lond.*, ser. 2, vol. vi, pp. 135–141, pl. xvi. 1842.

Contains lists of the Post-Pliocene shells of the neighbourhood of Quebec, with descriptive and general remarks thereon. The author compares these shells with those now living in the Gulf of St. Lawrence, and indicates their resemblance to the shells of the Glacial deposits of Uddevalla in Sweden.

Mis. Pub. No. 10——8

**Lyell, [*Sir*] Charles.** Travels in North America; with geological observations on the United States, Canada, and Nova Scotia. 2 vols. 8°. With maps and illustrations. London, 1845.

> The author gives numerous notes on the fossils which he collected in his travels, often with lists of species, and with many observations, comparing the forms collected with those found in corresponding formations in Europe.

**Lyell, [*Sir*] Charles.** Notes on the Cretaceous strata of New Jersey, and other parts of the United States bordering the Atlantic. < *Quart. Journ. Geol. Soc. Lond.*, vol. i, pp. 55–60. 1845.

> This memoir, though principally geological, contains various palæontological notes. The fossils collected were separately described by Prof. Edward Forbes and Mr. Lonsdale (*q. v.*).

**Lyell, [*Sir*] Charles.** Observations on the White Limestone and other Eocene or older Tertiary Formations of Virginia, South Carolina, and Georgia. < *Quart. Journ. Geol. Soc. Lond.*, vol. i, pp. 429–442, with 7 wood uts. 1845.

> Contains numerous observations on and lists of the fossils collected, several being figured. *Terebratula wilmingtonensis* and *Cerithium georgianum* are described as new species; and Prof. E. Forbes gives a description of a new Echinoid under the name of *Scutella jonesii*.

**Lyell, [*Sir*] Charles.** On the Miocene Tertiary strata of Maryland, Virginia, and of North and South Carolina. < *Quart. Journ. Geol. Soc. Lond.*, vol. i, pp. 411–429, with 2 engravings. 1845.

> The memoir contains numerous palæontological notes and lists of fossils. Lists of shells are given showing the number of Miocene species still existing, the species common to the American and European Miocene, &c. Prof. E. Forbes gives descriptions, accompanied with figures, of two new Echinoids (viz, *Amphidetus virginianus* and *Echinus ruffinii*). A list of the fossil Corals is given, and a note from Mr. Lonsdale is appended dealing with the indications of climate afforded by the Miocene Corals of Virginia.

**Lyell, [*Sir*] Charles.** On the newer deposits of the Southern States of North America. < *Quart. Journ. Geol. Soc. Lond.*, vol. ii, pp. 405–410. 1846.

> Besides scattered observations on various Invertebrate fossils met with, the author notes the occurrence on the shores of the Bay of Mobile of inland deposits of the shells of *Gnathodon cuneatus*.

**Lyell, [*Sir*] Charles.** On the structure and probable age of the coal-field of James River, near Richmond, Virginia. < *Quart. Journ. Geol. Soc. Lond.*, vol. iii, pp. 261–280. 1847.

> At pp. 274, 275, of this memoir, the author describes and figures a small *Estheria* [*Posidonomya*] as occurring in the Richmond strata referred to, and points out that the occurrence of these fossils would lead to the conclusion that the Richmond coal-field is of Triassic age.

**Lyell, [*Sir*] Charles.** On the relative age and position of the so-called Nummulite Limestone of Alabama. < *Quart. Journ. Geol. Soc. Lond.*, vol. iv, pp. 10–16. 1848.

> Numerous fossils are alluded to as occurring in the strata in question, and the memoir contains notes from Edward Forbes and Alcide D'Orbigny as to the zoological position of *Orbitoides* [*Nummulites*] *mantelli*.

**Lyell, *Sir* Charles,** *and* **J. W. Dawson.** On the remains of a reptile (Dendrerpeton acadianum, Wyman & Owen) and of a land-shell discovered in the interior of an erect fossil tree in the Coal-Measures of Nova Scotia. < *Quart. Journ. Geol. Soc. Lond.*, vol. ix, pp. 58–63, pls. ii–iv. 1853.

This memoir contains a description, with figures, of the first discovered specimen of the little Carboniferous land-shell since well known under the name of *Pupa (Dendropupa) vetusta*.

Marcou, Jules. Résumé explicatif d'une carte géologique des États-Unis et des provinces anglaises de l'Amérique du Nord, avec un profil géologique allant de la vallée du Mississippi aux côtes du Pacifique, et une planche de fossiles. < *Bull. de la Soc. Géol. de France*, vol. xii, pp. 813–936, pl. xxi and map. 1856.

This memoir contains lists of the fossils from the Lower Silurian to the Tertiary inclusive. Some Cretaceous *Ostreidæ* are figured.

Marcou, Jules. Geology of North America; with two reports on the prairies of Arkansas and Texas, the Rocky Mountains of New Mexico, and the Sierra Nevada of California. 1 vol. 4°. pp. 144, with 7 plates of fossils. Zurich, 1858.

Chapter iii of this work (pp. 32–53) is devoted to descriptions of fossils collected by the author from the Tertiary, Secondary, and Palæozoic deposits of the regions examined by him. *Ammonites shumardi, A. belknapii, A. novi-mexicani, Hamites fremonti, Inoceramus lerouxi, Isocardia washita, Holaster comanchesi, Orthoceras nova-mexicana, Myalina apachesi, Productus delawarii, Orthis pecosti, Spirifer rocky-montani, Terebratula rocky-montana, T. mormonii*, and *T. uta* are described as new species.

Marcou, Jules. Une reconnaissance géologique au Nébraska. < *Bull. de la Soc. Géol. de France*, 2e sér., vol. xxi, pp. 132–147. 1864.

Contains notes on the fossils.

Marcou, Jules. Le Terrain Crétacé des environs de Sioux-City, de la mission des Omaha et de Tekama, sur les bords du Missouri. < *Bull. de la Soc. Géol. de France*, ser. 2, vol. xxiv, pp. 56–71, pl. i. 1867.

The author gives some notes on the Invertebrate fossils of the Cretaceous deposits of Sioux City, Iowa.

Marcou, Jules. Untersuchungen in Californien. < *Verhandl. d. K. K. Geolog. Reichsanstalt*, 1875, pp. 215, 216.

Notes the occurrence near Fort Tejon of strata with Eocene fossils.

Mathew, G. F. On the Azoic and Palæozoic Rocks of Southern New Brunswick. < *Quart. Journ. Geol. Soc. Lond.*, vol. xxi, pp. 422–434. 1865.

Contains scattered notices of the fossils.

Mathew, G. F. Note sur les Mollusques de la formation Post-Pliocène de l'Acadie. < *Annales de la Soc. Malacologique de Belgique*, vol. ix, pp. 33–49, pl. i. (Translated from the author's MS. by Armand Thielens.) 1874.

Gives a general account of the Post-Pliocene formations, and furnishes notes on a large number of the fossil *Mollusca* which the author has met with in these beds in Acadia.

Meek, F. B. Fossils from the west coast of Kennedy Channel. < *Hayes's "Open Polar Ocean"*, London, 1867, p. 341; and < *Am. Journ. Sci. and Arts*, ser. 2, vol. xl, pp. 31–34.

Describes various fossils collected by Dr. Hayes on the west coast of Kennedy's Channel, from deposits of Lower Helderberg age. *Zaphrentis hayesi* and *Lozonema ? kanei* are described as new species.

**Meek, F. B.** Geology of the line of the great Pacific Railroad. [In a letter to Dr. J. J. Bigsby.] < *Geological Magazine*, Decade I, vol. vii, pp. 163, 164. 1870.

Notes the fossils obtained by Mr. Clarence King along the line of the Pacific Railway.

**Meek, F. B.** Remarks on the genus Lichenocrinus. < *Ann. and Mag. Nat. Hist.*, ser. 4, vol. viii, pp. 341–345. 1871.

A reprint from *Amer. Journ. Sci. and Arts*, 1871.

**Meek, F. B.** Supplementary note on the genus Lichenocrinus. < *Ann. and Mag. Nat. Hist.*, ser. 4, vol. ix, pp. 247, 248. 1872.

An additional description of the characters of *Lichenocrinus*, founded on a number of fresh specimens. The author concludes that it is an aberrant type of *Cystoidea*, representing a distinct family.

**Meek, F. B., and A. H. Worthen.** Notes on some points in the structure and habits of the Palæozoic Crinoidea. < *Canad. Nat.*, new ser., vol. iv, pp. 434–452. 1869.

Reprinted from the *Proc. Acad. Nat. Sci. Phila.*, 1869.

**Michelin, Hardouin.** Iconographie zoophytologique. Description par localités et terrains des Polypiers fossiles de France et pays environnants. Paris, 1840–47. pp. 348, with 78 plates.

A few American Corals are described in this work.

**Michelin, Hardouin.** Monographie des Clypéastres fossiles. < *Mém. de la Soc. Géol. de France*, vol. vii, pp. 101–147, pls. ix–xxxvi.

Amongst other forms, the author of this memoir describes various Clypeastroids from the Tertiary formations of the West Indies.

**Milne, John.** On the rocks of Newfoundland, with notes by Alexander Murray. < *Geol. Mag.*, Decade II, vol. iv, pp. 251–262. 1877.

Mr. Murray's notes to this paper contain various observations on the fossils found in the rocks of Newfoundland.

**Milne-Edwards, H.** Histoire naturelle des Crustacés, comprenant l'anatomie, la physiologie, et la classification de ces animaux. [Natural history of Crustacea, comprising their anatomy, physiology, and classification.] 3 vols. 8º. Paris, 1834–40.

Describes various species of American fossil *Crustacea* (Eurypterids and Trilobites).

**Milne-Edwards, H.** Histoire naturelle des Coralliaires ou Polypes proprement dits. 3 vols. 8º. Paris, 1857–60.

Describes a number of fossil Corals from North America.

**Milne-Edwards, H., and Jules Haime.** Mémoire sur les Polypiers appartenant aux groupes naturelles des Zoanthaires perforés et des Zoanthaires tabulés. < *Comptes Rendus*, 1849, t. xxix, pp. 257–263.

The authors found the genus *Dania* for the reception of the North American *D. huronica*.

**Milne-Edwards, H., and Jules Haime.** A monograph of the British Fossil Corals. Introduction, pp. i–lxxxv. < *Palæontographical Society*, 1850.

In the Introduction to their monograph of the British Fossil Corals, the authors found the genera *Anisophyllum*, *Baryphyllum*, *Hallia*, *Aulacophyllum*, *Trochophyllum*, *Hadrophyllum*, and *Eridophyllum*, principally or exclusively for the reception of American species.

**Milne-Edwards, H.**, *and* **Jules Haime.** Monographie des Poritides. <*Annales des Sciences Naturelles*, sér. 3, vol. xvi, pp. 21-70. 1850.

The only American Corals described are *Protaræa vetusta* Hall, sp.; *P. verneuili* E. & H.; and *Pleurodictyum problematicum* Goldf.

**Milne-Edwards, H.**, *and* **Jules Haime.** Monographie des Polypiers fossiles des Terrains Paléozoiques, précédée d'un tableau général de la classification des Polypes. [Monograph of the fossil Corals of the Palæozoic rocks, preceded by a general table of the classification of Polypes.] <*Archives du Muséum*, t. v, pp. 502, with 20 plates. Paris, 1851.

Owing to the classical position of this work amongst treatises dealing with the fossil Corals, it may be useful to subjoin a list of the species founded on American specimens therein described:—*Protaræa vetusta* Hall, sp.; *P. verneuili* E. & H.; *Plasmopora follis* E. & H.; *Lyellia americana* E. & H.; *L. glabra* Dale Owen, sp.; *Favosites favosa* Goldfuss; *F. troosti* E. & H.; *F. mamillaris* Castelnau, sp.; *Emmonsia hemispherica* Yand. & Shum., sp.; *E.? cylindrica* Mich., sp.; *Michelinia convexa* D'Orb.; *Chætetes filiosa* D'Orb.; *C. dalii* E. & H.; *C. ramosus* D'Orb.; *C. mammulatus* D'Orb.; *C. frondosus* D'Orb.; *C. pavonia* D'Orb.; *C. tuberculatus* E. & H.; *C. rugosus* E. & H.; *C. milleporaceus* E. & H.; *Dania huronica* E. & H.; *Dekayia aspera* E. & H.; *Constellaria antheloidea* Hall, sp.; *Syringopora tabulata* E. & H.; *S. verneuili* E. & H.; *S. verticillata* Goldf.; *S. tubiporoides* Yand. & Shum.; *Chonostegites clappi* E. & H.; *Columnaria alveolata* Goldf.; *Cyathaxonia cynodon* Raf. & Cliff.; *C. profunda* E. & H.; *Zaphrentis cornicula* Lesueur, sp.; *Z. centralis* E. & H.; *Z. rafinesquii* E. & H.; *Z. cliffordana* E. & H.; *Z. dalii* E. & H.; *Z. stokesi* E. & H.; *Z. desori* E. & H.; *Z. spinulosa* E. & H.; *Z. denticulata* Goldf., sp.; *Z. marcoui* E. & H.; *Z. gigantea* Lesueur, sp.; *Z. rameri* E. & H.; *Z. halli* E. & H.; *Amplexus yandelli* E. & H.; *Anisophyllum agassizi* E. & H.; *Baryphyllum verneuilanum* E. & H.; *Hallia insignis* E. & H.; *Aulacophyllum sulcatum* D'Orb., sp.; *Trochophyllum verneuilanum* E. & H.; *Hadrophyllum orbignyi* E. & H.; *Cyathophyllum lesueuri* E. & H.; *C. rectum* Hall, sp.; *C. distortum* Hall, sp.;'*C. rugosum* Hall, sp.; *Streptelasma corniculum* Hall; *S. ? expansa* Hall; *Ptychophyllum stokesi* E. & H.; *Heliophyllum halli* E. & H.; *Clisiophyllum danaanum* E. & H.; *Acervularia davidsoni* E. & H.; *Eridophyllum verneuilanum* E. & H.; *E. strictum* E. & H.; *Strombodes pentagonus* Goldf., sp.; *Lithostrotion mamillare* (=*L. canadensis*) Castelnau, sp.; *L. harmodites* E. & H.; *L. stokesi* E. & H.; *Phillipsastræa verneuili* E. & H.; and *Cystiphyllum americanum* E. & H. The new genera founded on American Corals are *Protaræa, Lyellia, Emmonsia, Dekayia,* and *Chonostegites.*

**Moore, J. Carrick.** On some Tertiary beds in the Island of San Domingo, with remarks on the fossils. <*Quart. Journ. Geol. Soc.*, vol. vi, pp. 39-44. 1850.

Contains lists of, and remarks upon, the Invertebrate fossils, principally dealing with the *Mollusca*.

**Moore, J. Carrick.** On some Tertiary Shells from Jamaica, with a note on the Corals, by P. Martin Duncan, M. B., F. G. S.; and a note on some Nummulinæ and Orbitoides, by Professor T. Rupert Jones, F. G. S. <*Quart. Journ. Geol. Soc. Lond.*, vol. xix, pp. 510-515. 1863.

**Morton, Samuel George.** Description of two new species of fossil Echinodermata from the Eocene strata of the United States. <*Ann. and Mag. Nat. Hist.*, ser. 1, vol. xviii, p. 357. 1846.

A reprint from *Silliman's American Journal*, September, 1846.

**Murchison, Sir Roderick I.** Siluria. A history of the oldest rocks in the British Isles and other countries. 5th ed. 8°. pp. 566, with 41 plates. London, 1872.

Contains notices of American palæozoic fossils (see especially chapter xviii, pp. 424-447).

**Murchison,** *Sir* **Roderick I., Edouard de Verneuil,** *and* **Count Alexander de Keyserling.** Geology of Russia in Europe and the Ural Mountains. Vol. ii. Troisième partie, Paléontologie. 4°. pp. 512. London and Paris, 1845.

> The authors note the occurrence of many of the Palæozoic fossils of Russia in deposits of corresponding age in North America.

**Murray, 'Alexander.** Report upon the Geological Survey of Newfoundland for the year 1871. St. John's, 1872. pp. 49.

> Contains a few notes on the fossils.

**Murray, Alexander.** Report upon the Geological Survey of Newfoundland for the year 1872. St. John's, 1873. pp. 34.

> Contains many notices of the fossils.

**Murray, Alexander.** Geological Survey of Newfoundland. Report of progress for the year 1873. Montreal, 1873. pp. 47.

> Contains notes on the fossils.

**Murray, Alexander.** Report upon the Geological Survey of Newfoundland for the year 1873. St. John's, 1873. pp. 69.

> Contains a few notes on the fossils.

**Murray, Alexander.** Geological Survey of Newfoundland. Report of progress for the year 1874. St. John's, 1875. pp. 74.

> The portion of this report by Mr. James P. Howley, on the Geology of Port-a-Port and St. George's Bay, contains notices of the fossils met with.

**Nelson, Richard J.** On the Geology of the Bermudas. < *Trans. Geol. Soc. Lond.*, ser. 2, vol. v, pp. 103-123, with 16 engravings. 1840.

> Contains numerous observations, dealing [with coral-reefs, formation of limestone, chalk, &c., of great interest to the palæontologist.

**Nelson, Richard J.** On the Geology of the Bahamas, and on Coral-formations generally. < *Quart. Journ. Geol. Soc. Lond.*, vol. ix, pp. 200-215. [Abstract.] 1853.

> Though not strictly palæontological, Major-General Nelson's memoir contains much matter of the highest interest to the philosophical palæontologist.

**Nicholson, H. Alleyne.** Migrations of the Graptolites. < *Quart. Journ. Geol. Soc. Lond.*, vol. xxviii, pp. 217-231. 1872.

> Treats in part of the distribution and range of the American species of *Graptolites.*

**Nicholson, H. Alleyne.** A monograph of the British Graptolitidæ. Part I. General introduction. pp. 133, with 74 engravings. Edinburgh, 1872.

> Notices various American forms of *Graptolites.*

**Nicholson, H. Alleyne.** On Ortonia, a new genus of fossil [Tubicolar Annelides, with notes on the genus Tentaculites. < *Geological Magazine,* Decade I, vol. ix, pp. 446-449, with engraving. 1872.

> Founds the genus *Ortonia,* with one species (*O. conica*), for the reception of some Tubicolous *Annelides* from the Cincinnati Group of Ohio.

**Nicholson, H. Alleyne.** On some Fossils from the Quebec Group of Point Lévis, Quebec. < *Ann. and Mag. Nat. Hist.*, ser. 4, vol. xi, pp. 133-143, with 3 engravings. 1873.

<small>Describes as new species *Dictyonema grandis, Tetragraptus approximatus, Dawsonia acuminata, D. rotunda, D. tenuistriata,* and *D. campanulata.* The genus *Dawsonia* is founded for the reception of bodies believed to be the generative capsules of *Graptolites*; and the genus *Clonograpsus* (Hall, MS.) is defined.</small>

**Nicholson, H. Alleyne.** Descriptions of two new species of fossil Tubicolar Annelides. < *Geological Magazine,* Decade I, vol. x, pp. 54-57, pl. iv, figs. 2 and 3. 1873.

<small>Describes *Ortonia minor* and *Conchicolites corrugatus,* from the Cincinnati Group of Ohio.</small>

**Nicholson, H. Alleyne.** Summary of recent researches on the Palæontology of Ontario, with brief descriptions of some new genera. < *Canad. Journ.,* new series, vol. xiv, pp. 125-136. 1873.

<small>Contains a summary of the palæontological researches in the Devonian formations of Ontario carried out by the author in 1873. A list of the fossils identified (160 species) is given, and the Polyzoan genera *Botryllopora, Carinopora, Tæniopora,* and *Cryptopora* are briefly described.</small>

**Nicholson, H. Alleyne.** On the species of Favosites of the Devonian rocks of Western Ontario. < *Canad. Journ.,* new ser., vol. xiv, pp. 38-50. 1873.

<small>A critical account of the genus *Favosites,* and of 6 of the species of this genus recognized by the author in the Devonian deposits of Ontario.</small>

**Nicholson, H. Alleyne.** On some new species of Stromatopora. < *Ann. and Mag. Nat. Hist.,* ser. 4, vol. xii, pp. 89-95, pl. iv. 1873.

<small>Describes as new species *S. ostiolata* (Guelph formation), and *S. tuberculata, S. granulata,* and *S. mammillata* (from the Corniferous Limestone).</small>

**Nicholson, H. Alleyne.** Descriptions of new fossils from the Devonian Rocks of Canada West. < *Geological Magazine,* Decade II, vol. i, pp. 10-16, 54-60, 117-126, 159-163, 197-201, pls. ii, iv, vi, ix, and 3 figures. 1874.

<small>The author describes and figures a number of new fossils from the Devonian rocks of Western Canada, preliminary to the publication of a more extended report on the organic remains of the Corniferous and Hamilton formations of this region. The species described comprise 12 Corals, 2 Brachiopods, 13 Polyzoa, and 2 Tubicolar Annelides. The two new Polyzoan genera *Botryllopora* and *Tæniopora* are defined.</small>

**Nicholson, H. Alleyne.** On Duncanella, a new genus of Palæozoic Corals. < *Ann. and Mag. Nat. Hist.,* ser. 4, vol. xiii, pp. 333-335, with 1 engraving. 1874.

<small>Founds the genus *Duncanella* for a simple Coral from the Niagara group of Indiana. The single species *D. borealis* is described.</small>

**Nicholson, H. Alleyne.** On Columnopora, a new genus of Tabulate Corals. < *Geological Magazine,* Decade II, vol. i, pp. 253-254, with engraving. 1874.

<small>Founds the genus *Columnopora,* with the single species *C. cribriformis,* for a Coral from the Cincinnati group of Ohio and the corresponding Hudson River formation of Ontario.</small>

**Nicholson, H. Alleyne.** Descriptions of new fossils from the Devonian rocks of Western Ontario. < *Canad. Nat.*, new ser., vol. vii, pp. 138–147. 1874.

<small>Describes as new *Zaphrentis fenestrata*, *Blothrophyllum decorticatum*, *Heliophyllum colbornense*, *Petraia* (?) *logani*, and *Alecto* (?) *canadensis*.</small>

**Nicholson, H. Alleyne.** On the affinities of the genus Stromatopora, with descriptions of two new species. < *Ann. and Mag. Nat. Hist.*, ser. 4, vol. xiii, pp. 4–13, with 3 engravings. 1874.

<small>Refers *Stromatopora* to the *Calcispongiæ*. The new species described are *S.* [*Caunopora*] *perforata* and *S. hindei*.</small>

**Nicholson, H. Alleyne.** Descriptions of two new genera and species of Polyzoa from the Devonian rocks. < *Ann. and Mag. Nat. Hist.*, ser. 4, vol. xiii, pp. 77–85, with 2 engravings. 1874.

<small>Describes the new genera *Cryptopora* and *Carinopora* as aberrant members of the *Fenestellidæ*. The known species, viz, *Cryptopora mirabilis* and *Carinopora hindei*, are from the Corniferous Limestone.</small>

**Nicholson, H. Alleyne.** Descriptions of species of Chætetes from the Lower Silurian rocks of North America. < *Quart. Journ. Geol. Soc. Lond.*, vol. xxx, pp. 499–515, pls. xxix, xxx. 1874.

<small>Treats of the species of *Chætetes* which the author had met with in the Cincinnati Group of Ohio and the Hudson River and Trenton formations of Canada. Nineteen species are recognized, of which several are described as new.</small>

**Nicholson, H. Alleyne.** Report upon the Palæontology of the Province of Ontario. Presented to the Legislative Assembly by command of His Excellency the Lieutenant-Governor. Toronto, 1874. 8°. pp. 133, with 8 plates and 58 woodcuts.

<small>In the introduction to this report, the author reviews the Devonian strata of the Province of Ontario, stratigraphically and as regards their palæontological relations. The remainder of the work is occupied with descriptions of 160 species of fossils from the Corniferous and Hamilton formations, comprising 6 species of *Protozoa*, 72 species of *Cœlenterata*, 43 species of *Brachiopoda*, 19 species of *Polyzoa*, 1 species of *Lamellibranchiata*, 1 species of *Pteropoda*, 12 species of *Gasteropoda*, 3 species of *Annelida*, and 4 species of *Crustacea*. Most of the new forms had been previously described by the author, but the following are here described for the first time:—*Clisiophyllum* [*Acrophyllum*] *pluriradiale*, *Heliophyllum proliferum*, *Favosites chapmani*, *Platyceras uniseriale*, *Strophostylus* (?) *subglobosus*, *S.* (?) *ovatus*, *S.* (?) *obliquus*, *Holopea eriensis*, *Helicotoma* (?) *serotina*, and *Syringopora intermedia*.</small>

**Nicholson, H. Alleyne.** On Favistella stellata and Favistella calicina; with notes on the affinities of Favistella and allied genera. < *Rep. British Assoc. for* 1874, *Sections*, pp. 89, 90.

<small>The new species *F. calicina* is founded for a Coral from the Hudson River Group of Ontario.</small>

**Nicholson, H. Alleyne.** Descriptions of species of Hippothoa and Alecto from the Lower Silurian rocks of Ohio, with a description of Aulopora arachnoidea, Hall. < *Ann. and Mag. Nat. Hist.*, ser. 4, vol. xv, pp. 123–127, pl. xi. 1875.

<small>Refers *Alecto inflata* Hall to *Hippothoa*, and describes as new species *Alecto auloporoides*, *A. frondosa* (James, MS.), and *A. confusa*.</small>

**Nicholson, H. Alleyne.** Descriptions of new species of Polyzoa from the Lower and Upper Silurian rocks of North America. <*Ann. and Mag. Nat. Hist.*, ser. 4, vol. xv, pp. 177-184, pl. xiv. 1875.

Ptilodictya falciformis, P. emucerata, P. flagellum, P. (?) arctipora, P. fenestelliformis, and Oeramopora ohioensis are described as new species from the Cincinnati formation, and Fenestella nervata from the Niagara (Guelph) formation of Ohio.

**Nicholson, H. Alleyne.** Notes on the Gasteropoda of the Guelph formation of Canada. <*Quart. Journ. Geol. Soc. Lond.*, vol. xxxi, pp. 543-551, pl. xxvi, with woodcut. 1875.

Treats of the Gasteropods which the author had collected in the Guelph Limestone of Canada. Sixteen forms are described, of which two (*Murchisonia boylei* and *Holopea ? occidentalis*) are determined as new.

**Nicholson, H. Alleyne.** Report upon the Palæontology of the Province of Ontario. Printed by order of the Legislative Assembly. Toronto, 1875. 8°. pp. 96, with 4 plates and 45 woodcuts.

This report is a continuation of one published in 1874, and contains an enumeration of 200 species of fossils collected by the author from the Trenton Limestone, Utica Slate, Hudson River formation, Niagara Limestone, Guelph formation, Corniferous Limestone, and Hamilton formation of Western Ontario. To many of the species nothing more than references are given; but descriptions, generally accompanied by figures, are given of all new species, as well as of those which have not been previously thoroughly examined or described in readily accessible works. In addition to a number of species for the first time enumerated as occurring in the Palæozoic deposits of Canada, the following new species are described:—*Ptilodictya falciformis* (Trenton Limestone), *Favistella calicina* (Hudson River Group), *Diplograpsus hudsonicus* (Hudson River Group), *Callopora minutissima* (Hamilton formation), *Stromatopora nulliporoides* (Hamilton), and *Spirorbis spinuliferus* (Hamilton).

**Nicholson, H. Alleyne.** On the Guelph Limestones of North America and their organic remains. <*Geological Magazine*, Decade II, vol. ii, pp. 343-348. 1875.

Gives a general account of the fossils of the Guelph formation.

**Nicholson, H. Alleyne.** Descriptions of new species of Cystiphyllum from the Devonian rocks of North America. <*Geological Magazine*, Decade II, vol. ii, pp. 30-33, pl. i. 1875.

The author describes 4 new species of *Cystiphyllum*, 2 (viz, *C. ohioense* and *C. squamosum*) from the Corniferous Limestone of Ohio, and 2 (*C. fruticosum* and *C. superbum*) from the Devonian of Ontario.

**Nicholson, H. Alleyne.** Descriptions of new species and of a new genus of Polyzoa from the Palæozoic rocks of North America. <*Geological Magazine*, Decade II, vol. ii, pp. 33-38, pl. ii. 1875.

Describes 4 new species of Polyzoa from the Devonian rocks of Canada and 1 (*Retepora trentonensis*) from the Trenton Limestone. The genus *Heterodictya* (with the single species *H. gigantea*) is founded, a form in most respects resembling *Ptilodictya*, but having the cells tabulate.

**Nicholson, H. Alleyne.** On some of the massive forms of Chætetes from the Lower Silurian. <*Geological Magazine*, Decade II, vol. ii, pp. 175-177. 1875.

Discusses the affinities of *Chætetes petropolitanus* Pand. and some allied forms, and provisionally suggests the name of *C. undulatus* for lobed and undulated masses, often regarded as a variety of *C. lycoperdon* Say.

**Nicholson, H. Alleyne.** On the mode of growth and increase amongst the Corals of the Palæozoic period. < *Trans. Royal Soc. Edin.*, vol. xxvii, pp. 237-249, pl. xvii. 1875.

Treats of the general and special peculiarities of growth and non-sexual reproduction exhibited by the Palæozoic Corals. The author's observations have principally reference to American forms.

**Nicholson, H. Alleyne.** On the bearing of certain Palæontological facts on the Darwinian theory of the origin of species and on the general doctrine of evolution. < *Trans. Vict. Inst.*, vol. ix, p. 307. 1875.

Amongst other subjects, the author examines the chief facts observable as to the succession of life in a series of conformable deposits; the Upper Silurian and Devonian Rocks of North America being selected for this purpose, and the question being specially investigated as regards the *Brachiopoda*.

**Nicholson, H. Alleyne.** Notes on the Palæozoic Corals of the State of Ohio. < *Ann. and Mag. Nat. Hist.*, ser. 4, vol. xviii, pp. 85-94, pl. v. 1876.

Gives details as to the microscopic characters of several species of *Chætetes*, *Constellaria*, and *Dekayia*. The minute structure of *Streptelasma corniculum* Hall is also described and figured.

**Nicholson, H. Alleyne.** On the minute structure of the Corals of the genera Heliophyllum and Crepidophyllum. < *Ann. and Mag. Nat. Hist.*, ser. 5, vol. i, pp. 44-54. 1878.

Describes the microscopical characters of the above genera.

**Nicholson, H. Alleyne, and R. Etheridge,** *jun.* Notes on the genus Alveolites, Lamarck, and on some allied forms of Palæozoic Corals. < *Journ. Linn. Soc.*, vol. xiii, pp. 353-370, pls. xix, xx. 1877.

Some American Corals are treated of in this memoir. The authors conclude, from a microscopical examination, that *Alveolites fischeri* Billings and *A. frondosa* Nich. from the Devonian of North America are truly referable to the genus *Pachypora* Lindström.

**Nicholson, H. Alleyne, and R. Etheridge,** *jun.* Contributions to Micro-Palæontology.—I. On the genus Tetradium, Dana, and on a British species of the same. < *Ann. and Mag. Nat. Hist.*, ser. 4, vol. xx, pp. 161-169, 161-169, with 1 engraving. 1877.

In the first part of this paper, the authors describe fully the microscopic characters of *Tetradium minus* Safford, from the Lower Silurian of Ohio and Canada.

**Nicholson, H. Alleyne, and R. Etheridge,** *jun.* On Ascodictyon, a new provisional and anomalous genus of Palæozoic fossils. < *Ann. and Mag. Nat. Hist.*, ser. 4, vol. xix, pp. 463-468, pl. xix. 1877.

The authors propose the generic title of *Ascodictyon* for some singular parasitic organisms, of uncertain affinities, found in the Devonian rocks of North America and the Carboniferous deposits of Britain. Two American species are described under the names of *A. fusiforme* and *A. stellatum*.

**Nicholson, H. Alleyne, and R. Etheridge,** *jun.* On the genus Palaeacis, and the species occurring in British Carboniferous rocks. < *Ann. and Mag. Nat. Hist.*, ser. 5, vol. i, pp. 206-227, pl. xii. 1878.

The authors deal in part with the American forms of the genus.

**Nicholson, H. Alleyne,** *and* **G. J. Hinde.** Notes on the fossils of the Clinton, Niagara, and Guelph formations of Ontario, with descriptions of new species. *Canad. Journ.*, new ser., vol. xiv, pp. 137-160, with 6 engravings. 1873.

Thirty-five species are recorded from the Clinton formation, including two new forms (*Ptilodictya ? punctata* and *Tentaculites neglectus*). From the Niagara formation are enumerated 49 species, including the new forms *Oenites lunata*, *Alveolites niagarensis*, *Asterophyllum gracile* (gen. nov.), *Cannapora annulata*, and *Clathropora intermedia*. Twenty species are recorded from the Guelph formation, the only new species being *Megalomus compressus*.

**Nicholson, H. Alleyne,** and **James Thompson.** Descriptions of some new or imperfectly understood forms of Palæozoic Corals. < *Proc. Royal Soc. Edin.*, vol. ix, pp. 149, 150. [Abstract.] 1876-77.

The authors propose the genus *Crepidophyllum* for Corals from the Devonian of Ontario, which possess the general structure of *Heliophyllum*, but have the central tabulate area enclosed by a distinct accessory wall. The genus includes *C. (Diphyphyllum) archiaci* [Bill., and some of the forms comprised under *C.* (*Heliophyllum*) *elegantulum* Nich. The genus *Lindströmia* is proposed for simple Corals from the Devonian of America, apparently referable to the *Aporosa*, and the single species *L. columnaris* is described.

**Nordenskiöld, A. E.** Bedegjörelse för en Expedition till Grönland, 1870. < *Svenska Vetenskaps-Akad. Öfversigter, Stockholm*, 1871.

The Danish original of a paper published by the author in the *Geol. Mag.*, Decade I, vol. ix, p. 289. Contains lists of subfossil shells by Lovén.

**Nordenskiöld, A. E.** Account of an expedition to Greenland in the year 1870. < *Geological Magazine*, Decade I, vol. ix, pp. 289-306, 355-368, 409-427, 449-463, 516-524. 1872.

At p. 411, the author gives a list of subfossil animals, almost exclusively *Mollusca*, collected in Greenland during the expedition of 1870, and determined by Prof. S. Lovén.

**Nugent, N.** Sketch of the geology of Antigua. < *Trans. Geol. Soc. Lond.*, ser. i, vol. v, pp. 459-469. 1821.

Contains notes on the fossils.

**Owen, David Dale.** On the geology of the Western States of North America. < *Quart. Journ. Geol. Soc. Lond.*, vol. ii, pp. 433-437, with map. 1846.

This is principally a geological memoir dealing with the States of Illinois, Indiana, Ohio, Kentucky, and Tennessee, but it contains numerous palæontological notes.

**Owen, Richard.** Description of the impressions on the Potsdam Sandstone discovered by Mr. Logan in Lower Canada. < *Quart. Journ. Geol. Soc. Lond.*, vol. vii, pp. 250-252. 1851.

Gives a description of the footprints found by Logan in the Potsdam Sandstone (see p. 112), and provisionally concludes that they were formed by Chelonians.

**Owen, Richard.** Description of the impressions and footprints of the Protichnites from the Potsdam Sandstone of Canada. < *Quart. Journ. Geol. Soc. Lond.*, vol. viii, pp. 214-225, pls. ix-xiv, A. 1852.

Describes and figures *Protichnites septem-notatus, P. octo-notatus, P. latus, P. multinotatus, P. lineatus*, and *P. alternans*. The general characters of the footprints are discussed, and the author concludes that they were formed by some Crustaceous animal.

**Owen, Richard.** [Note.] < *Quart. Journ. Geol. Soc. Lond.,* vol. viii, p. 213. 1852.

<blockquote>M. E. Desor having exhibited to the Geological Society of London a slab with footprints from the Clinton Group of the State of New York, Professor Owen gives a short note on their characters. They consisted of a double series of prints and a median track.</blockquote>

**Paisley, C. H.** Notes on the Marine Clays occurring at the railway-cutting on the left bank of the Tattagouch River. < *Canad. Nat.,* new ser., vol. vii, pp. 41–43. 1874.

<blockquote>Contains a list of the fossils determined by Principal Dawson.</blockquote>

**Paisley, C. H.** On the Post-Pliocene formation near Bathurst, New Brunswick. < *Canad. Nat.,* new ser., vol. vii, pp. 268–270. 1874.

<blockquote>Contains lists of the fossils.</blockquote>

**Payen, M.** Sur divers fossiles trouvés aux environs de la Basse-Terre (Guadaloupe). [On some fossils from Guadaloupe.] < *Bull. de la Soc. Géol. de France,* 2me sér., t. xx, p. 475. 1863.

**Poole, Henry.** On the characteristic fossils of the different coal-seams in Nova Scotia. < *Trans. Nova Scotia Inst. Nat. Sci.,* vol. i, part i, pp. 30–45. 1863.

<blockquote>Notices the occurrence of a few Invertebrates.</blockquote>

**Purves, J. C.** Esquisse stratigraphique et espèces fossiles de l'Ile d'Antigua. < *Ann. de la Soc. Malacologique de Belgique,* t. viii, *Bull. des Séances,* pp. xxv–xxviii. 1873.

<blockquote>Gives lists of, and notes on, the fossils.</blockquote>

**Reuss, A. E.** Die Foraminiferen des Senonischen Grünsandes von New Jersey. Palæontologische Beiträge. < *Sitzungsb. Math.-Naturw. Cl. Kais. Akad. Wiss. Wien,* vol. xliv, pp. 334–340, pl. vii, fig. 6, and pl. viii, fig. 1. 1861.

<blockquote>Describes and figures *Rotalia mortoni* and *Truncatulina dekayi.*</blockquote>

**Richardson, John.** Topographical and geological notices. Appendix to "Narrative of a second expedition to the shores of the Polar Sea, in the years 1825, 1826, and 1827, by John Franklin", pp. i–lviii. London, 1828.

<blockquote>Contains notes on the fossils (determined by Mr. Sowerby) collected by the expedition.</blockquote>

**Richardson, John.** Arctic searching expedition: a journal of a boat-voyage through Rupert's Land and the Arctic Sea, with an appendix on the physical geography of North America. 2 vols. 8°. London, 1851.

<blockquote>Contains notices of the fossils met with during the expedition.</blockquote>

**Rink, H.** Udsigt over Nord Grönland's Geognosi, isaer med Hensyn til Bjergmassernes mineralogiske Sammensaetning. [Sketch of the geognosy of North Greenland, with special reference to the mineralogical composition of the mountain masses.] < *Det Kongelige Danske Videnskabernes Selskabs Skriften,* ser. v, vol. iii, pp. 73–98. 1867.

<blockquote>This memoir is geological, but the author gives a list of Post-Pliocene shells, determined by Dr. Mörch.</blockquote>

**Roemer, Ferdinand.** Ueber eine neue Art der Gattung Blumenbachium (König) und mehrere unzweifelhafte Spongien in obersilurischen Kalkschichten der Grafschaft Decatur im Staate Tennessee in Nord-America. <*Neues Jahrb. für Min., Geogn., Geol. und Petrefaktenkunde,* Jahrg. 1844. pp. 680–686, pl. ix.

Describes and figures various *Amorphozoa*.

**Roemer, Ferdinand.** A sketch of the geology of Texas. <*Ann. and Mag. Nat. Hist.,* ser. 1, vol. xix, pp. 426–431. 1847.

A reprint from *Silliman's Journal,* November, 1846. Notes numerous Cretaceous fossils.

**Roemer, Ferdinand.** Ueber Hall's Palaeontologie des Staates New York. <*Neues Jahrb. für Min., Geogn., Geol. und Petrefaktenkunde,* Jahrg. 1848, pp. 169–178.

A critical review of vol. i of Hall's "Palæontology of the State of New York".

**Roemer, Ferdinand.** Ueber gegliederte aus Kalkstückchen zusammengesetzte Tentakeln, oder Pinnulae, auf den sogenannten Ambulakralfeldern der Pentremiten. <*Neues Jahrb. für Min., Geogn., Geol. und Petrefaktenkunde,* Jahrg. 1848, pp. 292–296, pl. v A.

The author describes specimens of *Pentremites* found in Alabama, in which jointed tentacles or "pinnulæ" are developed upon the ambulacral areas.

**Roemer, Ferdinand.** Texas. Mit besonderer Rücksicht auf deutsche Auswanderung und die physischen Verhältnisse des Landes mit eigener Beobachtung geschildert; mit einem naturwissenschaftlichen Anhange, und einer topographisch-geognostischen Karte von Texas. Bonn, 1849. pp. 464, with map.

The "naturwissenschaftlicher Anhang" (pp. 392–422) contains descriptions of fossils from the Cretaceous, Carboniferous, and Silurian rocks of Texas.

**Roemer, Ferdinand.** Ueber ein bisher nicht beschriebenes Exemplar von Eurypterus aus Devonischen Schichten des Staates New York in Nord-America. <*Palæontographica, Beiträge zur Naturgeschichte der Vorwelt, herausgegeben von Wilh. Dunker und H. von Meyer,* Bd. i, pp. 190–193, pl. xxvii. Cassel, 1851.

The author describes and figures a species of *Eurypterus* from the "Water-Lime Group" [not the Devonian] of the State of New York.

**Roemer, Ferdinand.** Die Kreidebildungen von Texas und ihre organischen Einschlüsse, mit einem die Beschreibung von Versteinerungen aus palaeozoischen und tertiären Schichten enthaltenden Anhange, und mit 11 von C. Hohe nach der Natur auf Stein gezeichneten Tafeln. Bonn, 1852. 4°. pp. 100.

The author gives a general account of the geology of Texas, with special reference to the Cretaceous rocks. A portion of the work (pp. 27–83) is occupied with the description of a large number of Cretaceous fossils; and in an appendix (pp. 83–94) the author enumerates and describes a number of Silurian and Carboniferous fossils.

**Roemer, Ferdinand.** Ueber Stephanocrinus, eine fossile Crinoiden-Gattung aus der Familie der Cystideen. <*Archiv für Naturgeschichte,* Jahrg. xvi, Bd. i, pp. 365–375, t. v. 1856.

Gives a full description of the characters of the genus *Stephanocrinus,* founded on specimens from the Niagara Limestone of the State of New York.

**Roemer, Ferdinand.** Monographie der fossilen Crinoiden-Familie der Blastoideen und der Gattung Pentrematites im Besondern. < *Archiv für Naturgeschichte,* Jahrg. xvii, Bd. i, pp. 326–397, with 5 plates. 1857.

> A monographic revision of the *Blastoidea.*

**Roemer, Ferdinand.** Dorycrinus, ein neues Crinoiden-Geschlecht aus dem Kohlenkalke Nord-Americas. < *Archiv für Naturgeschichte,* Jahrg. xix, Bd. i, pp. 207–220, pl. x. 1859.

> The author establishes the genus *Dorycrinus,* with a single species (*D. mississippiensis* F. Roemer), for the reception of a Crinoid from the Carboniferous Limestone of Warsaw Ill. The genus is related to *Amphoracrinus* and *Actinocrinus.*

**Roemer, Ferdinand.** Die silurische Fauna des westlichen Tennessee. Eine palaeontologische Monographie. [The Silurian Fauna of Western Tennessee. A palæontological monograph.] 4°. pp. 97, with 5 plates. Breslau, 1860.

> A large number of Silurian fossils from Tennessee are described in this important work, of which the following species and varieties are described as new:— *Calamopora (Favosites) forbesi,* var. *discoidea, Thecostegites hemisphæricus, Fenestella acuticosta, Platycrinus tennesseensis, Lampterocrinus tennesseensis, Oytocrinus lævis, Eucalyptocrinus ranifer, Coccocrinus bacca, Poteriocrinus pisiformis, Synbathocrinus tennesseensis, Oystocrinus tennesseensis, Orthis flssiplica, Spirifer niagarensis,* var. *oligoptycha, Rhynchonella tennesseensis,* and *Turbo tennesseensis.* Amongst the sponges, the genera *Astylospongia* and *Palæomanon,* and amongst the Crinoids the genera *Lampterocrinus* and *Oytocrinus,* are defined as new. In a concluding chapter, the author compares the Silurian fauna of Western Tennessee with that of corresponding deposits in other regions in North America and of Europe.

**Roemer, Ferdinand.** Ueber den Bau von Melonites multipora, ein Echinid des amerikanischen Kohlenkalkes. < *Archiv für Naturgeschichte,* Jahrg. xxi, Bd. i, pp. 312–330, pl. xii. 1861.

> A critical analysis of the characters of *Melonites.*

**Roemer, Ferdinand.** Lethæa paleozoica. Atlas, with 62 plates. Stuttgart, 1876.

> The text of this work is not yet published, but the atlas contains figures of many American fossils.

**Rogers, William B.** On the discovery of Paradoxides in the altered rocks of Eastern Massachusetts. < *Edinburgh New Philosophical Journ.,* new ser., vol. iv, pp. 301–304, 1856.

> Records the discovery of *Paradoxides harlani* Green (the locality of which was previously unknown) in the slates of Braintree, near Boston.

**Rominger, Carl.** On the true nature of Pleurodictyum problematicum. < *Ann. and Mag. Nat. Hist.,* ser. 3, vol. xi, pp. 390–391. 1863.

> A reprint from *Silliman's Journal,* January, 1863.

**Rössler, A. R.** Geologische Untersuchungen in Texas. < *Verhandl. der K. K. Geol. Reichsanstalt, Wien,* 1868, p. 188.

> Contains notices of the fossils.

**Rottermund, Count de.** Report on the exploration of Lakes Superior and Huron. Printed by order of the Legislative Assembly, April, 1856. Ottawa.

> Contains notes of the fossils, said to be from Lake Superior, but really derived from drifted boulders of Upper Silurian Limestone. Other notices of fossils seem to be of no value.

**Salter, J. W.** Journal of a voyage in Baffin's Bay and Barrow Strait in the years 1850-1, performed by H. M. ships "Lady Franklin" and "Sophia", under the command of Mr. William Penny, in search of the missing crews of H. M. ships "Erebus" and "Terror". By Peter C. Sutherland, M. D. London, 1852. 2 vols. 8°. Appendix, pp. ccxviii-ccxxxiii, pls. v and vi.

The author describes a number of *Crustacea, Mollusca,* and *Coelenterates* from the Silurian strata of the neighbourhood of Wellington Channel, &c. The new species described are:—*Orthoceras ommaneyi, Strophomena donneti, Rhynchonella phoca, Strephodes pickthornii, S.* (?) *austini, Favistella reticulata, F. franklini, Columnaria sutherlandi, Arachnophyllum richardsoni, Rhynchonella mansonii,* and *Calophyllum phragmoceras.*

**Salter, J. W.** On Arctic Silurian fossils. < *Quart. Journ. Geol. Soc. Lond.,* vol. ix, pp. 312–317. 1853.

Gives lists, with descriptive remarks, of a number of Upper Silurian fossils collected by the Arctic Expedition of 1850–51, chiefly from the entrance of Wellington Channel. The author also notes the occurrence of Pleistocene deposits, with marine shells of existing Arctic species, on Beechey and Cornwallis Islands, up to 500 feet.

**Salter, J. W.** Arctic Carboniferous fossils, collected by the expedition under Sir E. Belcher, C. B., 1852–54. In the "Last of the Arctic Voyages", by Sir Edward Belcher, C. B. 2 vols. 8°. London, 1855. Vol. ii, pp. 377, 391, pl. xxxvi.

Describes a number of Carboniferous fossils, of which the following are described as new species:—*Fusulina hyperborea, Zaphrentis ovibos, Clisiophyllum tumulus, Syringopora aulopora,* and *Fenestella arctica.*

**Salter, J. W.** Fossils from the base of the Trenton Limestone. < *Figures and Descriptions of Canadian Organic Remains,* Decade I, Montreal, 1859. pp. 47, pls. i-x.

In this work, Mr. Salter describes a number of fossils, mostly from the Trenton Limestone of Pauquette's Rapids on the Ottawa, in which there is a singular intermixture of the forms proper to the Black River and Chazy limestones with those characteristic of the higher part of the Trenton Group. Eighteen species of Gasteropods are described, referable to *Maclurea, Raphistoma, Helicotoma* (new subgenus), *Ophileta, Murchisonia, Cyclonema, Trochonema, Eunema,* and *Lozonema,* and comprising 12 new species. The characters and affinities of the genera are discussed at length. Two species of *Cyrtoceras,* and 5 of *Ctenodonta* (including 2 new species) are described. The characters of *Orthis tricenaria* Conr. are fully treated of; and lastly the author deals with the affinities and structure of the genus *Receptaculites,* referring the fossils of this group to the *Foraminifera,* and placing them in the neighbourhood of *Orbitolites.* Two new species are described, one, *R. occidentalis,* from the Trenton Limestone, and the other, *R. australis,* introduced for comparison, from the Silurian rocks of New South Wales.

**Salter, J. W.** On the fossils of the Lingula-flags or "Zone Primordiale". < *Quart. Journ. Geol. Soc. Lond.,* vol. xv, pp. 551–555, with 4 engravings. 1859.

Two new species of *Trilobites* are described and figured, viz, *Paradoxides bennettii,* from the Primordial beds of Newfoundland, and *Conocephalus antiquatus,* from a boulder of sandstone discovered in Georgia. An imperfect *Trilobite* from the Calciferous Sand-rock of Canada, formerly referred by the author to *Paradoxides,* is now doubtfully placed in *Asaphus.*

**Salter, J. W.** On some fossil Crustacea from the Coal-Measures and Devonian Rocks of British North America. < *Quart. Journ. Geol. Soc.*, vol. xix, pp. 75–80, figs. 1–12. 1863.

The genus *Amphipeltis*, with one species (*A. paradoxus*), is proposed for a Stomapod (?) Crustacean from the Devonian rocks of New Brunswick. The genus *Diplostylus*, with one species (*D. dawsoni*), is founded for an Amphipod (?) from the Coal-Measures of Nova Scotia. *Euryptus pulicaris* is described as new from the Devonian of New Brunswick, and other unnamed species of the same genus are noted from the Coal-Measures of Nova Scotia. There is also a note (with figures) as to three Lamellibranchs from the Coal-Measures of Nova Scotia, viz, *Anthracomya elongata* Dawson, sp., *A.* (*Naiadites*) *lævis* Dawson, sp., and *Anthracoptera* (*Naiadites*) *carbonaria* Dawson, sp.

**Slater, J. W., and E. Billings.** On Cyclocystoides, a new genus of Echinodermata from the Lower and Middle Silurian Rocks. < *Figures and Descriptions of Canadian Organic Remains: Decade III*. Montreal, 1858. pp. 86–90, pl. x bis.

The authors found the genus *Cyclocystoides* for some curious Echinoderms, in some respects intermediate between the Cystideans and the Star-fishes. Of the two species described, one (*C. halli* Bill.) is from the Trenton Limestone of Ottawa, and the other (*C. davisii* Salt.) is from the May Hill Sandstone of Presteign, Wales.

**Schomburgk, Sir Robert H.** The microscopical siliceous Polycystina of Barbados, and their relation to existing animals, as described in a lecture by Professor Ehrenberg of Berlin, delivered before the Royal Academy of Sciences on the 11th February, 1847. < *Ann. and Mag. Nat. Hist.*, ser. 1, vol. xx, pp. 115–127, pls. v and vi. 1847.

**Schomburgk, Sir Robert H.** The History of Barbados. 8°. pp. 772. London, 1848.

Contains notices of some of the Tertiary fossils, especially of the *Polycystina*. The new species *Scalaria ehrenbergi, Nucula packeri*, and *N. schomburgkii* are described by Prof. Edward Forbes.

**Schultze, Max.** Eozoön canadense. < *Ann. and Mag. Nat. Hist.*, ser. 4, vol. xiii, pp. 324, 326. [From a Report of the Meeting of the "Niederrheinische Gesellschaft für Natur- und Heilkunde" at Bonn, July 7, 1873, in the "Kölner Zeitung", August 14, 1873.] 1874.

A note in which this distinguished naturalist expresses his conviction that "there can be no serious doubt as to the Foraminiferous nature of *Eozoön canadense*".

**Scudder, Samuel H.** The fossil insects of North America. < *Geological Magazine*, Decade I, vol. v, pp. 172–177, 216–222. 1868.

The author gives a complete *résumé* of the known fossil insects of North America up to date (1868), accompanied by critical remarks on the species, and detailed statements as to the precise stratigraphical position of the remains in question.

**Scudder, Samuel H.** On the fossil Myriopods of the Coal-formations of Nova Scotia and England. < *Quart. Journ. Geol. Soc. Lond.*, vol. xxv, p. 441. [Abstract.] 1869.

The author recognizes six species of Chilognathous Myriopods in the Coal-Measures, five belonging to *Xylobius*, and one being the type of the new genus *Archiulus*. The family *Archiulidæ* is proposed for the reception of these forms.

**Scudder, Samuel H.** Two new Carboniferous Cockroaches from the Carboniferous of Cape Breton. < *Canad. Nat.*, new ser., vol. vii, pp. 271, 272, with 2 figures. 1874.

Describes *Blattina bretonensis* and *B. heeri* as new species.

II.—PUBLICATIONS MADE IN BRITISH AMERICA, ETC. 129

**Scudder, Samuel H.** Fossil Palæozoic Insects. < *Geological Magazine*, Decade II, vol. iii, pp. 519, 520. 1876.

Gives a complete list of the Carboniferous Insects of North America, arranged by families.

**Sharpe, Daniel.** Report on the fossil remains of Mollusca from the Palæozoic formations of the United States contained in the collection of Charles Lyell, Esq.; with remarks on the comparison of the North American formations with those of Europe. < *Quart. Journ. Geol. Soc. Lond.*, vol. iv, pp. 245–281. 1848.

This memoir is principally concerned with the identification of the fossils collected from the Silurian and Devonian Rocks of North America by Sir Charles Lyell, and the determination of such of these as appear to occur also in Europe. An elaborate list of the published species of *Mollusca* recognised in the collection is given, and detailed notes on a number of the species are appended.

**Smith, J. F.,** *jun.* Note on the more characteristic fossils of the Hudson River Group of Toronto and its environs. < *Canad. Journ.*, new ser., vol. iv, pp. 450–452. 1859.

**Stimpson, William.** Review of the Northern Buccinums, and remarks on some other northern marine Mollusks. < *Canad. Nat.*, new ser., vol. ii, pp. 364–389. 1867.

Descriptions of the northern species of *Buccinum*, including the forms found in the Post-Pliocene deposits of North America.

**Stokes, Charles.** On some species of Orthocerata. < *Proc. Geol. Soc. Lond.*, vol. ii, pp. 688–690. 1838.

Treats of the *Orthoceratites* found by Dr. Bigsby and other observers in Canada, and by various explorers in the Arctic regions. The generic types *Ormoceras* and *Huronia* are founded and defined, and the other forms are referred to *Actinoceras*.

**Stokes, Charles.** On some species of Orthocerata. < *Trans. Geol. Soc. Lond.*, ser. 2, vol. v, pp. 705–714, pls. lix, lx. 1840.

The specimens described are from Drummond Island and other Canadian localities, as well as from the Arctic regions. The author refers four species, all new, to the group *Actinoceras* Bronn., and describes three new species of the group to which he here gives the name of *Ormoceras*. The characters of these groups, and also of *Huronia*, are considered, and the latter is referred to the *Orthoceratidæ*.

**Thomson, James,** *and* **H. Alleyne Nicholson.** Contributions to the study of the chief generic types of Palæozoic Corals. < *Ann. and Mag. Nat. Hist.*, ser. 4, vol. xvii, p. 455. 1876.

In a note, the authors propose and define briefly the genus *Acrophyllum* for the reception of *A. (Clisiophyllum) oneidaense* Bill. and *A. (Clisiophyllum) pluriradiale* Nich., both from the Corniferous Limestone of Western Ontario.

**Toula, Franz.** Description of Mesozoic fossils from Kuhn Island. < *Die Zweite Deutsche Nordpolfahrt*, Bd. ii, *Wissenschaftliche Ergebnisse*, p. 497, with 2 plates. Leipzig, 1874.

[Not seen by the writer.] Describes a number of Jurassic fossils from Kuhn Island, of which *Perisphinctes payeri* is new.

**Tuomey, M.** Discovery of a chambered univalve shell in the Eocene Tertiary of James River, Virginia. < *Ann. and Mag. Nat. Hist.*, ser. 1, vol. x, pp. 156, 157. 1842.

A reprint from *Silliman's American Journal*, July, 1842.

**Van den Broeck,** [Ernest. Rapport sur un mémoire de M. G. F. Matthew intitulé: Notes on the Mollusca of the Post-Pliocene formation in Acadia. < *Ann. de la Soc. Malacologique de Belgique*, t. ix, *Bull. des Séances*, pp. cxliii–cli. 1874.

> See the original memoir under G. F. Mathew.

**Verneuil, Édouard Poulletier de.** Sur un Orthocératite gigantesque de [l'Amérique. < *Bull. de la Soc. Géol. de France*, vol. iv, pp. 556-559. 1846.

> Describes *Orthoceras herculaneus* from the Lower Silurian rocks of the United States.

**Verneuil, Édouard Poulletier de.** Note sur le parallélisme des roches des dépôts paléozoiques de l'Amérique septentrionale avec ceux de l'Europe, suivi d'un tableau des espèces fossiles communes aux deux continents, avec l'indication des étages où elles se rencontrent, et terminée par un examen critique de chacun de ces espèces. [Note on the parallelism of the Palæozoic rocks of North America with those of Europe, accompanied by a table of the fossil species common to the two continents, together with references to the horizons at which these occur, and a critical examination of each of these species.] < *Bull. de la Soc. Géol. de France*, vol. iv, pp. 646–709. 1846.

> The nature of this memoir is sufficiently indicated by its title. A large number of species of fossils is critically examined, and *Grammysia hamiltonensis* is described and figured as new.

**Verrill, A. E.** On the affinities of the Palæozoic Tabulate Corals. < *Ann. and Mag. Nat. Hist.*, ser. 4, vol. ix, pp. 355–364. 1872.

> A reprint from the *Amer. Journ. Sci. and Arts*, March, 1872.

**Vilanova y Peira, Juan.** Estructura de las rocas serpentinosas y el Eozoön canadense. < *Soc. Españ. Hist. Nat.*, vol. iii, parts 2 and 3. 1874.

> Concludes that *Eozoön canadense* is not the remains of an organism.

**Von Buch, Leopold.** Kreide am oberen Missouri. < *Zeitschrift d. Deutsch. Geol. Ges.*, Bd. v, p. 11. 1853.

> A note on Cephalopods from the Cretaceous formation of the Black Hills.

**Whiteaves, J. F.** Notes on the Cretaceous Fossils collected by Mr. James Richardson, at Vancouver and the adjacent islands. < *Geological Survey of Canada: Report of Progress for 1873-74*, pp. 260–268, with 1 plate.

> A number of Cephalopods, Gasteropods, and Lamellibranchs are noticed and in part described. The following species are described as new:—*Lucina richardsonii, Conchocele cretacea, Astarte cardinioides, A. vancouverensis, Tellina meekiana,* and *Fasciolaria nodulosa*.

**Whiteaves, J. F.** On some invertebrates from the coal-bearing rocks of the Queen Charlotte Islands, collected by Mr. James Richardson in 1872. Mesozoic fossils. Vol. i, part i. pp. 92, pls. i–x, with map and 9 engravings. < *Geological Survey of Canada*. Montreal, 1876.

> After a preliminary consideration of the deposits in which the fossils occur, and the general nature of their organic remains, the author proceeds to describe the spe-

cies. Many of the specimens were so poorly preserved as not to allow of complete specific determination, and others were identical with previously recorded forms. The following are the new species described:—*Ammonites perezianus*, *A. loganianus*, *A. richardsonii*, *A. skidegatensis*, *A. carlottensis*, *A. laperousianus*, *A. filocinctus*, *A. crenocostatus* (prov.), *Amauropsis tenuistriata*, *Pleurotomaria skidegatensis*, *Martesia* (?) *carinifera*, *Pleuromya* (?) *carlottensis*, *Pholadomya ovuloides*, *Callista* (?) *subtrigona*, *Trigonia diversicostata*, *Meleagrina amygdaloidea*, and *Syncyclonema merkiana*. In a concluding chapter, the author considers the palæontological relations and correlation of the Cretaceous deposits of Vancouver, and he arrives at the conclusion that the coal-bearing rocks of Queen Charlotte Islands, from which the fossils described were collected, can hardly be older than the Upper Jurassic or later than the Middle Cretaceous.

**Woodward, Henry.** Note on the palpus and other appendages of Asaphus, from the Trenton Limestone, in the British Museum. < *Quart. Journ. Geol. Soc. Lond.*, vol. xxvi, pp. 486-488, with woodcut. 1870.

The author records the discovery of the jointed palpus of one of the maxillæ in a specimen of *Asaphus platycephalus* from the Trenton Limestone.

**Woodward, Henry.** Note on a new British Cystidean. < *Geological Magazine*, vol. viii, pp. 71, 72, with engraving. 1871.

A short paper, with a letter from Mr. Billings, pointing out that *Placocystites forbesianus*, described by De Koninck (*Geol. Mag.*, vol. vii, p. 260) as a new British Cystidean, is really identical with *Ateleocystites huxleyi* Billings from the Lower Silurian of North America.

**Woodward, Henry.** On some new Phyllopodous Crustaceans from the Palæozoic rocks. < *Geological Magazine*, vol. viii, pp. 104-107, pl. iii. 1871.

The only American form described is the new *Dithyrocaris belli* from the Middle Devonian of Gaspé.

**Woodward, S. P.** Some account of Barrettia, a new and remarkable fossil shell from the Hippurite Limestone of Jamaica. < *The Geologist*, vol. vi, pp. 372-377, pls. xx, xxi. 1862.

The author describes and figures *Barrettia moniliformis* from the Cretaceous rocks of Jamaica.

**Woodward, S. P.** A manual of the Mollusca, being a treatise on recent and fossil shells. 3d ed. With an appendix on recent and fossil conchological discoveries, by RALPH TATE. 1875.

The body of this work contains numerous descriptions of American fossil *Mollusca*, and the chapters on distribution also contain palæontological information on the same subject.

**Zaphrinesque *and* Clifford.** Monographie des Turbinolides. < *Annals de Physique de Bruxelles*, 1820, tom. v.

[Not seen by the writer.] Describes various North American fossil Corals (*Zaphrentis phrygia* = *Z. cornicula* Lesueur, sp.; *Turbinolia buceros* = *Zaphrentis gigantea* Lesueur, sp.; *Omphyma verrucosa*). The authors also found the genus *Zaphrentis*.

**Zittel, Karl A.** Beiträge zur Systematik der fossilen Spongien. [Contributions to a systematic knowledge of fossil Sponges.] < *Neues Jahrbuch für Mineralogie, &c.*, 1877, pp. 40 [original pagination unknown], with 4 plates.

The structure and characters of various North American fossil Sponges are here discussed; and *Astylospongia* Roemer, *Calathium* Bill., (?) *Eospongia* Bill., and (?) *Trachyum* Bill. are referred to the *Hexactinellidæ*.

**Zittel, Karl A.,** *and* **W. Ph. Schimper.** Handbuch der Palaeontologie. 8°. Munich, 1876.

The first part of the first volume of this work (pp. 128, with 56 engravings) deals with the *Protozoa*, and may be more especially mentioned as containing definitions of the genera of *Polycystina* which occur in the "Barbadoes earth".

SUPPLEMENT TO THE FIFTH ANNUAL REPORT

OF THE

# UNITED STATES GEOLOGICAL SURVEY

OF

## THE TERRITORIES FOR 1871.

[Misc. publica.]

**F. V. HAYDEN,**
UNITED STATES GEOLOGIST IN CHARGE.

REPORT ON FOSSIL FLORA.—By Leo Lesquereux.

CONDUCTED UNDER AUTHORITY OF THE SECRETARY OF THE INTERIOR.

WASHINGTON:
GOVERNMENT PRINTING OFFICE.
1872.

# PREFATORY NOTE.

The materials composing the following report were not accessible at the time my annual report was printed, and are now issued in the form of a supplement. Full descriptions and illustrations of the new and little known species will appear in the final reports, now in an advanced state of preparation.

F. V. HAYDEN,
*United States Geologist in charge.*
OFFICE U. S. GEOLOGICAL SURVEY OF THE TERRITORIES,
*Washington, May* 13, 1872.

# AN ENUMERATION WITH DESCRIPTIONS OF SOME TERTIARY FOSSIL PLANTS, FROM SPECIMENS PROCURED IN THE EXPLORATIONS OF DR. F. V. HAYDEN, IN 1870.

BY LEO LESQUEREUX.

This enumeration may be considered as an appendix to the paper on the same subject, in the last report of Dr. F. V. Hayden. This report was just delivered and already in the hands of the printer when the materials on which the present notes are written were received. The specimens would have been reserved for a later examination, with that of others which may be procured this year. But as some of them give evidence of the age of formations at some localities which in the report are marked as unknown; as others represent new and remarkable forms; and others still have better preserved remains of species indifferently known as yet, it was advisable to examine them at once and to prepare and publish a short account of them.

In this paper the same plan is followed as in Dr. Hayden's report: 1st, description of species, grouped according to the localities where they have been found; 2d, some remarks on the analogy of these species, in relation to their geographical and stratigraphical distribution and to their typical characters, &c.

### 1. GREEN RIVER, ABOVE FISH-BEDS.

Fine-grained, buff-colored, hard shale, breaking more or less irregularly in horizontal layers.

HEMITELITES TORELLI, Heer (?). Represented by a very small fragment, only a single oblong leaflet, entire or slightly undulate on the borders, with nervation of this species as figured in Fl. Arc., 2, Pl. xl, Fig. 1–5. Identity cannot be positively ascertained from such a specimen.

ARUNDO GÖPPERTI, Munst. To this species I refer an irregularly, narrowly, striate stem with round knots, as in Fl. Ter. Helv., Pl. xxiii, Fig. 11. The same specimen bears a crushed fascicle of seeds of an *Arundo* (?). Other specimens still doubtfully referred to this species represent roots or root-stocks, varying from ¼ of an inch to 1½ inches in diameter, irregularly, more or less striate-wrinkled in the length, marked also, as in the first specimens, by round knots, placed at a distance from each other and without trace of articulations. These remains may belong as well to a *Phragmites* as to an *Arundo*. The comparison of the seeds may indicate their true relation.

PHRAGMITES OENINGENSIS, Al. Br. Fragments of doubly striated stems, marked by articulations as in Report, p. 284.*

JUNCUS, *species*. Fragments of stems of various size, like *Juncus retractus*, Heer, or *Juncus Scheuzeri*, Heer, in Fl. Ter. Helv., Pl. xxx, Figs. 2 *e* and 3 *c*.

---

* Quotations marked Report refer to my former paper in Dr. F. V. Hayden's last report, 1872.

SALIX ANGUSTA, Al. Br., in Heer's Fl. Ter. Helv., 2, p. 30, Pl. lxix, Fig. 3. One of the specimens represents a whole leaf 6 inches long 13 to 14 millimeters broad, in its widest part entire, linear, gradually tapering to a long point, and tapering also by a slightly curved line to the petiole. This leaf shows apparently its upper surface. The medial nerve is broadly marked, but the secondary veins are obsolete like their divisions. Another specimen of the same species has only one-half of a leaf of about the same width as the former, the under part, with secondary veins, very distinct, like their divisions, and surface evidently villose, it being marked by the impression of a thick coat of hairs. Heer, in his description of this species, rightlyc ompares it to *S. viminalis*, L., remarking, however, that his specimens do not indicate if the leaves were villose as in the living species.

SALIX MEDIA, Al. Br. For the form of the linear lanceolate leaves with entire borders, tapering upward to a point, obtuse at base, our specimens represent exactly this species as figured in Fl. Ter. Helv., Pl. lxviii, Figs. 14, 17, 19. But they do not show any trace of nervation, and identity is, therefore, uncertain. It is, however, generally the case in specimens of this species whose upper surface is smooth and do not bear any trace of secondary veins.

SALIX, *species*. Merely the base of two leaves still attached to a branchlet, alternate, with unequal base, just as in *S. inæquilatera*, Göpp., Schossnitz Fl., Pl. xxi, Fig. 6; very short-petioled, nearly sessile, with entire or undulately crenulate borders; apparently narrowly lanceolate-pointed; secondary veins open, thick like the intermediate shorter tertiary veins and nervilles; areolation distinct, of the same type as that of *S. Lavateri*, Heer. As much as can be seen, these leaves do not resemble any fossil species as yet published; but as the form of the leaves is not known, and as it is not seen if the borders are entire or denticulate, it is useless to attempt specification.

MYRICA NIGRICANS, *sp. nov*. Fragments of leaves, apparently narrowly lanceolate or linear-lanceolate, half an inch wide or less, passing down in an outward curve and cuneate to the petiole, distantly serrate, with short obtuse teeth; medial nerve thick, secondary veins open, (angle of divergence at least 60°,) distinct, branching downward two or three times in anastomosing with intermediate short tertiary veinlets. The nervation is analogous to that of the living *M. gale*, L., while by the form of the leaves it resembles *M. Vindobonensis*, Ung., as figured by Heer in Alaska Fl., Pl. iii, Fig. 5, differing, however, by the distant obtuse teeth of the borders. All the specimens of these leaves are blackened upon the yellow shale of ,this locality, and the surface appears dotted, as in our common *M. cerifera*, L., indicating a resinous compound in their texture. Some of the specimens bear small round seeds, which may be referred to this species.

MYRICA SALICINA, Ung. As far as identity can be ascertained from the outline of the leaves and with undistinct nervation, the leaf or part of leaf of the specimen (the point and base being destroyed) is the same as the one figured in Fl. Ter. Helv., Pl. lxxi, Fig. 2. The thin secondary veins, a few of which are discernible, have the same direction as in the European form and branch near the point as in species of this genus.

QUERCUS LONCHITIS, Ung. A small specimen, a narrow, lanecolate leaf, with serrate borders and secondary veins numerous, parallel, simple, craspedodrome, is referable to this species as figured in Fl. Ter. Helv., Pl. cli, Figs. 22 and 23.

FICUS POPULINA, Heer. A number of specimens agree with the forms of this species as described and figured in Heer, Fl. Ter. Helv., from

European specimens, presenting, however, some marked differences. The leaves are not long-acutely pointed, but obtusely so; though the primary and secondary nervation are alike, the ultimate divisions of the veins approach nearer to the borders, and sometimes the teeth of the borders appear rather pointed than round. As this species is very variable, these differences are not marked enough to authorize a separation. The general form of these leaves of ours rather resembles the variety in Heer's Fl. Ter. Helv., Pl. lxxxv, Figs. 1 and 2.

FICUS UNGERI, sp. nov. A splendid leaf, of which unluckily the point and lower part are destroyed. It is broadly lanceolate in outline, the borders nearly parallel in the middle of the leaf, apparently rounded to the petiole and also curving upward somewhat abruptly to a point. The part of the leaf as it is preserved is 8 inches long, 4 inches wide, with entire, slightly undulate borders, not coriaceous; medial nerve rather thick; secondary veins at a broad angle of divergence, (70° to 80°,) and tertiary nervation distinct, of the same type as that of *F. Americana*. The surface of the leaf is runcinate, as in *F. populina* and *F. tiliæfolia;* but the form of the leaf and the open, nearly horizontal secondary veins separate this species from any other known as yet in a fossil state. The leaf is larger than that of *F. Hercules*, Ett., or that of *F. Ruminiana*, Heer; comparable only, for the form and size, to the living *F. ferruginea*, which has also the secondary veins in an open angle. In the fossil species, these veins curve less abruptly and approach nearer to the borders in their ultimate curve.

CINNAMOMUM SCHEUZERI, Heer. I refer to this species two leaves of *Cinnamomum*, one of which is contracted above the base, as in some forms of *C. Buchi*, Heer; the other narrower, like a variety of *C. lanceolatum*, Heer. Both specimens are incomplete and have the nervation of *C. Scheuzeri*, as represented in many specimens from other localities of our Tertiary.

EUCALYPTUS AMERICANUS, sp. nov. Represented by good specimens. Leaves narrowly lanceolate, 5 to 6 inches long, $\frac{1}{2}$ to $\frac{3}{4}$ of an inch wide, entire, gradually tapering upward to a long point, tapering also, but less gradually, to the base of the flat, broad, medial nerve, which is merely enlarged at the point of attachment; secondary veins oblique, (divergence about 30°,) numerous, ascending nearly straight to near the borders, where they join a marginal vein, which follow the borders from the base to the point of the leaves, being scarcely bent to the point of union of the secondary veins, and thus forming a narrow, equal margin, marked by horizontal, thin, simple, parallel, and close veinlets. This fine species is distantly related to *E. Oceanica*, Heer, Fl. Ter. Helv., and may be still more so to *E. rhododendrifolia*, of Massalonga, which has, like ours, the true nervation of *Eucalyptus*, but is differing at least by its leathery texture, which is no coriaceous in ours. I know this Italian species merely from description, and cannot, therefore, indicate points of analogy.

AMPELOPSIS TERTIARIA, sp. nov. A digitate leaf, with five narrowly ovate, lanceolate-pointed leaflets, tapering downward to a short, slightly winged petiole, sharply serrate on the borders; medial nerve flat and broad; secondary veins in acute angle, curving along the borders, branching upward and anastomosing downward with branches of the upper veinlets. The nervation is similar to that of our living *A. quinquefolia*, Michx., the branches of the secondary veins entering the teeth, while the primary divisions follow the borders. It differs from it, however, by smaller and narrower leaves, short, winged petiole, &c.

The upper part of the leaflets is narrowed into a point, and the borders are serrate to the point.

ILEX AFFINIS, *sp. nov.* Leaf coriaceous, broadly ovate, round cuneate to the base, (point destroyed,) with borders narrowly margined, distantly dentate. Secondary veins open, nearly perpendicular to the medial nerve, curving near the borders, thin though distinct. Areolation and tertiary nervation like that of *I. coriacea*, Chap., of Florida. The fossil leaf differs from the living species by thinner, more open secondary veins, curving more gradually toward the borders, and by the teeth, rather turned upward, and not spiny. The spines, however, may have been destroyed by maceration. These differences are of not much account, and both species are closely related, if not identical.

ILEX STENOPHYLLA, Ung. The specimens represent the form figured by Heer, Fl. Ter. Helv., Pl. cxxii, Fig. 7. Leaf coriaceous, narrowly ovate, lanceolate, obtusely pointed, with entire borders; medial nerve strong; secondary veins thin, the inferior ones more oblique; areolation same as in Heer's Fig. 7. All the specimens of this species represent large leaves, none of them as small as those figured by Unger in the Chloris, and by Heer, *loc. cit.*, Figs. 8 and 8b. Except this, no point of difference is remarked.

CEANOTHUS CINNAMOMOIDES, Lsqx. Same form as described in Report, p. 289. The teeth are more sharply marked than in the first specimens examined.

RHUS ACUMINATA, *sp. nov.* A single leaf, ovate in outline, narrowed by an inward curve to a short, flat petiole, abruptly acuminate, with borders irregularly crenulate-lobed. Secondary veins open, strong, branching near the point, mostly craspedodrome in the lower part of the leaf, while in the upper part some abruptly curve near the borders and run along them. By its nervation, the species is like *R. Pyrrhœ*, Ung., except that the secondary veins are more numerous, in our specimen nearly as close to each other as in *R. Meriani*, Heer. It is distantly related to our living *R. aromatica*, Ait.

JUGLANS SCHIMPERI, *sp. nov.* A very fine species, represented by a number of specimens, all with the same characters. Leaves of a somewhat thick, but not coriaceous texture, lanceolate in outline, entire, largest near the base, about $1\frac{1}{2}$ inches broad, hence gradually tapering upward into a long acute point, abruptly rounded downward to the petiole; whole length of the leaves about 6 inches; from the broadest part to the point $4\frac{1}{2}$ inches. It is comparable to some forms of *J. rugosa*, Lsqx., but the form of the leaves, gradually decreasing to a point, is different, as also the nervation, which, like the areolation, is more distinct. The medial nerve is flat or grooved; the secondary veins more oblique, (angle of divergence, 42° to 45°,) more numerous and close to each other, 16 to 18 pairs in each leaf, curving slightly in ascending, and still more in coming to the borders, which they closely follow in their ultimate divisions.

JUGLANS ACUMINATA, Heer (?). The same leaf, in all its characters, as the one figured in Fl. Ter. Helv., Pl. cxxix, Fig. 6, and which is apparently far different from any other form of this species. Professor Heer, in his description, has no remarks about this peculiar form; rather comparable to *J. costata*, Ung., as figured by Ludwig in Pal., Vol. VIII, Pl. lvii, Fig. 7, and Pl. lvi, Fig. 7. In all the specimens of this locality, there is no leaf referable to *J. acuminata*, Heer, or to its relative, *J. rugosa*, Lsqx.

JUGLANS DENTICULATA, Heer, (?) Fl. Arc., 2, p. 483, Pl. lvi, Figs. 6–9. In describing this species, the author remarks that it is like *J. Bilinica*, Ung., with more delicate teeth and secondary veins curving nearer to the borders. The leaves, which I think referable to this species, are like Fig. 9, *loc. cit.*, obovate, gradually narrowed downward to the petiole and more abruptly pointed. Near the base, the borders are nearly entire or slightly serrulate, as in the leaves figured by Heer, *loc. cit.;* but from below the middle upward, they are coarsely and sharply serrate. The secondary veins are equidistant, parallel, gradually curving from the medial nerve to near the borders, where the curve becomes more marked, following the borders and sending strong branches to the point of the teeth. The nervation of this species is well marked and similar to that of some of our living species of *Juglans: J. rupestris*, Engl., for example, from California. One of the specimens bears three leaflets still apparently attached to a common petiole, and all have the same form, same size and nervation. In all our specimens the secondary veins are more curved than in any of the figures given by Heer. It is with this species as with *J. rugosa* compared to *J. acuminata;* identity is not more recognizable than characters to point out specific differences.

## 2. POINT OF ROCKS STATION, UNION PACIFIC RAILROAD.

Fine-grained, brown, ferruginous, very hard shale, with generally broken remains of leaves flattened in the plane of stratification.

ONOCLEA SENSIBILIS, L., as described by Dr. Newberry in Notes on The Later Extinct Floras, &c., p. 39, and figured, Pl. viii, ined. The specimen is upon a piece of white, hard limestone from near the mouth of the Yellowstone River.

*Populus arctica*, Heer. Same form as that of Fl. Arc., Pl. v, Fig. 9. The leaf is broken and its outline obsolete.

QUERCUS OLAFSENI, Heer(?). The specimen only shows the middle part of a leaf oval in outline, at least six inches long, four inches wide, with secondary veins oblique, parallel, straight, as represented for this species and for *Q. Grœnlandica*, Heer, in Fl. Arc., Pl. x, Figs. 3 and 5.

CORYLUS MCQUARRII, Forb. In many specimens, representing it in various forms of its leaves.

CORYLUS GRANDIFOLIA, Newy. It may be a variety of the former species, of which so many are described and figured by Heer in the Arctic Flora. The essential difference is not in the size of the leaves, but in the greater distance between the secondary veins, especially the two lower pairs. The nearest form to this one is that in Heer's Fl. Arc., Pl. ix, Fig. 3.

PLATANUS GUILLELMÆ, Heer,(?) apparently. The characters of the leaf are scarcely distinguishable.

ANDROMEDA, *species*. Two specimens representing the same part of a leaf: its lower part with the petiole. Its form is intermediate between that of *A. Grayana*, Heer, and *Diospiros lancifolia*, Lx.; ovate-lanceolate, one inch wide in the middle, where it is broken, gradually tapering to the petiole by an inward curved line; petiole one-half inch long, narrow, like the medial nerve; one pair only of secondary veins are discernible, ascending from the base of the leaves and following the borders. The other veins above are undistinctly seen, emerging in a more open angle, and curving to the borders.

CORNUS RHAMNIFOLIA, Heer, Fl. Ter. Helv., p. 28, Pl. cv, Figs. 22–25. It resembles somewhat *Juglans rugosa*, Lx., in some of its varieties, differing by shorter and broader leaves, two inches wide, scarcely two and a half inches long; secondary veins all simple, nearly straight, slightly diverging from each other in passing from the medial nerve to quite near the borders, where they curve abruptly; nervilles distinct, perpendicular to the veins, which preserve the same thickness in their whole length. Identical in characters with the European species.

VITIS ISLANDICA, (?) Heer, Fl. Arc., Pl. xxvi, Figs. 1 and 7*a*. Three broken undistinct specimens of lobate leaves, whose nervation is like that of Fig. 7*c*, *loc. cit.*, are doubtfully referred to this species, most of the outlines of the leaves being destroyed. They might be referable to *V. Olriki*, Heer, which has been obtained in better specimens at Evanston.

DOMBEYOPSIS ÆQUIFOLIA, Göpp., Fl. Ter. Schles., p. 22, Pl. iv, Fig. 4, and Pl. v, Fig. 2*a*. The leaf representing this species is only smaller than those figured by Göppert, *loc. cit*. The form, however, and the nervation are alike. It is broadly cordate, equal, entire on the borders, with 5 to 7 primary veins from the base; medial vein branching at a distance above the base; upper basilar veins much divided outside; fibrilles thick, parallel. The specimen shows only the lower half of one leaf.

JUGLANS RUGOSA, Lsqx. My remarks on *J. rhamnoides*, in Report, p. 294, apply to some forms of this species as represented by the numerous specimens of this locality. The discussion on the value of our American species is fallible as long as the descriptions are not elucidated by figures. I preserve this species on account of the small size and the form of the lateral leaflets, which are much shorter and broader toward the base, sometimes cordate, and also for the more deeply marked nervation. The surface of the leaves is generally runcinate by the depression of the veins and veinlets.

### 3. EVANSTON, ABOVE THE COAL.

Specimens on a hard, ferruginous shale of the same nature as that of Point of Rocks.*

PHRAGMITES OENENGENSIS, Al. Br. I refer to this species part of a stem about half an inch broad, with primary veins deep, strong, separated by intermediate very thin ones, articulated, marked at the articulation by the round scar of a branch. It is more deeply striated than in most of the specimens figured of this species. Sismonda in Pal. du Piémont, Pl. vi, Figs. 3–5, has a branch of the same kind.

POPULUS RICHARDSONI, Heer, Fl. Arc., p. 98. The specimen is of the same form as the one in Pl. lv, Fig. 3⁶, and still better preserved. It is a large ovate-cordate, pointed leaf with borders undulately, obtusely crenate; five primary basilar nerves, the exterior ones much branching outside, the two lowest curving in a very open angle toward the borders; the intermediate ascending more obliquely to near the point; tertiary nervation very distinct.

SALIX EVANSTONIANA, *sp. nov.* Leaf ovate-lanceolate, (?) (upper part broken,) rounded to the base, with apparently entire borders; lower pairs of veins (two pairs) shorter, nearly horizontal; superior ones longer, on a more acute angle of divergence, at various distances from each other, irregular in directions, curving near and along the borders, separated by shorter tertiary veins. This species has the nervation of *S. macrophylla*, Heer, especially as figured in Fl. Ter. Helv., Pl. lxvii, Fig. 4, and our specimen could be referred to it but for the form of the leaf appearing entire, merely ovate-pointed, much shorter, and by the medial nerve, which is narrow proportionally to the thick secondary veins and nervilles. These are distinct, perpendicular to the veins.

CORYLUS MCQUARRII, Heer, Report, p. 292. One specimen bears

---

* Report, p. 291.

a leaf of this species; another specimen, with leaves of *Juglans rugosa*, has a small nut which seems referable to the same, Hazel. It is slightly shorter and broader than the one figured as *C. McQuarrii*, in Heer's Fl. Arc., Pl. ix, Fig. 5.

MORUS AFFINIS, sp. nov. Leaf broadly ovate, truncate-cordate at base, abruptly pointed, with borders irregularly serrate,(?) (the stone is coarse-grained and the borders undistinct.) Secondary veins oblique, (angle of divergence, 30° to 35°,) nearly parallel, the basilar pair only approaching nearer to the superior one in ascending to the borders; all nearly straight, deeply marked, abruptly curving and anastomosing at a short distance from the borders; nervilles distinct, numerous, parallel, branching. The lowest pair, only of secondary veins, is much divided outside in oblique branches, parallel and curving near the borders, like the secondary ones; texture of the leaves apparently thin. Except that the nervilles are more numerous, the nervation and areolation of this species is in every point similar to that of our living *M. rubra*, L., as is also the form of the leaves which in one of the specimens, at least, appears to have one side slightly cut in one lobe. It is regretable that the borders are not distinctly seen. The four specimens of this species have the same characters.

FICUS GAUDINI, Lsqx., Report, p. 300. The specimen is a piece of fine-grained sandstone of the same kind and appearance as that from the unknown locality remarked upon in Report, p. 300, and which therefore should be referred to Evanston. The leaf is identical in characters with those formerly described.

PLATANUS ACEROIDES, Göpp. The leaf preserved nearly entire has the broad nearly truncate base of this species, with secondary basilar veins at an angle of 40°; the lateral lobes are long and pointed too, and therefore the identification is certain. The same specimen, however, bears two leaves of *P. Guillelma*, Göpp., whose characters are equally well marked by more oblique basilar veins, borders descending in an acute angle toward the petiole, along which they abruptly pass in a short wing. Heer, at first, united both species for the European specimens, and only admitted them as distinct in examining leaves from the North Greenland Tertiary, (Fl. Arc., II, p. 473.) I am as yet uncertain if this separation is sufficiently authorized. Some specimens of ours are referable to both forms, and, indeed, leaves of our living *P. occidentalis* show in their outlines, and even their nervation, differences which in a fossil state would authorize a separation of species, if seen from separate specimens, more legitimately than from the various forms referable to both the fossil ones. The presence, however, of leaves of a same type upon a same piece of shale, has no weight to decide the question of identity. The trees of the Tertiary, like those of our time, are generally grouped at the same place by a kind of family intimacy: *Juglans nigra* with *Carya alba*; *Acer saccharinum* and *A. rubrum* species of *Quercus*, &c., and of course their leaves are found side by side upon the ground, though coming from different trees.

CINNAMOMUM SCHEUZERI, Heer. Represented by a poor specimen. The lower part of the leaf is erased and no part of the nervation is distinguishable but the medial nerve and the two lateral veins, ascending to three-fourths of the leaf and curving inward along the borders. It might be referable to *C. polymorphum*, Heer, the leaf being larger than in the common forms of *C. Scheuzeri*; a true *Cinnamomum*, however.

CINNAMOMUM MISSISSIPPIENSE, Lsqx. Two leaves upon the same specimen. They are similar in their characters, even in size, to those figured from the Mississippi Tertiary in Trans. Am. Phil. Soc., vol. XIII, Pl. xix, Fig. 2.

MAGNOLIA HILGARDIANA, Lsqx.(?) Specimen showing the middle part only of a large leaf with undulate, entire borders and the nervation of this species. On one side of the leaf the secondary veins are slightly nearer to each other and also more oblique than on the other. It is apparently identical.

VITIS OLRIKI, Heer. One of the two leaves referable to this species is well preserved enough to show the nervation and the large entire obtuse teeth of the borders, which mark the specific characters. These leaves, however, are smaller than the fine one figured by the author in Fl. Arc., 1, Pl. xlviii, Fig. 1; broadly cordate, enlarged in a short obtuse lobe above the middle, then more abruptly pointed. It is palmately 5-nerved from the base, the lower pair of veins nearly horizontal; the lateral ones of the same angle as the divisions of the medial nerve, much branching outside; nervilles obsolete; leaf of a thin texture.

FICUS TILIÆFOLIA, (?) Al. Br. A large leaf whose mere outline and skeleton of veins are obscurely marked upon the stone. It is referable as well to *Dombeyopsis æquifolia*, Göpp. The lower part of the leaf is totaly erased.

ACER SECRETA, *sp. nov.* The leaf is seen only in its upper part; showing three deeply cut, lanceolate, long-pointed lobes with undulate borders marked by a few large teeth. The lobes are contiguous, nearly parallel and equal, separated by narrow but obtuse sinuses. The secondary veins are thin, very oblique, (angle of divergence, 25°;) Tertiary nervation obsolete. By its nervation and the mode of division of the borders, this leaf is comparable to *A. pseudoplatanus* var. *paucidentata*, as figured in Gaud., 3d Mem., Pl. iii, Fig. 2, differing, however, much by the deeply cut, lanceolate-pointed, nearly equal and parallel lobes.

RHAMNUS RECTINERVIS, Heer, Report, p. 295.

RHUS DELETA, Heer, Fl. Ter. Helv., III, p. 83, Pl. cxxvii, Fig. 8. Leaves membranaceous, ovate-lanceolate, obtusely pointed, entire; secondary veins open, camptodrome, thick near the base; tertiary nervation obsolete. The specimens agree with the description of the author, showing leaves of the same size more or less enlarged above the rounded base and of the same kind of nervation.

JUGLANS RUGOSA, Lsqx. Many leaves exactly similar in form and nervation to those of Point of Rocks Station. There is a large number of specimens of this species from both localities.

JUGLANS OBTUSIFOLIA, Heer. Leaves broader, enlarged in the middle, apparently obtusely pointed, rounded to the petiole, entire; surface of the leaves deeply runcinate by depression of the secondary veins, which curve near the borders and are equidistant; nervilles and tertiary nervation distinct; appear identical with Heer species, Fl. Ter. Helv., III, p. 89, Pl. cxxix, Fig. 9.

### 4. FISCHER'S PEAK, RATON MOUNTAINS.

A hard, greenish-yellow, metamorphic sandy shale, with distinct remains of plants, mostly flattened in the plane of stratification.

PTERIS EROSA, *sp. nov.* Leaflets apparently broadly lanceolate or ovate-lanceolate, (?) (the upper and lower part of the leaflet being destroyed,) with irregularly crenulate or lacerate borders; medial nerve thick; veinlets oblique, (angle of divergence, 60°,) straight, mostly simple, some forking, near or at the base, rarely above the middle, distant and parallel. By its nervation and the form of the leaflets, this species is a true *Pteris*, related by its characters to some varieties of *P. longifolia*, L., with serrate borders. The irregular laceration of the borders may be the result of maceration. The leaflet is not half preserved, the part seen being a little more than 2 inches long and half as broad. This species differs from *P. pennæformis*, Heer, by less oblique, less divided, and more distant veinlets.

PHRAGMITES OENINGENSIS, Al. Br. Stems 1 inch broad or less; coarsely striated with the same characters as those described above from Evanston.

SABAL CAMPBELII, Newy., Notes on Extinct Floras, p. 41, (Pl. x, ined.) There is a large number of specimens all with the same characters. They are referable to this species on account of the very thin, obscure striæ of the rays, whose surface in all the specimens, without exception, appears covered by a smooth, thick epidermis which obliterates the lines. The number of the rays, which are sharply folded, is proportionally very large, a character which, like the first, separates this species from *S. Grayana*, Lsqx., of the Mississippi Tertiary. The author describes the petiole as flat. The upper face is concave, nearly half-cylindrical, and striate like the leaves, except the middle, which is rugose and spongy-like; the lower is convex in the same degree; near its base the petiole flattens and enlarges. The specimens represent different parts of the plant—leaves, petioles, and their sheaths, trunks, fruits, &c.

CARPOLITHES PALMARUM, *sp. nov.* These fruits, described in Report, p. 295, from Evanston, (above the coal,) as *Carpolithes lineatus*, (?) Newby, are found agglomerated in large number upon the same specimens, and mixed with irregular striate woody filaments, thus apearing as derived from decayed bunches, the filaments representing pedicels. These fruits are round oval, varying in length from $1\frac{1}{2}$ to $2\frac{1}{2}$ centimeters, and in width from 1 to $1\frac{3}{4}$ centimeters. Most of them are more or less compressed; some nearly flat, some but little devious from the oval-cylindrical primitive form, which is slightly truncate on one side and conical obtuse on the other, narrowly striate, the lines converging to the truncate part, and there often becoming more inflated and distinct. These fruits are referable to species of Palms, not only on account of their connection with Palm leaves, on the same specimens, but especially in consideration of their form, their apparent texture, and their agglomeration in bunches. Their form is like that of the nuts of some species of *Iriartea—I. setigera*, Mart., for example; or of *Leopoldinia—L. pulchra*, M. and C. They appear to have been surrounded by a thin pulpous coating, under which there was a shelly envelope, still distinguishable on some of the specimens, with a compressible and therefore somewhat soft kernel. The best preserved specimens show differences in forms from conical obtuse to exactly oval except the small truncate point of attachment. These differences may indicate two species. Perhaps *C. lineatus*, Newy., is referable to the same kind of fruits; but none of these specimens are marked by a small point, as in Dr. Newberry's figure, *loc. cit.*

POPULUS MUTABILIS var. *repando-crenata*, Heer, Fl. Ter. Helv., p. 22, Pl. lxii, Fig. 2. A large leaf, the lower part of which is destroyed. It is broadly elliptical-lanceolate, obtusely pointed, with borders undulate-crenate and distant; alternate secondary veins very oblique and curved in ascending to and along the borders. The specimen is obscure, but the essential characters of this species are well preserved enough for identification.

POPULUS MONODON, Lsqx., Trans. Am. Phil. Soc., Vol. XIII, p. 413,

Pl. xv, Figs. 1 and 2. A large leaf, 4 inches broad in its widest part, at least 6 inches long, broadly ovate, lanceolate-pointed, rounded to the petiole; borders entire, undulate; medial nerve thick, secondary veins about 12 pairs, nearly equidistant and parallel, diverging from the medial nerve under an angle of 60°, slightly curved or nearly straight to the borders, where they become obsolete; lower secondary veins branching outside. This species is like the former by the general form of the still larger, longer leaves, from which it differs, however, by its secondary veins, more numerous, less distant, parallel, and by the borders entire. Its nervation is similar to that of *Populus balsamoides*, as figured by Gaudin, Fl. Ital., 1st Mem., Pl. iii, Fig. 1, for the branching and anastomosing of the secondary veins, and Fig. 4, for parallel, less distant veins; the leaf is of a thick texture.

QUERCUS CHLOROPHYLLA, Heer. A specimen, representing a coriaceous smooth leaf, runcinate horizontally, without trace of secondary veins or of tertiary nervation; apparently ovate and entire, the borders being imbedded in the stone. A small leaf upon the same specimen indicates more clearly its ovate form, marking identity with Heer's Fl. Ter. Helv. II, Pl. lxxv, Fig. 8. The medial nerve is proportionally broad.

FICUS ULMIFOLIA, *sp. nov.* Leaves round-oval, 3 inches wide, somewhat longer, with entire undulate borders, at least near the base, where only they are observable; medial nerve thick and grooved; petiole short and hooked; secondary veins more or less distant, parallel, open, (angle of divergence, 60°,) joining the medial nerve in a short, downward curve, or slightly decurrent, straight, or flexuous to near the borders, where they curve upward, with sometimes one outside branch; nervilles oblique to the veins, flexuous, undistinct. The borders of the leaves rounded downward, abruptly curve in descending to the petiole, the lower pair of veins following the same curve. The species is represented by a number of specimens, all more or less incomplete, with the upper part of the leaves mostly destroyed. Their general outline resembles that of some leaves of *Alnus Kefersteinii*, Göpp., differing, however, by entire borders and more open secondary veins. Its nearest relative is *F. borealis*, Heer, Fl. Balt., p. 74, Pl. xxi, Fig. 11, differing equally from this species by more open veins.

PLATANUS GUILLELMÆ, Göpp. The same form as the leaf figured in Heer's Fl. Arc., II, Pl. xlvii, Fig. 1.

LAURUS PADATA, (?) Lsqx., Trans. Am. Phil. Soc., vol. XIII, p. 418, Pl. xix, Fig. 1. All the specimens which I refer to this species have only the lower half of the leaves with obsolete nervation. They are most alike, 12 in number, indicating an obovate or oblanceolate coriaceous leaf, gradually tapering downward to a thick medial nerve. The few distinguishable secondary veins are thin, and have the same direction as in the species quoted above. This is not sufficient to warrant identity. These remains might be referrable to *Persea lancifolia*, Lsqx., *loc. cit.*, Figs. 3 and 4.

CINNAMOMUM MISSISSIPPIENSE, Lsqx., *loc. cit.*, p. 418, Pl. xix, Fig. 2. A good specimen, though merely a little more than the lower half of the leaf is preserved. The leaf is still larger than the one from Mississippi.

ANDROMEDA GRAYANA, Heer. Two specimens, one of which represents a whole leaf, with distinct nervation. The identity with Heer's species, Report, p. 298, is ascertained.

MAGNOLIA LESLEYANA, Lsqx., *loc. cit.*, p. 421, Pl. xxi, Figs. 1 and 2.

Two nearly entire leaves of this species, of exactly the same form and characters as those described from specimens of the Mississippi Tertiary.

MAGNOLIA HILGARDIANA, Lsqx., *loc. cit.*, p. 421, Pl. xx, Fig. 1. The borders of the leaves which I refer to this species are mostly erased. These leaves are oblong, not enlarged upward, as in the former species, abruptly rounded downward to the petiole; secondary veins numerous, parallel, open, curving at a short distance from the borders and along them. The general outline of these leaves and their nervation agree in in every point with description and figure, *loc. cit.*

Among the undeterminable fragments from this locality, there are still some referable to another species of *Magnolia*, especially resembling, by obtuse point and nervation, *Magnolia ovalis*, Lsqx., also of the Mississippi Tertiary.

TERMINALIA RADOBOJENSIS, Heer, not Ung. The same leaf, in all its characters, as the one figured in Fl. Ter. Helv., Pl. cviii, Fig. 12. It is entire, obovate, gradually tapering downward to the base of the medial nerve; secondary veins distant, opposite or alternate, irregular in distance and direction, at first curving outside from the medial nerve, and then ascending nearly straight to the borders, camptodrome. Traces of strong nervilles perpendicular to the secondary veins, and also of a few intermediate tertiary shorter veins, are obscurely seen on the specimen, the substance of the leaf appearing somewhat thick. Unger's figure of this species in Chloris, Pl. xlviii, Fig. 2, represents a much larger leaf, with secondary veins more numerous, equally distant, parallel, and an ultimate nervation finely marked, as in a leaf of a thin texture. These differences may be considered as specific.

RHAMNUS OBOVATUS, Lsqx. The leaf is smaller than those described from Marshall coal in Am. Jour. Sci. and Arts, vol. 45, p. 207. The peculiar form of the obovate or oblanceolate leaves with closely approached, parallel, thick secondary veins identify them easily.

RHAMNUS DELETUS, (?) Heer, Fl. Ter. Helv., p. 79, Pl. cxxiii, Figs. 19–23. Two broken specimens are referable to this species. They represent ovate, slightly cordate leaves, with 8 to 10 pairs of deeply marked secondary veins, slightly curving in passing to the borders, camptodrome with distinct fibrilles. The point of the leaf is destroyed and thus the essential character of this species—borders serrulate near the point—is not ascertainable.

BERCHEMIA PARVIFOLIA, Lsqx., Am. Jour. Sci. and Arts, vol. 45, p. 207. The name given to the species is not appropriate, as a new specimen from this locality has a leaf as large as in *B. volubilis*, D. C. From this it differs by broader leaves and secondary nervation more open, the veins slightly arched in ascending and bending upward before reaching as near the borders. This species is still more closely allied to *B. multinervis*, Heer, Fl. Ter. Helv., p. 77, Pl. cxxiii, Figs. 9–18, differing merely by the secondary veins, which, in the American species, are open from the medial nerve, while in Heer's species they join the nerve by a downward curve.

RHAMNUS FISCHERI, *sp. nov.* Leaves thickish, large, 4 inches long, 3 inches broad, rhomboidal, obtuse and entire; medial nerve, thick, grooved, secondary veins open, (angle of divergence, 60°,) equidistant, 10 to 12 pairs, parallel, straight to the borders, where they abruptly curve, camptodrome. By the form of the leaves and the straight secondary veins this species is related to *Rhamnus aizoon*, Heer. The nervilles are not distinguishable.

XANTHOXYLUM DUBIUM, *sp. nov.* A small oblong leaf 3 centimeters long, 1½ centimeters broad, with borders entire or wavy crenulate, nearly parallel in the middle, rounded downward, with an abrupt short descending curve to the base of the medial nerve. Secondary veins parallel, 8 pairs, open, (angle of divergence, 60°,) abruptly curving near the borders, camptodrome. The point of the leaf is destroyed. Related to *X. dentatum*, Heer, Fl. Ter. Helv., Pl. cxxvii, Fig. 21.

JUGLANS SMITHSONIANA, *sp. nov.* Leaves smooth, lanceolate, tapering into a long point, deeply undulate, abruptly curving downward, to the petiole, medial nerve flat and broad; lowest pair of secondary veins very oblique, running to and curving along the borders opposite; the other pairs alternate, distant, irregular in direction, curving also in ascending to and along the borders; tertiary nervation obsolete. A fine species represented by only one specimen, resembling by its nervation *J. Baltica*, Heer, Fl. Balt., Pl. xxix, Fig. 10, and by its general form *J. Schimperi*, Lsqx., described above, a true *Juglans*, though the leaf appears somewhat thick or coriaceous.

### 5. PLACER MOUNTAIN, NEW MEXICO.

A coarse, blackish, hard, metamorphic sandstone, with obscure remains of leaves; few of the specimens of this locality are distinct enough to allow positive identification of the leaves.

POPULUS BALSAMOIDES, Göpp. One leaf only, broadly ovate-cordate, abruptly narrowed to a point; medial nerve narrow; secondary veins numerous, 11 to 12 pairs, open, parallel, curving to and along the borders, (camptodrome.) The borders are apparently entire; but the coarseness of the stone prevents ascertaining it positively. It may represent a new species, differing from *P. balsamoides* by more numerous and parallel secondary veins. These veins appear to curve upward quite near the borders, and to join the superior divisions as in our *P. balsamifera*, L., var. *candicans*.

QUERCUS PLATANIA, (?) Heer. A mere fragment which agrees only by its nervation. Another broken specimen of the same character has the veins less distant, and agrees by its general outline and nervation with *Q. Olafseni*, Heer. Both appear to represent the same species of a *Quercus* as yet undeterminable.

FICUS TILIÆFOLIA, Heer. Only part of a leaf whose nervation is distinctly preserved and undoubtedly referable to this species. Another leaf of *Ficus* has the lateral basilar veins alternate as in *F. Morloti*, Heer, Fl. Ter. Helv., Pl. lxxxii, Fig. 8.

PLATANUS GUILLELMÆ, Heer. Represented by a number of specimens, all fragments, scarcely recognizable.

CINNAMOMUM MISSISSIPPIENSE, Lsqx. It differs by the secondary veins, not quite as thick, ascending, in the upper part of the leaves along the borders, as in some leaves of *C. Buchi*, Heer, Fl. Ter. Helv., Pl. xcv, Fig. 3. This difference is not characteristic. As remarked in my description of this species, *loc. cit.*, p. 418, the reversed figure of *C. Buchi*, represents exactly by its form that of *C. Mississippiense*.

MAGNOLIA! Species undeterminable, mere fragments.

CARPOLITHES SPIRALIS, *sp. nov.* A hard fruit of a remarkable form. It is oval-cylindrical, obtuse at one end, truncate at the other, 2 inches long, half as broad, obtusely narrowly ribbed, the ribs ascending in spiral around it from its truncate base, above which it is slightly contracted by two deep parallel lines, cutting the ribs at a right angle without changing their direction. I do not know any fruit to which this might be compared.

CARPOLITHES COMPOSITUS, *sp. nov.* It looks like a compound of flattened almonds, attached at their point and pressed together. It is divided upward in four unequal lobes, the two of the middle being longer and more flattened or narrower; the other shorter, more inflated, divided to half their length, which varies from $\frac{1}{4}$ to $\frac{1}{2}$ of an inch, and truncate at the lower end. The relation of this species is, like that of the former, unknown to me.

CARPOLITHES MEXICANUS, *sp. nov.* Much like some of the nuts described above as *C. palmarum*, differing, however, by its exactly ovate-cylindrical, pointed form.

### 6. HOT SPRINGS, MIDDLE PARK.

A piece of hard siliceous tufa or grit.

JUGLANS THERMALIS, *sp. nov.* Leaf ovate, lanceolate, cuneate-pointed, rounded in narrowing to the petiole, (broken,) 5 inches long, about 2 inches broad; medial nerve sharp and narrow; secondary veins irregular in distance and direction; the lowest pair more oblique, separated by horizontal tertiary veins anastomosing with branches of the secondary. Nervation analogous to that of *J. obtusifolia*, Heer, Fl. Ter, Helv., Pl. cxxix, Fig. 9; form of leaf like *J. longifolia*, Heer, *loc. cit.*, Fig. 10. It might be identical with this last species, of which the only leaf figured does not represent the tertiary nervation.

### GENERAL REMARKS.

#### GREEN RIVER, ABOVE FISH BEDS.

The geological station of this place, from indication of the fossil plants described, appears to be of a different stage from that of any of the other localities which have furnished materials for the present examination. In the former report, p. 289, the station of Green River is left indeterminate, one species only, *Ceanothus cinnamomoides*, being recognizable from the few specimens then on hand. Now we have besides this one, still found in the newly received lot of specimens, twenty-one species affording data for comparison. Except the omnipresent forms of the Tertiary, *Arundo*, *Phragmites*, and *Juncus*, all these plants bear a more recent facies than the species of Evanston, Point of Rocks, and Fischer's Peak, especially by their relation to living species—*Ceanothus cinnamomoides*, comparable to some of the numerous species of California; *Myrica nigricans*, allied to our *Myrica Gale*, L.; *Ficus Ungeri*, to *Ficus Americana*; *Ampelopsis tertiaria*, to the well-known *Ampelopsis quinquefolia*, Michx.; *Ilex affinis*, scarcely distinguishable from *Ilex coriacea*, Chap., of Florida; *Rhus acuminatd*, related to our common *Rhus aromatica*, L.; and *Eucalyptus Americanus*, to some species of this genus, inhabiting Australia. From these new species *Juglans Schimperi* is the only one which does not appear related to any of the present flora. Of the species of Green River described already from the Miocene of Europe, *Salix augusta*, apparently identical with the living *Salix viminalis*, L., and *Salix media*, are both from Oeningen, or from the upper stage of the Miocene; *Myrica salicina*, *Quercus lonchitidis*, and *Ilex stenophylla*, have representatives in both the Upper and the Middle Miocene; *Ficus populina*, only, belongs to the Lower Miocene; but as seen from the description, our American form differs in some points from the European, and may prove to be a different species. As related to Arctic types, we have only from Green River *Juglans denticulata*, (?) which, if not identical with the Greenland species, is at least closely allied to it.

2 s g s

The relation of all these species, therefore, except the *Cyperaceæ*, &c., found everywhere, is evidently with younger types, and indicates a higher station in the Tertiary measures. From the absence of the species which characterize the American formation considered as Eocene, and also from the absence of the Arctic types, which become less predominent in advancing toward our present epoch, the fossil plants of Green River apparently represent the Upper Miocene.

### POINT OF ROCK STATION.

The horizon of this station, like that of the former, was left undetermined in the Report, p. 308, the few specimens received from it indicating only one *Cyperites*, *Fagus Antipofi*, and indistinct leaves referable to *Juglans* and *Platanus*. Nine species have been added to this short list, from a new contribution of specimens; but as none of them is characteristic of a peculiar horizon, the geological station of this place is not positively ascertainable. Of these species, *Corylus McQuarrii*, *Populus arctica*, and *Platanus Guillelmœ* are represented in the formation considered as Eocene, the first at 6 miles above Spring Cañon, the two last at Evanston; but they have been found also in connection with strata referred to the lower Miocene—Medicine Bow, Washakie, and Junction Station. *Juglans rugosa* is distributed through the whole thickness of the American Tertiary, apparently at least; the other species, *Cornus rhamnifolia*, is found in all the stages of the European Miocene. From the presence of a number of Arctic types, *Populus arctica*, *Platanus Guillelmœ*, *Vitis Islandica*, *Fagus Antipofi*, which are absent from the Green River formation; I believe, however, that Point of Rocks occupies a lower stage in the Tertiary, though higher than Evanston, and that therefore its place is in the Lower Miocene. This supposition is essentially indicated by the absence of any of the species marked as characteristic of the American Eocene.

### EVANSTON.

A lot of specimens representing especially species of *Ficus* is marked in the former report, page 300, as of unknown origin. The lithological characters of these specimens and the analogy of the species which they bear, refer them to the same strata as those marked "*Evanston, below the coal.*" At the same place, the upper strata show evidently by their remains of plants, representatives of a flora of the same age as the lower ones; for two of the four species recognized above the coal are found also below it. Adding to this number the species described in these notes, we have a list of 42 species of fossil plants for Evanston; a larger number than from any other locality of the American Tertiary. This place may therefore be considered as a point of mark, used for future references and comparisons.

Considered in its whole or in its details, the large list of the species of Evanston do not indicate any character which might modify the opinion formerly advanced on the age of the formation. Except *Morus affinis*, closely allied to our living *Morus rubra*, all the other fossil plants represent older Tertiary types. It is undeniable that without any exception most of these types of ours compared with European fossil species should be referable to the Miocene. But as said in Report, pp. 313 and 314, either these species belong to the American Eocene or as yet this formation is unknown in our geology.

The relation of Evanston with the Mississippi Tertiary flora is now marked by three distinct species which they have in common—*Juglans appressa, Cinnamomum Mississippiense,* and *Magnolia Hilgardiana.* But it is evidently a geological and not an isothermal relation; for all the Arctic types described from Evanston—*Populus arctica, Populus Richardsoni, Corylus MacQuarrii, Vitis Olriki,* &c.—are absent from the Tertiary of the Mississippi.

### FISCHER PEAK, RATON MOUNTAINS.

By far the most interesting locality, on account of the data derived from it, for comparison of geological station as also of geographical distribution, is that of Fischer's Peak, in the Raton Mountains, north of the New Mexico Territory. On one side, the fossil flora of this locality affords evidence of the same age as that of Evanston and of the Mississippi, referable to both by the more remarkable species recognized from its specimens. With Evanston, it has in common, *Populus mutabilis, Platanus Guillelmæ, Cinnamomum Mississippiense, Andromeda Grayana, Magnolia Hilgardiana, Carpolithes palmarum,* or six species in the twenty-two determined from its remains. With the Mississippi Tertiary flora it has as identical species, *Populus mutabilus, Populus monodon, Quercus chlorophylla, Laurus pedata, Cinnamomum Mississippiense, Magnolia Lesleyana, Magnolia Hilgardiana, Juglans appressa,* or eight species. If we consider that this identity is for representatives of genera of distant affinity, which at the same time are all, except *Cinnamomum,* characteristic of our present flora—*Populus, Quercus, Magnolia, Juglans,* even *Palms;* if we consider still that this identity is rendered positive by the peculiar and easily ascertained characters of the species, we can but see here and acknowledge an evident proof of the homogeneity of the North American Tertiary flora in comparing it even at great distances under the same latitude. The difference between the two points of comparison is about 15° of longitude. On another side, this identity of species with Evanston by a few Arctic types—*Populus mutabilis, Platanus Guillelmæ, Andromeda Grayana,* and by southern types like *Quercus chlorophylla, Laurus pedata,* two *Magnolias,* fruits of the Palms—positively confirm the assertion of the former report, p. 311, that though the Tertiary flora of the Northwest is connected by identical forms with the Arctic flora of the same epoch, it already indicates, by a number of its species, climatic differences, according to latitude, as distinct as we see them in the arborescent vegetation of our time. Palm-trees at the Eocenic times were mixed to the flora, not only at Evanston but farther North at Fort Union. But at Fischer's Peak remains of Palms are more numerous nearly one-half of the specimens of this locality representing fragments of leaves, fruits, stems, &c., of a Sabal. In the Mississippi specimens, the remains of two species of Palm are equally abundant.

### REMARKS ON TYPICAL ANALOGY OF OUR PRESENT FLORA WITH THAT OF THE TERTIARY.

Little can be said on this question in addition to the remarks in Report, p. 314. The analogy of types of our present flora with those of the Tertiary becomes more evident in proportion to the progress of the researches. Two more of the North American genera of the present time are now recognized in the Northwest Tertiary—*Morus* and *Ampelopsis.* The discovery of a fossil species of Mulberry does not indicate for this country the origin of the numerous species of the same genus which have now representatives in the tropical regions of the whole world, but it proves at least that ours is truly indigenous. The similarity of the fossil leaves with those of the living species confirms the assertion. And the antiquity of race, too, may be indicated by the wide range of distribution and general prevalence of *Morus rubra*, from Florida to Lake Erie. No species of *Morus* has been as yet recognized in a fossil state. It is the same with *Ampelopsis*, a genus still more evidently North American than *Morus*; for no species of true *Ampelopsis* is known from another country.* The relation of form between the fossil species *Ampelopsis tertiaria* and the living *A. quinquefolia* is as distinctly marked as for the two species of *Morus*, and also its geographical distribution and its predominance in our flora. Both species are in intimate affinity to our North American vegetation. They are seen everywhere and known and liked by everybody. The one is the friend of the farmers by its shade, of his children delighted by the pleasantness of its fruits; the other adorns our dwellings when allowed to grow in our gardens. And when left to its own work, it covers with green foliage the dead trees and the barren rocks, tempering desolation and ruin by hiding them under elegant fringes and garlands painted of the richest colors. It is worth something to know that the origin of the Virginian Creeper and of the Red Mulberry is traceable to the Tertiary formations of North America.

There is still a number of genera from our arborescent flora which have not, as yet, any representatives recognized in the Tertiary—*Asimina*, for example, *Aesculus*, *Hamamelis*, some *Rosaceæ*, *Ericaceæ*, &c. The preservation and fossilization of leaves is more or less dependent upon the consistence of their texture, thin leaves being mostly destroyed by maceration too soon to leave distinct traces of their forms when imbedded in clay or sand deposits. In examining, upon the ground, the dead leaves of our forests in spring, the difference in the degree of preservation resulting of texture is easily remarked. For example, upon a lot occupied by Oak, Beach, Elm, and Maple trees, in nearly equal proportion, the leaves of the three first kinds will be found heaped everywhere and entire, while scarcely a few skeletons of decaying leaves of Maple are distinguishable. This probably explains the absence of some species, and also the disproportion of representatives of others in the Tertiary; as, for example, of the species of *Acer*, which, already predominant at the Cretaceous epoch, and having a large number of species in the present flora of our North American continent, have been as yet rarely found in our Tertiary formations. It must be said, too, that we know as yet but a very small part of the vegetation of the Tertiary, and that every new lot of specimens affords materials to modify suppositions which might be offered on the causes of the distribution of species. In the former report I alluded to the scarcity of the remains of Willows in our Tertiary, in comparison with their great number in the Cretaceous. In the present notes, four species of *Salix*, as yet unknown in our fossil flora, have been described, and probably a number of others will be found still.

However, it is true that some of our ancient types have disappeared, or show a tendency to disappear from our present flora, the types related to the present vegetation of Australia, for example, *Eucalyptus* of the Tertiary, which will be probably found in the Cretaceous with *Phillocladus* and *Proteoides;* some others also, now marked in the flora of Japan and China, which appear to have traveled westward, as *Cin-*

---

* *Ampelopsis botria*, D. C., is described from Zanzibar, Africa. As it has simple leaves and fruit eatable, it is probably referable to *Vitis*.

*namomum* and *Ficus* of the Tertiary, and the *Credneria*, with analogous types, of the Cretaceous. *Cinnamomum* and *Ficus*, however, have not left altogether our North American continent, but they have lost their importance in the vegetation of ours, at least compared with the place which they occupied in the Tertiary times.

Each formation, of course, has lost some of its vegetable types in acquiring new ones. The march of the increase and decrease of the typical representatives, the search for appreciable causes which may have fostered modifications of forms, is one of the most interesting parts of the study of vegetable paleontology.

On this subject, it is already evident, to my mind at least, that the *data* presented in these notes, and in the former report of Dr. Hayden, indicate a remarkable analogy of our present flora with that of the Tertiary, and of this, too, with the flora, considered as of the North American Cretaceous, pointing out its ancient origin. But the indications are not yet conclusive. The chain in the modifications of types from the oldest formations (Upper Cretaceous) to the newer ones, (Upper Tertiary,) and from these to our flora, appears especially defective in its last link, our knowledge with the Pliocene flora being as yet too limited. The only locality, known to me, where strata of this age, with remains of fossil plants, are xposed, is, as remarked in Report, p. 318, at Columbus, Kentucky, on what is called the chalk-banks of the Mississippi. The plants which I obtained there, in a too short tour of exploration, are, to my opinion, scarcely, if at all, distinguishable from species now living in the Southern States. I then identified, as far as identity can be ascertained from fossil leaves, *Quercus virens*, Michx.; *Castanea nana*, Muhl.; *Ulmus alata*, Michx.; *Planera Gmelini*, Michx.; *Prinos integrifolia*, Ell.; *Ceanothus Americanus*, L.; *Carya olivæformis*, Nutt; *Gleditchia triacanthos*, L.; and *Acorus calamus*, L. Professor Heer, to whom I sent sketches of the leaves representing these species, objected to my determinations, at least for some of them, and I have no doubt but that he is right in some points. However, the identity of a number, at least, of the species, is undeniable, indicating, therefore, an intimate relation of our arborescent flora with that of the Pliocene. It would be important to obtain a series of specimens numerous enough to give positive evidence of the degree of that relation. The deposits of leaves above Paducah belong to a more recent epoch, the Terrace epoch, apparently. All the specimens of leaves obtained from this formation represent, without doubt, even in the opinion of Heer, species of our time. In following, then, the researches for the purpose of studying the march in the flora from the Cretaceous times till ours, the strata of the West and those of the Mississippi could furnish documents for such a clear record as none other could be got elsewhere on the same subject.

For conclusion it is right to recall in a few words the essential points marked in this examination:

1st. It adds to our list of fossil species of the Tertiary 20 new forms, and describes 21 others, known already from the Miocene of Europe, but not as yet observed in our Tertiary flora. The number of its species is thus increased to 231.

2d. It fixes the geological horizon of three localities in different stages of the Tertiary, and marks the location of a group of specimens of as yet unknown origin.

3d. It more distinctly points out the relation of some important strata for ascertaining contemporaneity or difference of age.

4th. It indicates more positively modifications in the characters of the Tertiary flora of the North American continent according to climatic differences at different degrees of latitude, and at the same time recognizes identity of the characters of this vegetation at wide distances under the same latitude.

5th. It shows a more intimate relation between the present flora and that of the Tertiary by the discovery of new types identical in both.

The outlines of our Tertiary formations are, from former researches, recognized by their flora in Vancouver, Oregon, Alaska, Greenland, Connecticut, Kentucky, and Mississippi. Under the systematic and judicious directions of Dr. Hayden, its central area is diligently studied in the Northwestern Territories, and every year adds to the value and the importance of the materials furnished for the study of its fossil vegetation. And now Professor J. D. Whitney sends from California a large number of specimens obtained there from the Cretaceous and from different stages of the Tertiary formation. We may thus foresée that in a short time North America will contribute for the acquaintance of the flora of these formations documents reliable enough to afford a secure basis for its detailed and comparative history.

COLUMBUS, OHIO, *May* 4, 1872.

www.ingramcontent.com/pod-product-compliance
Lightning Source LLC
Chambersburg PA
CBHW031250250426
43672CB00029BA/1730